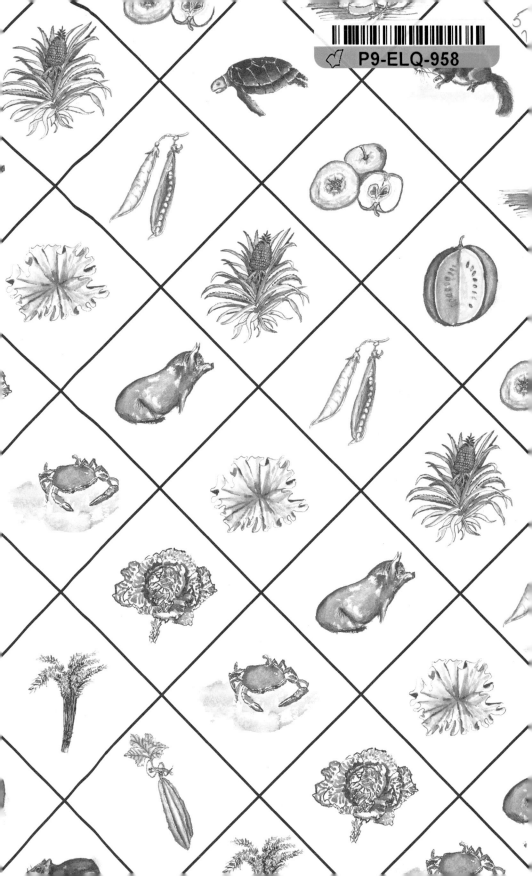

Choice Cuts

Other books by Mark Kurlansky

Salt: A World History
The Basque History of the World
Cod: A Biography of the Fish That Changed the World
A Chosen Few: The Resurrection of European Jewry
A Continent of Islands: Searching for the Caribbean Destiny

The White Man in the Tree and Other Stories (fiction)
The Cod's Tale (for children)

Choice Cuts

A Savory Selection of Food Writing

from Around the World

and Throughout History

Edited and illustrated by

MARK KURLANSKY

Ballantine Books

New York

A Ballantine Book
Published by The Ballantine Publishing Group

Copyright © 2002 by Mark Kurlansky

All rights reserved under International and Pan-American Copyright
Conventions. Published in the United States by The Ballantine Publishing
Group, a division of Random House, Inc., New York, and simultaneously in
Canada by Random House of Canada Limited, Toronto.

Ballantine and colophon are registered trademarks of Random House, Inc.

Owing to limitations of space, permission acknowledgments can be found on
pp. 469–474, which constitute an extension of this copyright page.

www.ballantinebooks.com

Library of Congress Cataloging-in-Publication Data is available from the
publisher upon request.

ISBN 0-345-45710-2

Text design by C. Linda Dingler

Manufactured in the United States of America

First Edition: November 2002

10 9 8 7 6 5 4 3 2 1

To Jack and Rubye Monet
for a hundred meals of roasts, red wine,
salad, cheese (with butter?), laughter,
and debate in two languages over three decades

My dear boy, when curds are churned,
the finest part rises upward and turns into butter.
So too, dear boy, when food is eaten the choice parts rise
upward and become mind.

—CHANDOGYA UPANISHAD

Contents

CHAPTER FOUR: *Favorite Restaurants*

CHAPTER FIVE: *Markets*

CHAPTER SIX: *Not Eating*

CHAPTER SEVEN: *Rants*

CHAPTER EIGHT: *On Bread Alone*

CHAPTER NINE: *The Mystery of Eggs*

CHAPTER TEN: *Eating Your Vegetables*

CHAPTER ELEVEN: *A Hill of Beans*

CHAPTER TWELVE: *The Fish That Didn't Get Away*

CHAPTER THIRTEEN: *Poultry, Fowl, and Other Ill-Fated Birds*

CHAPTER FOURTEEN: *The Meat of the Matter*

CHAPTER FIFTEEN: *Easy on the Starch*

CHAPTER SIXTEEN: *A Pinch of Seasoning*

CHAPTER SEVENTEEN: *Just a Salad*

CHAPTER TWENTY-SIX: *The English*

CHAPTER TWENTY-SEVEN: *The Americans*

CHAPTER TWENTY-EIGHT: *The Germans*

CHAPTER TWENTY-NINE: *The Politics of Food*

CHAPTER THIRTY: *What Does It Mean?*

Acknowledgments

THANKS TO MICHAEL MILLMAN, FOR COMING TO ME WITH the idea for this book; Nancy Miller, for pushing me to make the book better; and Charlotte Sheedy, for her enthusiastic backing. Thanks to Caroline Miller for much hard work and perseverance. A warm thanks to Rabbi Rolando Matalon for his guidance in the Talmud. Thanks also to Maya Baran, for introducing me to the wonderful work of her grandfather Angelo Pellegrini; to Matt Sartwell and Nach Waxman, for many valuable suggestions; to the wonderful chanteuse Daryl Sherman, for her advice; to Donald C. Kraus at Oxford University Press for his advice and assistance; and to Sarah Shanon, for a hundred helpful things. Thank you, John Ash, for your M.F.K. Fisher story. And most especially, thanks to Marian Mass across the table—thanks for the smile, the wit, the thoughts, that make eating dining.

Better Than Sex

FOOD, LIKE SEX, IS A WRITER'S GREAT OPPORTUNITY. IT OFFERS material that is both universal and intensely personal—something that illuminates the nature of humankind but also offers insights into the unique and intimate foibles of an individual.

To write only of the pleasures of eating would be pornography—a legitimate use of a writer's skills but, from the standpoint of both reader and writer, limited. The writer intuitively wants to explore the broader and more far-reaching effects of food, or for that matter sex, rather than the physical pleasure alone.

In the case of food—not usually the case with sex—the much sought after physical pleasure involves the acquisition of commodities. Sex only sometimes involves commerce and rarely is impacted by climate or land use. Food is about agriculture, about ecology, about man's relationship with nature, about the climate, about nation-building, cultural struggles, friends and enemies, alliances, wars, religion. It is about memory and tradition and, at times, even about sex. "Nothing is more agreeable to look at than a pretty gourmande in full battle-dress. . . . Her lips are soft and moist. . . ." wrote the nineteenth-century French food writer Jean Anthelme Brillat-Savarin. And as the twentieth-century American food writer M.F.K. Fisher explained about the erotic power of eating eel: "There is a phallic rightness about the whole thing, visual as well as spiritual, which has more to do with the structure of the fish than the possible presence of a mysterious and exotic spice."

TODAY, OUR INITIAL EXPECTATION OF FOOD WRITING IS THAT it will be about food, but the earliest food writers used food as one tool among many for illuminating broader subjects. The ancient Chinese wrote of food in terms of medicine and alchemy, as well as agriculture and ecology, but rarely simply as food. Food writing was often about land use and, by extension, sometimes about effective and incompetent government. "If you do not interfere with the busy season in the fields, then there will be more grain than people can eat; if you do not allow nets with too fine a mesh to be used in large ponds, then there will be more fish and turtles than one can eat," wrote Mencius (372–289 B.C.), a leading disciple of Confucius.

Much of the Old Testament is devoted to explaining what the Hebrew people should and should not eat. It was through this food, this specific diet, that the Hebrews were to define themselves as a distinct people. Food is an integral part of the moral code, the Mosaic law, and history's strongest expression of the often quoted Brillat-Savarin statement "Tell me what you eat, and I shall tell you what you are."

In the fifth century B.C., Herodotus, considered the first historian, would no doubt have agreed. Herodotus began his *Histories,* and with it the discipline of history, with the simple declaration "The purpose is to prevent the traces of human events from being erased by time." Among those traces were the food habits of bygone cultures. He observed how the Egyptians intertwined life and death, preserving their food in salt and curing their dead in much the same way. He described the food and gave recipes for mummification and explained how, after extravagant banquets, a carved wooden replica of a corpse in a coffin would be carried around the room, shown to each reveler with the words "Drink and make merry, but look on this, for such shalt thou be when thou art dead."

Perhaps the first true food writer was Archestratus, a poet who lived in the fourth century B.C. in the Grecian colony on what is today Sicily. Little more is known of him than that he wrote a poem called *The Life of Luxury,* which was characterized by Athenaeus, a later writer:

> Archestratus, in his love for pleasures, traveled over every land and sea with precision, in a desire, as it seems to me, to review with care the things of the belly; and imitating the writers of geographical descriptions and voyages, his desire is to set forth everything precisely, wherever the best to eat and the best to drink are to be found.

But among subsequent Greek and Roman writers, food continued to be merely an embellishment to discussions of broader topics. In the second century B.C., Cato wrote extensively about food in the earliest surviving complete book of Latin prose, but the central subject of this work is agriculture. In the first century A.D., Pliny the Elder wrote about food, though his principal subject was natural history. So he discussed the seas, their nature, the sea creatures that we eat, and then, without warning, launched into a tirade against eating seafood: "But why do I mention these trivial matters when shellfish are the prime cause of the decline of morals and the adaptation of an extravagant lifestyle? Indeed of the whole realm of Nature the sea is in many ways the most harmful to the stomach, with its great variety of dishes and tasty fish."

But what of this extravagant lifestyle that Pliny denounced? The whimsical Martial used food to describe his social life in first-century Rome, both praising and criticizing dinner parties, such as dinner at Cinna's:

> By daily making himself sick
> With minuscule drops of arsenic
> King Mithradates once built up
> Immunity to the poison-cup.
> In the same way, your small, vile dinner
> Saves you from death by hunger, Cinna.

Plutarch, the brilliant biographer, used food the way later novelists would. Just as Tomasi di Lampedusa brings us a vision of the faded aristocracy in his twentieth-century novel *The Leopard,* by describing their meals, Plutarch reveals the egocentric character of Lucullus, the aristocratic political leader, by describing the lavish manner in which he dined when alone. We also get to know something of Lucullus in the story of how servants came to him from Pompey's doctors. Pompey was ill and his doctor had prescribed thrush though the birds were out of season. But Lucullus had pens where he kept thrush for fattening. "So," said Lucullus smugly. "If Lucullus had not been an epicure, Pompey had not lived." Whereupon he ordered up a more common dish.

THE OLDEST COOKBOOK OF WHICH WE STILL HAVE A COPY is by Apicius and was probably produced in Rome in the first century A.D. Unfortunately, there seem to have been a number of people named Apicius living in Rome within that century, and at least three of them were noted gourmets. The leading candidate is M. Gabius Apicius who lived from 80 B.C. to A.D. 40. Gabius Apicius was a renowned gourmet in a society that admired gourmetism. He was known to be wealthy and eat well and many dishes were named after him, including several types of cheesecake, called apicians. If this is the same Apicius, apparently he was unimpressed, because he did not include a recipe for a single apician in his book. It is quite possible that the Apicius cookbook we have was not even written by its namesake, but is a collection of recipes in his honor, possibly compiled several centuries later.

It seems that after Gabius Apicius had spent most of his inheritance on food, he killed himself rather than face financial restraints. The dishes described in this book seem to the taste of someone who would eat his inheritance and then take his life. Its brief and barely explained recipes for sow's tits, stuffed dormice, and huge architectural centerpieces suggest the kind of extravagant cuisine that Plutarch said Lucullus ate.

It is surprising that the Greeks and Romans, known for producing hedonists, did not produce more pornography—both sexual and gastronomic. Imperial Rome seemed an age ideally suited for gastronomic pornography, with gourmetism appearing as a leitmotif in Roman writing. Some are denounced for their excess, others praised for it. Esoteric food debates run through the literature. Sow's tits and vulvae are the delicacies of choice for great occasions. But what was the appropriate sow? Many said it was a virgin, but Pliny argued for a pig whose first litter had been aborted.

Yet food writing remained more intellectual than sensual. In the following century, Galen, Marcus Aurelius's personal physician, wrote about food, diet, and health. "The humours from which animals and humans are composed," he stated, "are yellow bile, blood, phlegm and black bile." This unappetizing vision of four humors, whose balance was maintained by a proper diet, became one of the dominant medical beliefs in the Western world for more than a thousand years. The epicurean reader never completely recovers when the discussion of a delectable tidbit suddenly turns on the relative merits of phlegm and black bile.

Galen was that food writer from whom gourmets hoped not to hear. His descriptive powers were used for such subjects as "the stretching sensation" of flatulent wind. He informs that:

The nature of watermelons is generally rather chilling and contains a great deal of moisture, yet they possess a certain purgative quality, which means that they are also diuretic and pass down through the bowels more easily than large gourds and melons. Their cleansing action you can discover for yourself; just rub them on dirty skin. Watermelons will remove the following: freckles, facial moles, or epidemic leprosy, if anyone should have these conditions.

Care for a sweet, cool, juicy watermelon?

The influence of this black bile school of thought was felt for more than a thousand years. Platina, who wrote from Florence at the height of the fifteenth-century southern Renaissance, urged the eating of vinegar because "It represses bile and blood and also cuts phlegm with its intense acidity." This is a branch of food writing that has been continued by those who extol the virtues of high fiber and low salt.

But, with the thirteenth century, another branch of food writing emerged: the cookbook.

THE EARLIEST KNOWN MEDIEVAL COOKBOOK WAS A GERMAN manuscript from the first half of the thirteenth century. At the end of that century a twenty-nine-recipe manuscript was written in Anglo Norman. In 1300, a French manuscript was written. These cookbooks, usually in the form of rolled manuscripts, were the work of chefs recording the cuisine of a royal household, generally at the request of the lord, in order to document the splendor of the court. The recipes, like those of Apicius, were seldom more than a vague outline a few sentences long. They seemed to have been written by professional cooks for professional cooks who already knew the basic concepts and techniques. And they borrowed from one another despite being in different languages.

The most influential of these early cookbooks was *Le Viandier* by Guillaume Tirel, the head cook for King Charles V of France. Five different versions of this manuscript have been found, four of which are still in existence. The earliest of these is a rolled parchment dated from the second half of the thirteenth century. The latest version was issued in 1604. A consistent curiosity of cookbooks is that subsequent editions are almost always longer than earlier versions. It seems that no one ever shortens a cookbook. The author, Guillaume Tirel, is believed to have lived from about 1312 to 1395. So the first of his manuscripts was written before he was born and the last after he died. It appears that the author was the pivotal player in a collection of recipes that was continually enlarged over several centuries.

Tirel, like many medieval cooks, had picked up his lifelong nickname in his apprentice days. Taillevent, the name he was known by, was the word for a lightweight sail used for quick maneuvering, a jib, and may be a reference to his agility. In 1381, Taillevent became chef to Charles V, who, being well known as a promoter of culture, is thought to have urged his chef to compile the recipes.

Taillevent was the most famous chef of his epoch and his book dominated French cooking and French cookbooks for centuries. Among the works it influenced was *Le Mésnagier de Paris*. This book was written in 1393 by a bourgeois Parisian, sometimes said to be elderly but possibly no older than mid-fifties, as a guide for a teenage orphan he had recently married. It instructs her on morality, taking care of the home, managing the domestic staff, and gardening, and it includes a chapter on cooking.

THE RECIPE CHAPTER OF THE *MÉSNAGIER* IS TO A LARGE degree taken from Taillevent, and only occasionally, in deference to the fact that the intended reader is an amateur housewife, are things more elaborately explained. Taillevent's instruction for preparing peacocks begins, "They should be blown into and inflated like swans and roasted and glazed in the same way." Little additional information is offered in the swan section. *Le Mésnagier* uses this recipe word for word. It is easy to imagine the sad scene of the fifteen-year-old orphan bride, wanting to do well, peacock in one hand, husband's guide in the other, trying to inflate the heavy bird.

The *Mésnagier* was the first of a kind of cookbook that was to become commonplace until the twentieth century—the guide to young housewives. These cookbooks contained diverse chapters on such subjects as morality, gardening, running a household, and managing servants. Among the most famous English cookbook/guides to housewives were Eliza Smith's 1758 *The Compleat Housewife*, Margaret Dods's 1829 *Cook and Housewife's Manual,* and Isabella Beeton's 1861 *Beeton's Book of Household Management.* Among the leading American ones were Lydia Maria Child's 1829 *The American Frugal Housewife,* and Catherine Beecher's and her sister Harriet Beecher Stowe's 1869 *American Woman's Home.*

It is significant that these heirs to the *Mésnagier* were no longer a man's advice to his young wife but books by women for women. Behind each of these books is a woman's story. The most successful food book of eighteenth-century England was written by a woman, Hannah Glasse, but no less a figure than Dr. Johnson told Boswell that this was impossible and named a man as the true author. The accusation has been completely disproved. Like the recipient of *Le Mésnagier,* Isabella Beeton was a teenage bride, but she became a major figure in her husband's publishing company and published her own guide to young housewives, which, like *Le Mésnagier,* became a classic. The Beecher sisters had a sense of mission and saw the housewife's guide as an opportunity to write on their theory of the woman's role in upholding the morality of a society. Sarah Josepha Hale became one of the most influential women in nineteenth-century America by not only writing about food and household issues but by developing the "women's magazine."

From the nameless fifteen-year-old bride given book-length instructions on how to run her husband's home, to M.F.K. Fisher who dared to write about men the way Brillat-Savarin wrote about women, the history of food writing became the story of the long, slow struggle toward women's emancipation.

IN 1825 A NEW KIND OF FOOD BOOK WAS INVENTED. THE author was Jean Anthelme Brillat-Savarin, a French lawyer who fled the revolution and spent two years in New York struggling as both a language teacher and a violinist. Although fascinated with the scientific and even medical approach to food, his book *La Physiologie du goût,* despite its title, *The Physiology of Taste,* was more of a philosophic and literary musing on food than a scientific investigation. Appropriately, the chapters into which he divided his book were called "meditations." He meditated on sleep, overeating, undereating, on women, on obesity, on food and sexuality, and on food history. He philosophized, told anecdotes, and made pronouncements, such as "Every thin woman wants to grow plump" and "People predestined to gourmandism are in general of medium height; they have round or square faces, bright eyes, small foreheads, short noses, full lips and rounded chins" (surprisingly, this is not a description of the very tall Brillat-Savarin himself), or "Gourmandism, considered as a part of political economy, is a common tie which binds nations together by the reciprocal exchange of objects which are part of their daily food."

Yet, somehow, this seemingly meandering book held together, and still does, as a singular literary work.

Three years ahead of Brillat-Savarin, and some say more talented, was Karl Friedrich von Rumohr, a German contemporary who in 1822 had published *Geist der Kochkunst, The Essence of Cookery.* Baron von Rumohr was an erudite man, a well-traveled art historian, and the author of a four-volume novel and a wide range of other works that were generally praised for their prose craftsmanship. Typical of his ambitious nature, he decided to write a one-volume treatise on cooking, examining the different cooking techniques, the various foods and their uses, extolling the virtues of unpretentious traditional German food. It was written for German housewives to encourage them to maintain their traditions. But far from being a cookbook, it is a nonfiction masterpiece on a cuisine. It was written at a time when German nationhood was considerably behind much of Europe and it reflects, like so much nineteenth-century German literature and music, the search for a German national identity.

Yet the Baron's achievement has been dwarfed by the fame of Brillat-Savarin's book. It is sometimes suggested that the reason for this is that most of the world would rather listen to a Frenchman's gastronomic musings than those of a German.

In any case, the early nineteenth century was a fertile moment in food writing. A contemporary of Brillat-Savarin and the Baron, Alexandre-Balthazar-Laurent Grimod de la Reynière, became the first food journalist. His *Almanach des Gourmands,* packed with cooking information, food history, and a more than generous sprinkling of opinion and pet peeves, was published eight times between 1803 and 1813.

Due to a birth defect, Grimod wrote with mechanical hands with which he demonstrated his extraordinary dexterity at elaborate feasts. He was celebrated for his somewhat cynical wit, saying of doctors, "It is other people's indigestion that prevents them from having to diet themselves." He said of a good soup that "Like the overture of a comic opera, it should announce the subject of the work." And he left us this warning: "Beware of people who don't eat; in general they are envious, foolish, or nasty. Abstinence is an anti-social virtue." He was also the first restaurant critic, having established a jury to rate them, a process that, inevitably, was deemed corrupt.

The literary influence of Brillat-Savarin and von Rumohr continued, and nineteenth-century novels are particularly rich in food description. Alexandre Dumas *père* who always considered himself a food commentator, left behind 303 volumes of literature. Volume 304 was his posthumously published food dictionary. Dumas seemed certain that this book, and not *The Three Musketeers* or *The Count of Monte Cristo,* would secure his reputation for posterity. The book is outrageously inaccurate. It perpetuated, or perhaps even started, such myths as the ancients driving ducks across the Alps to furnish Roman feasts, a pointless feat that would have taken years. Dumas ignored the numerous edible crabs of the Brittany coast and asserted only two were edible, and that "negroes feed" on the eggs of one of them. He then bizarrely declared that Caribbean people live "almost exclusively" on crabs. He describes haddock, a fish that has rarely attained one meter in length, as seven meters long. And some of his recipes, such as "shark pie made from the stomach of young sharks," seem fanciful. He did write that he had no opinion on the dish since he had never eaten it "and have no wish to do so." An esteemed man of letters at the end of an illustrious career, on the subject of food, Dumas did, said, and wrote as he pleased, including rejecting all wine and extolling the qualities of water.

By the mid-nineteenth century, all the genre of food books found on contemporary shelves had already been established. There were a few Catos, including Thomas Jefferson, who talked about food in their discussions of agriculture; an occasional Pliny, including Henry David Thoreau, who included food in their observations on natural phenomena; and there are always the Galens, the health writers. But most books were either versions of Taillevent's cookbook, *Le Mésnagier's* guide to young housewives, Brillat-Savarin's literary musings, von Rumohr's definition of national cuisine—a particularly popular genre among Basques, French, Italian, and British food writers—or journalism in the tradition of Grimod de la Reynière.

A YOUNG WOMAN NAMED FANNIE MERRITT FARMER, HANDicapped from a childhood ailment that may have been polio, was not expected to be a forceful influence on anything when she graduated from the Boston Cooking-School and became an instructor. The decade-old school had been founded in 1879 and offered women a two-year program that would qualify them to earn a living as a cook. Farmer was known for relentlessly testing recipes for exact times and ingredients. In 1896, when she published her *Boston Cooking-School Cook Book,* she for all time took a great deal of the fun out of cookbooks by insisting that recipes were a scientific and not an artistic expression. No longer would a recipe be a paragraph or two that attempted to express the concept of the dish. Farmer's book was not the first to specify measurements, but it was the first to list the ingredients at the top of the recipe and was the first to introduce such notions as a level measure. Every recipe was to be a formula, which began with a list of ingredients. While this new style offered little to writers or readers, amateur cooks liked it. With about four million copies sold, it is still in print, still being revised, and has remained the model for recipe writing.

IT WAS GRIMOD—WITTY, QUICK, AND UNABASHEDLY OPIN-ionated—who is the forefather of the great majority of today's food writers, those who fill the food pages of newspapers and magazines. Grimod once wrote of journalists, "They are recognizable by the apoplectic throats, their bushy moustaches and their puffy, bibulous visages." Since Grimod, they have remained, puffy faces and all, if not the most respected then at least the best-known and most read of food writers. In the 1920s and 1930s a new and prolific species appeared, the American journalist loose in Europe with an expense account. These were not food writers, but they ate well and they wrote well, and in time, usually as they grew fatter, they began to feel as if they had something to say about food. The tradition has continued. The problem with it was well explained by one such food writer, A. J. Liebling. Himself a journalist who wrote for *The New Yorker,* earning a comfortable but not lavish living, Liebling maintained that a true gourmet had a middling income: poverty bars too many experiences and an unlimited budget does not develop curiosity or discrimination. "A man who is rich in his adolescence is almost doomed to be a dilettante," Liebling wrote. "This is not because millionaires are stupid but because they are not impelled to experiment." A gourmet, he believed, needed to be a scrounger, not a frequenter of the most famous and expensive.

Liebling was by nature such a scrounger. Exploring the back streets, he ate and ate and ate and became enormous. He was a close friend of Waverley Root, a fellow American journalist who was sent to Paris to cover news for the European edition of the *Chicago Tribune.* Liebling wrote of his friend, "A kindly and humorous man of wide and disparate interests, he could talk well of many things, but our conversations, from the time I met him, were preponderantly about what we had eaten, or were about to eat—a topic varied by what we had drunk or were about to drink with it."

It is a fallacy, and one perpetuated by many of their successors, that eating a lot is sufficient education for a profound knowledge of food. Liebling got a great deal of his food facts from Root and it has remained a mystery where Root got his information. They were both occasionally wrong, though certainly less frequently than Alexandre Dumas. What distinguished Liebling and Root is their prose style. Very different, they were both wonderful writers, the kind of writers who seduce their readers after two sentences. Liebling began a piece:

> *Mens sana in corpore sano* is a contradiction in terms, the fantasy of a Mr. Have-your-cake-and-eat-it. No sane man can afford to dispense with debilitating pleasure; no ascetic can be considered reliably sane. Hitler was the archetype of the abstemious man. When the other krauts saw him drink water in the Beer Hall they should have known he was not to be trusted.

Root began an entry on dandelion, "Whoever first called the dandelion 'a tramp with a golden head' captured nicely the humble rustic nature of this eminently edible plant, which probably accounts for the fact that very little attention is paid to it in literature." At the end of his life Root gave up news for food writing, contributing a regular column to the *International Herald Tribune,* where I was a young journeyman journalist.

WITH INTERESTING PROSE NOW LARGELY OMITTED FROM cookbooks because of Fannie Farmer's almost universal influence, the mid–twentieth century, the time of Root and Liebling, became a golden age of food writing in English. The British were producing von Rumohrs—such writers as Elizabeth David and Jane Grigson, who were writing encyclopedic volumes aimed at preserving the fast-fading traditions of British food—while the Americans were turning out Grimods and Brillat-Savarins. At the same time, Europeans came to America and brought European sensibilities to the craft. Joseph Wechsberg, an Austrian writer; Ludwig Bemelmans, the Austrian writer and illustrator best known for his children's books about Madeline; Angelo Pellegrini, an Italian who mastered English so beautifully he was renowned for his Shakespeare lectures at the University of

Washington—these writers, like Brillat-Savarin and von Rumohr, were literary people who sometimes wrote about food.

Mary Frances Kennedy Fisher, M.F.K. Fisher, born in 1908, was the American-born master of this genre of literary food musings. Her food writing, in the tradition of Brillat-Savarin, is seldom entirely about food. Fisher wrote about cultures, people she met, people she loved. She wrote a great deal about herself. She was a writer. But whatever she wrote about, food was always in some way a part of it. Her 1949 translation of Brillat-Savarin's *The Physiology of Taste* was instrumental in securing his place, perhaps an overly exalted one, in America. Fisher conveyed a love of food, among other physical and emotional pleasures. Though sometimes surrounded by snobs, she always rejected food snobbery. While she spent years in France and frequently wrote about it, she never participated in the American food writing of the time, which insisted that everything French was orgasmic and everything American a disgrace.

In 1954 Clifton Fadiman wrote, in an introduction to Fisher's compendium *The Art of Eating*, "We Americans, however, do not as a rule take gladly to the literature of gastronomy. Perhaps a native puritanism is at fault. Though things are on the mend, we still plump ice cream into carbonic acid gas, rank steak and potatoes just below the Constitution, and contrive the cafeteria." Fisher always opposed such a mentality. "All around are signs of it," she wrote. "Everywhere, little trickles of snobbish judgment, always changing, ever present." I think she would have agreed that plumping ice cream into carbonic acid gas is a creative American idea. In point of fact, the egg creams of Avenue A in New York and the root beer float, still done particularly well off Harvard Square in Cambridge, are among the high points of American gastronomic inventiveness. And Americans are less embarrassed about steak and potatoes since the world has grown smaller and we have discovered that the French rank *steak-frites* slightly higher than the Declaration of the *droit de l'homme*.

When contemplating food, Fisher found sex more interesting than snobbery, as in her discussion of the cooking of single men: "Their approach to gastronomy is basically sexual, since few of them under seventy-nine will bother to produce a good meal unless it is for a pretty woman. Few of them at any age will consciously ponder on the aphrodisiac qualities of the dishes they serve forth, but subconsciously they use what tricks they have to make their little banquets, whether intimate or merely convivial, lead as subtly as possible to the hoped-for bedding down."

The enduring popularity of food books shows that we do take gladly to the literature of gastronomy, as do readers everywhere else in the world. There is simply no better way for a writer to approach the fundamental subjects of the human condition than to talk about the food we choose to ingest.

—M.K.

CHAPTER ONE

Gourmets and Gourmands

MARK KURLANSKY ON GOURMETS

NO ONE EVER KNOWS WHEN HE IS WELL-OFF. WHENEVER I WAS called a gourmet, I suspected I was being accused of something at least slightly unpleasant. But that was before I heard the term "foodie." I am still not sure that a gourmet is a good thing to be, but it must be better than a foodie.

Although I cannot say exactly what a gourmet is, like Justice Stewart said of pornography, I know it when I see it, and I am slipping into contemplation of the meaning of the word "gourmet" because I am clearly in the company of a couple of them. The two gourmets who have invited me to lunch in a rural Basque restaurant in the green mountains of Vizcaya province are a small, red-faced, and energetic author of a popular Spanish food guide and an enormously round and well-fed man of unclear profession whose business card labels him as "gastronomic adviser."

The enthusiastic author rates all his food from one to ten. He wants all of us to do the same. He gives the lomo, the thinly sliced burgundy-colored prime cut of cured pork, only an eight. The gastronomic adviser had ventured a nine, and so they turned to me, the indecisive Hamlet of the group, who requested clearer definitions of both eight and nine.

A gourmet, according to Webster's dictionary, is "a judge of choice foods." It comes from an old French word for a wine-tasting servant and is generally confused with the word "gourmand"—an old French word meaning glutton. From this it appears that medieval Frenchmen knew the difference between a judge—someone guided by intellect—and a glutton—someone guided by appetite. But contemporary Americans are somehow getting the two notions confused. In French, by the way, the two words are still distinct. When I wrote for the *International Herald Tribune* in Paris, the French accountant who processed my expenses used to delight in pointedly calling me "Monsieur Gourmand."

Is it a lingering Puritanism that causes Americans to suspect the analysis of a physical pleasure? In 1901, Picasso depicted in blue paint a little girl reaching up to a table to scrape a bowl. It is usually labeled by its French title, *le gourmet.* But at a recent show in New York it was translated into English as *The Greedy Child.* Is a gourmet greedy? In truth, most people who are labeled gourmets, like my two lunch companions, go beyond the act of judging and analyzing. They are arriving at their judgments by eating a lot of food. Is the discussion an excuse for the real act, which is eating? Picasso's little girl did eat all the contents of the bowl.

My gourmets are discussing the lobster. The red-faced author has given it a ten and is trying to get me to concede that these tough little clawed creatures shipped from northern Europe are far better than the lobster that come from what he does not realize is my native New England, which in fact they are not.

Plato would not have thought much of these two. He mistrusted any interest in the preparation or presentation of food. In *The Republic* he states that the enjoyment of food is not a true pleasure because the purpose of eating is to relieve pain—hunger. To turn it into more than that through culinary skills, to him, was the use of artifice to disguise the true nature of food and eating. In *Gorgias* he states that cooking "is a form of flattery . . . a mischievous, deceitful, mean and ignoble activity, which cheats us by shapes and colors, by smoothing and draping. . . ." Was Plato right that gourmetism is morally and intellectually suspect or was he simply one of those unfortunates with a rubber palate incapable of appreciating food's pleasures? Or both?

Gourmet is a word with dangerous boundaries. In itself it may be a worthwhile pursuit. Food is a central activity of mankind and one of the single most significant trademarks of a culture. Shouldn't someone be examining it? But the discipline risks perilous proximity to both physical and intellectual overindulgence. In his 1996 novel *The Debt to Pleasure,* John Lancaster toys with our suspicion of gourmets. The narrator of the book is a man who, as the character himself puts it, is engaged in "the application of intelligence to pleasure." While telling the story of his life he rambles on about soups, stocks, and curry. Discussion of the perfect vinaigrette leads to analysis of the perfect seven-to-one martini. The perfect everything must be espoused, declared, and examined. By instinct, the reader does not like this rambling dilettante full of unsolicited opinions. The beauty of this novel is that the writer makes the readers doubt themselves. At first we struggle to like him and the book, but we find him pompous, then unbearable. Just as we are growing angry with this book and its smug narrator, we start to realize that he is obsessive. The fault is not with the book nor with the reader. There truly is something "not right" about this man. His gourmetism is not about a universal pleasure, the common human experience of eating, but about setting himself apart, eating special foods, having special pleasures, being answerable only to special laws. Finally we realize that we were right to have suspected this gourmet, that he truly is deranged, in fact, a dangerous psychopath.

My tablemates don't like the monkfish, and only give it a five.

What should a gourmet look like? I'm afraid most Chinese would not accept my friend the fat gastronomic adviser as a gourmet. A true gourmet—a judge—has the wisdom to know when to stop eating. From Confucius to Mao, most Chinese philosophy has contended that excess is unnatural, wasteful, and alien to proper dining. Chinese food writing emphasizes the healthiness of gourmets and their choices. Otherwise gourmetism is suspect. The contemporary Chinese writer Lu Wenfu in his novella "The Gourmet" writes: "The word gourmet is pleasing to the ear, perhaps also to the eye. If you explain it in simple everyday language, however, its not so appealing. A gourmet is a person who is totally devoted to eating."

Karl Friedrich von Rumohr, an early-nineteenth-century gourmet, known in his language as a *feinschmecker,* literally a fine taster, not only separated gourmands and gourmets but perhaps shed some light on Plato when he wrote in 1822, "Dull witted brooding people love to stuff themselves with quantities of heavy food, just like animals for fattening. Bubbly intellectual people love foods which stimulate the taste buds without overloading the belly. Profound, meditative people prefer neutral foods which do not have an assertive flavor and are not difficult to digest, and therefore do not demand too much attention."

Jean Anthelme Brillat-Savarin, the French lawyer, politician, and self-declared gourmet, also insisted that a true gourmet was health conscious. It is interesting to note that in France, gourmets, like intellectuals, are often self-declared. Curiously Brillat-Savarin rejected any distinction between the words "gourmet" and "gourmand," consistently calling the epicurean judges of food gourmands but denying that it had anything to do with gluttony. He did not have the American awkwardness about celebrating physical pleasure.

But plump men were of little appeal to Brillat-Savarin and so he denounced overeating by men while stating that women gourmets "are plump, chubby, pretty rather than beautiful, with a slight tendency to fullness of figure." In another work he wrote, "Gourmandism is far from unbecoming to women," and so we have a good idea of how Brillat-Savarin liked his gourmets.

Having finished and rated a light fruity young Basque Rioja, my well-fed, arithmetical lunch-mates opened a big imposing garnet-colored Rioja just as a thick, rare, salted, and grilled steak, a chuleta, is brought to our table. After giving it a ten, the food guide author placed the bone on my plate. "Take that," he says. "It's the best part, but you have to pick it up with your hands and gnaw on it." And he was right. A gourmet knows that the best part is not always the expensive part, and he will find that part, and then he will share it. A gourmet should want to share. Brillat-Savarin insisted on gourmets sharing.

I took the bone in my hands.

Judging foods without regard to price is a rich man's game, and yet poor people can be gourmets able to discern a good potato from a bad one. As though to underscore this point, the steak was followed by an oxtail stew, and this black-sauced peasant dish met with the double-digit rating as well. But not everyone could afford to be so tested. Only the rich can follow a thick, aged, choice steak with a stew from the tail. And so I sometimes wonder if it does not behoove those who have that luxury to talk less about it. It comes back to Plato's point. Fundamentally, gourmetism, unlike judging the fine points of art or music, is focused on a biological need designed to ease the pain of hunger, and lifting it above this level implies overlooking the sad fact that some people do not have the means to assuage that pain.

Dessert arrives, a white mousse with a berry sauce, and my two friends are engaged in lively discourse over whether it contains *queso de filadelfia,* which further descends into competing eulogies in praise of cream cheese.

I wonder: Are people who spend all their time meticulously dissecting a physical pleasure far from needing a twelve-step program? In 1997 the American Academy of Neurology announced the discovery of something called gourmet syndrome: "a new eating disorder in which some patients with right anterior brain lesions suddenly become compulsively addicted to thinking about and eating fine foods." In this study of 723 patients with brain lesions, 36 were observed becoming gourmets, and of those, 34 were found to have lesions in the right anterior part of the brain. A businessman who preferred a good tennis match to dinner suffered a brain hemorrhage and afterward "couldn't stop talking or writing about food." One patient had been a political journalist until a brain hemorrhage led him to become a food writer. Maybe I should go to a doctor now for my scan.

Things are getting worse at the table. Over brandy and Cuban cigars they have turned from the cream cheese debate to the rating of Cuban versus Brazilian woman. I notice by the physical descriptions offered to bolster their arguments that they both like their women pretty much the way Brillat-Savarin did. That must be what gourmets like. Or is it gourmands?

—based on an article from *Food & Wine* magazine, October 1999

BEN SIRA AGAINST GLUTTONY

In the second century B.C., *according to legend, Simeon Ben Sira was born already speaking and with his teeth fully formed. After reaching a more acceptable age he began writing a series of maxims and proverbs.*   —M.K.

IF YOU ARE SITTING AT A GRAND TABLE, DO NOT LICK YOUR lips and exclaim, "What a spread!"

Remember, it is a vice to have a greedy eye.

There is no greater evil in creation than the eye; that is why it must shed tears at every turn.

Do not reach for everything you see, or jostle your fellow-guest at the dish; judge his feeling by your own and always behave considerately.

Eat what is set before you like a gentleman; do not munch and make yourself objectionable.

Be the first to stop for good manners' sake and do not be insatiable, or you will give offense.

If you are dining in a large company, do not reach out your hand before others.

A man of good upbringing is content with little, and he is not short of breath when he goes to bed.

The moderate eater enjoys healthy sleep; he rises early, feeling refreshed.

But sleeplessness, indigestion, and colic are the lot of the glutton.

If you cannot avoid overeating at a feast, leave the table and find relief by vomiting.

—*The Wisdom of Ben Sira,*
second century B.C.,
translated from the Hebrew

LE MÉSNAGIER DE PARIS
ON GLUTTONY

THIS SIN OF GLUTTONY HAS TWO ASPECTS AND IS DIVIDED into five types. The first type is when someone eats sooner than is appropriate, that is to say too early in the morning or before the hour of praying, or before going to church, before having heard the words and commandments of God. Every creature should have the good sense and discretion to know that you shouldn't eat before the hour of tierce, except in cases of sickness, weakness, or some such constraint.

The second type of gluttony is eating more often than one should or when there is no need to eat. The Scriptures say, "To eat once a day is angelic, eating twice a day is human, eating three, four, or more times a day is living like an animal and not a human being."

The third type of gluttony is eating and drinking so much during the course of a day that it makes one sick, so ill as to be bedridden.

The fourth type of gluttony is eating so greedily that one doesn't stop to chew the food but swallows it whole and soon becomes, as the Scriptures say of Esau, the first born of his brothers, that he ate with such haste that he nearly choked.

The fifth type of gluttony is the search for delicacies, no matter what the price, when one could do with less and thereby afford to help one or a few people who are in need. We read of this sin in the Gospels—the evil rich man, dressed in purple, who ate copiously every day but had nothing to give to poor lepers. It is said that he was damned for having lived too delicately while refusing to share in the name of God as was his duty.

—from *Le Mésnagier de Paris,* 1393,
translated from the French by Mark Kurlansky

JEAN ANTHELME BRILLAT-SAVARIN ON GOURMETS

I HAVE THUMBED EVERY DICTIONARY FOR THE WORD *gourmandism,* without ever being satisfied with the definitions I have found. There is a perpetual confusion of *gourmandism* in its proper connotation with *gluttony* and *voracity*: from which I have concluded that lexicographers, no matter how knowing otherwise, are not numbered among those agreeable scholars who can munch pleasurably at a partridge wing *au suprême* and then top it off, little finger quirked, with a glass of Lafitte or Clos Vougeot.

They have completely, utterly forgotten that social gourmandism which unites an Attic elegance with Roman luxury and French subtlety, the kind which chooses wisely, asks for an exacting and knowing preparation, savors with vigor, and sums up the whole with profundity: it is a rare quality, which might easily be named a virtue, and which is at least one of our surest sources of pure pleasure.

Definitions

Let us make a few definitions, for a clearer understanding of this subject.

Gourmandism is an impassioned, considered, and habitual preference for whatever pleases the taste.

It is the enemy of overindulgence; any man who eats too much or grows drunk risks being expelled from its army of disciples.

Gourmandism includes the love of delicacies, which is nothing more than a ramification of this passion for light elegant dishes of little real sustenance, such as jams, pastries, and so on. This is a modification introduced into the scheme of things for the benefit of the ladies, and of such men as are like them.

No matter how gourmandism is considered, it deserves praise and encouragement.

Physically, it is the result as well as the proof of the perfect state of health of our digestive organs.

Morally, it is an implicit obedience of the rules of the Creator, who, having ordered us to eat in order to live, invites us to do so with appetite, encourages us with flavor, and rewards us with pleasure.

Advantages of Gourmandism

Gourmandism, considered as a part of political economy, is a common tie which binds nations together by the reciprocal exchange of objects which are part of their daily food.

It is something which makes wines, brandies, sugars, spices, vinegars and pickles, and provisions of every kind, travel from one end of the world to the other.

It gives a corresponding price to mediocre or good or excellent supplies, whether these qualities come to them artificially or by nature.

It sustains the hopes and ambitions and performances of that mass of fishermen, hunters, gardeners and such, who each day fill the most luxurious pantries with the results of their labors and their discoveries.

It is, finally, the means of livelihood of an industrious multitude of cooks, bakers, candymakers and other preparers of food with varying titles who, in their own ways, employ still more workers of every kind to help them, all of which causes a flow of capital whose movement and volume could not be estimated by the keenest of calculators.

And note well that any industry which has gourmandism for its object is but the more fortunate since it both has the fattest fortunes behind it and depends on the commonest daily human needs.

In the social state to which we have come today, it is hard to imagine a nation which would live solely on bread and vegetables. This nation, if it existed, would inevitably be conquered by a meat-eating enemy, as with the Hindus, who have fallen time after time before any armies that wished to attack them; or on the other hand it would be subjugated by the cooking of its neighbors, like the Boeotians of long ago, who became gourmands after the battle of Leuctra.

More Advantages

Gourmandism offers great resources to the government: it adds to taxes, to duties, and to indirect fiscal returns. Everything that we swallow must be paid for, and there is not a single treasury which does not owe part of its real strength to our gourmandizing.

What shall we say of the hundreds of cooks who, for several centuries now, leave France every year to exploit the appetites of other lands? Most of them are successful men, and bring back to their own country the fruits of their labors, in obedience to an instinct which never dies in a true Frenchman's heart. This importation of wealth is more than might be guessed, and its bearers will influence posterity.

What could be fairer, if nations honored their great men, than a temple with altars raised to gourmandism by the natives of our own France?

Powers of Gourmandism

In 1815, the treaty of the month of November imposed on France the condition of paying seven hundred and fifty million francs in three years to the Allies.

To this duty was added the one of making good the reclamations of inhabitants of the different countries, whose united rulers had set forth the amounts, coming altogether to more than three hundred million.

And finally to all this must be added the requisitions of every possible kind made by the enemy generals, who heaped wagons with goods which they headed for the frontiers, and which the public was later forced to pay for; all this came to more than fifteen hundred millions.

It was possible, and in fact rightful, to fear that such considerable payments, which moreover were made every day in bullion, would put a fearful strain on the treasury, and would cause a depreciation in all paper values and be followed by that misery which hovers over a penniless and helpless nation.

"Alas!" cried the moneyed fellows who watched the ominous wagon going to be loaded at the bank in the Rue Vivienne, "alas, there is our silver, flowing out of the country in a flood. By next year we'll kneel before a crownpiece if we ever see one; we'll be living like beggars; business will be dead; there will be nothing left to borrow; we'll have famine, plague, a civil death."

What actually happened gave the lie to all these fears, and to the great astonishment of everyone who was connected with finance, the national payments were easily met, credit increased, people borrowed eagerly, and during the whole period of this SUPERPURGATION the exchange, that infallible measure of the circulation of money, was in our favor: that is to say, we had the arithmetical proof that more money came in to France than left it.

What power is it that came to our aid? What godlike thing was it that caused this miracle? It was gourmandism.

When the Britons, Germans, Huns, Cimmerians, and Scythians poured into France, they brought with them a rare voracity, and stomachs of uncommon capacity.

They were not long satisfied with the official fare which was offered to them by an enforced hospitality; they hungered for rarer delicacies, and before long the Queen of Cities was no more than an immense mess hall. These invaders ate in the restaurants, in the cook shops, in the taverns and the bars, in the stores, and even in the streets.

They stuffed themselves with meat, fish, game, truffles, cakes, and above all with our fruits.

They drank with a thirst as abysmal as their hunger, and always demanded the best wines, hoping to discover unknown pleasures in them, which they were inevitably astonished not to recognize.

Superficial observers did not know what to think of this endless, meaningless eating; but the real Frenchmen chuckled and rubbed their hands together as they said: "Look at them, under our spell! They have spent more crowns tonight than the Government paid them this morning!"

It was a happy period for everyone who catered to the pleasures of the palate. Véry built up his fortune; Achard began his; Beauvilliers made a third lucky one, and Madame Sullot, whose shop in the Palais-Royal was not more than ten feet square, sold as many as twelve thousand little tarts a day.

This still lasts: foreigners flood into our country from every part of Europe, to carry on in peacetime the pleasant habits they formed during the war; they feel helplessly drawn to Paris, and once there they must enjoy themselves at any price. And if our public stock is high, it is less because of the good rate of interest it carries than because of the innate confidence which is felt in a country where gourmands are made happy.

—from *The Physiology of Taste,* 1825,
translated from the French by M.F.K. Fisher

ALEXANDRE-BALTHAZAR-LAURENT GRIMOD DE LA REYNIÈRE ON GOURMETS AND GLUTTONS

MR. BARTHE [NICHOLAS-THOMAS BARTHE, WHO DIED IN 1785 at age fifty-one, it is said from a life of overindulgence], the ingenious author of *Fausses Infidelités,* who was as egotistical as he was gourmand, had the habit of eating something from every dish on the table. His sight being poor, he suffered from the constant fear of having missed something; consequently he was constantly turning to his servant and asking, "Have I had any of this? Have I eaten any of that?" All of which was extremely amusing to the other guests. Barthe died of indigestion, aggravated by a fit of temper: for he was irascible, too. Had he only been a gourmet [though Grimod uses the older word, *gourmand*] he might still be alive today, like his enemy Mr. Cailhava [Jean-Claude Cailhava, who died in 1813 at the age of eighty-two].

A voracious appetite is all that is required to be a glutton. To merit the title of gourmet requires an exquisite judgment, a profound knowledge of every side of the gastronomic art, a sensual and delicate palate, and a thousand other qualities which are difficult to find in the same person at the same time.

—from *Almanach des Gourmands,* 1804,
translated from the French by Mark Kurlansky

AUGUSTE ESCOFFIER
ON THE ART OF COOKING
IN MODERN SOCIETY

It is ironic that Auguste Escoffier (1846–1935), who defined French cooking for several generations, did so in London after moving there in 1890. From his base at the Savoy Hotel and later the Ritz-Carlton, he was the most famous chef of the turn of the century, an epoch marked by opulence. His 1903 book Le guide culinaire *became the professional cook's textbook, explaining French cuisine for the next seventy years, until he was dethroned by nouvelle cuisine. Interestingly, in the introduction to the 1907 edition, he forecast nouvelle cuisine, accurately describing the kind of cooking that would replace him.* —M.K.

THE ART OF COOKING DEPENDS ON THE PSYCHOLOGICAL state of society, and it is not possible to separate the two. Where life is relaxed and easy and not troubled, where the future is certain and protected from the whims of fortune, the art of cooking becomes considerably developed because it provides one of the most agreeable pleasures that can be bestowed on a man of taste.

On the other hand, where life is active, where the thousand anxieties of industry and business consume a man's spirit, there cannot be a life of luxury. Usually, the need for nutrition seems, to people driven by the whirlwind of business, no longer a pleasure but a burden; they consider the time spent at the dinner table as lost, and they demand of those charged with serving them that they are never left waiting.

One can, and one should, deplore such habits. From the perspective of the diners' health, the stomach will pay the consequences, and they are to blame. But it is completely beyond our power to stop them: All that can be done with culinary science is to counteract the foolishness of man, in whatever measure possible, with the perfection of products.

If the customer demands to be served quickly, we have no choice but to do what he asks or to lose him: that which we refuse him our competitors will provide. We are therefore forced to be in the service of his fantasy. If our customary methods of working, if our service does not comply with this requirement, we must retrain ourselves. Only one thing has to remain unchangeable: that is the quality of the dishes; it is the value that is at the root of cooking, the foundation of our work. The presentation has already begun to change. Much of the paraphernalia and frills have vanished or will vanish, replaced by modern service: the pedestal, the fringes, etc. We will go even further down this path. We will take simplicity to its limits, but at the same time we will improve both the taste and nutritional value of dishes; we will make them lighter, and more digestible for weakened stomachs; we will concentrate them; we will strip them of most of their nonessential ingredients. In a word, cooking, without ceasing to be an art, will become scientific and will be elaborate in formulas, in the service too often of a method and a precision which leaves nothing to chance.

—from *Le guide culinaire* (2nd edition), 1907, translated from the French by Mark Kurlansky

HENRI GAULT AND CHRISTIAN MILLAU ON NOUVELLE CUISINE

The October 1973 issue of Le nouveau guide Gault-Millau, *the fifty-fourth issue of Henri Gault and Christian Millau's hip food and travel magazine, featured on the cover a fat, worried old hen with*

bloodshot eyes staring helplessly while her egg hatched a brash young rooster who crowed "Vive la Nouvelle Cuisine Française." A new food term was born, soon to be misused for all sorts of inventions.

Gault and Millau were talking specifically about French food. Younger chefs, among them Paul Bocuse, Alain Senderens, the Trois-gros brothers, and Michel Guérard, they contended, were rethinking French cuisine for the first time since Escoffier and introducing new approaches, and especially new products, many of which, such as avocados, were already commonplace in the United States. The cuisine that was described in 1973 became the standard way to cook in France. Nouvelle cuisine was so specifically French that it was, and still is, misunderstood in the rest of the world. You have to be dominated by Escoffier before rejecting him becomes meaningful.

While the emphasis was on lighter food, it should be remembered that they were talking about lighter than Escoffier's sumptuous cuisine for the worry-free, nineteenth-century elite who ate at their leisure. It was the cuisine Escoffier had predicted in 1907, with simple presentation, quicker preparation, and an emphasis on good products. Inside the magazine, an article was marked by an illustration of a fallen pot-bellied older chef, medals on chest, haggard ruddy face bespeaking excess and abuse. Over him stood a thin young chef in the kind of pose once used by hunters who had bagged their big-game quarry. The article offered the following "ten commandments" of nouvelle cuisine Française. —M.K.

1. *Reduced cooking time* (like the Chinese) for most fish dishes and all shellfish and crustaceans, dark meat fowl, game roasts, veal, some green vegetables, pasta. Roasted lobster and veal rack chez Denis, the green beans of Bocuse, the fish at Le Duc, the frog legs at Haeberlin, the duck at Guérard, the shrimp at Troisgros, the woodcock at Minot, among others, are outstanding examples.

2. *New uses of products* It is undeniable that our era of overproduction and debasing technology is poisoning, even eliminating, many products. Gastronomically speaking, there is practically no more chicken, veal, beef, game, trout, cheese, etc. Old-fashioned cooking, even the best, continues to use these antiseptic and rigorously insipid products without wavering. New chefs try to eliminate rather than cover up the bad quality with overly aggressive sauces. They have two solutions.

   a. To make what we are calling "market cuisine," which is made with the products bought the same morning (the new chefs get up very early) or duly ordered. They uncover among the best markets rare and precious (and expensive) chickens, veal, shrimp, partridge, frogs, tomatoes, eggs, truffles, etc.

b. They make do with what the modern world has not yet destroyed, or things that have been made more accessible and fresher: seafood (oysters are better than ever); butter, generally respectable; vegetables, in spite of pesticides; Israeli foie gras; California asparagus; etc.

3. This approach has led modern chefs to *reduce the choices on their menu.* This has been done for a long time now in the provinces, where regular customers return more often. In Paris, fewer of those giant menus are being seen that offer an absurdly varied choice and impose the necessity of stockpiling food in the cold. (God knows in what condition "fresh" products were in those restaurants with five hundred dishes in the time of our grandparents.) With the new way, there is the means for stocking fresh food, a more immediate cuisine, more inventive, fresher, less routine, always cooked to order. And the fortunate end to sauce bases worked in the bain-marie, the glory of the prewar epoch.

4. The new chefs *are not systematically modernist.* They know of the dangers threatening products—fish and crustaceans especially, as soon as they are chilled, whether they be raw or cooked.

Unlike the old school that served you a cluster of frozen shrimp and soles Dugléré dried on ice, the new chefs use a refrigerator delicately.

5. However, they do not let out the cry of raped virgins on the subject of every piece of equipment for cooking or preserving or cleaning that offers them *avant-garde techniques.* Their stoves are new (and clean) and have easy temperature control. There are hot counters for their dishes. They work in a climate that is not stiflingly hot, without unbearable smells, in a well-lit and ample space. They use mixers and ice cream makers and automatic rotisseries and peelers and trash bailers. . . .

6. They have banished from their cooking the so-called culinary principle (actually just a sorry way of preserving) that calls for game (and certain domestic meat that is passed off for game) to be marinated in

oil, alcohol, wine, or spices for days, not to mention the horrible practice of hanging meat (Curnonsky's contemporaries prepared rotten birds). The new chefs serve *game cured but fresh,* and the spices designed to conceal the shameful rot are gone.

7. Little by little, the new chefs recognize the pretension, the inanity, the mediocrity of rich and heavy sauces. *Those terrible brown and white sauces, espagnoles, perigueux, financières, the grand veneur, béchamel, mornay* that have murdered many a liver and covered up so much tasteless meat. Those beef reductions, red wine, madeira, blood, roux, gelatine, flour, cheese, and starch are no longer carved in stone. The chefs go gently with stocks, cream, butter, pure juice, eggs, truffle, lemon, fresh herbs, and pepper and cherish light sauces, sauces that blend, that exalt, and leave the spirit light and the stomach comfortable.

8. *They do not ignore dieting.* Without bowing to the inconsistencies of men in a hurry and women health food followers, they have discovered the grace of light food, of clever salads, of fresh vegetables simply cut, of rare meat. The steak at Troisgros is less fattening than macrobiotic soup. And tomatoes are no longer peeled just for the taste but for the good of the stomach.

9. They have also understood *the danger of gaudy presentations,* wastefulness, which the venerable Carême made fashionable 150 years ago. They still like to embellish, but they know the limits and don't pass them, and have discovered the aesthetics of simplicity.

10. Finally. *They invent.* It is said that since the nineteenth century everything has been tried and created, all the tools, cooking, combinations. Well, that isn't true. (Sixty years ago, Jules Maincave, ingenious inventor, imagined replacing vinaigrette with a mixture of pork juice and rum, married the chicken to the lily of the valley, veal with absinth. . . .) There remain millions of dishes to invent, and probably hundreds to revive.

—from *Le nouveau guide Gault-Millau,* no. 54, October 1973,
translated from the French by Mark Kurlansky

LUDWIG BEMELMANS ON BEING A GOURMET

THERE IS A LOT OF TALK ABOUT THE GOURMET THESE DAYS and about the rules and the art of eating—in fact, several magazines are devoted to this subject. Any restaurant that would try to satisfy the true gourmet would be bankrupt in a matter of weeks. The popular concept of the gourmet is that of a seal-like, happy creature of Gargantuan appetite, who sticks a napkin inside his collar, dunks bread into the sauces and throws on the floor plates that are not properly heated. His nourishment is catalogued as caviar, pâté de foie gras, truffles, pheasant and crêpes Suzette. He drinks only the proper wine, but on closing his eyes and rinsing it in and out through his teeth he is able to tell you not only the age of the wine but also the number on the barrel in which it has been aged. He is thought of as a middle-aged man (never a woman), portly and jolly, given to reciting toasts that are spiked with French terms. His extravagant dinners take on the aspect of an eating contest rather than a good meal.

Actually, the true gourmet, like the true artist, is one of the unhappiest creatures existent. His trouble comes from so seldom finding what he constantly seeks: perfection.

To be a gourmet you must start early, as you must begin riding early to be a good horseman. You must live in France; your father must have been a gourmet. Nothing in life must interest you but your stomach. With hands trembling, you must approach the meal about which you have worried all day and risk dying of a stroke if it isn't perfect.

The last time I was at the Ritz in Paris I noticed a novice waiter, called a *piccolo,* standing in the dining room. He was about fourteen years old, with a student's pale face. Every so often he hid behind a marble column while he popped into his mouth, one by one, strawberries that he had swiped from the breakfast buffet. The captain on duty surprised him in the act and pulled him into the room, holding him gingerly by one ear. There in front of the buffet he delivered a long lecture, the gist of which was that the good things displayed there were only for the distinguished guests of the house. The captain, seeing that I had observed the scene, came to the table. "Very good boy, otherwise," he said. "He will be all right once he gets the hang of things." The boy, he explained, was the son of the owner of a tavern in

Rouen; this man had a brother who was a maître d'hôtel at the Tour d'Argent, the famous Paris restaurant. When the boy was born, his father had written his brother to reserve for the boy a place as an apprentice, and because Monsieur the Maître d'Hôtel of the Tour d'Argent was a great friend of Monsieur the Maître d'Hôtel of the Ritz, the fortunate connection had been made, and the boy was thus in line for a fine career—after several years' apprenticeship. His counterpart below stairs, the one who becomes an apprentice in the kitchen, starts with peeling potatoes and scrubbing. In this climate the gourmet can survive. The climate of democracy is fatal to him.

At one time the gourmet had a chance in America. A horde of European chefs, maîtres d'hôtel, managers, waiters and cooks came to America.

Walking off the boats, they went straight to the newly erected large hotels, some of which, for several years, matched the standards of the European hotel de grand luxe.

One of the greatest hotels and restaurants of that time was the old Knickerbocker, owned and managed by a man named Regan, who walked through his hotel with two detectives because he was afraid that some foreign waiter might knife him. A complaint from a customer, in these days, was followed by immediate discharge.

When employees of the old Waldorf reported sick, they actually had to be in bed, for it was Mr. Boldt's habit to send detectives to their homes to check up.

As for hiring new help—that was no problem for management; outside the doors of every New York employment office were long lines of job seekers, each with a dossier of references from the best European houses.

As immigration became restricted, trained hotel personnel became fewer. Now virtually all of the old-timers have disappeared. Replacing them, particularly those employed in the kitchen, is one of the great problems of hotel keeping, for Americans don't like to be cooks.

Hotel managers tell you Americans make poor cooks. They say they lack the—"I don't know what." By the same rule it is said that no American makes a good musician or painter, but he does—once he is interested.

The fault is that no one has taken the trouble to make the profession of cooking attractive to young Americans—to inform them that being a good chef is one of the most satisfying, honored and remunerative callings. Another deterrent, perhaps, is the costume. The chef's traditional white hat, jacket and apron probably seem like sissy stuff to the prospective kitchen candidate.

America is a land of healthy appetites. It is not in the American character to live in order to eat. Rather, the reverse is true. Many try, but just as Americans don't make good gigolos, neither do they make good gourmets.

The desperate rituals of the various food fraternities and gourmet clubs are as authentic as the war dances Indians stage for tourists at Western railroad depots. The food served at the dinners of the societies is relatively good, as banquets go. The trouble with these affairs is not so much the cooking as the commercial note that is injected throughout the meal. You are accosted by salesmen for newly invented salad dressings, deep-frying fats or starchless spaghetti. These fellows are followed by liquor and champagne salesmen who creep around the table taking orders.

Such get-togethers fail to do anything for the cause, mainly because no good chef can prepare a truly superb meal for more than a dozen people.

Occasionally I am looked upon as a gourmet and when I go out with friends, they say, "Oh, let him order—he knows everything about food and wine."

Having been born in Europe and lived in hotels most of my life, I do know how to read a menu and can usually tell a poor restaurant by instinct. As for being a gourmet, I disqualify in every respect. I eat too much, drink too much and love company at the table. I use the menu without attention to rules. The geography of my stomach is antigourmet in the extreme. For example, I long for a small shack along the Danube, at the side of the old stone bridge in Regensburg, Bavaria. There, over an open fire, in a kitchen two hundred years old and by a secret recipe kept in the family, sausages the size of a small finger are broiled.

They are served on a bed of sauerkraut, with the same brown beer my grandfather brewed. On a good day, I can eat a dozen of these for my second breakfast, around ten in the morning, and drink two quarts of that beer.

I remember with sadness an old fisherman in Miami on whose boat I worked long ago. There was a shack there, also on a pier, where we sold the fish. But we always kept one for ourselves, which we cooked in the shack. No fish has ever been better.

In the whole world there are no better lobsters than those that come from Maine. There are no better steaks anywhere than in America. I often go to the seafood bar on the lower level of the Grand Central Station in New York to eat a clam pan roast. For Italian food I like Angelo's in Mulberry Street, or Tony's San Marino in East 53rd Street; for fish, Sweet's Restaurant near the fish market in downtown New York. The best German food is served by Luchow's, whose proprietor tries to keep the specialties of the house as authentically indigestible as they must be. The sauerbraten and potato pancakes there are superb, the red cabbage and lentil soup expertly cooked. Geese, venison and *Hasenpfeffer* are done as if Herr Walterspiel himself were at the oven, and you leave satisfied. If a prize were given for the treatment of beer, then it would go to this place. The pipes are kept clean, it's not too cold and there is enough of it drawn so that it is always fresh.

—from *La Bonne Table,* 1964

A. J. Liebling on Boxing
Away Gluttony

In 1926, though, I had another route to keeping my weight within bounds. I liked to box, and I had an illusion that if I boxed a lot, I could eat and drink a great deal and even stay up late with the girls. The exercise would burn all that out. I was too young to know that if you do those three things often you will feel with increasing infrequency like boxing, and boxing is no fun unless you feel like it. This is because boxing makes you want to eat, but eating does not make you want to box. I had not yet heard the great Sam Langford say: "You can sweat out beer and you can sweat out whiskey, but you can't sweat out women." Sam had never had to contend with my toughest opponent of all, sheer gluttony.

—from *Between Meals,* 1959

CHAPTER TWO

Food and Sex

Food and sex are inevitably linked because they are the two great physical pleasures that writers most want to write about. A. J. Liebling once complained that the perfect specimens of female anatomy, all the perfect parts, were never found together on the same woman: "So just as in a restaurant, you had to pick a modest but satisfying agenda." However, he gallantly cautioned, "It was trickier than that because a woman, unlike a navarin de mouton, has a mind." Men, when not in mixed company, often start by talking about food and end up talking about sex. I can only suppose that the same is true of women. What has changed is that until the twentieth century, only men put these thoughts in print.   —M.K.

JOHN ASH ON M.F.K. FISHER'S WARM SANDWICH

Mostly remembered today for the beauty of her prose, in her lifetime M.F.K. Fisher was known to be a seductively attractive woman. John Ash, a California chef and food commentator, only knew her when she was fairly elderly, but he still recalls her as stunningly beautiful.   —M.K.

USUALLY WHEN I VISITED MARY FRANCES I BROUGHT lunch, but on one particular day she said she would fix lunch for us. I arrived in the morning and, as we chatted, she took a loaf of good local crusty French bread, split it in half lengthwise and proceeded to slather both sides with a good amount of homemade mayonnaise and coarse Dijon mustard. She then proceeded to layer on slices of a tasty smoked ham; thick slices of a creamy jack cheese from Ig Vella, whose cheese company was and still is in nearby Sonoma; and topped it all with some leaves of spicy arugula.

What she did then was mysterious, at least for the moment. She took this big old sandwich and wrapped it tightly in several layers of plastic wrap. I confess I thought she maybe was getting a little "forgetful." She then pronounced ". . . lunch will be ready in an hour" and then gave me the wrapped sandwich and instructed me to sit on it! We continued to chat even though I was a little distracted by my "cushion." In about an hour she said "lunch is ready" and instructed me to stand up. She unwrapped the loaf, which was now highly compressed and warm from my body heat. She sliced it into nice little finger sandwiches, and served it with some little cornichon pickles on the side and a glass of nice Sonoma Pinot Noir, as I recall. She remarked that this sandwich had many attributes. Not only was it delicious, but it was also a wonderful tool to use with overactive children to get them to sit still and in one place for a little while. I'm not sure if I fell into that category or not, but I've never forgotten that great lady or her sandwich!

—from a personal communication with Mark Kurlansky, 1999

M.F.K. FISHER ON THE VIRILITY OF TURKISH DESSERTS

SABRI, THE HOMESICK TURKISH LAWYER, INVITED US FOR tea. We drank too much of it, and ate, ravenously or discreetly, according to our nationalities, at a large cake like a macaroon. Sabri had made it, and he told us how.

"Cook finest vermicelli thoroughly," he instructed, a cold polite smile on his face and his eyes very warm and melancholy. "Then when it is done spread it in a large shallow baking-dish and drip honey and sweet oil upon it until the dish brims.

"Throw slivers of pistachio nuts upon it, as many as you like—I like very many. And then bake it slowly. It will shrivel down to a brown crusty cake with a moist inside, like the one you did not eat much of."

"Sabri, it's—we——"

"I know. It's too sweet for you, eh, Al?"

"Yes. It makes every tooth in my head quiver like a stricken doe." Sabri almost smiled.

"For myself," he remarked, distantly, "it is barely sweet. And these icings and bonbons you eat! They are tasteless as dust to a Turk.

"Of course, in our world, the Near East, we like anything with starch in it, too. There is a good reason." He looked glumly and perhaps a little maliciously at me.

"Yes, a very good reason—for us, that is. We Easterners eat viscous, sticky foods to make ourselves more virile!

"Perhaps that's what ails us," he added, austerely. Then he grinned, and broke the last chunk of cake in his fat, too-sensitive hands. "Young men try to increase what they have; old men look for what they've passed by—but is it only in Turkey?"

—from *The Art of Eating,* 1937

<hr>

EMILE ROUMER ON PEASANT LOVE

Emile Roumer was born in Haiti in 1908. Educated in France, he wrote poetry in French from 1930 to 1935, and then stopped writing entirely. —M.K.

The Peasant Declares His Love

High-yellow of my heart, with breasts like tangerines,
you taste better to me than eggplant stuffed with crab,
you are the tripe in my pepper-pot,

the dumpling in my peas, my tea of aromatic herbs.
You are the corned beef whose customhouse is my heart,
my mush with syrup that trickles down the throat.
You are a steaming dish, mushrooms cooked with rice,
crisp potato fries, and little fish fried brown. . . .
My hankering for love follows you wherever you go.
Your bottom is a basket full of fruits and meat.

—Translated from the French by John Peale Bishop, c.1930

Brillat-Savarin on Women Gourmets

GOURMANDISM IS FAR FROM UNBECOMING TO THE LADIES:
it agrees with the delicacy of their organs, and acts as compensation
for certain pleasures which they must deny themselves, and certain ills
to which nature seems to have condemned them.

Nothing is more agreeable to look at than a pretty gourmande in
full battle-dress: her napkin is tucked in most sensibly; one of her
hands lies on the table; the other carries elegantly carved little morsels
to her mouth, or perhaps a partridge wing on which she nibbles; her
eyes shine, her lips are soft and moist, her conversation is pleasant,
and all her gestures are full of grace; she does not hide that vein of co-
quetry which women show in everything they do. With so much in her
favor, she is utterly irresistible, and Cato the Censor himself would be
moved by her.

Anecdote

Here, however, I must recall a bitter memory.

One day I found myself seated at the dinner table next to the
lovely Mme. M . . . d, and I was silently congratulating myself on such
a delightful accident when she turned suddenly to me and said, "To
your health!" At once I began a compliment to her in my prettiest
phrases; but I never finished it, for the little flirt had already turned to
the man on her left, with another toast. They clicked glasses, and this

abrupt desertion seemed to me a real betrayal, and one that made a scar in my heart which many years have not healed over.

Women Are Gourmandes

The leanings of the fair sex toward gourmandism are in a way instinctive, for it is basically favorable to their beauty.

A series of precise and exhaustive observations has proved beyond doubt that a tempting diet, dainty and well prepared, holds off for a long time the exterior signs of old age.

It adds brilliancy to the eyes, freshness to the skin, and more firmness to all the muscles; and just as it is certain, in physiology, that it is the sagging of these muscles which causes wrinkles, beauty's fiercest enemy, so it is equally correct to say that, other things being equal, the ladies who know how to eat are comparatively ten years younger than those to whom this science is a stranger.

Painters and sculptors have long recognized this truth, and they never portray subjects who, through choice or duty, practice abstinence, such as anchorites or misers, without giving them the pallor of illness, the wasted scrawniness of poverty, and the deep wrinkles of enfeebled senility.

—from *The Physiology of Taste,* 1825,
translated from the French by M.F.K. Fisher

Grimod de la Reynière on Why Blondes Go Better Than Brunettes with Food

WITH A FEW EXCEPTIONS, FAIR SKIN DENOTES A DISTINguished lineage, a delicate mind, and a soft and fine skin (a characteristic much admired by connoisseurs, for being as sensitive in the dark as in light). Normally it is a sign of softness, and of all the pleasing qualities of the fair sex. A blonde seems humbly to beseech your heart, while a brunette tends to ravish it. There is no question that people prefer to receive prayers than orders.

Whether you think this analogy is fair or not, a meal of blonde food is in every way superior to a meal of brunette food. Any cook can easily do an acceptable job on the latter, but the former can only be realized by a first-rate cook.

—from *Manuel des Amphitryons,* 1808,
translated from the French by Mark Kurlansky

M.F.K. FISHER ON
BACHELOR COOKING

B IS FOR BACHELORS . . . AND THE WONDERFUL DINNERS they pull out of their cupboards with such dining-room aplomb and kitchen chaos.

Their approach to gastronomy is basically sexual, since few of them under seventy-nine will bother to produce a good meal unless it is for a pretty woman. Few of them at any age will consciously ponder on the aphrodisiac qualities of the dishes they serve forth, but subconsciously they use what tricks they have to make their little banquets, whether intimate or merely convivial, lead as subtly as possible to the hoped-for bedding down.

Soft lights, plenty of tipples (from champagne to straight rye), and if possible a little music, are the timeworn props in any such entertainment, on no matter what financial level the host is operating. Some men head for the back booth at the corner pub and play the juke-box, with overtones of medium-rare steak and French-fried potatoes. Others are forced to fall back on the soft-footed alcoholic ministrations of a Filipino houseboy, muted Stan Kenton on the super-Capehart, and a little supper beginning with caviar malossol on ice and ending with a soufflé au kirschwasser d'Alsace.

The bachelors I'm considering at this moment are at neither end of the gastronomical scale. They are the men between twenty-five and fifty who if they have been married are temporarily out of it and are therefore triply conscious of both their heaven-sent freedom and their domestic clumsiness. They are in the middle brackets, financially if not emotionally. They have been around and know the niceties or amenities or whatever they choose to call the tricks of a well-set table and a well-poured glass, and yet they have neither the tastes nor the pocketbooks to indulge in signing endless chits at Mike Romanoff's or "21."

In other words, they like to give a little dinner now and again in the far from circumspect intimacy of their apartments, which more often than not consist of a studio-living-room with either a disguised letdown bed or a tiny bedroom, a bath, and a stuffy closet called the kitchen.

I have eaten many meals prepared and served in such surroundings. I am perhaps fortunate to be able to say that I have always enjoyed them—and perhaps even more fortunate to be able to say that I enjoyed them because of my acquired knowledge of the basic rules of seduction. I assumed that I had been invited for either a direct or an indirect approach. I judged as best I could which one was being contemplated, let my host know of my own foreknowledge, and then sat back to have as much pleasure as possible.

I almost always found that since my host knew I was aware of the situation, he was more relaxed and philosophical about its very improbable outcome and could listen to the phonograph records and savor his cautiously concocted Martini with more inner calm. And I almost always ate and drank well, finding that any man who knows that a woman will behave in her cups, whether of consommé double or of double Scotch, is resigned happily to a good dinner; in fact, given the choice between it and a rousing tumble in the hay, he will inevitably choose the first, being convinced that the latter can perforce be found elsewhere.

The drinks offered to me were easy ones, dictated by my statements made early in the game (I never bothered to hint but always said plainly, in self-protection, that I liked very dry Gibsons with good ale to follow, or dry sherry with good wine: safe but happy, that was my motto). I was given some beautiful liquids: really old Scotch, Swiss Dézelay light as mountain water, proud vintage Burgundies, countless bottles of champagne, all good too, and what fine cognacs! Only once did a professional bachelor ever offer me a glass of sweet liqueur. I never saw him again, feeling that his perceptions were too dull for me to exhaust myself, if after even the short time needed to win my acceptance of his dinner invitation he had not guessed my tastes that far.

The dishes I have eaten at such tables-for-two range from home-grown snails in home-made butter to pompano flown in from the Gulf of Mexico with slivered macadamias from Maui—or is it Oahu? I have found that most bachelors like the exotic, at least culinarily speaking: they would rather fuss around with a complex recipe for Le Hochepot de Queue de Boeuf than with a simple one called Stewed Ox-tail, even if both come from André Simon's *Concise Encyclopædia of Gastronomy*.

They are snobs in that they prefer to keep Escoffier on the front of the shelf and hide Mrs. Kander's *Settlement Cook Book*.

They are experts at the casual: they may quit the office early and make a murderous sacrifice of pay, but when you arrive the apartment is pleasantly odorous, glasses and a perfectly frosted shaker or a bottle await you. Your host looks not even faintly harried or stove-bound. His upper lip is unbedewed and his eye is flatteringly wolfish.

Tact and honest common sense forbid any woman's penetrating with mistaken kindliness into the kitchen: motherliness is unthinkable in such a situation, and romance would wither on the culinary threshold and be buried forever beneath its confusion of used pots and spoons.

Instead the time has come for ancient and always interesting blandishments, of course in proper proportions. The Bachelor Spirit unfolds like a hungry sea anemone. The possible object of his affections feels cozily desired. The drink is good. He pops discreetly in and out of his gastronomical workshop, where he brews his sly receipts, his digestive attacks upon the fortress of her virtue. She represses her natural curiosity, and if she is at all experienced in such wars she knows fairly well that she will have a patterned meal which has already been indicated by his ordering in restaurants. More often than not it will be some kind of chicken, elaborately disguised with everything from Australian pine-nuts to herbs grown by the landlady's daughter.

One highly expert bachelor-cook in my immediate circle swears by a recipe for breasts of young chicken, poached that morning or the night before, and covered with a dramatic and very lemony sauce made at the last minute in a chafing dish. This combines all the tricks of seeming nonchalance, carefully casual presentation, and attention-getting.

With it he serves chilled asparagus tips in his own version of vinaigrette sauce and little hot rolls. For dessert he has what is also his own version of riz à l'Impératrice, which he is convinced all women love because he himself secretly dotes on it—and it can be made the day before, though not too successfully.

This meal lends itself almost treacherously to the wiles of alcohol: anything from a light lager to a Moët et Chandon of a great year is beautiful with it, and can be well bolstered with the preprandial drinks which any bachelor doles out with at least one ear on the Shakespearean dictum that they may double desire and halve the pursuit thereof.

The most successful bachelor dinner I was ever plied with, or perhaps it would be more genteel to say served, was also thoroughly horrible.

Everything was carried out, as well as in, by a real expert, a man then married for the fifth time who had interspersed his connubial adventures with rich periods of technical celibacy. The cocktails were delicately suited to my own tastes rather than his, and I sipped a glass of Tio Pepe, properly chilled. The table, set in a candle-lit patio, was laid in the best sense of the word "nicely," with silver and china and Swedish glass which I had long admired. The wine was a last bottle of Chianti, " 'stra vecchio."

We ate thin strips of veal that had been dipped in an artful mixture of grated parmigiano and crumbs, with one of the bachelor's favorite tricks to accompany it, buttered thin noodles gratinés with extra-thin and almond-brown toasted noodles on top. There was a green salad.

The night was full of stars, and so seemed my eager host's brown eyes, and the whole thing was ghastly for two reasons: he had forgotten to take the weather into his menu planning, so that we were faced with a rich, hot, basically heavy meal on one of the worst summer nights in local history, and I was at the queasiest possible moment of pregnancy.

Of course the main mistake was in his trying to entertain a woman in that condition as if she were still seduceable and/or he still a bachelor: we had already been married several months.

—from *An Alphabet for Gourmets,* 1949

CHAPTER THREE

Memorable Meals

EATING AT CAB CALLOWAY'S

Everybody Eats When They Come to My House

Have a banana, Hannah,
Try the salami, Tommy,
Give with the gravy, Davy,
Everybody eats when they come to my house!

Try a tomato, Plato,
Here's cacciatore, Dorie,
Taste the baloney, Tony,
Everybody eats when they come to my house!

I fix your favorite dishes,
Hopin' this good food fills ya!
Work my hands to the bone in the kitchen alone,
You better eat if it kills ya!

Pass me a pancake, Mandrake,
Have an hors-d'oeuvre-y, Irvy,
Look in the fendel, Mendel,
Everybody eats when they come to my house!

Hannah! Davy! Tommy! Dora! Mandrake!
Everybody eats when they come to my house!

Pastafazoola, Talullah!
Oh, do have a bagel, Fagel,
Now, don't be so bashful, Nashville,
Everybody eats when they come to my house!

Hey, this is a party, Marty
Here, you get the cherry, Jerry,
Now, look, don't be so picky, Micky,
'Cause everybody eats when they come to my house!

All of my friends are welcome,
Don't make me coax you, moax you,
Eat the tables, the chairs, the napkins, who cares?
You gotta eat if it chokes you!

Oh, do have a knish, Nishia,
Pass me the latke, Macky,
Chile con carne for Barney,
Everybody eats when they come to my house!

Face! Buster! Chair! Chops! Fump!
Everybody eats when they come to my house!

Everybody eats when they come to my house!

—1948

MARTIAL'S DINNER INVITATION

Marcus Valerius Martialis, commonly known as Martial, was born in A.D. *40 in Spain. He moved to Rome at the age of twenty-three and spent the next thirty-five years there, among all classes of Romans, observing and wryly commenting on Roman life, one of the first poets of urbanism. He died in* A.D. *104 in Spain.* —M.K.

Toranius, if the prospect of a cheerless, solitary dinner
Bores you, eat with me—and get thinner.
If you like appetite-whetters,
There'll be cheap Cappadocian lettuce,
Pungent leeks, and tunny-fish
Nestling in sliced eggs. Next, a black earthenware dish
(Watch out—a finger-scorcher!) of broccoli just taken
From its cool bed, pale beans with pink bacon,
And a sausage sitting in the centre
Of a snow-white pudding of polenta.
If you want to try a dessert, I can offer you raisins (my own),
Pears (from Syria), and hot chestnuts (grown
In Naples, city of learning)
Roasted in a slow-burning
Fire. As for the wine, by drinking it you'll commend it.
When this great feast has ended,
If, as he well might,
Bacchus stirs up a second appetite,
You'll be reinforced by choice Picenian olives fresh from the trees,
Warm lupins and hot chick-peas.
Let's face it,
It's a poor sort of dinner; yet, if you deign to grace it,
You'll neither say nor hear
One word that's not sincere,
You can lounge at ease in your place,
Wearing your own face,
You won't have to listen while your host reads aloud from some
        thick book
Or be forced to look
At girls from that sink, Cadiz, prancing
Through the interminable writhings of professional belly-dancing.
Instead, Condylus, my little slave,
Will pipe to us—something not too rustic, nor yet too grave.
Well, that's the 'banquet'. I shall invite
Claudia to sit on my left. Who would you like on my right?

—from *Epigrams,* first century A.D.,
translated from the Latin by James Michie

HERODOTUS ON EGYPTIAN DINING

*Herodotus, considered the first historian, was a Greek born in 484
B.C. His principal subject was the enmity between East and West
and he wrote of these cultures, especially Egypt, in great detail. He
is thought to have visited Egypt about 460 B.C., but beyond that little is known of the date of this manuscript.* —M.K.

AMONG THE EGYPTIANS THEMSELVES, THOSE WHO DWELL IN THE
cultivated country are the most careful of all men to preserve the memory of the past, and none whom I have questioned have so many chron-
icles. I will now speak of the manner of life which they use. For three
following days in every month they purge themselves, pursuing after
health by means of emetics and drenches; for they think it is from the
food which they eat that all sicknesses come to men. Even without this,
the Egyptians are the healthiest of all men, next to the Libyans; the reason of which to my thinking is that the climate in all seasons is the same;
for change is the great cause of men's falling sick, more especially
changes of seasons. They eat bread, making loaves which they call
"cyllestis"* of coarse grain. For wine, they use a drink made of barley;
for they have no vines in their country. They eat fish uncooked, either
dried in the sun or preserved with brine. Quails and ducks and small
birds are salted and eaten raw; all other kinds of birds, as well as fish (except those that the Egyptians hold sacred) are eaten roast and boiled.

At rich men's banquets, after dinner a man carries round a wooden
image of a corpse in a coffin, painted and carved in exact imitation, a
cubit or two cubits long. This he shows to each of the company, saying
"Drink and make merry, but look on this; for such shalt thou be when
thou art dead." Such is the custom at their drinking-bouts.

—from *The Persian Wars,* fifth century B.C.,
translated from the Greek by A. D. Godley

---

*Loaves twisted to a point, apparently.

Plutarch on Lucullus Dining with Himself

For the administration of public affairs has, like other things, its proper term, and statesmen, as well as wrestlers, will break down when strength and youth fail. But Crassus and Pompey, on the other hand, laughed to see Lucullus abandoning himself to pleasure and expense, as if luxurious living were not a thing that as little became his years as government of affairs at home or of an army abroad.

And, indeed, Lucullus's life, like the Old Comedy, presents us at the commencement with acts of policy and of war, at the end offering nothing but good eating and drinking, feastings, and revellings, and mere play. For I give no higher name to his sumptuous buildings, porticos, and baths, still less to his paintings and sculptures, and all his industry about these curiosities, which he collected with vast expense, lavishly bestowing all the wealth and treasure which he got in the war upon them, insomuch that even now, with all the advance of luxury, the Lucullean gardens are counted the noblest the emperor has. Tubero the stoic, when he saw his buildings at Naples, where he suspended the hills upon vast tunnels, brought in the sea for moats and fish-ponds round his house, and built pleasure-houses in the waters, called him Xerxes in a gown. He had also fine seats in Tusculum, belvederes, and large open balconies for men's apartments, and porticos to walk in, where Pompey coming to see him, blamed him for making a house which would be pleasant in summer, but uninhabitable in winter; whom he answered with a smile, "You think me, then, less provident than cranes and storks, not to change my home with the season." When a prætor, with great expense and pains, was preparing a spectacle for the people, and asked him to lend him some purple robes for the performers in a chorus, he told him he would go home and see, and if he had got any, would let him have them; and the next day asking how many he wanted, and being told that a hundred would suffice, bade him to take twice as many: on which the poet Horace observes, that a house is but a poor one where the valuables unseen and unthought of do not exceed all those that meet the eye.

Lucullus's daily entertainments were ostentatiously extravagant, not only with purple coverlets, and plate adorned with precious stones, and dancings, and interludes, but with the greatest diversity of dishes and the most elaborate cookery, for the vulgar to admire and envy. It was a happy thought of Pompey in his sickness, when his physician prescribed a thrush for his dinner, and his servants told him that in summer-time thrushes were not to be found anywhere but in Lucullus's fattening coops, that he would not suffer them to fetch one thence, but observing to his physician, "So if Lucullus had not been an epicure, Pompey had not lived," ordered something else that could easily be got to be prepared for him. Cato was his friend and connection, but, nevertheless, so hated his life and habits, that when a young man in the senate made a long and tedious speech in praise of frugality and temperance, Cato got up and said, "How long do you mean to go on making money like Crassus, living like Lucullus, and talking like Cato?" There are some, however, who say the words were said, but not by Cato.

It is plain from the anecdotes on record of him that Lucullus was not only pleased with, but even gloried in his way of living. For he is said to have feasted several Greeks upon their coming to Rome day after day, who of a true Grecian principle, being ashamed, and declining the invitations, where so great an expense was every day incurred for them, he with a smile told them, "Some of this, indeed my Grecian friends, is for your sakes, but more for that of Lucullus." Once when he supped alone, there being only one course, and that but moderately furnished, he called his steward and reproved him, who professing to have supposed that there would be no need of any great entertainment, when nobody was invited, was answered, "What, did not you know, then, that to-day Lucullus dines with Lucullus?" Which being much spoken of about the city, Cicero and Pompey one day met him loitering in the forum, the former his intimate friend and familiar, and, though there had been some ill-will between Pompey and him about the command in the war, still they used to see each other and converse on easy terms together. Cicero accordingly saluted him, and asked him whether to-day were a good time for asking a favour of him, and on his answering, "Very much so," and begging to hear what it was, "Then," said Cicero, "we shall like to dine with you to-day, just on the dinner that is prepared for yourself." Lucullus being surprised, and requesting a day's time, they refused to grant it, neither suffered him to talk with his servants, for fear he should give order for more than was appointed before. But thus much they consented to, that before their faces he might tell his servants, that to-day he would sup in the Apollo (for so one of his best dining-rooms was called), and by this evasion he outwitted his guests. For every room, as it seems, had its own assessment of expenditure, dinner at such a price, and all else in accordance; so that the servants, on knowing where he would dine, knew also how much was to be expended, and in what style and form dinner was to be served. The expense for the Apollo was fifty thousand drachmas, and thus much being that day laid out, the greatness of the cost did not so much amaze Pompey and Cicero, as the rapidity of the outlay. One might believe Lucullus thought his money really captive and barbarian, so wantonly and contumeliously did he treat it.

—from *Lives of the Noble Grecians and Romans,* first century A.D.,
translated from the Greek by John Dryden

FRANCES CALDERÓN DE LA BARCA ON MEXICAN FOOD

*Frances Erskine Inglis was born in Edinburgh in 1804 to an afflu-
ent family. When her father went bankrupt, Fanny moved to Boston
with four of her ten siblings to become schoolteachers. Scottish
schoolteachers were prized in New England. Her teaching career
ended in a scandal caused by a satire performed at a charity event
that may or may not have been written by Fanny. They then moved
to Staten Island, where she met her future husband, Angel Calderón
de la Barca, fourteen years her senior and born in Buenos Aires to
Spanish diplomats. They married in 1838 and the Spanish government sent the newlywed husband to Mexico as the first Spanish
minister. While there, the couple researched sources for William
Hickling Prescott, a respected historian who was planning a history
of the conquest of Mexico. When they returned, Prescott, whose
Mexican history was to give him enduring fame, urged Fanny to
publish her letters, which she did in 1842.   —M.K.*

WHEN WE ARRIVED, WE FOUND DINNER LAID FOR FORTY persons, and the table ornamented by the taste of the gardener, with pyramids of beautiful flowers.

I have now formed acquaintance with many Mexican dishes; *molé* (meat stewed in red chile), boiled nopal, fried bananas, green chile, etc. Then we invariably have *frijoles* (brown beans stewed), hot tortillas— and this being in the country, pulque is the universal beverage. In Mexico, tortillas and pulque are considered unfashionable, though both are to be met with occasionally, in some of the best old houses. They have here a most delicious species of cream cheese made by the Indians, and ate with virgin honey. I believe there is an intermixture of goats' milk in it; but the Indian families who make it, and who have been offered large sums for the receipt, find it more profitable to keep their secret.

Every dinner has *puchero* immediately following the soup; consisting of boiled mutton, beef, bacon, fowls, garbanzos (a white bean), small gourds, potatoes, boiled pears, greens, and any other vegetables; a piece of each put on your plate at the same time, and accompanied by a sauce of herbs or tomatoes.

As for fruits, we have mameys, chirimoyas, granaditas, white and black zapotes; the black, sweet, with a green skin and black pulp, and with black stones in it; the white resembling it in outward appearance and form, but with a white pulp, and the kernel, which is said to be poisonous, is very large, round, and white. It belongs to a larger and more leafy tree than the black zapote, and grows in cold or temperate climates; whereas the other is a native of *tierra caliente.* Then there is the chicozapote, of the same family, with a whitish skin, and a white or rose-tinged pulp; this also belongs to the warm regions. The capulin, or Mexican cherry; the mango, of which the best come from Orizaba and Cordova; the cayote, etc. Of these I prefer the chirimoya, zapote blanco, granadita, and mango; but this is a matter of taste.

—from *Life in Mexico,* 1842

LADY NUGENT ON OVEREATING IN COLONIAL JAMAICA

Maria Skinner was born in the British colony of New Jersey in 1771. In 1797, at the age of twenty-six, she married George Nugent, a forty-year-old British officer who had fought for Britain in

*the American Revolution. Lady Nugent lived in Jamaica from 1801
to 1805, during which time her husband was lieutenant governor
and commander in chief. She wrote her journal for herself and it was
not published until 1839, four years after her death, and then only
privately for a few friends.*   —M.K.

THE ADMIRAL, &C. SET OFF FOR PORT HENDERSON, AND
we for Bushy Park estate, Mr. Mitchell's, where we breakfasted in the
Creole style.—Cassada* cakes, chocolate, coffee, tea, fruits of all sorts,
pigeon pies, hams, tongues, rounds of beef, &c. I only wonder there
was no turtle. Mr. M.'s delight is to stuff his guests, and I should think
it would be quite a triumph to him, to hear of a fever or apoplexy, in
consequence of his good cheer. He is immensely rich, and told me he
paid £30,000 per annum for duties to Government. His house is truly
Creole. The wood-work mahogany—galleries, piazzas, porticoes, &c.
In front a cane-piece, and sugar works, with plenty of cocoa-nut trees
and tamarind trees, &c. He seems particularly indulgent to his negroes,
and is, I believe, although a very vulgar, yet a very humane man.

After breakfast, set off to Spring Gardens, to review the militia of
St. John's parish and St. Dorothy's. Spring Gardens was formerly a
fine place, but its owner now lives in England, and the house and every
thing are neglected. The situation is beautiful. I saw an immense fig-
tree, with a palm growing out of the top; it had a most singular appearance, but how the palm was engrafted, no one could tell me. The
house has carved mahogany doors, &c. and many remains of its former magnificence.

On the lawn we found the regiments assembled, and spectators of
all colours crowding the place. Kittereens,† horses, and mules, in
abundance, attending.—The whole review, in fact, was most funny.
Not one of the officers, nor their men, knew at all what they were
about, and each had displayed his own taste, in the ornamental part
of his dress. They were indeed a motley crew, and the Colonel whispered me—"Ah, ma'am, if the General did but know half the trouble

---

*Or Cassava.

† Kittereen—a kind of covered vehicle. In the west of England formerly applied to a
kind of omnibus, and in the West Indies to a one-horse chaise or buggy. Gardner, in his "History of Jamaica," states in error that it took its name from its being made in Kettering. The
derivation from the car ran by Christopher (Kit) Treen between Penzance and Truro is also
doubtful. In Jamaica Lady Brassey, when she visited the island in 1883, applied it to a vehicle something like the modern buggy, but simpler in construction.

I have had to draw up the men as you see them, he would not ask me to change their position; for what they will do next I don't know. You see I have drawn a line with my cane for them to stand by, and it is a pity to remove them from it." Poor man! I did pity him, for at the first word of command they stared, and then moved in every direction, and such a scene of confusion at any review I believe was never beheld.— A magnificent second breakfast, which succeeded this display, proved that, at Spring Gardens, the business of ménage, or eating and drinking, was better understood than military tactics.

After their repast, Colonel Ogilvy wished me to receive the thanks of the corps, for attending the review; but I begged leave to decline the display, and as soon as possible we all returned to Bushy Park, where we arrived to rest ourselves about 4. Had a profuse dinner at 5.—Sick of so much eating and fatigue, and get rid of the remembrance of it all by going soundly to sleep at 9 o'clock.

I don't wonder now at the fever the people suffer from here—such eating and drinking I never saw! Such loads of all sorts of high, rich, and seasoned things, and really gallons of wine and mixed liquors as they drink! I observed some of the party, to-day, eat of late breakfasts, as if they had never eaten before—a dish of tea, another of coffee, a bumper of claret, another large one of hock-negus; then Madeira, sangaree, hot and cold meat, stews and fries, hot and cold fish pickled and plain, peppers, ginger sweetmeats, acid fruit, sweet jellies—in short, it was all as astonishing as it was disgusting.

—from *Lady Nugent's Journal,* February 4, 1802

GIUSEPPE TOMASI DI LAMPEDUSA
ON SICILIAN DINING

Tomasi di Lampedusa, the last male of a Sicilian noble family with important land holdings, including the island of Lampedusa, died in Rome in 1957 without an heir and with barely a penny. Among his few possessions was the manuscript for a novel that had been twice rejected.

In 1885, the head of the house had died without a will, and the fights among his nine children destroyed most of the value of the estate. The last prince, Giuseppe, was born in 1896. In 1934, Guiseppe's father died and left him only a palace in Palermo, which was later bombed into ruins by the Allies. Giuseppe salvaged what furniture remained and most of his books and moved them to a small house along Palermo's crumbling waterfront. For about twenty years he thought about writing a novel about his vanished world. He was spurred on when his cousin and closest friend won a poetry prize in 1954. In 1955, Giuseppe completed four chapters and sent them to the publisher Mondadori with the title Il Gattopardo *(The Ocelot). He later added two more chapters, but the manuscript was rejected in 1956 on the advice of Sicilian author Elio Vittorini. Giuseppe continued working on the book even though he was dying of lung cancer. Several days before his death Vittorini rejected it again.*

Leaving instructions to his adopted son that he was to pursue publication, he also instructed that under no circumstance was his son to accept the humiliation of paying for self-publication. The manuscript continued to circulate. Only months later the young writer Giorgio Bassani announced that he had discovered a master-piece. A year and a half after the author's death it was accepted for publication and won Italy's most prestigious fiction award. While Italians continue to argue about it, The Leopard *has continued to sell and have many admirers.*   —M.K.

THE CENTRAL DOORS OF THE DRAWING-ROOM WERE FLUNG open and the butler declaimed mysterious sounds announcing that dinner was ready: 'Prann' pronn'.' The heterogeneous group moved towards the dining-room.

The Prince was too experienced to offer Sicilian guests, in a town of the interior, a dinner beginning with soup, and he infringed the rules of *haute cuisine* all the more readily as he disliked it himself. But rumours of the barbaric foreign usage of serving an insipid liquid as first course had reached the notables of Donnafugata too insistently for them not to quiver with a slight residue of alarm at the start of a solemn dinner like this. So when three lackeys in green, gold and powder entered, each holding a great silver dish containing a towering macaroni pie, only four of the twenty at table avoided showing pleased surprise; the Prince and Princess from foreknowledge, Angelica from affectation and Concetta from lack of appetite. All the others (including Tancredi, I regret to say) showed their relief in varying ways, from the fluty and ecstatic grunts of the notary to the sharp squeak of Francesco Paolo. But a threatening circular stare from the host soon stifled these improper demonstrations.

Good manners apart, though, the aspect of those monumental dishes of macaroni was worthy of the quivers of admiration they evoked. The burnished gold of the crusts, the fragrance of sugar and cinnamon they exuded, were but preludes to the delights released from the interior when the knife broke the crust; first came a spice-laden haze, then chicken livers, hard boiled eggs, sliced ham, chicken and truffles in masses of piping hot, glistening macaroni, to which the meat juice gave an exquisite hue of suède.

The beginning of the meal, as happens in the provinces, was quiet. The arch-priest made the sign of the Cross and plunged in head first without a word. The organist absorbed the succulent dish with closed eyes; he was grateful to the Creator that his ability to shoot hare and woodcock could bring him ecstatic pleasures like this, and the thought came to him that he and Teresina could exist for a month on the cost of one of these dishes; Angelica, the lovely Angelica, forgot little Tuscan black-puddings and part of her good manners and devoured her food with the appetite of her seventeen years and the vigour given by grasping her fork half-way up the handle. Tancredi, in an attempt to link gallantry with greed, tried to imagine himself tasting, in the aromatic forkfuls, the kisses of his neighbour Angelica, but he realised at once that the experiment was disgusting and suspended it, with a mental reserve about reviving this fantasy with the pudding; the Prince, although rapt in the contemplation of Angelica sitting opposite him, was the only one at table able to notice that the *demi-glace* was overfilled, and made a mental note to tell the cook so next day; the others ate without thinking of anything, and without realising that the food seemed so delicious because sensuality was circulating in the house.

—from *The Leopard*, 1958,
translated from the Italian by Archibald Colquhoun

Chiquart on Preparing a Royal Feast

In 1420, Chiquart Amizco, chief cook to Duke Amadeus VIII of Savoy—the future Pope Felix V—wrote a manuscript of culinary advice, Du fait de cuisine. *As chef he was called upon on numerous occasions to mount huge feasts to entertain visiting royalty. One such event was in 1397 and another in 1403 on the occasion of Mary of Burgundy leaving home. This occurred one Friday and Saturday, fast days on which good Catholics were required to deny themselves. Chiquart was charged with preparing one of those peculiar medieval contradictions, a lenten feast, consisting of four meals, almost fifty different dishes, without using meat or meat products. The feat is still remembered. His manuscript is particularly valuable to food historians because, while all other fifteenth-century French cookbooks reflect the dominance of Taillevent, Chiquart's book documents a different regional cuisine. His cooking was French, and therefore Taillevent-like, but, being in Savoy, also reflected local Alpine cooking and introduced Italian ideas and products. Also, Chiquart's writing gives the most extensive explanation of cooking techniques of any fifteenth-century cookbook.* —M.K.

To begin with, God having granted that a very honorable feast be given, at which there may be kings, queens, dukes, duchesses, counts, countesses, princes, princesses, marquesses, marchionesses, barons, baronesses and prelates of various classes, and nobles, too, in large number, the following things are necessary both to cook for the regular household and to do the feast honorably and to the honor of the lord who gives it.

And firstly, one hundred fat oxen, some one hundred and thirty sheep, also fat, six score of pigs; and, for each day during the feast, one hundred small piglets, both for roasting and for other uses, and sixty large fat pigs, salted, for larding and cooking.

To this end, the butcher would be well advised to have a good provision of meats so that, should it happen that the feast lasts longer than is intended, all that is needed will be immediately available. Even if there should be any surplus meat, that will not matter because nothing will be wasted.

For each day of the aforesaid feast you need two hundred kids and lambs, one hundred calves and two thousand head of poultry.

And your purveyors of game should be able, diligent and foresighted enough to have forty horses to get to various places for deer, hares, rabbits, partridge, pheasants, small birds (whatever they can find of these without number), doves, cranes, herons, any wild fowl—whatever sort of game they can get. They should set about this two months or six weeks before the feast; and all of them should bring or send whatever they have been able to get at least three or four days before the feast so that this game can be hung and properly prepared in each case.

And for each day of the feast they should be provided with six thousand eggs.

Furthermore, for the aforesaid feast they must have two charges of gross spices, that is, white ginger, Mecca ginger, cinnamon, grains of paradise and pepper.

Of minor spices, that is, nutmeg (6 lbs), cloves (6 lbs), mace (6 lbs), galingale (6 lbs); thirty loaves of sugar, 25 lbs of saffron, six charges of almonds, one charge of rice, 30 lbs of starch, twelve *cabas* of candied raisins, twelve *cabas* of good candied figs, twelve *cabas* of candied prunes, a *quintal* of dates, 40 lbs of pinenuts, 18 lbs of Orchil lichen, 18 lbs of alkanet, 18 lbs of goldleaf and, yet furthermore, one lb of camphor, one hundred *aunes* [130 yds] of good, fine bolting-cloth: these things are solely for cooking purposes. Moreover, for the feast you need two hundred boxes of all sorts and colors of dragees to garnish the dishes. And if the feast should last longer, additional materials should be available.

For the profit of the lord who is offering the feast, and to expedite its preparation as much as possible, the abovementioned spices, in whatever generous amount is necessary for the feast, should be ground into powder, and each should be set aside in good big leather bags.

In order to do this feast as well as possible and without blame or fault, the Household Stewards, the Kitchen Squires, and the Chief Cook should meet to locate, inspect and organize good, adequate places to carry out the cooking activities. This space should be large enough that great double work-tables can be set up in such a way that the Kitchen Squires can move comfortably between the serving-tables and the work-tables, in order to pass the dishes on and to receive them back again.

There should be a provision of good big cauldrons to boil large cuts of meat, and a great number of moderate-sized ones for making pottages and for other cooking operations, and great suspended pans for cooking fish and other things, and a great number of large and ordinary-sized boilers for pottages and other things, and a dozen good big mortars. Decide on the place where sauces will be prepared. And you will need some twenty large frying pans, a dozen great kettles, fifty pots, sixty two-handled pots, a hundred hampers, a dozen grills, six large graters, a hundred wooden spoons, twenty-five holed spoons, both large and small, six pot-hooks, twenty oven-shovels, twenty roasters, both those with turnable spits and those with spits mounted on andirons. You should not put your trust in wooden skewers or spits, because you could spoil all your meat, or even lose it; rather, you should have six score iron spits which are strong and thirteen feet long; and you need three dozen other spits which are just as long but not as thick, in order to roast poultry, piglets and water birds: *Si volucris verrat, qui torret eam procul errat; volucrem a torre procul de flumine torre.* And besides this, four dozen slender skewers for doing glazing and for fastening things.

You need two *boces* of vinegar, one white and the other claret, each of eight *sommes;* one good twenty-*somme boce* of good verjuice; and a ten-*somme boce* of oil.

You need one thousand cart-loads of good dry firewood, and a large barnful of coal; and you should always know where to get more so as not to run out.

So that the workers not be idle or lack anything, ample money should be assigned to the Kitchen Squires to get salt, ingredients and any other things which might be necessary for cooking—of which I shall make no mention at present.

For the sake of decency and cleanliness, and to speed the service as much as possible, you must have a great supply of dishes, of gold, silver, pewter and wood, that is to say, four thousand or more of them, in such quantity that when you have presented the first serving you will have enough for the second serving and still some left over; and in the meantime you can wash and clean the dishes used in that first serving.

Since at such a feast there may be very high, mighty, noble, venerable and honorable lords and ladies who will not eat meat, it is necessary to have similar amounts of sea-fish and fresh-water fish, both fresh and salted, and these in as varied preparations as can be.

And because the dolphin is king of all the other sea-fish, it will be put first, then congers, grey mullet, hake, sole, red mullet, John Dory, plaice, turbot, lobsters, tuna, sturgeon, salmon, sprats, sardines, sea-urchins, mussels, eels, bogues, ray, calamary, weever and anchovies; the eels, both fresh and salted.

Of fresh-water fish: large trout, large eels, lampreys, filets of char, great pike filets, great carp filets, great perch, dace, pollacks, greylings, burbots, crayfish, and all other fish.

Because there are at this feast a few great lords or ladies, as was mentioned before, who will have with them their Chief Cook whom they will order to arrange and cook particular things for them, that Chief Cook should have supplied and dispensed to him, quickly, fully, generously and cheerfully, anything he may ask for or that may be necessary for his lord or lady, or for the both of them, so that he may serve them as he should.

In addition, you must have six score *quintals* [3600 lbs] of fine cheese; six hundred *aunes* [750 yds] of good, fine white cloth to cover the serving tables and the fish, meat and roasts; sixty *aunes* [75 yds] of linen to make the strainers for jellies; and enough fine white sheeting to make a dozen strainers similar in nature to a hippocras strainer.

You need two large two-handed knives to cut up the oxen, a dozen dressing knives for dressing, and two dozen knives for cutting up ingredients for pottages and for stuffings, and to prepare poultry and fish; and, as well, a half-dozen rasps to clean the work-tables and the chopping blocks, a hundred baskets for carrying meat to the pots and vats, both raw meat and cooked meat that is being borne to or from the work-tables; and also to carry coal for roasts and for whatever other purpose; and also to carry and to gather the dishes.

If it should happen that the feast is held in winter, each night for cooking you will need sixty torches, twenty lbs of tallow candle, and sixty lbs of suet tapers to inspect the butchery, the pastry kitchen, the fish kitchen, and all of the activities of the kitchen.

And, as for the pastry kitchen you must have a good big room as close as possible to the kitchen to hold two good big ovens for baking meat- and fish-pies, tarts, flans, custards, and *ratons,* and all other things that are necessary in cooking.

And for this the workers should be supplied with thirty *sommes* [3600 lbs] of fine flour for the abovementioned purposes, and they should be sure of being able to get more if the feast should last longer.

Since by the pleasure of the blessed Holy Trinity, which unfailingly grants us freely of everything, we shall have good, fine, great provisions to do our feast in grand fashion, we must get Chief Cooks and workers who will make the dishes and *entremets* for that feast; and if it should turn out that these cooks and workers are not available, send someone to look for some in places where they can be found, so that the feast can be done in a grand and honorable fashion.

Now that we have the chief workers that we need for the feast, it remains to organize them, which ones will be handling meats, and which fish. And let them be well instructed on how to make fish dishes of colors similar to those of the meat dishes for each serving, as will be explained.

—from *On Cookery,* 1420,
translated from the French by Terence Scully

ERNEST HEMINGWAY ON HOW HE LIKES TO EAT

No, people are funny in the way they are constructed. I only like to eat at sea or in the hills where I get hungry. What I really like is good fresh fish, grilled, good steaks (not these comic steaks they have bred for slobs to eat so they have no taste but only size) but good steaks with the bone and very rare. Good lamb, rare. Elk, mountain sheep, venison and antelope in that order and grouse, young sage-hen, quail and teal, canvasback and mallards in that order. With mashed potatoes and gravy. For vegetables I like celery and artichokes best; artichokes cold with sauce vinagreat (mis-spelled), Brussels sprouts, Swiss chard, broccoli and all fruits.

To eat when you write is just a stupefyeing bore unless they have some of the above.

So don't worry about me down here eating nothing and makeing an ass of myself. I have had strange eating habits since I was a boy. It is nothing to be proud of, ashamed of nor alarmed about. Bears don't eat all winter and Harry Wills fasts a month each year.

Best always,
Ernest

—Letter to Charles Scribner, 18–19 May, 1951

SARAH JOSEPHA HALE ON THANKSGIVING DINNER

Sarah Josepha Hale was said to be one of the most influential American women of her day. She pioneered the women's magazine—she edited Ladies Magazine *from 1827 to 1836, and then* Godey's Lady's Book *from 1837 to 1877—which is not to say that she was in the forefront of all the major issues of the day. During the Civil War,* Godey's *barely mentioned that there was a war because such was not the affair of a lady. But through her magazines, her novel, short stories, and articles, Hale did have a tremendous impact. One of her most visible imprints on American culture is that she was the great promoter of the holiday of Thanksgiving and had much to do with not only the fact that Americans celebrate it but the turkey-and-cranberry way in which they do it.* —M.K.

AND NOW FOR OUR THANKSGIVING DINNER.

The roasted turkey took precedence on this occasion, being placed at the head of the table; and well did it become its lordly station,

sending forth the rich odor of its savory stuffing,
and finely covered with the froth of the
basting. At the foot of the board, a
sirloin of beef, flanked on either
side by a leg of pork and loin of
mutton, seemed placed as a
bastion to defend the innumerable bowls of gravy and plates of
vegetables disposed in that quarter.

A goose and pair of ducklings occupied side stations on the table; the
middle being graced . . . by that rich burgomaster of the provisions,
called a chicken pie. This pie, which is wholly formed of the choicest
parts of fowls, enriched and seasoned with a profusion of butter and
pepper, and covered with an excellent puff paste is, like the celebrated
pumpkin pie, an indispensable part of a good and true Yankee Thanksgiving.

Plates of pickles, preserves and butter, and all the necessaries for
increasing the seasoning of the viands to the demands of each palate,
filled the interstices on the table, leaving hardly sufficient room for the
plates of the company, a wine glass and two tumblers for each, with a
slice of wheat bread lying on one of the inverted tumblers. A side table
was literally loaded with the preparations for the second course.

There was a huge plum pudding, custards and pies of every name
and description known in Yankee land; yet the pumpkin pie occupied
the most distinguished niche. There were also several kinds of rich
cake, and a variety of sweetmeats and fruits.

—from *The Good Housekeeper,* 1841

NELSON ALGREN ON THE LAND
OF MIGHTY BREAKFASTS

*In the 1930s, Nelson Algren, a young fiction writer who in 1949
would win the first National Book Award for* The Man with the
Golden Arm, *joined the Illinois Writers Project, part of the federal*

Works Progress Administration (WPA). Other writers who joined included Saul Bellow and Richard Wright. They were to document American foodways for a national program called "America Eats," a series of guides showing the impact of immigration and customs on the food traditions of each region. Algren's assignment, which he completed, was the Midwest. But "America Eats" was never completed because of World War II.   —M.K.

FOLLOWING THE CIVIL WAR, A CONSIDERABLE MIGRATION into the lumber country of Michigan occurred. Houses were rudely built in these areas, and settlement was transitory. Hundreds of small communities would spring up, only to disappear when the land was cut over and the sawmills removed to new timberland. Such conditions did not encourage variation in diet; food monotony reached a new high in lumber-operating sections of the state during the last three decades of the nineteenth century.

Paul Bunyan felt there were two kinds of Michigan lumber-camp cooks, the Baking Powder Buns and the Sourdough Stiffs. One Sourdough Sam belonged to the latter school. He made everything but coffee out of sourdough. He had only one arm and one leg, the other members having been lost when his sourdough barrel blew up.

The hyperbole serves to emphasize a truth. The sourdough pancake has always been a favorite among lumberjacks everywhere. To the camp cook a continuous supply of sourdough is an indispensable part of camp equipment, and he is never without his batch of starter. The starter is a portion of dough reserved from previous mixtures and stored in the kind of barrel that proved disastrous to Sourdough Sam. Zealously guarded, the starter can be kept for weeks in ordinary temperatures.

The night before the pancakes are to be fried, the cook assembles his batter, using the starter as a leavening agent. Flour and water are added to the starter, and the mixture is left near the stove to rise. By morning it is a light and frothy mass, smelling pungently of fermentation. After reserving from the batch a starter for the next morning's pancakes, the cook adds salt, sugar, eggs, a little fat, and a pinch of soda. He pours large spoonfuls of the batter on a huge, fire-blackened griddle, abundantly greased with smoking pork rind and very hot. Then, after the griddle cake has fried a few moments, he flips it expertly and it's as good as done.

In the old camps it was customary for the cook to install near the door of the shanty a crock containing sourdough batter in various stages of fermentation. Into the crock went all leftover batter and scraps of bread, doughnuts, cake, or pancakes, which quickly attained the semiliquid consistency of the batter.

Standing in a box sled among steaming kettles of beans, beef stew, and tea, the bull cook drove over a road to a central point in the woods to blow his dinner horn. The call carried five miles through the snowy forest. Then he howled like an Irish wolf: "Ye-ow!'s goin' to waste." The men swarmed toward the box sled from every direction. Though they ate around a big fire of slash, the beans froze on their plates and the tea froze in their whiskers.

At night they came into camp stamping with cold and grim with hunger. In the cookhouse the long tables were loaded with food— smoking platters of fresh mush, bowls of mashed potatoes, piles of pancakes and pitchers of corn syrup, kettles of rich brown beans, pans of prunes, dried peaches, rice pudding, rows of apple pies. The big camps fed the men bountifully and well.

> Run here, men, it's bilin' hot,
> Sam 'n Dave's both eatin' out the pot.
> Old Uncle Jake says, "I'll be damn,
> If I can't get a foreleg I'll take a ham."

The jacks ate silently, with great speed. If a greenhorn was tempted to make conversation, he was reminded by a placard on the wall: "No talking at the table."

The cook was the king bee of the camp. He was well paid and well worth his pay, handling prodigious quantities of food, baking, roasting, frying, stewing for a hundred men who ate like horses, feeding them lavishly on an allowance of thirty cents a day per man.

The preparation of beans verged on ritual. A deep hole was dug on one side of the fire and filled with glowing embers. When the beans had been soaked for twenty-four hours, they were taken out and scalded. With deliberation the cook now chose the right kind of onion and placed it on the bottom of the pot. Then the beans were poured in until the pot was filled within six inches of the top. Slices of fat pork were laid across this, a sufficiency of molasses was poured upon the whole, and the pot sealed. The embers were now taken from the hole in the floor and the pot inserted. All space around the sides was filled and packed with hot coals and the bean hole covered up. The fire was made over it and kept burning twenty-four hours, when the cooking was complete. This made a rich and golden breakfast dish.

—from *America Eats*, c. 1940

W. H. AUDEN AND LOUIS MACNEICE ON ICELANDIC FOOD

In the summer of 1936, two young British poets, W. H. Auden and Louis MacNeice, spent three months in Iceland. They produced one of the most whimsical and quirky, perhaps even goofy, pieces of travel writing of all times. The book includes poetry and prose, a verse letter to Lord Byron, and a jointly written last will and testament, which begins:

> We, Wystan Hugh Auden and Louis MacNeice
> Brought up to speak and write the English tongue
> Being led in the eighteenth year of the Western Peace
> To the duck-shaped mountainous island with a Danish King, . . .

Years later, Auden would write, "As to the merits of the book, if any, I am in no position to judge. But the three months in Iceland upon which it is based stand out in my memory as among the happiest in a life which has so far been unusually happy. . . ."
Here is their assessment of the local Icelandic food.   —M.K.

Food.

In the larger hotels in Reykjavik you will of course get ordinary European food, but in the farms you will only get what there is, which is on the whole rather peculiar.

Breakfast: (9.0 a.m.). If you stay in a farm this will be brought to you in bed. Coffee, bread and cheese, and small cakes. Coffee, which is drunk all through the day—I must have drunk about 1,500 cups in three months—is generally good. There is white bread, brown bread, rock-hard but quite edible, and unleavened rye bread like cake. The ordinary cheese is like a strong Dutch and good. There is also a brown sweet cheese, like the Norwegian. I don't like cakes so I never ate any, but other people say they are good.

Lunch and Dinner: (12 noon and 7 p.m.). If you are staying anywhere, lunch is the chief meal, but farmers are always willing to give you a chief meal at any time of the day or night that you care. (I once had supper at 11 p.m.)

Soups: Many of these are sweet and very unfortunate. I remember three with particular horror, one of sweet milk and hard macaroni, one tasting of hot marzipan, and one of scented hair oil. (But there is a good sweet soup, raspberry coloured, made of bilberry. L.M.)

Fish: Dried fish is a staple food in Iceland. This should be shredded with the fingers and eaten with butter. It varies in toughness. The tougher kind tastes like toe-nails, and the softer kind like the skin off the soles of one's feet.

In districts where salmon are caught, or round the coast, you get excellent fish, the grilled salmon particularly.

Meat: This is practically confined to mutton in various forms. The Danes have influenced Icelandic cooking, and to no advantage. Meat is liable to be served up in glutinous and half-cold lumps, covered with tasteless gravy. At the poorer farms you will only get Hángikyrl, *i.e.* smoked mutton. This is comparatively harmless when cold as it only tastes like soot, but it would take a very hungry man indeed to eat it hot.

Vegetables: Apart from potatoes, these, in the earlier part of the summer are conspicuous by their absence. Later, however, there are radishes, turnips, carrots, and lettuce in sweet milk. Newish potatoes begin to appear about the end of August. Boiled potatoes are eaten with melted butter, but beware of the browned potatoes, as they are coated in sugar, another Danish barbarism.

Fruit: None, except rhubarb and in the late summer excellent bilberries.

Cold Food: Following the Scandinavian custom, in the hotels, following the hot dish there are a number of dishes of cold meats and fishes eaten with bread and butter. Most of these are good, particularly the pickled herring. Smoked salmon in my opinion is an overrated dish, but it is common for those who appreciate it.

Sweets: The standard sweet is skyr, a cross between Devonshire cream and a cream cheese, which is eaten with sugar and cream. It is very filling but most people like it very much. It is not advisable, however, to take coffee and skyr together just before riding, as it gives you diarrhoea.

Tea: (4 p.m.). Coffee, cakes, and if you are lucky, pancakes with cream. These are wafer-thick and extremely good. Coffee and cake are also often brought you in the evening, about 10 p.m. Those who like tea or cocoa should bring it with them and supervise the making of it themselves.

—from *Letter from Iceland,* 1936

HOOKER ON ICELANDIC FOOD

ON THE CLOTH WAS NOTHING BUT A PLATE, A KNIFE AND fork, a wine glass, and a bottle of claret, for each guest, except that in the middle stood a large and handsome glass-castor of sugar, with a magnificent silver top. The dishes are brought in singly; our first was a large tureen of soup, which is a favourite addition to the dinners of the richer people, and is made of sago, claret, and raisins, boiled so as to become almost a mucilage. We were helped to two soup plates full of this, which we ate without knowing if anything was to come. No sooner, however, was the soup removed, than two large salmon, boiled and cut in slices, were brought on and, with them, melted butter looking like oil, mixed with vinegar and pepper; this, likewise, was very good and when we had with some difficulty cleared our plates, we hoped we had finished our dinners. Not so, for there was then introduced a tureen full of eggs of the Cree, a great tern, boiled hard, of which a dozen were put upon each of our plates; and for sauce, we had a large basin of cream, mixed with sugar, in which were four spoons, so that we all ate out of the same bowl, placed in the middle of the table. We devoured with difficulty our eggs and cream, but had no sooner dismissed our plates, than half a sheep, well roasted, came on with a mess of sorrel called by the Danes, scurvy-grass, boiled, mashed and sweetened with sugar. However, even this was not all; for a large dish of waffels as they are here called, that is to say, a sort of pancake made of wheat flour, flat, and roasted in a mould, which forms a number of squares on the top, succeeded the mutton. This was not more than half an inch thick and about the size of an octavo book. Then bread, Norway biscuit and loaves made of rye were served up: for our drink we had nothing but claret, of which we were all compelled to empty the bottle that stood by us, and this too out of tumblers rather than wine-glasses. The coffee was extremely good and we trusted it would terminate the feast; but all was not yet over; for a large bowl of rum punch was brought in and handed round in glasses pretty freely, and to every glass a toast was given. Another bowl actually came which we were with difficulty allowed to refuse to empty entirely; nor could this be done but by ordering our people to get the boat ready for our departure, when, having concluded this extraordinary feast by three cups of tea each, we took our leave and reached Reykjavik about ten o'clock, but did not for some time recover from the effects of this most involuntary intemperance.

—from *Journal of a Tour in Iceland,* 1809

MARTIAL ON APPLAUSE
FOR POMPONIUS

Pomponius, when loud applause
Salutes you from your client-guests,
Don't fool yourself: good food's the cause
And not your after-dinner jests.

—from *Epigrams,* first century A.D.,
translated from the Latin by James Michie

CHARLES DICKENS DINES AT DELMONICO'S, NEW YORK

MENU

Huitres sur coquille

Potages

Consommé Sévigné   Crème d'asperges à la Dumas

Hors-d'oeuvre chaud

Timbales à la Dickens

Poissons

Saumon à la Victoria   Bass à l'Italienne

Pomme de terre Nelson

Relèves

Filet de boeuf à la Lucullus   Laitues braisées demi-glace

Agneau farci à la Walter Scott   Tomatoes à la Reine

Entrées

Filet de brants à la Seymour

Petits pois à l'Anglaise

Croustades de ris de veau à la Douglas

Quartier d'artichauts Lyonnaise

Epinards au velouté

Côtelettes de grouses à la Fenimore Cooper

Entrées Froid

Galantine à la Royale   Aspics de foies-gras historiés

Intermède

Sorbet à l'Americaine

Rôtis

Bécassines   Poulet de grains truffés

Entremets Sucrés

Pêches à la Parisienne (chaud)

Macédoine de fruits   Muscovite à l'abricot

Lait d'amandes rubané de chocolat

Charlotte Doria

Viennois glacé à l'orange   Corbeilles de biscuits Chantilly

Gâteau Savarin au Marasquin

Glaces forme fruits Napolitaine

Parfait au Café

Pièces Montées

Temple de la Littérature   Trophée à l'Auteur

Pavillion international   Colonne Triomphale

Les Armes Britanniques   The Stars and Stripes

Le Monument de Washington   La Loi du destin

Fruits   Compote de pêches et de poirs   Petit fours

Fleurs

Dessert

—April 1867

CHAPTER FOUR

Favorite Restaurants

IRVING BERLIN ON LUNCHING AT THE AUTOMAT

Times are not so sweet,
But the bluebloods have to eat,
So the best of families meet
At the Automat.
All the millionaires
Who were lunching at Pierre's
Have been occupying chairs
At the Automat.
The Morgans and the Whitneys
And other big shots
Change dollars into jitneys
And drop them in the slots.
Times are on the fritz,
So they all have left the Ritz
And the social column sits
In the Automat.

Take your lunch at the Automat
And you'll find that it's become high-hat.

You'll see
Members of society,
Missus Belmont passing by,
Putting mustard on a Swiss-on-rye;
Ev'ry day with a tray in hand,
You can see those high-toned babies stand
In line.
Take a look at Missus Ryan
Pushing Missus Randolph Hearst,
Saying, "That's my place—I got here first."
The Goulds and Biddles
And the Rockefellers too
Enjoy their griddles
Like the rest of us do,
And a plate of beans will fill their hearts with glee.
Come along and you will see
Missus Astor with a grin
And a dab of ketchup on her chin.
With pearls around her neck
Missus Woolworth eats her mutton,
And then she splits the check
With her girlfriend Missus Hutton;
And the scandal that will be spilt
When a Gould and Vanderbilt
Take a bit of a Swiss-cheese sandwich
And begin to chat
While lunching at the Automat.
Times are not so sweet,
But the bluebloods have to eat,
So the best of families meet
In the Automat.

While the panic's on,
If you look for Otto Kahn,
You will find that Otto's gone
To the Automat.
A Whitney with a pickle
Is not very swell,
But pickles for a nickle
Are cheap, so what the hell!

Berenice Abbott, *Automat, 977 Eighth Avenue,* 1936

Times are on the fritz,
So they all have left the Ritz,
And the social column sits
In the Automat.

—from *Face the Music,* 1932

GEORGE G. FOSTER ON NEW YORK OYSTER CELLARS

George G. Foster wrote features for Horace Greeley's New York Tribune. *He was a new kind of urban writer who spent his time in*

*slums and wrote colorfully, and sometimes factually, about street
culture.*   —M.K.

THE OYSTER-CELLARS, WITH THEIR BRIGHT LAMPS CASTING
broad gleams of red light across the street, are now in full tide, and every
instant sees them swallow up at one entrance a party of rowdy and half-
drunken young men, on their way to the theater, the gambling-house, the
bowling-saloon, or the brothel—or most likely to all in turn—while another is vomited up the other stairway, having already swilled their fill of
oysters and bad brandy, and garnished their reeking mouths each with an
atrocious cigar, which the bar-keeper recommended as "full-flavored." If
we step down one of these wide entrances we shall see a long counter
gorgeously decked with crystal decanters and glasses, richly carved and
gilt, and the wall ornamented with a voluptuous picture of a naked
Venus—perhaps the more seductive from being exquisitely painted. Before the long marble bar are arranged some dozen or score of individuals, waiting their turns for liquor—while on the other side a man with his
shirt-sleeves rolled up and his face in a fiery glow, seems to be pulling
long ribbons of julep out of a tin cup. At the other end of the room is a
row of little stalls, each fitted up with its gas-burner, its red curtain, its little table and voluptuous picture, and all occupied with busy eaters. In the
rear of these boxes is a range of larger apartments called "private rooms,"
where men and women enter promiscuously, eat, drink and make merry,
and disturb the whole neighborhood with their obscene and disgusting
revels, prolonged far beyond midnight. The women of course are all of
one kind—but among the men, you would find, if you looked curiously,
reverend judges and juvenile delinquents, pious and devout hypocrites,
and undisguised libertines and debauchees. Gamblers and fancy men,
high-flyers and spoonies, genteel pick-pockets and burglars, even, sometimes mingle in the detestable orgies of these detestable caverns; and the
shivering policeman who crawls sleepily by at the dead of night, and mechanically raps his bludgeon upon the pavement as he hears the boister-
ous mirth below, may be reminding a grave functionary of the city that it
is time to go home to his wife and children after the discharge of his "arduous public duties."

—from *New York by Gas-Light and Other Urban Sketches*, 1850

JOSEPH WECHSBERG ON TAFELSPITZ AT MEISSL & SCHADN IN VIENNA

IT WAS PERHAPS NOT ALTOGETHER AN ACCIDENT THAT THE first disappointment of my career as an officer was caused by boiled beef. Few Americans think of boiled beef as the gastronomic treat it is known for in central Europe. In Vienna there was a restaurant that was held in high esteem by local epicures for its boiled beef—twenty-four different varieties of it, to be exact.

The restaurant was Meissl & Schadn, an eating-place of international reputation, and the boiled-beef specialties of the house were called *Tafelspitz, Tafeldeckel, Rieddeckel, Beinfleisch, Rippenfleisch, Kavalierspitz, Kruspelspitz, Hieferschwanzl, Schulterschwanzl, Schulterscherzl, Mageres Meisel* (or *Mäuserl*), *Fettes Meisel, Zwerchried, Mittleres Kügerl, Dünnes Kügerl, Dickes Kügerl, Bröselfleisch, Ausgelöstes, Brustkern, Brustfleisch, Weisses Scherzl, Schwarzes Scherzl, Zapfen,* and *Ortschwanzl.*

The terminology was bound to stump anybody who had not spent the first half of his adult life within the city limits of Vienna. It was concise and ambiguous at the same time; even Viennese patriarchs did not always agree exactly where the *Weisses Scherzl* ended and the *Ortschwanzl* began. Fellow Austrians from the dark, Alpine hinterlands of Salzburg and Tyrol rarely knew the fine points of distinction between, say, *Tafelspitz, Schwarzes Scherzl,* and *Hieferschwanzl*—all referred to in America as brisket or plate of beef—or between the various *Kügerls.* Old-time Viennese butchers with the steady hand of distinguished brain surgeons were able to dissect the carcass of a steer into thirty-two different cuts, and four qualities, of meat. Among the first-quality cuts were not only tenderloin, porterhouse, sirloin, and prime rib of beef, as elsewhere, but also five cuts used exclusively for boiling; two *Scherzls,* two *Schwanzls,* and *Tafelspitz.* Unlike in present-day America, where a steer is cut up in a less complicated, altogether different manner, in Vienna only the very best beef was good enough to be boiled.

You had to be a butcher, a veterinarian, or a Meissl & Schadn habitué of long standing to know the exact characteristics of these *Gustostückerln.* Many Viennese had been born in the Austro-Hungarian monarchy's provinces of Upper Austria, Serbia, Slovakia, South Tyrol, Bohemia, or Moravia. (Even today certain pages of the Vienna telephone directory contain as many Czech-sounding names as the Prague directory.) These ex-provincials were eager to obliterate their un-Viennese past; they tried to veneer their *arrivisme;* they wanted to be more Viennese than the people born and brought up there. One way to show one's *Bodenständigkeit* was to display a scholarly knowledge of the technical terms for boiled beef. It was almost like the coded parlance of an exclusive club. In Vienna a person who couldn't talk learnedly about at least a dozen different cuts of boiled beef, didn't belong, no matter how much money he'd made, or whether the Kaiser had awarded him the title of *Hofrat* (court councilor) or *Kommerzialrat.*

The guests of Meissl & Schadn were thoroughly familiar with the physical build of a steer and knew the exact anatomical location of *Kügerls, Scherzls,* and *Schwanzls.* At Meissl & Schadn, precision was the keynote. You didn't merely order "boiled beef"—you wouldn't step into Tiffany's and ask for "a stone"—but made it quite clear exactly what you wanted. If you happened to be a habitué of the house, you didn't have to order, for *they* would know what you wanted. A Meissl & Schadn habitué never changed his favorite cut of boiled beef.

The restaurant was part of the famous Hotel Meissl & Schadn on Hoher Markt, which was popular with incognito potentates for its discreet, highly personalized service. The chambermaids looked like abbesses and knew the idiosyncrasies of every guest. If a man came to Meissl & Schadn who hadn't been there for ten years, he might find a small, hard pillow under his head because the abbess hadn't forgotten that he liked to sleep hard.

There were two restaurants, the *Schwemme* on the ground floor—a plebeian place with lower prices and checkered tablecloths—and the de-luxe *Restaurant* on the second floor, with high prices and snow-white damask tablecloths. The upper regions were under the command of the great Heinrich, who was already a venerable octogenarian when I first saw him in the late twenties.

HE WAS A MASSIVE, CORPULENT MAN WITH THE PINK CHEEKS of a healthy baby and the wisdom of a Biblical patriarch. His hands and jowls were sagging and he had serious trouble keeping his eyes open. He never budged from his command post near the door, from where he could overlook all tables, like an admiral on the bridge of his flagship surveying the units of his fleet. Few people in Vienna had ever seen an admiral in the flesh, but everybody agreed that Heinrich looked more an admiral than many a real one. Once in a while his pulse would stop beating and his eyelids would droop, and he would remain suspended between life and death, but the *défilé* of the waiters carrying silver plates with various cuts of boiled beef never failed to revive him.

Heinrich had spent his life in the faithful service of emperors, kings, archdukes, *Hofräte,* artists, and generals, bowing to them, kissing the hands of their ladies, or wives. His bent back had taken on the curvature of the rainbow, reflecting the fine nuances of his reverence, from the impersonal half-bow, with which he would dispose of the *nouveaux riches,* to the affectionate deep-bow, which was reserved for his old habitués, impoverished court councilors, and aristocrats living from the sale of one painting to the next.

Between Heinrich and his habitués there ruled a highly civilized, strictly regulated protocol. Upon entering the restaurant the guest would be greeted by Heinrich—or, rather, by Heinrich's bent back expressing the exact degree of respect in which the guest was held. The depth of Heinrich's bow depended upon the guest's social standing, his taste for, and his knowledge of, boiled beef, and his seniority. It took a man from twenty-five to thirty years to earn the full deep-bow. Such people were greeted by *"Meine Verehrung, küss die Hand,"* which was breathed rather than whispered, and never spoken; Heinrich wasn't able to speak any more.

The guest would be taken to his table by one of Heinrich's captains. Each guest always had the same table and the same waiter. There was mutual respect between waiter and guest; when either one died, the other would go to his funeral. The waiter would hold the chair for the guest; he would wait until the guest was comfortably seated. One of Heinrich's axioms was that "a man doesn't enjoy his beef unless he sits well."

When the guest was seated, the waiter would stand in front of him, waiting for the guest's order. That was a mere formality, since the waiter knew what the guest wanted. The guest would nod to the waiter; the waiter, in turn, would nod to the *commis;* and the *commis* would depart for the kitchen.

The *commis's* order to the cooks had the highly personal flavor that distinguished all transactions at Meissl & Schadn. It would be "The *Schulterscherzl* for General D." or "Count H. is waiting for his *Kavalierspitz."* This implied a high degree of finickiness on the part of the habitué, who wouldn't be satisfied with so narrow a definition as the

Kavalierspitz; his refined palate demanded that he get his private, very special part of a *Kavalierspitz.*

After a suitable interval the *commis* would bring in the meat on a massive, covered silver plate. Some people would have a consommé before the meat; clear consommé was the only preceding dish Heinrich approved of. The *commis* was followed by the *piccolo,* an eight-year-old gnome wearing a tiny tuxedo and a toy bow tie. The *piccolo's* job was to serve the garniture: grated horseradish, prepared with vinegar *(Essigkren),* with apple sauce *(Apfelkren),* or with whipped cream *(Oberskren);* mustard, pickles, boiled potatoes, boiled cabbage, spinach, or anything else the guest wanted with the meat.

An elaborate ritual would ensue. The waiter had been standing motionless, watching his subordinates as they put the various plates on a small serving-table next to the guest's table. Now the waiter would step forward, lift the cover off the silver plate, and perform the "presentation" of the meat. This was another mere motion, since the guest's enthusiastic approval was a foregone conclusion. The waiter would serve the meat on a hot plate, place it on the table in front of the guest, make a step back, and glance at Heinrich. Then the guest, in turn, would glance at Heinrich.

There followed a minute heavy with suspense. From his command post Heinrich would review the table, with a short, sweeping glance taking in the meat, the garniture, the accessories, the setting, the position of chair and table. It was hard to understand how he managed to see anything through the narrow slit of his almost closed eyelids; but see he did. He would give a slight nod of approval to the waiter, and to the guest. Only then would a genuine habitué start to eat.

WORDS OF ORDINARY PROSE HAVE GENERALLY BEEN HELD inadequate to express the delights of boiled beef at Meissl & Schadn. Many Austrian poets were moved to rhymed praise while they regaled themselves on a well-nigh perfect *Hieferschwanzl.* But poets, especially Austrian poets, are rarely given to tenacity of purpose, and somehow the poets didn't bother to write down their poems after leaving the restaurant. Richard Strauss, an ardent devotee of the *Beinfleisch,* often considered writing a tone poem about his favorite dish, but after he finished his ballet *Schlagobers (Whipped Cream),* he thought that another major composition devoted to an Austrian food specialty might be misinterpreted by posterity and resented by his admirers in Germany, who, like most Germans, heartily disliked Vienna.

Strauss, not unaware of his considerable German royalties, dropped the project.

"Too bad he did," a Viennese music-critic and Strauss-admirer said not long ago. "A tone poem on *Beinfleisch* might have surpassed even the transcendental beauty of *Death and Transfiguration.*"

THERE WAS A REASON FOR THE EXCELLENCE OF THE BEEF served at Meissl & Schadn. The restaurant owned herds of cattle that were kept inside a large sugar refinery in a village north of Vienna. There the steers were fed on molasses and sugar-beet mash, which gave their meat its extraordinary marble texture, taste, tenderness, and juice. The animals were slaughtered just at the right time, and the meat was kept in the refrigerators from one to two weeks.

In Vienna, in those days, boiled beef was not a dish; it was a way of life. Citizens of the Danube capital, venturing into hostile, foreign lands where boiled beef was simply boiled beef, would take Viennese cookbooks along that contained the anatomical diagram of a steer, with numbered partitions and subdivisions indicating the *Gustostückerln.* This was a wise precaution. Even in German-speaking lands the technical expressions denoting various cuts of beef differ from land to land. Vienna's *Tafelspitz* (brisket), for instance, is called *Tafelstück* by the Germans and *Huft* by the German-speaking Swiss. A Viennese *Beinfleisch* is called *Zwerchried* in Germany and *plat-de-côte* among the Swiss.

VIENNA'S BOILED-BEEF-EATERS ARE VEHEMENT CHAUVINISTS. They don't recognize the American New England dinner, the French *pot-au-feu,* or the *petite marmite.*

"The meat of the *petite marmite* is cooked in an earthenware stock-pot," a *Tafelspitz* scholar explained to me. "And the necks and wings of fowl are added. Incredible!" He shuddered slightly.

The Viennese experts take a dim view of *bœuf saignant à la ficelle,* rare beef with a string, a great French dish. A piece of fillet is tightly wrapped around with a string, roasted quickly in a very hot oven, and dipped for sixty seconds—not for fifty-eight or sixty-two, but for sixty—in boiling consommé, just before it is served. The juice is kept inside the pinkish meat by the trick of quick roasting and boiling.

But the Viennese do recognize *Tellerfleisch,* another local specialty. *Tellerfleisch* (the name means "plate meat") is eaten only *between* meals. It consists of a soup plate filled two thirds with clear beef soup, boiled carrots, split green onions, chopped parsley, with a piece of almost but not quite boiled beef and several slices of marrow, sprinkled with chopped chive.

There were two schools of cooking beef in Vienna. People who cared more about a strong soup than about the meat put the raw meat into cold water and let it cook gently, for hours, on a slow fire. They would add parsley, carrots, green onions, celery, salt, and pepper. After an hour the white foam that had formed on top was skimmed off. Sometimes half an onion, fried on the open range plate, was put in to give the soup a dark color. Others, who wanted their beef juicy and tender, put it straight into boiling water and let it simmer. This would close the pores of the meat and keep the juices inside.

The Meissl & Schadn was hit by American bombs in March 1945. A few weeks later, Red Army liberators tossed gasoline-soaked rags and gas cans into the half-destroyed building and set fire to it. The hotel burned down. But the tradition that had made Meissl & Schadn a great restaurant had come to an end long before. The restaurant was a creation of the Habsburg monarchy; its prosperity and decay reflected the greatness and decline of the Danube empire. With the help of Heinrich, it survived the hectic twenties, but when he died, the restaurant was doomed.

"People would come in and ask for 'boiled beef,' " an ex-habitué now remembers. "It was shocking."

Vienna's butchers have forgotten the fine points of cutting up a steer, and the chefs don't know how to slice a *Tafelspitz*. The small pieces at the pointed end of the triangular *Tafelspitz* are cut lengthwise, but the large, long, fibrous, upper end must be cut along its breadth.

Today most Viennese restaurants serve *Rindfleisch* or *Beinfleisch*, without any specification. The cattle are raised, and the meat is cut and cooked without the loving care that made it such a treat. It is often tough and dry, and served by ignorant waiters who recommend to their customers expensive "outside" dishes, such as Styrian pullet or imported lobster. The waiters are more interested in the size of their tips than in the contentment of the guest's palate. Restaurant-owners, operating on the get-rich-quick principle, no longer keep herds of cattle inside sugar refineries. It wouldn't be profitable, they say; besides, many refineries are located in the Soviet Zone of Austria.

—from *Blue Trout and Black Truffles*, 1948

A. J. Liebling on Restaurant
Maillabuau in Paris

In the twenties, the Rue Sainte-Anne, a narrow street running from near the Théâtre Français end of the Avenue de l'Opéra to the Rue Saint-Augustin and skirting the Square Louvois *en passant,* had been rendered illustrious by a man named Maillabuau, a gifted restaurateur but a losing horse-player who had no money to squander on décor. He turned his worn tablecloths into an asset by telling his customers that he wasted none of their contributions on frills—all went into the supreme quality of his materials and wines. A place with doormen in uniforms, he would say—a place with deep carpets and perhaps (here a note of horror would enter his voice) an orchestra— was *ipso facto* and *prima facie* a snare. He would then charge twice as much as any other restaurant in Paris. My memories of visits to Maillabuau's—visits that I had enjoyed only by stratagem—were so pleasant that I had chosen the Hôtel Louvois in order to be near it.

All during my year at the Sorbonne, the *Guide du Gourmand à Paris* had served as the Baedeker for my exploratory splurges when I had money enough to try restaurants off my usual beat. The author addressed his book to the gourmand, rather than to the gourmet, he said, because it was impossible to like food if you did not like a lot of it; "gourmet" was therefore a snob word, and a silly one. This predisposed me in his favor. But it was his subject matter that held me captive. The restaurants were categorized as "of great luxury," "middling-priced," "reasonable," and "simple," but all were warranted "good," and there were about a hundred and twenty-five of them. At the head of the "luxury" group was a "first platoon" of six restaurants (of which today only one survives, and that scarcely worthy of mention). Maillabuau, despite the worn tablecloths, figured among the ten others in the "luxury" group. In my own forays, "reasonable" was my ceiling, but I liked to read about the others—those financially unattainable Princesses Lointaines. I knew the description of Maillabuau's by heart:

> Sombre, almost lugubrious front. If the passerby is not warned, never will he suspect that behind that façade, having crossed that modest threshold, he can know the pure joys of gastronomy! How to know, if one is not a gourmand, that here the sole is divine, that the *entrecôte Bercy* has singular merits, that the pâté of venison is beyond

equal, that the burgundies (especially the Chambertin) are of the year that they should be, and that the *marc* resembles embalmed gold? How to know that only here, in all Paris, are made ready the fat squab guinea-hens anointed with all the scents of the Midi? Staggering bill, which one never resents paying.

I had no thought of crossing that modest threshold myself until one warm morning in the late spring of 1927, when it occurred to me that my father, mother, and sister would be arriving in Paris in a few weeks—they were waiting only for the beginning of the summer holiday at the Connecticut College for Women, where my sister was now a sophomore—and that in the natural course of events they would ask me, the local expert, where to dine. My mother and sister favored the kind of restaurant where they saw pretty dresses and where the *plat du jour* was likely to be called "Le Chicken Pie à l'Américaine," but my father had always been a booster for low overhead and quality merchandise; they were the principles that had guided his career as a furrier. Russian sable and ermine—with baum or stone marten if a woman couldn't afford anything better—had always been his idea of decent wear. His views on fur were a little like J. P. Morgan's on yachts—people who had to worry about the cost shouldn't have them. Foxes began and ended, for him, with natural blacks and natural silvers; the notion of a fox bred to specifications would have filled him with horror. Seal had to be Alaskan seal, not what was called Hudson seal, which meant muskrat. Persian lamb had to be *unborn* Persian lamb, not mutton.

As I had anticipated, when my family arrived in Paris they did indeed consult me about the scene of our first dinner together. So Maillabuau's it was. When we arrived before the somber, almost lugubrious front, my mother wanted to turn back. It looked like a store front, except for a bit of scrim behind the plate glass, through which the light from within filtered without éclat.

"Are you sure this is the right place?" she asked.

"It's one of the best restaurants in the world," I said, as if I ate there every day.

My father was already captivated. "Don't give you a lot of hoopla and ooh-la-la," he said, with approval. "I'll bet there are no Americans here."

We crossed the modest threshold. The interior was only half a jump from sordid, and there were perhaps fifteen tables. Old Maillabuau, rubicund and seedy, approached us, and I could sense that my mother was about to object to any table he proposed; she wanted some place like Fouquet's (not in the *Guide du Gourmand*). But between her and Maillabuau I interposed a barrage of French that neither she nor my sister could possibly penetrate, though each chirped a few tentative notes. "I have brought my family here because I have been informed it is the most illustrious house of Paris," I told him, and, throwing in a colloquialism I had learned in Rennes, a city a hundred years behind the times, I added, "We desire to knock the bell."

On hearing me, old Maillabuau, who may have thought for a moment that we were there by mistake and were about to order waffles, flashed a smile of avaricious relief. Father, meanwhile, regarding the convives of both sexes seated at the tables, was already convinced. The men, for the most part, showed tremendous *devantures*, which they balanced on their knees with difficulty as they ate, their wattles waving bravely with each bite. The women were shaped like demijohns and decanters, and they drank wine from glasses that must have reminded Father happily of beer schooners on the Bowery in 1890. "I don't see a single American," he said. He was a patriotic man at home, but he was convinced that in Paris the presence of Americans was a sign of a bunco joint.

"Monsieur my father is the richest man in Baltimore," I told Maillabuau, by way of encouragement. Father had nothing to do with Baltimore, but I figured that if I said New York, Maillabuau might not believe me. Maillabuau beamed and Father beamed back. His enthusiasms were rare but sudden, and this man—without suavity, without a tuxedo, who spoke no English, and whose customers were so patently overfed—appeared to him an honest merchant. Maillabuau showed us to a table; the cloth was diaphanous from wear except in the spots where it had been darned.

A split-second *refroidissement* occurred when I asked for the *carte du jour.*

"There is none," Maillabuau said. "You will eat what I tell you. Tonight, I propose a soup, trout *grenobloise,* and *poulet* Henri IV— simple but exquisite. The classic *cuisine française*—nothing complicated but all of the best."

When I translated this to Father, he was in complete agreement. "Plain food," he said. "No *schmier.*" I think that at bottom he agreed that the customer is sure to be wrong if left to his own devices. How often had the wives of personal friends come to him for a fur coat at the wholesale price, and declined his advice of an Alaskan seal—something that would last them for twenty years—in favor of some faddish fur that would show wear in six!

The simplicity of the menu disappointed me; I asked Maillabuau about the *pintadou,* fat and anointed with fragrance. "Tomorrow," he said, posing it as a condition that we eat his selection first. Mother's upper lip quivered, for she was *très gourmande* of cream sauces, but she had no valid argument against the great man's proposal, since one of the purposes of her annual trips to Europe was to lose weight at a spa. On the subject of wines, M. Maillabuau and I agreed better: the best in the cellar would do—a Montrachet to begin with, a Chambertin with the fowl.

It was indeed the best soup—a simple *garbure* of vegetables— imaginable, the best trout possible, and the best boiled fowl of which one could conceive. The simple line of the meal brought out the glories of the wine, and the wine brought out the grandeur in my father's soul. Presented with one of the most stupendous checks in history, he paid with gratitude, and said that he was going to take at least one meal a day *chez* Maillabuau during the rest of his stay. The dessert, served as a concession to my sister, was an *omelette au kirsch,* and Maillabuau stood us treat to the *marc,* like embalmed gold. Or at least he said he did; since only the total appeared on the check, we had to take his word for it. The *omelette au kirsch* was the sole dessert he ever permitted to be served, he said. He was against sweets on principle, since they were "not French," but the *omelette* was light and healthy. It contained about two dozen eggs.

The next day we had the *pintadou,* the day after that a *pièce de bœuf du Charolais* so remarkable that I never eat a steak without thinking how far short it falls. And never were the checks less than "staggering," and never did my father complain. Those meals constituted a high spot in my gastronomic life, but before long my mother and sister mutinied. They wanted a restaurant where they could see some dresses and eat *meringues glacées* and *homard au porto.*

SO IN 1939, ON MY FIRST EVENING IN WARTIME PARIS, I WENT straight from the Louvois to the Rue Sainte-Anne. The Restaurant Maillabuau had vanished. I did not remember the street number, so I walked the whole length of the Rue Sainte-Anne twice to make sure. But there was no Maillabuau; the horses at Longchamp had eaten him.

—from *Between Meals,* 1959

M.F.K. FISHER ON
MONSIEUR PAUL'S

"LET ME SUGGEST," SHE INTERRUPTED FIRMLY, "OUR SPECIAL dry sherry. It is chosen in Spain for Monsieur Paul."

And before I could agree she was gone, discreet and smooth.

She's a funny one, I thought, and waited in a pleasant warm tiredness for the wine.

It was good. I smiled approval at her, and she lowered her eyes, and then looked searchingly at me again. I realized suddenly that in this land of trained nonchalant waiters I was to be served by a small waitress who took her duties seriously. I felt much amused, and matched her solemn searching gaze.

"Today, Madame, you may eat shoulder of lamb in the English style, with baked potatoes, green beans, and a sweet."

My heart sank. I felt dismal, and hot and weary, and still grateful for the sherry.

But she was almost grinning at me, her lips curved triumphantly, and her eyes less palely blue.

"Oh, in *that* case a trout, of course—a *truite au bleu* as only Monsieur Paul can prepare it!"

She glanced hurriedly at my face, and hastened on. "With the trout, one or two young potatoes—oh, very delicately boiled," she added before I could protest, "very light."

I felt better. I agreed. "Perhaps a leaf or two of salad after the fish," I suggested. She almost snapped at me. "Of course, of course! And naturally our *hors d'oeuvres* to commence." She started away.

"No!" I called, feeling that I must assert myself now or be forever lost. "No!"

She turned back, and spoke to me very gently. "But Madame has never tasted our *hors d'oeuvres*. I am sure that Madame will be pleased. They are our specialty, made by Monsieur Paul himself. I am sure," and she looked reproachfully at me, her mouth tender and sad, "I am sure that Madame would be very much pleased."

I smiled weakly at her, and she left. A little cloud of hurt gentleness seemed to hang in the air where she had last stood.

I comforted myself with sherry, feeling increasing irritation with my own feeble self. Hell! I loathed *hors d'oeuvres*! I conjured disgusting visions of square glass plates of oily fish, of soggy vegetables glued together with cheap mayonnaise, or rank radishes and tasteless butter. No, Monsieur Paul or not, sad young pale-faced waitress or not, I hated *hors d'oeuvres*.

I glanced victoriously across the room at the cat, whose eyes seemed closed.

II

Several minutes passed. I was really very hungry.

The door banged open, and my girl came in again, less discreet this time. She hurried toward me.

"Madame, the wine! Before Monsieur Paul can go on—" Her eyes watched my face, which I perversely kept rather glum.

"I think," I said ponderously, daring her to interrupt me, "I think that today, since I am in Burgundy and about to eat a trout," and here I hoped she noticed that I did not mention *hors d'oeuvres*, "I think I shall drink a bottle of Chablis 1929—*not* Chablis Village 1929."

For a second her whole face blazed with joy, and then subsided into a trained mask. I knew that I had chosen well, had somehow satisfied her in a secret and incomprehensible way. She nodded politely and scuttled off, only for another second glancing impatiently at me as I called after her, "Well cooled, please, but not iced."

I'm a fool, I thought, to order a whole bottle. I'm a fool, here all alone and with more miles to walk before I reach Avallon and my fresh clothes and a bed. Then I smiled at myself and leaned back in my solid wide-seated chair, looking obliquely at the prints of Gibson girls, English tavern scenes, and hideous countrysides that hung on the papered walls. The room was warm; I could hear my companion cat purring under the ferns.

The girl rushed in, with flat baking dishes piled up her arms on napkins, like the plates of a Japanese juggler. She slid them off neatly in two rows on to the table, where they lay steaming up at me, darkly and infinitely appetizing.

"*Mon Dieu!* All for me?" I peered at her. She nodded, her discretion quite gone now and a look of ecstatic worry on her pale face and eyes and lips.

There were at least eight dishes. I felt almost embarrassed, and sat for a minute looking weakly at the fork and spoon in my hand.

"Perhaps Madame would care to start with the pickled herring? It is not like any other. Monsieur Paul prepares it himself, in his own vinegar and wines. It is very good."

I dug out two or three brown filets from the dish, and tasted. They were truly unlike any others, truly the best I had ever eaten, mild, pungent, meaty as fresh nuts.

I realized the maid had stopped breathing, and looked up at her. She was watching me, or rather a gastronomic X-ray of the herring inside me, with a hypnotized glaze in her eyes.

"Madame is pleased?" she whispered softly.

I said I was. She sighed, and pushed a sizzling plate of broiled endive toward me, and disappeared.

I had put a few dull green lentils on my plate, lentils scattered with minced fresh herbs and probably marinated in tarragon vinegar and walnut oil, when she came into the dining room again with the bottle of Chablis in a wine basket.

"Madame should be eating the little baked onions while they are hot," she remarked over her shoulder as she held the bottle in a napkin and uncorked it. I obeyed meekly, and while I watched her I ate several more than I had meant to. They were delicious, simmered first in strong meat broth, I think, and then drained and broiled with olive oil and new-ground pepper.

I was fascinated by her method of uncorking a vintage wine. Instead of the Burgundian procedure of infinite and often exaggerated precautions against touching or tipping or jarring the bottle, she handled it quite nonchalantly, and seemed to be careful only to keep her hands from the cool bottle itself, holding it sometimes by the basket and sometimes in a napkin. The cork was very tight, and I thought for a minute that she would break it. So did she; her face grew tense, and did not loosen until she had slowly worked out the cork and wiped the lip. Then she poured an inch of wine in a glass, turned her back to me like a priest taking Communion, and drank it down. Finally some was poured for me, and she stood with the bottle in her hand and her full lips drooping until I nodded a satisfied yes. Then she pushed another of the plates toward me, and almost rushed from the room.

I ate slowly, knowing that I should not be as hungry as I ought to be for the trout, but knowing too that I had never tasted such delicate savory morsels. Some were hot, some cold. The wine was light and cool. The room, warm and agreeably empty under the rushing sound of the stream, became smaller as I grew used to it.

My girl hurried in again, with another row of plates up one arm, and a large bucket dragging at the other. She slid the plates deftly on to the table, and drew a deep breath as she let the bucket down against the table leg.

"Your trout, Madame," she said excitedly. I looked down at the gleam of the fish curving through its limited water. "But first a good slice of Monsieur Paul's *pâté*. Oh yes, oh yes, you will be very sorry if you miss this. It is rich, but appetizing, and not at all too heavy. Just this one morsel!"

And willy-nilly I accepted the large gouge she dug from a terrine. I prayed for ten normal appetites and thought with amused nostalgia of my usual lunch of cold milk and fruit as I broke off a crust of bread and patted it smooth with the paste. Then I forgot everything but the exciting faint decadent flavor in my mouth.

I beamed up at the girl. She nodded, but from habit asked if I was satisfied. I beamed again, and asked, simply to please her, "Is there not a faint hint of *marc*, or perhaps cognac?"

"*Marc*, Madame!" And she awarded me the proud look of a teacher whose pupil has showed unexpected intelligence. "Monsieur Paul, after he has taken equal parts of goose breast and the finest pork, and broken a certain number of egg yolks into them, and ground them *very*, very fine, cooks all with seasoning for some three hours. *But,*" she pushed her face nearer, and looked with ferocious gloating at the *pâté* inside me, her eyes like X-rays, "he never stops stirring it! Figure to yourself the work of it—stir, stir, never stopping!

"Then he grinds in a suspicion of nutmeg, and then adds, very thoroughly, a glass of *marc* for each hundred grams of *pâté*. And is Madame not pleased?"

Again I agreed, rather timidly, that Madame was much pleased, that Madame had never, indeed, tasted such an unctuous and exciting *pâté*. The girl wet her lips delicately, and then started as if she had been pin-struck.

"But the trout! My God, the trout!" She grabbed the bucket, and her voice grew higher and more rushed.

"Here is the trout, Madame. You are to eat it *au bleu,* and you should never do so if you had not seen it alive. For if the trout were dead when it was plunged into the *court bouillon* it would not turn blue. So, naturally, it must be living."

I knew all this, more or less, but I was fascinated by her absorption in the momentary problem. I felt quite ignorant, and asked her with sincerity, "What about the trout? Do you take out its guts before or after?"

"Oh, the trout!" She sounded scornful. "Any trout is glad, truly glad, to be prepared by Monsieur Paul. His little gills are pinched, with one flash of the knife he is empty, and then he curls in agony in the *bouillon* and all is over. And it is the curl you must judge, Madame. A false *truite au bleu* cannot curl."

She panted triumph at me, and hurried out with the bucket.

III

She *is* a funny one, I thought, and for not more than two or three minutes I drank wine and mused over her. Then she darted in, with the trout correctly blue and agonizingly curled on a platter, and on her crooked arm a plate of tiny boiled potatoes and a bowl.

When I had been served and had cut off her anxious breathings with an assurance that the fish was the best I had ever tasted, she peered again at me and at the sauce in the bowl. I obediently put some of it on the potatoes: no fool I, to ruin *truite au bleu* with a hot concoction! There was more silence.

"Ah!" she sighed at last. "I knew Madame would feel thus! Is it not the most beautiful sauce in the world with the flesh of a trout?"

I nodded incredulous agreement.

"Would you like to know how it is done?"

I remembered all the legends of chefs who guarded favorite recipes with their very lives, and murmured yes.

She wore the exalted look of a believer describing a miracle at Lourdes as she told me, in a rush, how Monsieur Paul threw chopped chives into hot sweet butter and then poured the butter off, how he added another nut of butter and a tablespoonful of thick cream for each person, stirred the mixture for a few minutes over a slow fire, and then rushed it to the table.

"So simple?" I asked softly, watching her lighted eyes and the tender lustful lines of her strange mouth.

"So simple, Madame! But," she shrugged, "you know, with a master—"

—from *The Gastronomical Me*, 1943

JAMES BEARD ON
MEIER & FRANK'S IN PORTLAND

James Beard was born in Portland, Oregon, at the turn of the last century. An enormous man, his dream was to be an opera singer. His long career in food was marked by his love of an audience, but also by an unpretentious gift for words. No one ever explained a dish better. —M.K.

THE SECOND GREAT PORTLAND RESTAURANT, WHICH STILL exists in different and more elaborate form, is located in Meier & Frank's department store, run by the two families since the early 1850s. It is a landmark and has a personality unlike that of any other store in America. My father's family traded there in bartering days. Mother had one of the lowest account numbers on the books and felt as much at home there as she did in her own house.

The restaurant began as a novelty and became for a long time the best eating place in all of Portland. It was as hard to get a table there as it is now at "21" in New York. The men's grill has some regulars who have been going there for thirty and forty years or more—every day! This year Meier & Frank opened another fine restaurant in their new shopping-center store, which serves dinner and has a bar, grill and dining room.

One of the best chefs I ever knew was the chef at Meier & Frank's for a number of years, Don Daniels. He was paid extremely well for a chef by those days' standards and was worth it, for he produced food of rare quality—veal birds with a rich, creamy sauce, flavored with dill or tarragon; a beautiful salmi of duckling; and a remarkably good salmon soufflé with a hollandaise sauce. And he did superb clams, shipped from Seaside and Gearhart as fast as possible, which were sautéed *meunière* or with parsley butter and served with an excellent tartar sauce.

Don also served good caviar and wonderful salads, among them one which included chicken, walnuts and his own mayonnaise. His curry of crab was unforgettable, as was his little boned squab with a rice stuffing. Desserts were beyond belief. His Frankco is still one of the greatest frozen desserts ever created. It is made with the heaviest cream possible, whipped and then frozen at a very low temperature. Then it is scooped out in jagged crystalline portions. In my day, this came in maple, cognac, lemon and strawberry, according to the season, and it is still a major attraction at Meier & Frank's. Don also made rich home-style coffeecakes with almond toppings and *streusel,* using butter by the ton. And there was a remarkable black bottom pie. It had a crumb crust and was really two different types of Bavarian cream on a chocolate base. If you cared for that sort of dessert, then it was your dish and a sublime one.

This man was unique, and fortunately the Meiers and Franks understood his genius. He had a true sense of the seasonal aspect of menu building and was one of the first restaurant men to feature seasonal foods when they were at their height. He had an established clientele who wanted the best and paid for it, and he ran the restaurant according to his own gastronomic pleasure. (They are the same ideas, on a smaller scale, which Joseph Baum applied so successfully to the Four Seasons.) I am glad I knew this man and grateful that, for a period of time, I could eat in his restaurant four or five times a week.

—from *Delights & Prejudices,* 1964

LAWRENCE FERLINGHETTI'S CAFÉ

Recipe for Happiness in Karbaraovsk or anyplace

One good boulevard with trees
with one grand café in sun
with strong black coffee in very small cups

One not necessarily very beautiful
man or woman who loves you

One fine day

—1972

CHAPTER FIVE

Markets

ÉMILE ZOLA ON THE
TRIPERIE AT LES HALLES

A triperie is a place where not only tripe but all kinds of offal are prepared and sold.   —M.K.

HE FIRST MET CLAUDE LANTIER IN THE *TRIPERIE*. THEY HAD been going there every day, drawn by the taste of blood, the cruelty of street urchins amused by the sight of severed heads. A rust-colored stream ran around the pavilion. They dipped the tips of their shoes in it and made dams with leaves, which caused little bloody puddles. They were fascinated by the arrival of cartloads of offal, which stank even after thorough washings. They watched the unloading of bundles of sheep's feet, which were piled on the ground like dirty paving stones; huge stiff tongues still bleeding where they had been ripped from the throat; and beef hearts, like huge church bells, unmounted and silent. But what most made them shudder with pleasure were the big baskets, dripping in blood, filled with sheep heads, their greasy horns and black muzzles and strips of woolly skin left hanging from bleeding flesh. They looked at these bloody hampers and imagined guillotines lobbing off countless heads and throwing them in baskets.

They followed the baskets to the bottom of the cellar, watching them

Robert Doisneau, *Untitled* (Robert Doisneau/Rapho)

glide along the rails laid over the steps, and listening to the wheezing cry made by the casters as the wagons went down. Below was exquisite horror. They entered into the scent of death, walked between dark, cloudy puddles sometimes appearing to be lit by glowing purple eyes. The floor felt sticky on the soles of their shoes as they splashed through, revolted and yet entranced by this horrifying muck. The gas jets had low flames like the batting lid of a bloodshot eye. Near the water taps, in the pale light that came through the grates, they came to the chopping blocks. Mesmerized, they watched the butchers, their aprons stiffened with gore, smashing sheep heads with mallets. They lingered for hours until all the baskets were empty, held by the crack of bones, until the last tongue was torn out, the last brain knocked loose by blows to the skull. Sometimes a worker walked behind them, hosing down the cellar floor, water bursting out with the roar of an open floodgate. But although the flood was so powerful that it wore away at the floor, it did not have the power to remove either the stain or the stench of blood.

—from *The Belly of Paris,* 1873,
translated from the French by Mark Kurlansky

Edna Ferber on a Chicago Market Window

JUST OFF STATE STREET THERE IS A FRUITERER AND IMPORTER who ought to be arrested for cruelty. His window is the most fascinating and the most heartless in Chicago. A line of open-mouthed, wide-eyed gazers is always to be found before it. Despair, wonder, envy, and rebellion smolder in the eyes of those gazers. No shop window show should be so diabolically set forth as to arouse such sensations in the breast of the beholder. It is a work of art, that window; a breeder of anarchism, a destroyer of contentment, a second feast of Tantalus. It boasts peaches, dewy and golden, when peaches have no right to be; plethoric, purple bunches of English hothouse grapes are there to taunt the ten-dollar-a-week clerk whose sick wife should be in the hospital; strawberries glow therein when shortcake is a last summer's memory, and forced cucumbers remind us that we are taking ours in the form of dill pickles. There is, perhaps, a choice head of cauliflower, so exquisite in its ivory and green perfection as to be fit for a bride's bouquet; there are apples so flawless that if the garden of Eden grew any as perfect it is small wonder that Eve fell for them. There are fresh mushrooms, and jumbo cocoanuts, and green almonds; costly things in beds of cotton nestle next to strange and marvelous things in tissue wrappings. Oh, that window is no place for the hungry, the dissatisfied, or the man out of a job. When the air is filled with snow there is that in the sight of muskmelons which incites crime.

—from *Maymeys from Cuba,* 1912

Claude McKay on a Fruit Stand in Harlem

In 1890, Claude McKay was born in a thatch-roofed house in the lush green slopes of central Jamaica. In 1912, he came to America to attend an agricultural college in Kansas. His plan was to learn modern farming techniques and return to Jamaica. But two years later he had left school. Although he became one of the leading voices in the Harlem Renaissance, renowned for both novels and poetry, a part of him always remembered that verdant, red-soiled farmland he had left behind. —M.K.

The Tropics in New York

Bananas ripe and green, and ginger-root,
   Cocoa in pods and alligator pears,
And tangerines and mangoes and grape fruit,
   Fit for the highest prize at parish fairs,

Set in the window, bringing memories
   Of fruit-trees laden by low-singing rills,
And dewy dawns, and mystical blue skies
   In benediction over nun-like hills.

My eyes grew dim, and I could no more gaze;
   A wave of longing through my body swept,
And, hungry for the old, familiar ways,
   I turned aside and bowed my head and wept.

—1930

SAMUEL CHAMBERLAIN ON THE FISH MARKET IN MARBLEHEAD, MASS.

Samuel Chamberlain, author and illustrator of almost fifty books on gastronomic subjects, wrote Clémentine in the Kitchen *about the experiences of his family's Burgundian cook when they took her with them to America at the outbreak of World War II.* —M.K.

BUT ONE LOCAL INSTITUTION IN MARBLEHEAD WAS PITCHED precisely to Clémentine's old-world viewpoint—the fish store of Mr. Job

Stacy. Repeated coats of white paint, inside and out, could not disguise the antiquity of Stacy's Fish Shop, installed in a low frame building that resembled a pure Cape Cod cottage. Back in the 1870s, Job's grandfather had cut a many-paned shop window in the street façade of the house and established the business. Job and his brothers (who do most of the fishing) inherited it as a matter of course. Job takes charge of the shop, and his brothers, who are distinctly less personable and given to Saturday night bacchanals, preside at the picturesque old fishermen's shanty at the water's edge, where the nets, lobster pots, and Newburyport rum are stored.

There is no hint of pretension in Stacy's Fish Shop. The window contains the same exhibition of giant sea shells, coral curiosities, mounted lobsters, and stuffed fish that has been there for years. Once you are inside you will observe a Spartan exhibit of cod liver oil flanked by a few wooden boxes of salted cod fillets and a lonely squad of catsup bottles. Clean sawdust is on the floor. Before you is a small white marble counter, covered with chopped ice that all but conceals a few freshly caught haddock and cod. That is all you see as you enter Mr. Stacy's shop, except a blackboard. It isn't impressive.

But there is one hint that indisputable treasures are concealed in icy bins in the back room. It is on that blackboard, upon which Job lavishes a fine Spencerian flourish. When the Beck family studied this handsome document for the first time, a ray of pure rapture burst through the clouds. We began to realize our enormous good fortune in choosing this New England seaport as our home. For Job Stacy lists upon his blackboard an almost utopian stock of freshly caught fish. He has haddock, mackerel, and young cod at excursion rates. And there are handsome butterfish, rock bass, perch, and bluefish. He has fillets of cusk, plaice, and flounder, besides smoked fillets and finnan haddie of unimpeachable integrity. His bins hide an ample supply of halibut, swordfish, and salmon. He has clams—soft-shelled ones for steaming, cherrystones for appetizers, and for your chowder ponderous quahaugs. He has oysters—bluepoints, Cotuits, and Narragansetts. His lobsters are so alive they are athletic, but he has lobster meat if you prefer it. In season you can find tender young soft-shelled crabs, or you can have shrimps or crab meat at any time. He has not only the large sea scallops, but those rarities of the American *gourmandise,* small Cape scallops as well.

It was natural that Clémentine should share our enthusiasm, once we introduced her to Mr. Stacy and his well-stocked back room. Here was a shop that reminded her of France and of the amiable Monsieur

Chollet, who used to sell us *merlan,* turbot, and sole. Clémentine began to pay almost daily visits to Mr. Stacy's shop, chattering affably in French, a language that he obviously did not understand, until she finally thawed out his Yankee reserve very perceptibly. Meanwhile the Becks saw the beginning of a dream come true. Our table became beautified with the freshest of Atlantic fish, cooked as a French *Cordon Bleu* would do it.

Here I would like to share our good fortune with you by tearing a few leaves from Clémentine's notebook. There is nothing brilliantly original about any of these recipes. They merely follow the old French fundamentals. But to judge by the comments of our dinner guests, they have opened up a new vista to at least a few New England hostesses. And since they can be achieved rather easily in an American home, we hope that they merit your sympathetic consideration.

Clémentine's approach to preparing New England fish was refreshing and direct. It never occurred to her to fry fish in deep fat. Fried scallops, fried oysters, fried clams, fried "fillet of sole"—the inevitable vocabulary of the restaurant cook in these parts—did not become a part of her culinary jargon, and we were certainly just as glad. Clémentine took the simplest and most obvious French path, which was to bake this clean saltwater fish in white wine with mushrooms. The unassuming haddock and baby cod take on surprising distinction when prepared in this rudimentary manner:

HADDOCK AU VIN BLANC

Place haddock fillets in a shallow buttered baking dish. Add at your discretion thinly sliced mushrooms and thin slices of small white onions, though chopped shallots are best. Season with a little salt, pepper from the pepper mill, a bay leaf, and a sprig of thyme. Sprinkle with fine bread crumbs and dot well with butter. Pour a generous glass of dry white wine into the baking dish and bake the fish in a moderate (350°) oven until just firm, basting now and then—it should not take more than 20 minutes. Serve with steamed potatoes and a trickle of lemon juice.

—from *Clémentine in the Kitchen,* 1943

Wole Soyinka on an Evening Market in Nigeria

Wole Soyinka is a Nigerian playwright, novelist, and poet who won the Nobel Prize for Literature in 1986. Aké is his autobiographical account of growing up in a western Nigerian village. —M.K.

Edun, who lived on the other side of Ibarapa morning market, was inducted at the same time. We celebrated the occasion as yet another liberating step from the demands of our households. In addition to lessons, scouting, and a few fictions, there was now the legitimate escape through choir practice. And although I lived nearer to the church, it was somehow accepted that it was I who should go past the church, cross the street between Aké square and Ibarapa market, go through the market, pick my way through the intervening *agbole* and return with Edun through the same passages to the church for choir practice and, when we began to robe, for church services.

We varied the course. The evening market was normally out of our way since it lay on the other side of the road to Iberekodo, but the morning market was mostly bare and devoid of interest by the hour of choir practice. Going through the sister market only added some ten or fifteen minutes to the walk and I made sure that I set out early enough to make up the time for it. The flavours of the market rose fully in the evenings, beckoning us to a depletion of the *onini* and halfpennies which we had succeeded in saving up during the week. For there they all were, together, the *jogi* seller who passed, in full lyrical cry beneath the backyard wall at a regular hour of the morning, followed only moments later by the *akara* seller, her fried bean-cakes still surreptitiously oozing and perfuming the air with groundnut oil. In the market we stood and gazed on the deftly cupped fingers of the old women and their trainee wards scooping out the white bean-paste from a mortar in carefully gauged quantities, into the wide-rimmed, shallow pots of frying oil. The lump sank immediately in the oil but no deeper than an inch or two, bobbed instantly to the surface and turned pinkish in the oil. It spurted fat globules upwards and sometimes beyond the rim of the pot if the mix had too much water. Then, slowly forming, the outer crust of crisp, gritty light brownness which masked the inner core of baked bean-paste, filled with green and red peppers, ground crayfish or chopped.

Even when the *akara* was fried without any frills, its oil impregnated flavours filled the markets and jostled for attention with the tang of roasting coconut slices within farina cakes which we called *kasada;* with the hard-fried lean meat of *tinko;* the 'high,' rotted-cheese smell of *ogiri;* roasting corn, fresh vegetables or *gbegiri.* *Akàmu,* the evening corn pap, was scooped into waiting bowls from a smooth, brown gourd sitting in enamelled trays on bamboo trestles, presided over by women who daily improvised new praise-chants. An *onini,* even a halfpenny did not fulfil every craving but the sights and the smells were free. Choir practice became inseparable from the excursion through Ibarapa's sumptuous resurrection of flavours every evening. When, a few months later, our apprenticeship was over and we became full-fledged choristers, I continued to leave early on Sundays and other church seasons to call on Edun for both morning and evening services. The morning market was not open on Sundays but, there was a woman who appeared to have converted all the smells and textures of both morning and evening markets in her pot of stew, a crayfish and locust-bean biased concoction which queened it over rice and a variety of yams. Apart from a few stalls of fresh vegetables, she alone defied the claims of Sunday to a market-free gesture of respect. The consequence was predictable. Breakfast at home was not niggardly, so it was not a question of hunger. It was even special on Sundays—yams, fish stew, omelette, bread, butter and the inevitable tea or lemon grass infusion. But it was not yet breakfast on Sunday until I had picked my way through the stalls of Ibarapa, cassock and surplice thrown over the shoulder, rescued Edun from his home and, robbing God to pay Iya Ibarapa, used up the pennies we were given for offering on the steaming, peppery, glutinous riot of liver, of chunks and twists of cows' insides served by the old woman as church bells signalled the half-hour before confronting God. Once or twice, probably a little oftener, we were struck by the fear that God might object to this weekly deprivation of his rightful dues, but I think I lightened our apprehensions by suggesting that we sang better after the richness of the markets in our throats than we ever did with the delicacies of the parsonage alone. In any case, we watched for signs of disapproval from the designated owner of those Sunday pennies, but received none.

When I asked Ibidun, Mrs Lijadu's niece, what our Aunt put in her stews to make it taste so peculiar she said, *pasmenja*. It was a strange word but one which was perfectly suited to the flavour of the meals we had with our Aunt who, we had decided, belonged to the vague Brazilian side of some of our relations. An axis of tastes and smells was formed between her and our grandmother, Daodu's sister, who lived alone in Igbein almost on the other side of Abeokuta. We did not visit her much but, when we did, I would realize with a start—and not just at mealtime—that I was not at Mrs Lijadu's but in the home of our maternal grandmother, the mysterious elder sister of Rev A. O. Ransome-Kuti. It remained one of the mysteries of the family relationships over which Wild Christian spent so much time trying to educate us. Were the Olubi our cousins and did this mean blood or marriage relations? I listened, understanding none of the elaborate and intricate family history. Links were formed of far more tangible matters. Our Igbein grandmother had nothing in common, as far as I ever discerned, with her formidable brother Daodu. Equally stern and just as affectionate perhaps, but I was more ready to accept, and indeed continued to believe for a long time that she was Beere's mother. And I thought that she and Mrs Lijadu were sisters because they both cooked with *pasmenja,* both homes were constantly wreathed in the smell of *pasmenja.* Even their buns and *chin-chin* had identical flavours; as for food in both homes, it could only have been cooked, not merely by sisters, but by two people who had been sisters all their lives. Daodu's wife, Beere, I never associated with any form of cooking. Eating, that was a different matter.

Beere had a passion for *moin-moin* and she was so fond of *moin-moin* made by Wild Christian that she often sent one of her elder children, Koye or Dolupo, all the way from Igbein to Aké for Wild Christian's *moin-moin.* When she came in person and joined our parents at table, a shriek of outrage was wrung from her if an overzealous maid had unwrapped the steamed delicacy from the leaves. For her, the sublime parts of *moin-moin* were those wafer-thin truants which leaked into the folds of leaves and were now steamed into light, independent slivers, to be peeled leisurely from their veined beds and sucked smoothly through the lips in-between, or, as a finale to the chunky mouthfuls of the full-bodied *moin-moin.* The hapless maid produced *moin-moin* paraded in all its steamy, but naked glory and Beere would confidently insist that the leaves be retrieved. There was no danger; she knew very well that they had not been thrown into the dust-bin. We watched her glide meticulously through every leaf, prise through the stuck-together leaves with a skin-surgeon's care. She levered apart the baked veins of the leaf-wraps, casually picking up the oiled wafers along the way and licking her lips in ostentatious enjoyment. She acknowledged our unvoiced stares of protest by remarking loudly—if she happened to be in the mood—that anyone who really believed that such tidbits should be left to children was either a fool or an Englishman. Then, with a roguish look on her bespectacled face, she measured off a slice from the centre of the *moin-moin,* pushed it aside for us and winked, remarking afterwards that she would sooner forgo the main lump than lose those insubstantial slivers with their Wild-Christian flavour, sealed in secret corners cunningly pinched by her practised fingers.

The hawkers' lyrics of leaf-wrapped *moin-moin* still resound in parts of Aké and the rest of the town but, along Dayisi's Walk is also a shop which sells *moin-moin* from a glass case, lit by sea-green neon lamps. It lies side by side with McDonald's hamburgers, Kentucky Fried Chicken, hot dogs and dehydrated sausage-rolls. It has been cooked in emptied milk-tins and similar containers, scooped out and sliced in neat geometric shapes like cakes of soap. And the newly-rich homes stuff it full of eggs, tinned sardines from Portugal and corned beef from the Argentine. The fate of *wara,* among others, is however one without even this dubious reprieve. The vendor of milk-curds, floated in outsize gourds has been banished by chromium boxes with sleek spouts which dispense yellowish fluids into brittle cones. If it were, at least, ice *cream!* But no. The quick-profit importer of instant machines is content to foist a bed-pan slop of diabetic kittens on his youthful customers and watch them lick it noisily, biting deeper into the cone. Even Pa Delumo's Sunday school children knew better; the ice cream king of Dayisi's Walk would have been dethroned, through neglect, by the *wara* queen.

Our teeth were cut on *robo,* hard-fried balls of crushed melon seeds, and on *guguru-and-epa,* the friend and sustainer of workers on the critical countdown towards pay day. A handful of guguru was washed down in water, palm-wine or pito and hunger was staved off for the rest of the working day. Evening, and *konkere* department took over, a bean-pottage with a sauce of the darkest palm-oil and peppers, and of a soundly uncompromising density. Mixed with *gari,* it fully justified the name of concrete whose corrupted version it proudly bore. The Hausa women who sold *guguru* carefully graded their corn; we combined in our purchases the hard-roasted teeth-breakers, the fluffy, off-white floaters and the half-and-half, inducing variations into taste-buds with slices of coconut or measures of groundnuts. Today's jaws on Dayisi's Walk appear no less hard-worked, indeed they champ endlessly—on chewing-gum. Among the fantasy stores lit by neon and batteries of coloured bulbs a machine also dispenses popcorn, uniformly fluffed. Urchins thrust the new commodity, clean-wrapped, in plastic bags in faces of passengers whose vehicles pause even one moment along the route. The blare of motor-horns compete with a high-decibel outpouring of rock and funk and punk and other thunk-thunk from lands of instant-culture heroes. Eyes glazed, jaws in constant, automated motion, the new habituees mouth the confusion of lyrics belted out from every store, their arms flapping up and down like wounded bush-fowl. Singly, or in groups of identical twins, quad- or quintuplets they wander into the stereo stores, caress the latest record sleeves and sigh. A trio emerge with an outsize radio-cassette player in full blast, setting up mobile competition with the already noise-demented line of stores.

—from *Aké,* 1981

CHAPTER SIX

Not Eating

SHOLOM ALEICHEM ON YOM KIPPUR

Both eating and not eating are essential to the ritual of Judaism. The most important day of fast is Yom Kippur, the day of atonement after the New Year. Many stories emerge about this important festival of not eating. In the Talmud, there is the story of R. Joseph, the son of Raba, who became so engaged in an argument with his father that they missed the last meal before sundown. It being Yom Kippur, they would have to wait another twenty-four hours before eating.

Sholom Aleichem, the pen name of Solomon Rabinowitz, one of a number of nineteenth-century writers who developed a literature in the Yiddish language, tells a different story of fasting for Yom Kippur in "The Search." —M.K.

"NOW, LISTEN TO ME," SAID A MAN WITH ROUND BOVINE eyes, who had been sitting in a corner by the window, smoking and taking in stories of thefts, holdups, and expropriations. "I'll tell you a good one, also about a theft, which happened in my town, in the synagogue of all places, and on Yom Kippur too! You'll like it.

OUR KASRILEVKE—THAT'S WHERE I COME FROM—IS A SMALL town and a poor one. We have no thieves and no stealing, for there is nobody to steal from and nothing to steal. And aside from all that, a Jew just isn't a thief. I mean to say, even if a Jew is a thief, he is not the kind of thief who sneaks in through a window or goes at you with a knife. He may twist you and turn you, outtalk you and outsmart you—granted; but he won't crawl into your pockets, he won't be caught red-handed and led down the street in disgrace. That may happen to a thieving Ivan but not to a Jew. Imagine, then, someone stealing in Kasrilevke, and quite a bit of money too—eighteen hundred rubles at one stroke!

One day a stranger arrived in our town, a Jew, some sort of contractor from Lithuania. He appeared on the evening of Yom Kippur, just before the time for prayer. He left his bundle at the inn and hurried out to look for a place to pray and found the old synagogue. He arrived in time to attend the evening prayer and ran into the trustees with their collection box.

"*Sholom aleichem!*"

"*Aleichem sholom!*"

"Where are you from?"

"From Lithuania."

"And what's your name?"

"What difference does that make to your grandmother?"

"Well, after all, you've come to our synagogue!"

"Where else do you want me to go?"

"You surely want to pray here?"

"Have I any choice?"

"Then put something in the box."

"Of course. Did you think I was going to pray for nothing?"

Our stranger took three silver rubles out of his pocket and put them in the box. Then he put a ruble in the cantor's plate, gave a ruble for the rabbi, another for the school, and threw half a ruble into the poor box; in addition, he handed out coins to the beggars standing at the door—we have so many poor people in our town, God bless them, that if you really went at it you could distribute Rothschild's fortune among them.

When we saw the kind of stranger he was we gave him a place right at the east wall. You will ask how one could be found for him when all the places were occupied. Some question! Where does one find a place at a celebration—a wedding, say, or a circumcision feast—after all the guests have been seated at the table and suddenly there is a commotion—the rich guest has arrived! Well, all the others squeeze together until a place is made for the rich man. Jews have a habit of squeezing—when no one else squeezes us, we squeeze one another.

The round-eyed man paused for a moment, looked at the audience to see what impression his quip had made, and resumed his tale.

In short, the stranger occupied a place of honor. He asked the *shammes* for a prayer stand and, donning his cloak and prayer shawl, began to pray. Bending over his stand, he prayed and prayed, always on his feet, never sitting down, let alone lying down. He did not leave his stand for a minute, that Litvak, except when the Eighteen Blessings were recited and everyone had to face the Ark, and during the kneeling periods. To stand on one's feet on a day of fasting without ever sitting down—only a Litvak can do that.

After the *shofar* was blown for the last time, and Chaim-Chune the teacher, who always conducts the first night prayer after the holiday, began to chant, *"Ha-mai-riv a-a-arovim,"* we suddenly heard a cry, "Help, help, help!" We looked around and saw the stranger lying on the floor in a faint. We poured water on him to bring him to, but he fainted again.

What had happened? A fine thing! He had on him—the Litvak, that is—eighteen hundred rubles; and he had been afraid, so he said, to leave his money at the inn. You think it's a trifle, eighteen hundred rubles? To whom could he entrust such a sum in a strange town? Nor did it seem right to keep it in his pocket on Yom Kippur. So, after thinking the matter over, he decided quietly to slip the money into his stand—yes, a Litvak is quite capable of such a thing! Now do you understand why he did not leave his stand for a minute? Someone had apparently snatched his money during the Eighteen Blessings or one of the kneeling periods.

In short, he screamed, he wept, he lamented—what would he do now without the money? It was, he said, someone else's, not his, he was only an employee in some office, a poor man, burdened with many children. All he could do now, he said, was to jump into the river or hang himself right here in the synagogue in front of everybody.

On hearing such talk the whole congregation stood paralyzed, forgetting that they had been fasting for twenty-four hours and were about to go home to eat. It was a disgrace before a stranger, a shameful thing to witness. Eighteen hundred rubles stolen, and where? In a place of worship, in the old synagogue of Kasrilevke! And when? On Yom Kippur! Such a thing was unheard of.

"*Shammes,* lock the door!" our rabbi ordered. We have our rabbi—his name is Reb Yosefel—a true and pious Jew, not oversubtle but a kindly soul, a man without gall, and sometimes he has brilliant ideas, such as wouldn't occur even to a man with eighteen heads! When the door was locked the rabbi addressed the congregation. His face was white as the wall, his hands were trembling and his eyes burning.

"Listen carefully, my friends," he said. "This is an ugly business, an outrage, unheard of since the creation of the world, that in our town, in Kasrilevke, there should be such an offender, such a renegade from Israel, who would have the impudence to take from a stranger, from a poor man, a supporter of a family, such a large sum of money. And when? On a holy day, on Yom Kippur, and perhaps even during the closing prayer! Such a thing has been truly unheard of since the creation of the world! I can't believe such a thing is possible, it just can't be! Nevertheless—who can tell?—some wretched man was perhaps tempted by this money, particularly since it amounted to such a fortune. The temptation, God have mercy on us, was great enough. So if it was decreed that one of us succumb to the temptation—if one of us has had the misfortune to commit such a sin on a day like this—we must investigate the matter, get to the bottom of it. Heaven and earth have sworn that truth must come to the top like oil on water, so we must search each other, go through each other's garments, shake out the pockets of everyone here—from the most respectable member of the congregation to the *shammes,* sparing no one. Begin with me: here, my friends, go through my pockets!"

Thus spoke our rabbi, Reb Yosefel, and he was the first to open his caftan and turn all his pockets inside out. After him, all the members of the congregation loosened their girdles and turned out their pockets, and each of them in turn was searched, and felt all over, and shaken out. But when they came to Laizer Yosl he turned all colors and began to argue. The stranger, he said, was a swindler; the whole thing was a Litvak's trick, no one had stolen any money from him. "Can't you see," he said, "that the whole thing is a lie, a fraud?"

The congregation broke out in loud protests. "What do you mean?" they said. "Respectable citizens have submitted to a search—why should you be excepted?" The whole crowd clamored, "Search him, search him!"

Laizer Yosl saw that things were going badly for him, and he began to plead with tears in his eyes, begging that he be spared. He swore by every oath: may he be as pure of all evil as he was innocent of stealing. And on what grounds was he to be spared? He couldn't bear the disgrace of being searched, he said, and implored the others to have pity on his youth, not to subject him to such an indignity. Do anything you want, he said, but do not go through my pockets. How do you like such a scoundrel? Do you think anyone listened to him?

But wait a minute, I have forgotten to tell you who this Laizer Yosl was. He was not a native of Kasrilevke; he came from the devil knows where to marry a Kasrilevke girl. Her father, the rich man of our town, had unearthed him somewhere and bragged that he had found a rare gem, a real genius, for his daughter, a man who knew by rote a thousand pages of the Talmud, who was an expert in Scriptures, a Hebraist, and a mathematician who could handle fractions and algebra, and who wielded the pen like nobody's business—in short, a man with all seventeen talents. When his father-in-law brought him, everyone went to look at this gem, to see what kind of rare bargain the rich man had acquired. Well, if you just looked at him he was nothing special, a young man like many others, fairly good-looking, only the nose a little too long, and a pair of eyes like two glowing coals, and a mouth with a sharp tongue in it. He was examined; they made him explain a page of the Talmud, a chapter from the Bible, a passage from Rambam, this and that, and he passed the test with flying colors—the dog was at home everywhere, he knew all the answers! Reb Yosefel himself said that he could be a rabbi in any Jewish community—not to mention his vast knowledge of worldly things. Just to give you an idea, there is in our town a subtle scholar, Zeidel Reb Shaye's son, a crazy fellow, and he doesn't even compare with Laizer Yosl. Moreover no one in the world could equal him as a chess player. Talk about cleverness!

Needless to say, the whole town envied the rich man such a genius, although people said that the gem was not without its flaws. To begin with, he was criticized for being too clever (and what there's too

much of isn't good), and too modest, too familiar with everyone, mingling too easily with the smallest among the smallest, whether it be a
boy or a girl or even a married woman. Then he was disliked because
of the way he walked around, always absorbed in thought. He would
come to the synagogue after everyone else, put on his prayer shawl,
and page the *Well of Life* or *Ebn Ezra*, with his skullcap on askew—
never saying a word of prayer. No one ever saw him doing anything
wrong; nevertheless it was whispered that he was not a pious man—
after all, no one can have all the virtues!

And so when his turn came to be searched his refusal was at once
interpreted as a sign that he had the money on him. "Make me swear
an oath on the Bible," he said. "Cut me, chop me to pieces, roast me,
burn me alive, anything, but don't go through my pockets!"

At this point even our Rabbi Yosefel, though the gentlest of men,
lost his temper and began to scold. "You so-and-so," he cried, "you deserve I don't know what! What do you think you are? You see what all
these men have gone through—all of them have accepted the indignity of a search, and you want to be an exception! One of the two—
either confess and give back the money, or show your pockets! Are you
playing games with an entire Jewish community? I don't know what
we'll do to you!"

In short, they took this nice young man, laid him on the floor by
sheer force, and began to feel him all over and shake out his pockets. And then they shook out—guess what?—chickenbones and a
dozen plum pits; everything was still fresh, the bones had recently
been gnawed, and the pits were moist. Can you imagine what a
pretty sight it was, all this treasure shaken out of our genius's pockets? You can picture for yourselves the look on their faces, he and his
father-in-law, the rich man, and our poor rabbi too. Our Reb Yosefel
turned away in shame; he could look no one in the face. And later,
when the worshipers were on their way home, to eat after the fast,
they did not stop talking about the treasure they had discovered in
the young man's pockets, and they shook with laughter. Only Reb
Yosefel walked alone, with bowed head, unable to look anyone in the
eyes, as though the remains of food had been shaken out of his own
pockets.

The narrator stopped and resumed his smoking. The story was
over.

"And what about the money?" we all asked in one voice.

"What money?" the man said with an uncomprehending look as he blew out the smoke.

"What do you mean, what money? The eighteen hundred—"

"O-o-o-oh," he drawled. "The eighteen hundred? Vanished without a trace."

"Vanished?"

"Without a t-r-a-c-e."

—from *A Treasury of Yiddish Stories,* 1902,
translated from the Yiddish by Norbert Guterman

JOHN STEINBECK ON STARVATION
IN CALIFORNIA'S HARVEST

THE SPRING IS RICH AND GREEN IN CALIFORNIA THIS YEAR. In the fields the wild grass is ten inches high, and in the orchards and vineyards the grass is deep and nearly ready to be plowed under to enrich the soil. Already the flowers are starting to bloom. Very shortly one of the oil companies will be broadcasting the locations of the wildflower masses. It is a beautiful spring.

There has been no war in California, no plague, no bombing of open towns and roads, no shelling of cities. It is a beautiful year. And thousands of families are starving in California. In the county seats the coroners are filling in "malnutrition" in the spaces left for "causes of death." For some reason, a coroner shrinks from writing "starvation" when a thin child is dead in a tent.

For it's in the tents you see along the roads and in the shacks built from dump heap material that the hunger is, and it isn't malnutrition. It is starvation. Malnutrition means you go without certain food essentials and take a long time to die, but starvation means no food at all. The green grass spreads right into the tent doorways and the orange trees are loaded. In the cotton fields, a few wisps of the old crop cling to the black stems. But the people who picked the cotton, and cut the peaches and apricots, who crawled all day in the rows of lettuce and beans, are hungry. The men who harvested the crops of California, the women and girls who stood all day and half the night in the canneries, are starving.

It was so two years ago in Nipomo, it is so now, it will continue to be so until the rich produce of California can be grown and harvested on some other basis than that of stupidity and greed.

—from *America and Americans*, 1938

MENCIUS ON FEEDING CHINA

Confucius, who lived from 551 to 479 B.C., was considered China's first moral philosopher. He was troubled by the nature of mankind and wanted to raise the standard of human behavior. One of the leading sources of Confucianism is a book called The Mencius, *written by Mencius, who was a student of Confucius's grandson and lived from 372 to 289 B.C.*

Mencius went further than Confucius in some basic beliefs. Both criticized government, but Mencius said that people had the right to rebel against bad government. One of the first environmentalists, Confucius had great concerns about ecology and food production. Mencius was even more outspoken on these issues. The following passage is unusual in ancient Chinese literature for the directness of its criticism of government policy. Lesser figures were executed for such candor.   —M.K.

IF YOU DO NOT INTERFERE WITH THE BUSY SEASON IN THE fields, then there will be more grain than the people can eat; if you do not allow nets with too fine a mesh to be used in large ponds, then there will be more fish and turtles than they can eat; if hatchets and axes are permitted in the forests on the hills only in the proper seasons, then there will be more timber than they can use. When the people have more grain, more fish and turtles than they can eat, and more timber than they can use, then in the support of their parents when alive and in the mourning of them when dead, they will be able to have no regrets over anything left undone. This is the first step along the Kingly way.

If the mulberry is planted in every homestead of five mu of land, then those who are fifty can wear silk; if chickens, pigs and dogs do not miss their breeding season, then those who are seventy can eat meat; if each lot of a hundred mu is not deprived of labour during the busy seasons, then families with several mouths to feed will not go hungry. Exercise due care over the education provided by the village schools, and discipline the people by teaching them the duties proper to sons and younger brothers, and those whose heads have turned grey will not be carrying loads on the roads. When those who are seventy wear silk and eat meat and the masses are neither cold nor hungry, it is impossible for their prince not to be a true King.

Now when food meant for human beings is so plentiful as to be thrown to dogs and pigs, you fail to realize that it is time for garnering, and when men drop dead from starvation by the way-side, you fail to realize that it is time for distribution. When people die, you simply say, "It is none of my doing. It is the fault of the harvest." In what way is that different from killing a man by running him through, while saying all the time, "It is none of my doing. It is the fault of the weapon." Stop putting the blame on the harvest and the people of the whole Empire will come to you.

—from *Mencius,* third century B.C.,
translated from the Chinese by D. C. Lau

BRILLAT-SAVARIN'S ADVICE
TO WOMEN WHO ARE THIN

EVERY THIN WOMAN WANTS TO GROW PLUMP: THAT IS AN avowal which has been made to us a thousand times. Therefore it is in order to pay final homage to the all-powerful sex that we are going to try here to tell how to replace with living flesh those pads of silk or cotton which are displayed so profusely in novelty shops, to the obvious horror of the prudish, who pass them by with a shudder, turning away from such shadows with even more care than if it were actuality they looked upon.

With a suitably adapted diet, the usual prescriptions relative to rest and sleep can almost be ignored without endangering the net results: if you do not take any exercise, you will be inclined to grow fat; if you exercise, you will still grow fat, since you will eat more than usual. When hunger is knowingly satisfied, you not only restore what energy you have used up, but you add to what you already have, whenever there is need for it.

If you sleep a great deal, it will be fattening; if you sleep little, your digestion will take place faster and you will eat more.

The only problem, then, is to indicate to those who wish to fill out their curves what foods they must always choose for their nourishment; and this task need not be a difficult one if the various principles which we have already established are followed.

In sum, it is necessary to introduce into the stomach foods which will occupy it without tiring it, and to the assimilative powers foods they can best turn into fat.

Let us try to outline the day's fare of a sylph, whether male or female, who has been seized by the desire to materialize into solid flesh.

Basic plan. Eat plenty of bread, baked fresh each day, and take care not to discard the soft inside of the loaf.

Before eight o'clock in the morning, and in bed if that seems best, drink a bowl of soup thickened with bread or noodles, but not too much of it, so that it may be eliminated quickly; or, if you wish, take a cup of good chocolate.

At eleven, lunch on fresh eggs scrambled or fried in butter, little meat pies, chops, and whatever you wish; the main thing is that you have eggs. A cup of coffee will do no harm.

The dinner hour depends on how well your luncheon has been assimilated: we have often said that when the ingestion of one meal follows too quickly upon the digestion of another, it is, in legal terms, a form of malpractice.

After luncheon you must take a little exercise: the gentlemen, only if their professions allow it, for attention to business comes first; the ladies will go to the Bois de Boulogne, the Tuileries, their dressmakers, the shops, and finally to their friends' houses, to chat of what they have seen. We hold that such conversation is highly beneficial, because of the great pleasure which accompanies it.

At dinner take soup, meat, and fish, as much as you wish; but add to them dishes made with rice or macaroni, frosted pastries, sweet custards, creamy puddings, etc.

For dessert eat Savoy biscuits, babas, and other concoctions which are made of flour, eggs, and sugar.

This diet, although it seems very rigid, is really capable of great variety; it has place in it for the whole animal kingdom, and you must take especial care to change the use and preparation and seasoning of the different starchy foods which you will be served and which you will enliven in every possible way, so that you may avoid being surfeited by them, an event which would prove an invincible obstacle to any improvement in your appearance.

You should drink beer by preference, or wines from Bordeaux or the French Midi.

Avoid all acids except in salads, which refresh the digestion. Sweeten whatever fruits need it; avoid taking baths which are too cold; try to breathe from time to time the pure air of the open countryside; eat plenty of grapes in season; and do not exhaust yourselves by dancing too much at the balls.

Go to bed about eleven o'clock on ordinary days, and not later than one in the morning on special occasions.

If you follow this plan with care and determination, you will soon repair the ravages of nature; your health as well as your beauty will improve; sensual pleasure will profit from the two of them, and the Professor's ears will ring agreeably to the music of grateful confidences.

We fatten sheep, calves, oxen, poultry, carp, crayfish, and oysters; and from this fact I have deduced the following general maxim: *Everything that eats can grow fat, as long as its food is sensibly and suitably chosen.*

—from *The Physiology of Taste*, 1825,
translated from the French by M.F.K. Fisher

MARTIAL ON NOT BEING FED

Last night, Fabullus, I admit,
You gave your guests some exquisite
Perfume—but not one slice of meat.
Ironic contrast: to smell sweet
And yet be desperate to eat.
To be embalmed without being fed
Makes a man feel distinctly dead.

—from *Epigrams,* first century A.D.,
translated from the Latin by James Michie

CHAPTER SEVEN

Rants

PELLEGRINO ARTUSI AGAINST FRYING SALT COD

Pellegrino Artusi was an affluent nineteenth-century silk merchant from Florence. He collected recipes and thoughts about food from a lifetime of entertaining, but no one would publish it. Unlike Giuseppe Tomasi di Lampedusa, he was willing to publish it himself, which he did in 1891. Since then, La Scienza in Cucina e l'arte di Mangiar Bene, The Science of Cooking and the Art of Eating Well, *has had 111 printings. The American edition was titled simply* The Art of Eating Well. —M.K.

THE FRYING PAN CAN BE PUT TO MANY WONDERFUL USES in the kitchen, but I feel that *baccalà* comes to a horrid end in it: Since it must first be boiled and then dipped in batter, there isn't a sauce on earth capable of giving it a pleasant flavor. This is the reason that some people, perhaps because they don't know of any better techniques, do the following. To boil the *baccalà*, put it in a pot of cold water on the stove, and remove it as soon as the water comes to a boil. (It can be eaten as is, at this stage, if you just season it with oil and vinegar *[mayonnaise and lemon are also quite good]*.) However, we now come to the technique I mentioned above, which you are perfectly free to try, and then damn to hell both the recipe and the person who wrote it. After boiling the *baccalà,* marinate it whole in red wine for several hours. Dry it with a cloth, clean it, removing the scales and spines, and cut it into pieces. Lightly flour the pieces and dip them in an unsalted batter made with water, flour, and a drop of oil. Fry the *baccalà* in oil and dust it with sugar after it's cooled somewhat. The taste of the wine is barely perceptible if the fish is eaten hot; remember—you wanted to prepare this dish against my best advice.

—from *The Art of Eating Well,* 1891,
translated from the Italian by Kyle M. Phillips III

ELIZABETH DAVID AGAINST THE GARLIC PRESS

ACCORDING TO THE BRITISH RESTAURANT GUIDES, DINING at John Tovey's Miller Howe Hotel on Lake Windermere is an experience akin to sitting through the whole Ring cycle in one session. Perhaps, but in Tovey's latest book, *Feast of Vegetables,* there is little sign of excess or eccentricity. His recipes are basically conventional, the novelty, and it is a useful one, lying in the seasonings. Carrots may be spiced with coriander or caraway seed, or green ginger. Orange juice and rind go into grated beetroot. Marsala and toasted almond flakes give courgettes a new look and a new taste. Chicory or Belgian endives are braised in orange juice, the grated peel added. A celeriac soup is again flavoured with orange juice and the grated rind. A celeriac, courgette and potato mixture is cooked in a frying pan into a flat cake—a useful recipe for non–meat eaters. Another in the same category is for individual moulds of cooked carrots and turnips, whizzed to a purée with hazelnuts, egg yolks, cream and seasonings of onion salt (something I can myself at all times do without) and ground ginger. Whisked egg whites are folded in, the mixture is transferred to buttered ramekins lined with lettuce leaves, baked in a water bath in a hottish oven, and turned out for serving. All oven temperatures are given in

Fahrenheit, centigrade and gas marks, and timing is always carefully worked out, in many cases with three alternatives, according to whether you want your vegetables crisp—Mr Tovey steers clear of the idiotic term crispy—firm or soft.

It is when we get to the subject of garlic that I really warm to Mr Tovey. What he has to say about its preparation is alone worth the price of his book. The passage should be reproduced in large type, framed and sold in gift shops for the enlightenment of gadget-minded cooks the length and breadth of the land. In the manner of those pious thoughts which once adorned the walls of cottage parlours, proclaiming that God is Love, or Drink is the Pick-me-up which lets you Down, Mr Tovey's text is concise and to the point. Readers, heed him *please:* "I give full marks to the purveyors of garlic presses for being utterly useless objects."

I'd go further than that. I regard garlic presses as both ridiculous and pathetic, their effect being precisely the reverse of what people who buy them believe will be the case. Squeezing the juice out of garlic doesn't reduce its potency, it concentrates it and intensifies the smell. I have often wondered how it is that people who have once used one of these diabolical instruments don't notice this and forthwith throw the thing into the dustbin. Perhaps they do but won't admit it.

Now here's John Tovey again. The consistency you're looking for when adding garlic to a dish is "mushy and paste-like." Agreed. It is quickly achieved by crushing a peeled clove lightly with the back edge of a really heavy knife blade. Press a scrap of salt into the squashed garlic. That's all. Quicker, surely than getting the garlic press out of the drawer, let alone using it and cleaning it. As a one-time kitchen-shop owner who in the past has frequently, and usually vainly, attempted to dissuade a customer from buying a garlic press, I am of course aware that advice not to buy a gadget which someone has resolved to waste their money on is usually resented as bossy, ignorant, and interfering. At least now I am not alone.

Now a word of dissent. If there's one thing about expensive restaurant cooking which to my mind spoils vegetable soups, it's the often unnecessary and undesirable use of chicken or meat-based stock as a foundation. John Tovey uses just one basic chicken or turkey and vegetable stock for every one of his soups, from asparagus, courgette, fennel, Jerusalem artichoke, to parsnip, sweet corn, tomato, turnip. I suppose that passes in a hotel restaurant where you're feeding different people every day, but in household cooking such a practice soon results in deathly monotony.

That's one, just one, of the reasons stock cubes are so awful. They give the same underlying false flavour to every soup. It can't be sufficiently emphasised that many vegetable soups are best without any stock at all. It's not a question of lazy cooking. Donkeys years ago I learned from Boulestin not to diminish and distort the indefinably strange and alluring flavour of Jerusalem artichoke purée with stock. A year or two ago, when Raymond Blanc was still at the Quat' Saisons in Oxford, I had there a creamy pumpkin soup which I'd be happy to eat every other day. He told me he used a very light vegetable stock as a base for his delectable creation. The information seems worth passing on.

—from *Tatler,* February 1986

ALEXIS SOYER IN DEFENSE OF THE FRYING PAN

Alexis Soyer, born in the cheeseworthy village of Meaux-en-Brie, France, was an original man. He not only became London's most celebrated chef, especially from 1837 to 1850 when he was head chef at the Reform Club, but he was also an inventor and social activist. He believed that an interest in food should be more than the development and preparation of great dishes. It should be an interest in taking on the world's nutritional problems and in ending hunger. And he did more than write about these ideas. When he heard of the Irish famine he went to Dublin with a portable kitchen he had invented. Though a cook for the wealthy, his book Soyer's Shilling Cookery for the People *was one of many projects to reach poor and middle-class people.* —M.K.

THIS USEFUL UTENSIL, WHICH IS SO MUCH IN VOGUE IN ALL parts of the world, and even for other purposes besides cookery—for I have before me now a letter, written, at the Ovens' diggings, on the back of a frying-pan, for want of a table; but in your letter you suggest

Unidentified photographer, *Pancake Race, Shrove Tuesday*, c. 1950

the necessity of paying particular attention to it, as it is the utensil most in vogue in a bachelor's residence. I cannot but admire your constant devotion to the bachelors: you are always in fear that this unsociable class of individuals should be uncomfortable. For my part, I do not pity them, and would not give myself the slightest trouble to comfort them, especially after they have passed the first thirty springs of their life. Let them get married, and enjoy the troubles, pleasures, and comforts of matrimony, and have a wife to manage their home, and attend to more manly pursuits than cooking their supper when they get

home at night, because the old housekeeper has gone to bed; or light-
ing the fire when they get up in the morning, because the old dame
has a slight touch of lumbago and should he require something substantial for his breakfast, and want that utensil of all work, the frying-
pan, finds it all dirt and fishy, not having been cleaned since he last
dined at home.

No, my dear Eloise, I assure you I do not feel at all inclined to add
to their comforts, though you may do what you like with the following
receipts, which are equally as applicable to them, as to the humble
abode of the married fraternity.

You will also find, in these receipts, that the usual complaint of
food being greasy by frying, is totally remedied, by sautéing the meat
in a small quantity of fat, butter, or oil, which has attained a proper
degree of heat, instead of placing it in cold fat and letting it soak while
melting.

I will, in as few words as possible, having my frying-pan in one
hand and a rough cloth in the other, with which to wipe it (considering that cleanliness is the first lesson in cookery), initiate you in
the art of producing an innumerable number of dishes, which can be
made with it, quickly, economically, relishing, and wholesome. But I
must first tell you, that the word fry, in the English language, is a
mistake; according to the mode in which all objects are cooked
which are called fried, it would answer to the French word *sauté,* or
the old English term *frizzle;* but to fry any object, it should be immersed in very hot fat, oil, or butter, as I have carefully detailed to
you in our "Modern Housewife." To frizzle, sauté, or, as I will now
designate it, semi-fry, is to place into the pan any oleaginous substance, so that, when melted, it shall cover the bottom of the pan by
about two lines; and, when hot, the article to be cooked shall be
placed therein. To do it to perfection requires a little attention, so
that the pan shall never get too hot. It should be perfectly clean—a
great deal depends on this.

I prefer the pan, for many objects, over the gridiron; that is, if the
pan is properly used. As regards *economy,* it is preferable, securing all
the fat and gravy, which is often lost when the gridiron is used.

All the following receipts can be done with this simple *batterie de
cuisine,* equally as well in the cottage as in the palace, or in the bachelor's chamber as in the rooms of the poor.

1st Lesson. To Semi-fry Steak.—Having procured a steak about three quarters of an inch thick, and weighing about one pound, and two ounces of fat, place the pan on the fire, with one ounce of butter or fat; let it remain until the fat is melted, and rather hot; take hold of the steak at one end by a fork, and dip it in the pan, so that one side is covered with fat; then turn the other side in it, and let it remain for two or three minutes, according to the heat of the fire; then turn it: it will take about ten or twelve minutes, and require to be turned on each side three times, taking care that the pan is not too hot, or it will burn the gravy, and perhaps the meat, and thus lose all the nutriment; in fact, the pan should never be left, but carefully watched; on this depends the advantages of this style and mode of cookery. If the object is not turned often, it will be noticed that the gravy will come out on the upper surface of the meat, which, when turning over, will go into the pan and be lost, instead of remaining in the meat. Season with a teaspoonful of salt and a quarter of pepper; then feel with the finger that it is done, remove it with a fork, inserted in the fat, and serve very hot.

So much for the first lesson, the details of which must be learnt as it will then simplify every other receipt.

2nd Lesson.—Remember that the thickness is never to exceed one inch, nor be less than half an inch, and to be as near as possible the same thickness all over. A good housewife will object to one cut in any other way; but if it cannot be avoided, press it out with the blade of the knife, to give it the proper thickness. When done, wipe the pan clean, and place it on a hook against the wall, with the inside of the pan nearest the wall, to prevent the dust getting in.

Now, dear Eloise, you will perhaps say that the foregoing lessons are too long for so simple a thing as a steak, as everybody think themselves capable of cooking it without tuition, but having now given these directions, I hope those who fancy they can cook without learning will know better for the future, and pay a little attention to so important a subject.

The above lesson may be varied by adding to the pan, with the seasoning, a few chopped onions, or eschalots, parsley, mushrooms, pickles, semi-fried at the same time or after, and poured over the steak; or when the steak is dished up, a little butter, or chopped parsley and butter, or two spoonfuls of either Relish, Harvey's, or any other good sauce that may be handy. Pour the fat of the steak into a basin for future use. Some fried potatoes may be served with it, or the following additions made: after the steak is done, slice a quarter of a pound of onions to each pound of steak, and a little more fat; fry quickly, and when brown place round the steak; pour the gravy over.

Some mushrooms, if small, whole, if large, sliced, put in the pan and fried, are excellent.

Two tablespoonfuls of mixed pickle, put into the pan after the steak is removed, fried a little, then add two tablespoonfuls of the liquor and two of water; when on the point of boiling pour over the steak. The same may be done with pickled walnuts and gherkins, or two ounces of tavern-keepers' butter rubbed over, or half a pint of oyster sauce, or mussel sauce, or horseradish sauce; or a little flour dredged over the steak, and a little water added in the pan, when the steak is done, and a little colouring or ketchup, and then poured over the steak.

—from *Soyer's Shilling Cookery for the People,* 1860

GRIMOD DE LA REYNIÈRE
AGAINST PEACOCKS

OF ALL THE TWO-FOOTED CREATURES THAT LIVE IN THIS lowly world, the peacock is, without exception, the stupidest and the most vain. No technique of killing or tiring out renders it usable. It is good neither boiled nor roasted and it is so denounced in Paris that it cannot be put on a table in good company. The peacock is to cooking what is to literature a hopelessly ignorant journalist who lacks tact, taste, manners, and salt.

—from *Almanach des Gourmands,* 1804,
translated from the French by Mark Kurlansky

LUDWIG BEMELMANS AGAINST PARIS WAITERS

MY FIRST VISIT TO PARIS DEPRESSED ME. I HATED IT. I WAS then a bus boy in a New York hotel and my mortal enemies were waiters, waiter captains and headwaiters. I worked my way over on the old *S.S. Rotterdam* and dutifully made my way to Paris. It seemed filled with battalions of my enemies. I left after two days and swore never to return. (I even circled around it to get back to New York.) I fled to my native Tyrol, got into buckskin shorts and a green hat with the shaving brush. A photograph taken of me at that time is referred to by my daughter Barbara as the "Bing Crosby picture of Pappy." The buckskin pants have got too tight for me, the mood has changed. I have developed a tolerance for hotel personnel, and now my favorite city is Paris.

—from *La Bonne Table,* 1964

GEORGE ORWELL ON PARIS COOKS AND WAITERS

UNDOUBTEDLY THE MOST WORKMANLIKE CLASS, AND THE least servile, are the cooks. They do not earn quite so much as waiters, but their prestige is higher and their employment steadier. The cook does not look upon himself as a servant, but as a skilled workman; he is generally called *"un ouvrier,"* which a waiter never is. He knows his power—knows that he alone makes or mars a restaurant, and that if he is five minutes late everything is out of gear. He despises the whole noncooking staff, and makes it a point of honour to insult everyone below the head waiter. And he takes a genuine artistic pride in his work, which demands very great skill. It is not the cooking that is so difficult, but the doing everything to time. Between breakfast and luncheon the head cook at the Hôtel X. would receive orders for several hundred dishes, all to be served at different times; he cooked few of them himself, but he gave instructions about all of them and inspected them before they were sent up. His memory was wonderful. The vouchers were pinned on a board, but the head cook seldom looked at them; everything was stored in his mind, and exactly to the minute, as each dish fell due, he would call out, *"Faites marcher une côtelette de veau"* (or whatever it was) unfailingly. He

Sylvia Plachy, *Cappuccino*, 1987

was an insufferable bully, but he was also an artist. It is for their punctuality, and not for any superiority in technique, that men cooks are preferred to women.

The waiter's outlook is quite different. He too is proud in a way of his skill, but his skill is chiefly in being servile. His work gives him the mentality, not of a workman, but of a snob. He lives perpetually in sight of rich people, stands at their tables, listens to their conversation, sucks up to them with smiles and discreet little jokes. He has the pleasure of spending money by proxy. Moreover, there is always the chance that he may become rich himself, for, though most waiters die poor, they have long runs of luck occasionally. At some cafés on the Grand Boulevard there is so much money to be made that the waiters actually pay the *patron* for their employment. The result is that between constantly seeing money, and hoping to get it, the waiter comes to identify himself to some extent with his employers. He will take pains to serve a meal in style, because he feels that he is participating in the meal himself.

I remember Valenti telling me of some banquet at Nice at which he had once served, and of how it cost two hundred thousand francs and was talked of for months afterwards. "It was splendid, *mon p'tit, mais magnifique!* Jesus Christ! The champagne, the silver, the orchids— I have never seen anything like them, and I have seen some things. Ah, it was glorious!"

"But," I said, "you were only there to wait?"

"Oh, of course. But still, it was splendid."

The moral is, never be sorry for a waiter. Sometimes when you sit in a restaurant, still stuffing yourself half an hour after closing time, you feel that the tired waiter at your side must surely be despising you. But he is not. He is not thinking as he looks at you, "What an overfed lout"; he is thinking, "One day, when I have saved enough money, I shall be able to imitate that man." He is ministering to a kind of pleasure he thoroughly understands and admires. And that is why waiters are seldom Socialists, have no effective trade union, and will work twelve hours a day—they work fifteen hours, seven days a week, in many cafés. They are snobs, and they find the servile nature of their work rather congenial.

—from *Down and Out in Paris and London,* 1933

A. J. Liebling Against Food That Does Not Know Its Own Mind

I like tastes that know their own minds. The reason that people who detest fish often tolerate sole is that sole doesn't taste very much like fish, and even this degree of resemblance disappears when it is submerged in the kind of sauce that patrons of Piedmontese restaurants in London and New York think characteristically French. People with the same apathy toward decided flavor relish "South African lobster" tails—frozen as long as the Siberian mammoth—because they don't taste lobstery. ("South African lobsters" are a kind of sea crayfish, or *langouste,* but that would be nothing against them if they were fresh.) They prefer processed cheese because it isn't cheesy, and synthetic vanilla extract because it isn't vanillary. They have made a triumph of the Delicious apple because it doesn't taste like an apple, and of the Golden Delicious because it doesn't taste like anything. In a related field, "dry" (non-beery) beer and "light" (non-Scotchlike) Scotch are more of the same. The standard of perfection for vodka (no color, no taste, no smell) was expounded to me long ago by the then Estonian consul-general in New York, and it accounts perfectly for the drink's rising popularity with those who like their alcohol in conjunction with the reassuring tastes of infancy—tomato juice, orange juice, chicken broth. It is the ideal intoxicant for the drinker who wants no reminder of how hurt Mother would be if she knew what he was doing.

—from *Between Meals,* 1959

KARL FRIEDRICH VON RUMOHR ON EMOTIONS TO BE AVOIDED WHILE EATING

THERE ARE SOME EMOTIONS WHICH OCCASION AN EXCESsive surge of bile; others excite the nervous system and cause harmful contractions of the digestive system; some states of mind actually impair the function of these organs.

The following emotions will have the effects mentioned:

Firstly: Indignation. In this case the provocation occurs when an unexpected occurrence gives offence to our own person, to our friends or even to our opinions. Anyone with proper feelings will not inflict a personal insult on someone else without good reason but it is particularly important that intentional insults be totally avoided during mealtimes. Inexperienced people who are not accustomed to social intercourse are, however, very likely to fall into the trap of unintentionally insulting others. Any intelligent person who notices them should therefore not take them too seriously. He should control himself, so that he does not himself become the victim of pointless indignation. On the other hand, it is easy to offend people quite unintentionally if they are not very bright and do not have the capacity to interpret correctly every nuance of an expression. When speaking to stupid people, intelligent guests will therefore measure their words much more precisely, taking special care to avoid irony, which is usually completely lost on the simple-minded. If everyone at the table is stupid, it is most fortunate if they are all of a phlegmatic temperament. If the reverse is true, it will be useful to play loud music during the meal, a practice which I reject as harmful and disruptive in any other circumstances.

We tend to be much more ambivalent about insults offered to friends than about those which affect ourselves. It is, however, impossible to suggest any firm rule here because the social nuances of friendship are so very varied. Suffice it to say that we should take particular care to protect both very new friends and our long-established, well-tried friends. This is because those friends who are neither brand new, nor semi-retired, tend to be more ambivalent towards us.

Insulting a man's opinions is a most delicate matter which should be avoided if at all possible. For people have the highest opinion of their own opinions; they treasure them like children; in fact, the more they feel unable to formulate different or new opinions, the more they will value the existing ones.

There are two distinct types of opinion. One type will gradually become firmly embedded in the soul during a man's lifetime while the second type will strike the soul like a flash of lightning. The first type should never ever be approached too closely but the second type can always be assailed through jokes and other intellectual artillery, so that they explode and rumble around as they did originally.

Secondly: Anger. Anger is aroused by provocative speech which imperceptibly increases a man's indignation until it becomes a lasting mood. Therefore anger is no more than a state of prolonged indignation and is induced by the same factors. If one refrains from arousing indignation, anger will also be avoided. Once a man's indignation has been aroused, however, there is still time to divert his anger. As we may occasionally prevent a conflagration by tearing down a building, a state of indignation can likewise be soothed by calm and indulgence, together with appropriate apologies. The threat of approaching anger will then be quelled.

Thirdly: Annoyance. This is a state of suppressed anger which is again induced by the same factors as the above. The difference here is that the angry man is unable to express his feelings, either because he is overexcited or because he is nervous and afraid. As the vicious hyena is the most terrible of the hunting animals, so this particular mood will be the most detrimental to a meal.

The following states of mind will cause contractions of the stomach:

Firstly: Embarrassment. This normally arises from conversations in which no-one succeeds in expressing his opinion properly. The people most prone to this harmful state of mind are married couples and friends who are harbouring some sort of mistrust, grudge or resentment against each other but are not yet ready to give vent to their feelings. It is best in such cases if the parties concerned have a good, frank discussion some time before the meal and, if they find themselves unable to iron out the misunderstandings, they should not eat together. Embarrassment may also arise where the people around a table are not equally endowed from an intellectual point of view, or where their standards of education and cultivation are too disparate, so that no one person is willing to drop his guard before his fellows. During a meal therefore, no-one should boast and press his superior knowledge, nor should he hold forth in languages which are not adequately understood by the other guests. I should even like to advise people against vague, half-baked attempts at making their fellows aware of any class differences because this can cause a certain degree of embarrassment where their intellectual capacity is otherwise equal. Embarrassment will reach its most dangerous extreme where people get involved in conversations in which they find themselves unable either to agree wholeheartedly or to openly disagree. In such circumstances it is useful to call upon people such as diplomats who are accustomed to not speaking their minds too openly in their tinpot political discussions. In this particular case, it will be a great advantage if such a person is well schooled in the art of charming others and is graced with a lively and sociable sense of humour. He will then find it quite easy to engage others in innocent, amusing conversation which will not dry up.

Secondly: Humiliation. A table-fellow will feel humiliated if attention is drawn to any of his physical or spiritual defects or weaknesses, infirmities or even vices, which are not suitable for mention in polite company. We all encounter some unfortunate incidents during our lives and allusions to these can be most unpleasant. We tend to feel much more ashamed about specific incidents in our lives simply because we feel that others then consider us capable of, or likely to, cause such incidents. People who have an exalted opinion of themselves, or who at least consider themselves superior to others should never be made to feel their vacuousness and negativity during the course of a meal. If action becomes unavoidable, corrective sermons should be preached during the hours of the morning. Unless the offenders are totally inured, they will necessarily feel very ashamed. People who are very foolish will also feel ashamed if they are made aware of a superiority of rank or wealth.

It is merciful to spare people other forms of humiliation and, when at the table, it is wise to harden oneself against all types of shame.

Thirdly: Uneasiness. This arises when conversation is fickle and irrelevant; when everyone tries to speak at once; when no-one has any accurate knowledge of the topic of conversation and, finally, when illogical people try to debate a subject, even if they do have some knowledge of it.

The threat of uneasiness can easily be avoided during a meal if people try to control themselves and restrain their own vanity and egotism.

Fourthly: Stress. This is caused when people try to express concepts which others find irksome and difficult to understand. Conversations touching upon metaphysics and mathematics should be banned forever from our tables. Admittedly, the Greeks had quite different ideas on this subject but we poor Germans even find it difficult to express ourselves clearly and succinctly on matters of domestic and public life.

The following states of mind may impair the function of the digestive organs:

Firstly: Sleepiness. This dangerous mood may be caused by a

person's own thoughtlessness but is more likely to arise when one particular guest monopolises the conversation, rolling out meaningless thoughts in a wearisome tone.

Secondly: Stupefaction. This is the result of excessive noise or meaningless, confused talk, violent laughter and other exaggerated behaviour. Playing music during meals tends to stupefy people and is therefore reprehensible. Many years ago, Shakespeare accused the Germans of being too noisy at the table. Nowadays this reproach applies only to the public rooms in German inns or to the civic banquets held in some areas, rather than to the German nation as a whole.

—from *The Essence of Cookery,* 1822,
translated from the German by Barbara Yeomans

MARTIAL AGAINST POETRY AT THE TABLE

Whether or not Apollo fled from the table
Thyestes ate his sons at, I'm unable
To say; what I *can* vouch for is our wish
To escape your dinner parties. Though each dish
Is lavish and superb, the pleasure's nil
Since you recite your poems. To hell with brill,
Mushrooms and two-pound turbots! I don't need
Oysters: give me a host who doesn't read.

—from *Epigrams,* first century A.D.,
translated from the Latin by James Michie

CHAPTER EIGHT

On Bread Alone

GALEN ON REFINED BREAD

THOSE WHO HAVE DEVOTED THOUGHT TO THE PREPARATION of refined bread have discovered a food with little nourishment, but it does avoid, as far as is possible, the harm that comes from blockages. This bread is the least thick and viscous, since it is more airy than earthy. Its lightness is observed from its weight and from it not sinking in water, but rather bobbing on the surface like a cork.

Although the people who live in the countryside around me cook large quantities of wheat flour with milk, it should be understood that this food causes blockages. All such foods that contain good juices and are nourishing, harm those who use them constantly, by creating blockages in the liver and generating stones in the kidneys. For when the raw juice acquires viscosity—whenever the passages through the kidneys are in some people by nature rather narrow— whatever is very thick and viscous is ready to generate the sort of scale that forms on pots in which water is heated, and is deposited around stones in many of the waters that are naturally hot. The

Robert Doisneau, *Picasso and the Loaves,* 1952 (Robert Doisneau/Rapho)

temperament of the kidneys is a contributory factor, especially when its heat is fiery and sharp.

In this category lies the scale that forms in diseased joints. For everything superfluous always flows into the weakest areas and causes whatever condition is appropriate to the nature of the individual. There will shortly be a discussion on its complete use in the section about milk, just as there will be one on fattening foods, since there are some other foods that contain the same power.

—from *On the Powers of Foods,* A.D.180,
translated from the Latin by Mark Grant

PLATINA ON BREAD

In 1421, Platina was born to a poor family in Piadena, a village near Cremona. His original name was Bartolomeo Sacchi, but he was known by many other names. He called himself Platina, though it is not certain why. He served as a soldier of fortune in the wars between great Italian Renaissance princes. In his thirties, he turned to writing and moved to Florence, the heart of the southern Renaissance at its height. De honesta voluptate et Valetudine, On Right Pleasure and Good Health, *was written about 1465. Some 40 percent of the recipes were lifted directly from the leading Renaissance chef, Martino, and among the other involuntary contributors is Pliny. But Platina admitted these debts openly. He was in particular an admirer of Martino and his only goal was a lively compendium on food.* —M.K.

AMONG THE FRUITS OF EARTH DISCOVERED FOR MAN'S USE, grain is the most useful. According to Celsus, its kinds are considered spelt, rice, pearl barley, starch, wheat, winter wheat, and the kind of spelt which the ancients called *adoreum,* from which we get the word "adore," so called because offerings of cakes made from *adoreum* were proferred to the gods. Nothing is more productive and pleasant or more nourishing than wheat, which nourishes much more if it is grown in the hills and not on the plain.

Barley is considered the noblest grain of all because it wants to be sown in dry, loose earth, because it matures quickly, and because of the slenderness of its stalk, it is cut before all other grains. Polenta and a sweetened broth are more advantageously made from it than from bread for those who are ill. I do not believe that the African winter wheat whose bread the ancients praised was in any way like that which our own age eats, because there is no kind of bread more unpalatable than this, and because it represses the appetite to no purpose.

Anyone, therefore, who does baking should use flour *[farina]* which is well-ground from wheat, although *farina* is so-called from *far,* ground grain. From this, he should separate the bran and the inferior flour with a very fine flour sieve, then put the flour, with warm water and some salt, on a baker's table closed in at the sides, as the people at Ferrara in Italy are accustomed to do. If you live in damp places and a bit of leaven is used, [the baker], with help from his associates, kneads to that consistency at which bread can be made fairly easily. Let the baker be careful not to put in too much or too little leaven, for, from the former, bread can acquire a sour taste, and, from the latter, it can become too heavy to digest and too unhealthy, since it binds the bowels. Bread should be well-baked in an oven and not used the same day, nor is it especially nourishing when made from very fresh wheat and if it is digested slowly.

—from *On Right Pleasure and Good Health,* c. 1465, translated from the Latin by Mary Ella Milham

MARJORIE KINNAN RAWLINGS ON HOT BISCUITS AND DUTCH OVEN ROLLS

Marjorie Kinnan Rawlings was born in Washington, D.C. At the age of thirty-two she moved to Cross Creek, Florida, and began writing about rural life there. Her best-known novel is The Yearling. Cross Creek, *about her adopted home, is rich in food lore and revealed the already established novelist to be one of the great American food writers. It was followed by a cookbook,* Cross Creek Cookery. —M.K.

THE HOT BISCUIT RUNS A POOR SECOND TO CORNBREAD, but is considered of higher social caste. We abrogate and deprecate cornbread when we have guests, but we should consider ourselves deficient in hospitality if we served a company meal without hot biscuits. We cannot conceive of a guest's not relishing them, and a tale is told of a visitor to the South who never got to taste a hot biscuit, solely from his hostess' zeal in trying to provide them hot. It seems that the visitor was a great conversationalist, and as the hot biscuits were passed him by the maid, he would take one, butter it, and delve into talk. He would pause, reach for his biscuit, and the hostess would say, "Oh, but that one is cold. You must have a hot one." She would ring for fresh biscuits, the guest would take one and butter it, make conversation, and again, his biscuit would be snatched from him as he was about to eat it. The story goes that he left the South without ever having tasted a hot southern biscuit. It sounds like one of Irvin Cobb's yarns, but it is more than plausible. We do not have here the beaten biscuit of Kentucky, but we make our biscuits much shorter than northern biscuits, and while I sometimes think longingly of my mother's and grandmother's biscuits, light, flaky, falling apart in layers, I bite into a Florida biscuit, crisp as Scotch shortbread, and no longer recall my ancestry. The sorriest Negress, who can turn out nothing else fit to eat, can make hot biscuits that would have melted the hard heart of Sherman.

We have a wonderful recipe in these parts for ice box rolls, whose yeast-rising dough may be prepared in advance, kept in the icebox, and brought out to be raised and baked when needed. It is perhaps exceptional or local only in that we bake it by preference in a Dutch oven with live coals for heat. Cast iron is so superior for cooking utensils to our modern aluminum that I not only cannot grieve for the pioneer hardship of cooking in iron over the hearth, but shall retire if necessary to the back yard with my two Dutch ovens, turning over all my aluminum cookers for airplanes with a secret delight. The Parker House in its hey-day could not have made rolls as good as those we make on camps in the Dutch oven. I make the rolls a trifle larger than is usual and tuck them in tightly in their buttered iron nest. I put on the heavy cover and set the oven with its three short legs either within faint warming distance of the camp fire, or out in the sun. The heat for baking, when they have risen and are ready in an hour or so, must be handled as carefully as a munitions plant handles its powder. Too little heat in baking means pale wan doughy rolls, and too much means rolls of charcoal. Only experience teaches the number and depth of hot glowing oak coals both under the oven and on the lid. When properly done, the rolls are light as feathers, done to a great flakiness, hazel-nut brown, and of a flavor achieved under no other circumstances.

My most successful Dutch oven rolls were prepared in the middle of the St. John's River. The doctor and his wife Dessie and I were on a fishing trip on a warm winter day down the Ocklawaha River to its junction with the St. John's, through little Lake George, to the mouth of Salt Springs Run, where we planned to cook supper and camp for the night. I had brought along my large Dutch oven and a big bowl of dough for my rolls. We fished late into the afternoon and it was plain that by the time we reached our camping place, it would be too late to set my dough to rise. There would be time enough for the baking, for the fish must be cleaned and fried. We estimated the time to the landing, and an hour and a quarter beforehand, I brought out my bowl of dough, my extra flour, my butter and my Dutch oven from under a seat of the rowboat, and while spray from the wind-swept river dashed into my face, I mixed the dough in the bowl in my lap, shaped my rolls and placed them tenderly in the Dutch oven. I put the oven far forward where the late afternoon sun would rest on the lid, and by the time we reached Salt Springs Run and the camp fire was built, the rolls had risen and were ready for the baking. They had never been so delicious. Supper was superb, the fresh-caught bass white and sweet and firm, the coffee strong and good as it can only be in the open.

We were on a little promontory at the mouth of the run, with great live oaks around us, and palms tall against the aquamarine evening sky. A full moon rose in front of us and we felt ourselves favored of all mortals. After so much delight, we might have expected to pay the piper. The night was hideous. Because the time was winter, we had assumed there would be no mosquitoes. But because the winter was warm, they had hatched, and as we lay on blankets on the sand, they descended in swarms. We built up the camp fire to make smoke to drive them away and the smoke was more annoying than the mosquitoes. Hoot owls settled in the oaks over our heads and cried jeeringly all night. Wood roaches came in and awakened us from our spasms of slumber with their sharp nibbling on our ears. When we arose at dawn, the doctor said, "You know, the only thing that kept me going through the night was remembering those rolls."

—from *Cross Creek*, 1942

Clementine Paddleford on the Best Buns of 1949

In 1949, This Week Magazine, *a Sunday magazine included in numerous newspapers across the country, published a booklet of the twenty best recipes in American regional cooking. The recipes were selected and tested by the food editor, Clementine Paddleford. The selection included Gloucester codfish balls, chicken hash with flannel cakes, lemon pie, Iowa ice cream, and Philadelphia cinnamon buns.*

—M.K.

Sticky cinnamon buns belong to Philadelphia as do Independence Hall and the Twelfth Street Market. This is a bun of true cinnamon flavor, of a stickiness incarnate.

A pilgrimage to Philadelphia in search of the bun traditional led down Race Street to the kitchen of Harriet E. Worrell. A native Philadelphian, although born in Ogden—a town named for her grandfather—scarcely a stone's throw from Rittenhouse Square. The Ogdens and the Worrells, she told us, are cinnamon-bun families from way back—meaning they like sticky buns daily, baked at least three times a week.

Philadelphia Cinnamon Buns

1¼ cups milk	2 eggs
¼ cup lukewarm water	¼ cup butter or margarine
1 package dry granular yeast	½ cup brown sugar
5 cups sifted all-purpose flour	2 teaspoons cinnamon
1½ teaspoons salt	½ cup black walnut meats
1 tablespoon sugar	½ cup raisins or currants
½ cup shortening	1 cup dark or light corn syrup
¾ cup sugar	

Scald milk, cool to lukewarm. Dissolve the yeast in water for 10 minutes and combine with milk. Make a sponge by adding two cups of flour, salt and one tablespoon sugar, beating until smooth. Set aside in a warm place. Beat shortening until light, whip in three-fourths cup sugar and add eggs one at a time, beating each in thoroughly. When the sponge is bubbly, gradually beat in shortening mixture, then knead in remaining three cups of flour. Cover and let rise in a warm place until double in bulk.

Roll a portion of the dough to one-fourth-inch thickness. Spread with softened butter or margarine, sprinkle with a mixture of brown sugar and cinnamon. Scatter on the nuts and raisins or currants and dribble with a part of the syrup. Roll as a jelly roll and cut in one-and-one-half-inch lengths. Stand buns in two deep nine-inch pans that have been well buttered and filled with syrup to a depth of one-fourth inch. Cover and let rise until double in bulk. Bake in a moderate oven (350°F.) until brown, about 45 minutes. Turn out of pans immediately. Yield: 2 dozen buns.

—from *Best Recipes of 1949*

ELIZABETH DAVID ON TOAST

'No bread. Then bring me some toast!'

—*Punch*, 1852

' "Toast" said Berry, taking the two last pieces that stood in the rack. "I'm glad to get back to toast. And a loaf of brown bread that isn't like potter's clay." '

—Dornford Yates, *Adèle & Co.*, Ward, Lock, 1931

IT ISN'T ONLY FICTIONAL HEROES TO WHOM TOAST MEANS home and comfort. It is related of the Duke of Wellington—I believe by Lord Ellesmere—that when he landed at Dover in 1814, after six years' absence from England, the first order he gave at the Ship Inn was for an unlimited supply of buttered toast.

In *The Origin of Food Habits* (1944), H. D. Renner makes an attempt to explain the English addiction to toast. 'The flavour of bread,' he says, 'can be revived to some extent by re-warming and even new flavours are created in toasting.' This is very true, but leaves the most important part unsaid. It is surely the *smell* of toast that makes it so enticing, an enticement which the actuality rarely lives up to. In this it is like freshly roasted coffee, like sizzling bacon—all those early morning smells of an intensity and deliciousness which create far more than those new flavours, since they create hunger and appetite where none existed. Small wonder that the promise is never quite fulfilled. 'Village life,' Renner continues, 'makes stale bread so common that toasting has become a national habit restricted to the British Isles and those countries which have been colonized by Britain.' Surely England was not the only country where villages were isolated and bread went dry and stale? I wonder if our open fires and coal ranges were not more responsible than the high incidence of stale bread for the popularity of toast in all classes of English household. For toasting bread in front of the fire and the bars of the coal-burning range there were dozens of different devices—museums of domestic life are crammed with them, Victorian cookery books show any number of designs—as many as there are varieties of electric toaster in our own day; apart from toasters for bread, there were special racks for toasting muffins and crumpets, and special pans for toasting cheese. And, as recorded in the recipe for potato bread, there were, in the nineteenth century, eminent medical men writing grave advice as to the kind of bread which, when toasted, would absorb the maximum amount of butter. That buttered toast goes back a long way in English life, and was by no means confined to country places where fresh bread was a rarity is shown by the following quotation: 'All within the sound of Bow Bell,' wrote Fynes Morison in *Itinerary*, Volume 3 (1617), 'are in reproch called cochnies, and eaters of buttered tostes.'

Buttered toast is, then, or was, so peculiarly English a delicacy—and I use the term delicacy because that is what in our collective national memory it still is—that the following meticulous description of how it was made, at least in theory, reads poignantly indeed. It is from the hand of Miss Marian McNeill, author of that famous work *The Scots Kitchen*, on this occasion writing in an enchanting volume, long out of print, called *The Book of Breakfasts*, published in 1932:

'Sweet light bread only a day old makes the best toast. Cut into even slices about quarter of an inch thick. It may be toasted under the grill, but the best toast is made at a bright smokeless fire. Put the slice on a toasting-fork and keep only so near the fire that it will be heated through when both sides are well browned. Move the toast about so as to brown evenly. Covered with an earthen bowl, toast will keep warm and moist.

'If very thin, crisp toast is desired, take bread that is two days old, cut it into slices about three-eighths of an inch thick, and toast them patiently at a little distance from a clear fire till delicately browned on both sides. With a sharp knife divide each slice into two thin slices, and toast the inner sides as before. Put each slice as it is done into a toast rack.

'For hot buttered toast, toast the bread more quickly than for ordinary toast, as it should not be crisp. Trim off the crusts and spread the toast liberally with butter that has been warmed but not allowed to oil. Cut in neat pieces, pile sandwichwise, and keep hot in a covered dish over a bowl of hot water. Use the best butter.'

I have my own childhood memories of toast-making in front of the schoolroom fire. Although I fancy that more toast fell off the fork into the fire and was irretrievably blackened than ever reached our plates, I can recall the great sense of achievement when now and again a slice did come out right, evenly golden, with a delicious smell and especially, as I remember, with the right, proper texture, so difficult to describe, and so fleeting. Only when it was hot from the fire and straight off the fork did that toast have the requisite qualities. Perhaps young children are better qualified than grown-ups to appreciate these points. And perhaps that is why buttered toast is one of those foods, like sausages, and potatoes baked in their skins, and mushrooms picked from the fields, which are never as good as they were.

Nowadays my toast is usually made on one of those ridged metal plates which goes over a gas flame or an electric burner. This produces crisp toast, very different from the kind made in front of the fire, but in its way almost as good. These lightweight metal toasters are very cheap. There is no need to buy an expensive iron one. Rye bread or 100 per cent whole wheatmeal bread both make excellent toast, but for buttered toast a light white bread is best. I prefer to make this kind of toast under the grill, electric toasters being machines with which I cannot be doing. In this I must be in a very small minority, for electric toasters are one of the most popular of all wedding presents, and in May 1975 *Which?* published a report on no fewer than thirteen different electric toasters. 'Some like it well done,' declared *Which?*, 'others pale brown; some like it done slowly to give a crisp finish, others done quickly so it's still soft inside.' All of these pronouncements are no doubt correct, as indeed is the statement that 'you don't want your piece of toast to be black in the middle and white round the edges.' That is to say, I don't. But I know plenty of people who actually *like* their toast to be charred. Perhaps they prefer it charred at the edges and white in the middle, and I'm not sure how this would be achieved. Another of the report's dictums, 'however you like your toast, you want all pieces to be more or less the same,' is one I don't agree with, perhaps fortunately, for it is not easy to get all your pieces more or less the same. Unless, that is, you have a caterers' toasting machine and caterers' sliced bread which between them produce what I call restaurateurs' toast, that strange substance cut in triangles and served with the pâté, and for breakfast, in all English hotels and restaurants. This English invention has in recent years become popular in France where, oddly enough, it goes by the name of toast, as opposed to real French toast which is called *pain grillé,* and is just what it says, grilled bread. That brings me back to the toast-making device I myself use, the metal plate or grill over the gas burner. Part of the charm of the toast produced on this device is that every piece is different, and differently marked, irregularly chequered with the marks of the grill, charred here and there, flecked with brown and gold and black . . . I think that the goodness of toast made in this way does depend a good deal on the initial quality of the bread, and the way it is cut. Thin slices are useless, and I don't think that white sliced bread would be very successful—there is too much water to get rid of before the toasting process starts, and steamy bread sticks to the toaster. Thickish slices are best, preferably rather small ones which can be easily turned with grill tongs. Like most other toast, this kind is best straight from the grill. 'If allowed to stand and become sodden, dry toast becomes indigestible. From the fire to the table is the thing,' wrote the delightfully named Lizzie Heritage in *Cassell's Universal Cookery Book* (first published 1894). And if the toast is to be buttered, I suppose we must remember Marian McNeill's 'use the best butter.' What *is* the best butter? Unsalted, some would say. I'll settle for any butter that's good of its kind. The very salt butter of Wales can be perfectly delicious eaten with the right kind of toast (no marmalade for me), and here is Flora Thompson describing toast with salt butter and celery, and toast with cold boiled bacon. Toast-resistant though I am, she makes me long for that fresh hot toast and crisp celery, a wonderful combination, and how subtle:

'In winter, salt butter would be sent for and toast would be made and eaten with celery. Toast was a favourite dish for family consumption. "I've made 'em a stack o' toast as high as up to their knees," a mother would say on a winter Sunday afternoon before her hungry brood came in from church. Another dish upon which they prided themselves was thin slices of cold, boiled streaky bacon on toast, a dish so delicious that it deserves to be more widely popular.'

—from *English Bread and Yeast Cookery*, 1977

MIMI SHERATON ON BIALYS

Mimi Sheraton, a former New York Times *restaurant critic, traveled to the town of Bialystok, Poland, in search of the origin of the bialystoker kuchen, or, as it is now known in America, the bialy. So thoroughly was the Jewish community extinguished in this eastern Poland town that there was not even a trace of their famous bread, and it was suggested that it was a myth, that bialys did not come from Bialystok. But they did, and Sheraton persevered, and through the memory of Jews in communities throughout the world, she pieced together the bialy's story.*   —M.K.

As I BEGAN TO RECEIVE BIALY MEMOIRS, I WANTED TO KNOW more about how these humble onion rolls are made and how they evolved in the eighty or so years of their existence in New York and elsewhere around the United States. Danny Scheinin kindly let me hang around Kossar's and take notes. In the winter of 1998 he sold the bakery to Juda Engelmayer and Danny Cohen, two energetic, thirty-something brothers-in-law, who still follow the traditional methods for baking bialys and also uphold the custom of a baker's dozen that includes thirteen pieces.

I always love walking into Kossar's, a wide, bright store that, in an

old-fashioned way, is really a bakery with a small, makeshift sales counter. The air is veiled in flour, and the scent of yeast, onions, and baking bread warmly engulfs visitors. Silent bakers in white T-shirts work with professional assurance, rolling, kneading, shaping, smearing on onions, and taking baked bialys from the oven. Passersby on Grand Street peer through the big front windows, and shoppers idle in and out, schmoozing, making purchases, and usually, buying one extra bialy to be eaten out of hand.

Danny Scheinin explained that too often in the United States today, bialys and bagels are made in the same bakeries, both from the same bagel dough. But a true bialy requires much more yeast than do bagels, so that it will rise quickly and its rim will be gently soft. Also, bialys are made without the malt or sugar that is added to bagels to produce a golden crust, and unlike bagels, they are not boiled before being baked. (If authentic bialy bakeries sell bagels, they usually buy them from a bagel baker.)

For the most part, good bialys come from dedicated bialy bakeries, where the only other products are different shapes of bialy dough, such as bulkas—long, oval rolls topped with onions or garlic and poppy seeds—and pletzls that are ten-to-twelve-inch flat rounds, liberally sprinkled with poppy seeds and onions.

Kossar's bialy dough is made authentically with only four ingredients: high-gluten flour, salt, ice water, and bakers' yeast. Forget about sugar, eggs, or oil, all of which are recommended in various cookbooks. Kossar's recipe for a dough batch that makes seventy to eighty dozen bialys, includes 100 pounds of high-gluten flour, 7 gallons of ice water, 2 pounds of salt, and about 1 pound of yeast, depending on the weather, more yeast being necessary on colder days. Until early 2000, the mixing and shaping went as follows: These ingredients were quickly, briefly combined in a huge commercial electric mixer and allowed to rise in the mixer bowl for two to three hours, or until the dough began to come together but was still very sticky. The dough was then turned out on a lightly floured board and divided into about nine 6-pound mounds. Each was kneaded by hand, that step being impossible with older machines because the dough was so sticky.

Next, the shaping began. With an experienced eye and hand, the bakers divided the large mounds of dough into roughly thirty smaller balls, each weighing about three ounces to make bialys that are four inches in diameter. After rising for one hour, each ball was lightly rolled between the baker's floured palms and was then gently flattened onto a board. Now the mixing, kneading, and balling are done by machine, with barely noticeable differences in the final results.

Forming the identifying center indentation is still done by hand. Working at lightning speed, the bakers shape the center well by placing both thumbs on top of the center of each round of dough, with their index and middle fingers underneath. They then press and slightly stretch the dough to form the well. Invited to try my hand, I found the ball of gentle dough almost cuddly to work with, and so delicate that if I pressed my thumb against my fingers too firmly, I tore through the dough. After struggling to shape about six bialys, I gained much respect for the bakers like Whitey Aquanno, who has been at Kossar's since 1973 and who forms the wells with almost invisible motions at a dazzling rate.

This hand method of shaping is relatively new to bialy baking, as the well used to be impressed with a small rolling pin. Danny Scheinin recalls that in 1956, when he joined the bakery, his father-in-law, Morris Kossar, bought the wooden rolling pins used in Orthodox communities for making Passover matzohs. Such matzoh baking is done only from January to Passover, and since each year's rolling pins have to be new, the used ones must be discarded or sold cheaply. Bakery owners used to cut the longer pins into the two- to three-inch lengths they required, or as an alternative, they ordered small rolling pins from neighborhood carpenters. The traditional rolling pin used for bialys in Bialystok had two thin rod handles and a thicker center cylinder, so that the center of the bialy would be depressed while the rim remained high. That rolling pin closely resembled the type still used for making dim sum in China.

Saving time is one reason for the switch from rolling pin to hands. In addition, according to Danny Scheinin, the brick-lined gas ovens that replaced the old coal- and wood-fired ovens bake so rapidly that the compressed, thick dough formed by a rolling pin cannot bake thoroughly before the onions and the top crusts burn.

I agree with those who insist that the rolling pins produced a more tantalizing texture, with a firmer, densely packed, and crackly center. As skillful as a baker may be, even at Kossar's, the center wells are not always compressed enough and so rise in the oven, leaving little or, sometimes, no indentation.

Thus formed, the bialys are ready for the topping of onions (and poppy seeds when they were used). In the best of all possible worlds, the onions will be large, white, and sweet and will be chopped by hand, not ground by a meat grinder. Understandably, in commercial bakeries, grinding is more practical. To absorb the water in the onions, Kossar's grinds seven- or eight-hour-old bialys (hard but not stale) into crumbs and mixes them with the onions (one bialy to ten onions) to achieve a spreadable mixture much like wet sand. The onions should be ground no more than two days in advance of use. Freezing them to ensure a steady supply is understandable for a high-volume bakery, but some flavor and aroma will be lost. In any case, the onions should be absolutely raw, never sautéed, steamed, or salted down, despite such instructions in many cookbooks. A common practice in many bialy bakeries is to use dehydrated onions that tend to burn into acrid, black flecks unless they are first soaked in water, in which case, they generally turn unpleasantly pink and have a stale, metallic flavor. I found that all garlic used in bialy bakeries, including Kossar's, is dehydrated or freeze-dried and, therefore, tastes stale and unpleasantly acidic.

The onion mixture is quickly smeared by hand into the well and on top of each shaped, unbaked bialy. The kuchen are all then placed on big wooden peels and slid onto the revolving iron shelves of a brick-lined, 500-degree gas oven. Undoubtedly old-timers are right in their claims that bialys had a more richly burnished, smokier flavor when baked in a wood-fired oven.

Now, another choice is necessary. Obviously, the longer the bialys bake, the darker brown and crispier they will be. As someone who likes very well-done bialys with nice dark brown blistered tops and crisp toasted bottoms, I find myself increasingly frustrated by the mostly whiter and softer bialys sold today. The choice appears to be generational. Customers over fifty-five or sixty generally choose the dark rolls, while the younger customers prefer the light. Danny Cohen and Juda Engelmayer, Kossar's new owners, also prefer the light bialys and caution their bakers to stop "burning" them. They feel, probably correctly, that the lighter ones keep longer and also that the younger clientele they must attract shares their preference. Recently they must have reconsidered, because they now always seem to have a batch or two of the crisp, dark-brown beauties that I cherish.

—from *The Bialy Eaters,* 2000

CHAPTER NINE

The Mystery of Eggs

A BAGHDAD RECIPE FOR ONIONS AND EGGS

CUT UP ONIONS WELL, THEN STRAIN AWAY THEIR JUICE, then throw them in the *tajine,* and pour over them a sufficiency of fresh sesame oil, then fry them in that sesame oil. Then pour eggs upon them, after beating them well until the yolks are mixed with the whites. Put a little salt and spices with them, and do not stop observing the fire and stirring until it is pleasing.

> —from *Kitab Wasf al-At'ima al-Mu'tada*
> (The Description of Familiar Foods), 1373,
> translated from the Arabic by Charles Perry

HANNAH GLASSE
ON MAKING EGGS LARGE

Hannah Glasse (1708–1770) was the best-known and most influential English cookbook writer of the eighteenth century. Her 1747 The Art of Cookery, Made Plain and Easy; Which far exceeds any Thing of the Kind ever yet Published *was kept in print for decades, both in England and America. But the cookbook was also famous because in the more famous Boswell's* Life of Johnson, *Johnson erroneously suggests that she did not write her book. In fact, she did write it, though her subtitle seems an exaggeration, since a good third of her recipes were taken from other books.*

Still, Glasse did improve English cooking by replacing suet with butter. And although her cooking seems heavy by today's standards, she did do much to make the cooking of the period lighter. —M.K.

To Fry Eggs as round as Balls.

Having a deep Frying-pan, and three Pints of clarified Butter, heat it as hot as for Fritters, and stir it with a Stick, till it runs round like a Whirlpool; then break an Egg into the Middle, and turn it round with your Stick, till it be as hard as a poached Egg, the Whirling round of the Butter will make it as round as a Ball, then take it up with a Slice, and put it in a Dish before the Fire. They will keep hot half an Hour, and yet be soft; so you may do as many as you please. You may serve these with what you please, nothing better than stewed Spinage, and garnish with Orange.

To make an Egg as big as Twenty.

Part the Yolks from the Whites, strain them both separate through a Sieve, tye the Yolks up in a Bladder, in the Form of a Ball; boil them hard, then put this Ball into another Bladder, and the Whites round it; tye it up oval Fashion, and boil it. These are used for grand Sallads. This is very pretty for a Ragoo, boil five or six Yolks together, and lay in the Middle of the Ragoo of Eggs; and so you may make them of any Size you please.

A Grand Dish of Eggs

Break as many Eggs as the Yolks will fill a Pint Bason, the Whites by themselves, tye the Yolks by themselves in a Bladder round; boil them hard, then have a wooden Bowl that will hold a Quart, make like two Butter-dishes, but in the Shape of an Egg, with a Hole through one at

the Top. You are to observe, when you boil the
Yolks to run a Pack-thread through it, and a
quarter of a Yard hanging out. When the
Yolk is boiled hard, put it into the Bowl-
dish; but be careful to hang it so as to be
in the Middle. The String being drawn
through the Hole, then clap the two Bowls
together, and tye them tight, and with a
fine Tunnel pour in the Whites through
the Hole; then stop the Hole close,
and boil it hard, it will take an Hour.
When it is boiled enough, carefully
open it, and cut the String close. In the
mean time take twenty Eggs, beat them
well, the Yolks by themselves, and the Whites by themselves; divide
the Whites into two, and boil them in Bladders the Shape of an Egg.
When they are boiled hard, cut one in two long-ways, and one cross-
ways, and with a fine sharp Knife cut out some of the White in the
Middle, lay the great Egg in the Middle, the two long Halves on each
Side, with the hollow Part uppermost, and the two round flat between.
Take an Ounce of Truffles and Morells, cut them very small, boil them
in half a Pint of Water till they are tender, then chop a Pint of fresh
Mushrooms clean picked and washed, chopped small, put into the
Truffles and Morells; let them boil, add a little Salt, a little beaten Nutmeg, a little beaten Mace, and add a Gill of pickled Mushrooms
chopped fine. Boil fourteen of the Yolks hard in a Bladder, then chop
them and mix them with the other Ingredients; thicken it with a Lump
of Butter rolled in Flour, shaking your Sauce-pan round till hot and
thick, then fill the round with Whites, and turn them down again, and
fill the two long ones; what remains, save to put into the Sauce-pan.
Take a Pint of Cream, a quarter of a pound of Butter, the other four
Yolks beat fine, a Gill of White Wine, a Gill of pickled Mushrooms, a
little beaten Mace, a little Nutmeg, put all into the Sauce-pan, to the
other Ingredients, stir all well together one way, till it is thick and fine;
then pour it over all, and garnish with notched Lemon.

This is a grand Dish at a second Course. Or you may mix it up
with Red Wine and Butter, and it will do for a first Course.

—from *The Art of Cookery, Made Plain and Easy*, 1747

LYDIA MARIA CHILD
ON POACHED EGGS

Lydia Maria Child's The American Frugal Housewife *was published in Boston in 1829. She believed that no cookbooks existed for the middle-class American housewife. In the tradition of* Le Mésnagier de Paris, *her book was a guide for setting up the home with recipes, and it became the book of the nineteenth-century New England woman working, for the first time, in the textile mills. In what has become a New England cliché, she emphasized frugality, not wasting a scrap of anything.* —M.K.

THE BEAUTY OF A POACHED EGG IS FOR THE YOLK TO BE seen blushing through the white, which should only be just sufficiently hardened to form a transparent veil for the egg. Have some boiling water in a tea kettle; pass as much of it through a clean cloth as will half fill a stewpan; break the egg into a cup and when the water boils, remove the stewpan from the heat and gently slip the egg into it; it must stand until the white is set; then put it over a very moderate fire, and as soon as the water boils, the egg is ready; take it up with a slice, and neatly round off the ragged edges of the white; send them up on bread toasted on one side only, with or without butter.

—from *The American Frugal Housewife,* 1829

PELLEGRINO ARTUSI
ON DRINKING EGGS

AFTER MEAT, EGGS ARE THE MOST NUTRITIOUS FOOD. Maurizio Schiff, the famous physician who held a chair at the University of Florence, showed that the white is more nutritious than the yolk, which consists of fats, and that raw or barely cooked eggs are

harder to digest because the stomach has to perform two operations simultaneously: first, coagulate them, and second, absorb them. It is therefore best to avoid extremes, i.e., eat them neither raw nor overcooked.

Eggs taste best in the spring. Fresh eggs are given to young mothers to drink, and popular wisdom holds them to be good for newlyweds too.

The son of an innkeeper I once knew, a big, foolish young man who ruined his health in the pursuit of vices, went to a doctor, who told him to drink two fresh eggs every morning. He was both lucky and unfortunate that the inn had a large henhouse where he could go drink freshly laid eggs, for after a few days he got to thinking, "If two eggs are good, four are better." Then the simpleton decided, "If four are better, six are better still." Following this line of reasoning, he got to twelve to fourteen eggs per day, which brought about a gastritis that kept him in bed for I don't know how long, hatching the eggs he'd drunk.

—from *The Art of Eating Well,* 1891,
translated from the Italian by Kyle M. Phillips III

JAMES BEARD ON
SCRAMBLED EGGS

WHEN PEOPLE INVITE YOU IN FOR A QUICK MEAL, OR IF something goes wrong in the kitchen, they are apt to say, "Oh well, I'll just scramble some eggs," as if "just scrambling some eggs" couldn't be simpler. As a matter of fact, scrambling eggs is one of the more complex kitchen processes, and there are various schools of egg scrambling. There are those who believe eggs should be scrambled in a double boiler over simmering water, those who believe they should be scrambled quickly, and those who believe that it takes slow and most accurate timing to make the curds tender, delicious, and of varied sizes. Every person regards his particular fashion of scrambling an egg as a mark of his culinary skill, and so it is. My good friend Julia Child once demonstrated her theory of scrambling eggs on television. She lifted the pan from the burner and then lowered it, to adjust the heat and the scrambling process, then as the final moment arrived, she accelerated her tempo to make the eggs come to just the right point. Hers is an extremely good method, provided you have the patience and dexterity.

Scrambled eggs can be so delicious, so creamy and rich and eggy, if I may use the word, that it is too bad we don't use them more. They combine well with many things—chopped sautéed mushrooms, finely chopped ham, crisp bacon bits, little slices of sausage, freshly grated Parmesan or Gruyère cheese, chopped herbs, finely chopped peeled and seeded tomatoes—as well as being perfectly splendid on their own.

Depending upon the number of eggs to be scrambled, I like to use a small or large Teflon-coated pan. I have a cast-aluminum Teflon-lined 9-inch omelet pan with rounded sides that I use for up to 4 or 5 eggs and a 10-inch pan for larger quantities, which are much harder to make. I disagree completely with those who say you can scramble one egg well. It is an impossibility.

For scrambled eggs I think you should gauge at least 2 eggs per person. Add salt, freshly ground black pepper, and 1 or 2 dashes of Tabasco, and then beat lightly with a fork. For lighter scrambled eggs, I beat in 1 teaspoon of water for every two eggs. I don't like cream or milk added to scrambled eggs, but if I want them extraordinarily rich, I mix in softened butter, as I will describe later on.

If I am adding ham or bacon, I would use 2 slices of Canadian bacon about 3 inches in diameter and 2 pieces of ham of the same size and ¼ inch thick, precook it lightly, cut into thin shreds, and toss into the pan with a tablespoon or two of butter. Let this warm over low heat, then add, for two servings, 4 beaten eggs and, as you do, increase the heat to medium high. As soon as the coagulation starts, make pushing strokes with a rubber or wooden spatula so you get curled curds. I'm not quite as definite in my movements as Julia Child. I lift the pan off the burner from side to side with sort of a circular motion, while pushing with the spatula. As the heat in the cooking eggs increases, the curds form much faster, and there you have to remove the pan from the heat and work faster with your pushing. That's the ticklish point. You have to know the exact moment to cease applying any heat and rush your eggs from pan to plate, or they will be overcooked, hard, coarse-textured and disagreeable.

Now, if you want very rich eggs, as you push curds in the pan add little bits of softened butter, which will melt in and give you delicious, heavily buttered scrambled eggs such as you have seldom experienced. In some places, they are called "buttered eggs," and that's a very good term.

If you are adding chopped herbs or mushrooms, lace them in as you scramble the eggs so they become a part of the amalgamation of the creamy curds. Of course, there is nothing wrong with adding chopped parsley or chives or other bits and pieces after you have transferred the eggs from the pan to a plate or platter.

If you have never tried the combination, try scrambled eggs with sliced smoked fish for your next Sunday brunch or luncheon. A platter of smoked salmon, smoked eel, smoked sturgeon, or smoked whitefish, with lemon wedges, good rolls or bagels, and a huge pile of creamy eggs—that's good eating. If you like, you can scramble the eggs at the table in an electric skillet or chafing dish, guiding them to a perfect conclusion as you chat with your guests.

I have had, in my time, memorable meals of scrambled eggs with fresh truffles, scrambled eggs with caviar and other glamorous things, but to me, there are few things as magnificent as scrambled eggs, pure and simple, perfectly cooked and perfectly seasoned.

—from *On Food,* 1974

ANGELO PELLEGRINI ON CHICKEN INTESTINE OMELETTES

M.F.K. Fisher described her first meeting with Angelo Pellegrini with typical Fisher suggestiveness: "Although I have known few men of letters intimately, excluding my husband, of course, Angelo Pellegrini is the only one I have ever shared a spit-bucket with."

Among the judges at a California wine tasting, they were assigned to share a spittoon. She was crushed when this man, whom she regarded as the best food writer on the West Coast, her native and much loved region, treated her with disdain and brutal rudeness. He complained that women should not be on wine panels and that she smelled. He insisted her perfume was interfering with his palate, and she argued that she was not wearing perfume. A day later he apologized profusely, realizing that it was the hotel soap on his hands that confused his delicate taste buds. The two became lifelong friends. Fisher referred to Pellegrini as "the great god Pan of this Western world."

He was an immigrant from Italy who moved to Seattle and became a professor of English literature, writing occasionally about food and wine and often about "the good life." Known for his erudition and eloquence, he also notoriously enjoyed female companionship. Fisher said she was his friend, "with the full consent of his wife, and the tacit agreement of scores of other fellow females in every direction from Seattle." Relatives remember his pièce de résistance as the day he brought Italian sex goddess Anne Bancroft home to meet the family. —M.K.

I LEARNED FROM MY FATHER TO MAKE A RATHER DAINTY omelet with the intestines of a fryer. Of all the men I have ever known, he had the most perfect sense of the value of bread and wine. Every week end he took charge of the kitchen. On Saturday afternoon he prepared the meat, usually rabbit, less frequently fowl, for the Sunday dinner. When the choice was chicken he always dry-picked it in order to leave undisturbed the precious oils in the skin which he considered, and rightly so, the most savory part of the bird. He was never impatient or in a hurry; and when he had cleaned the chicken with that care for which he had so much talent, it was smooth and glossy as a slab of marble. He cast away nothing except the feathers, beak, crop, claws, outer skin of the feet, and the contents of the intestines and gizzard. When he had squeezed out the excrement from the intestines, he would go to the kitchen sink and, by utilizing the cascading water, turn them deftly inside out. After they had been thoroughly washed he left them overnight in a pan in slowly running water.

On Sunday morning, the woodstove was his altar and he the officiating priest. Clean-shaven, in white shirt with sleeves rolled to the elbow, he would go to the cupboard from whence he fetched his vermouth. He poured the measured drink, touched it up with *Ferro China* bitters, and gave it to his stomach, taking care to leave enough in the glass for me if I happened to be around, as of course I was. Then he would smack his lips, suck in at his mustache, and go to work on the omelet. The intestines, white as snow, were taken from the water, carefully dried, and cut into small pieces. They were then fried very slowly in a combination of butter and olive oil, with finely minced parsley, chives, thyme, a bit of lemon rind, a touch of garlic, salt, pepper, and cayenne. After a final benediction of dry muscatel, they were folded into the egg and brought to the table. A basket of crisp bread and a pot of coffee, flanked by a bottle of brandy, were added, and he then proceeded to minister to the little flock that clustered about him. I have heard many sermons, Protestant and Catholic. None has impressed me more than my father's reverent care for the food that sustains our body.

I was once discovered by some friends while in the act of cleaning the intestines of a fowl. When I told them that I was going to use them in an omelet, they were first incredulous and then mildly shocked. For their breakfast they had had, very likely, link sausage, a dubious hodge-podge encased in tougher guts than would grace my omelet. Fortunately, what people don't know, doesn't hurt them.

I do not expect my American friends to run to the poultry dealer and ask for a bag of guts. And of course they won't; for even if they could get over the horror of eating such things, they would hesitate to undertake their preparation. One can't just simply take the insides of a chicken—or of any other animal—and cast them into a frying pan as one does a cutlet. Tripe, kidneys, and sweetbreads must be prepared with special care, some skill, and with a reasonable indifference to time. And that, I suppose, must be another reason why the American housewife will not bother about them.

—from *The Unprejudiced Palate*, 1948

CHAPTER TEN

Eating Your Vegetables

CATO ON PRESERVING
GREEN OLIVES

Cato was a major Roman political figure in the second century B.C. He was known for his speaking skills and wrote numerous widely praised books, but On Farming *is the only one to survive in its entirety into modern times. It is the oldest surviving complete book of Latin prose.*

This recipe for curing olives remains the standard practice even today. There is a substance called oleuropein, unique to olives, which is extremely bitter. The olives are soaked to remove it before being fermented. —M.K.

HOW GREEN OLIVES ARE CONSERVED. BEFORE THEY TURN BLACK, they are to be broken and put into water. The water is to be changed frequently. When they have soaked sufficiently they are drained, put into vinegar, and oil is added. ½ lb. salt to 1 peck olives. Fennel and lentisk are put up separately in vinegar. When you decide to mix them in, use quickly. Pack in preserving-jars. When you wish to use, take with dry hands.

—from *On Farming,* second century B.C.,
translated from the Latin by Andrew Dalby

Pliny the Elder on Onions

ONIONS DO NOT GROW WILD. CULTIVATED ONES PROVIDE A cure for poor vision through the tears caused by their very smell. Even more effective is the application of some onion-juice to the eyes. Onions are said to be a soporific and, eaten with bread, to be capable of healing mouth-sores.

The school of Asclepiades claims that eating onions promotes a healthy complexion, and that if they are eaten every day on an empty stomach they maintain good health, are beneficial for the stomach, and ease the bowels by moving gas along; when used as a suppository they disperse haemorrhoids. Finally, added to that extracted from fennel, onion-juice is marvellously efficacious when used in the early stages of dropsy.

—from *Natural History,* first century A.D., translated from the Latin by John F. Healy

M.F.K. Fisher on the Dislike of Cabbage

THE WAITRESS, FAT AND SILENT, STAGGERED IN UNDER A tray, her knees bending slightly outwards with its weight. She put down a great plate of steaks, with potatoes heaped like swollen hay at each end. We looked feebly at it, feeling appetite sag out of us suddenly.

Another platter thumped down at the other side of the table, a platter mounded high with purple-red ringed with dark green.

"What—*what* is that beautiful food?" Mrs. Davidson demanded, and then quickly mended her enthusiasm, with her eyes still sparkling hungrily. "I mean, beautiful as far as food could be."

My own appetite revived a little as I answered: "That's a ring of spinach around chopped red cabbage, probably cooked with ham juice."

At the word spinach her face clouded, but when I mentioned cabbage a look of complete and horrified disgust settled like a cloud. She pushed back her chair.

"Cabbage!" Her tone was incredulous.

"Why not?" James asked, mildly. "Cabbage is the staff of life in many countries. You ought to know, Mrs. Davidson. Weren't you raised on a farm?"

Her mouth settled grimly.

"As *you* know," she remarked in an icy voice, with her face gradually looking very old and discontented again, "there are many kinds of farms. My home was *not* a collection of peasants. Nor did we eat such—such peasant things as this."

"But haven't you ever tasted cabbage, then, Mrs. Davidson?" I asked.

"Never!" she answered proudly, emphatically.

"This is delicious steak." It was a diplomatic interruption. I looked gratefully at James. He grinned almost imperceptibly, and went on, "Just let me slide a little sliver on your plate, Mrs. Davidson, and you try to nibble at it while we eat. It will do you good."

He cut off the better portion of a generous slice of beef and put it on her well-emptied plate. She looked pleased, as she always did when reference was made to her delicacy, and only shuddered perfunctorily when we served ourselves with the vegetable.

As the steak disappeared, I watched her long old ear-lobes pinken. I remembered what an endocrinologist had told me once, that after rare beef and wine, when the lobes turned red, was the time to ask favours or tell bad news. I led the conversation back to the table, and then plunged brusquely.

"Why do you really dislike cabbage, Mrs. Davidson?"

She looked surprised, and put down the last bite from her bowl of brandied plums.

"Why does anyone dislike it? Surely you don't believe that I think your eating it is anything more than a pose?" She smiled knowingly at my nephew and me. He laughed.

"But we *do* like it, really. In our homes we cook it, and eat it, too, not for health, not for pretence. We like it."

"Yes, I remember my husband used to say that same sort of thing. But he never got it! No fear! It was the night I finally accepted him that I understood why my family had never had it in the house."

We waited silently. James filled her glass again.

"We missed the last train, and couldn't find a cab, and of course Mr. Davidson, who thought he knew everything, wandered down the wrong street. And there, in that dark wet town, lost, cold, miserable—"

"Oh, night of rapture, when I was yours!" James murmured.

"—cold, miserable, we were suddenly almost overcome by a ghastly odour!"

I repressed my instinctive desire to use the word "stink" and asked maliciously, "A perfume, or a smell?"

"A dreadful *odour*," she corrected me, with an acidulous smile at my coarseness. "It was so terrible that I was almost swooning. I pressed my muff against my face, and we stumbled on, gasping.

"When finally I could control myself enough to speak, I murmured, 'What was it? What was that gas?' My husband hurried me along, and I will say he did his best to apologize for what he had done—and well he should have!—by saying, 'It was cabbage, cooking.'

" 'Oh!' I cried. 'Oh, we're in the *slums!* ' "

—from *Serve It Forth*, 1937

CATO ON CABBAGE EATERS

IN ADDITION, STORE THE URINE OF ANYONE WHO HABITUALLY eats cabbage; warm it, bathe the patient in it. With this treatment you will soon restore health; it has been tested. If you wash feeble children in this urine they will be weak no longer. Those who cannot see clearly should bathe their eyes in this urine and they will see more. If the head or neck is painful, wash in this urine, heated: they will cease to be painful.

Also, if a woman foments her parts with this urine, they will never irritate. Foment as follows: boil in a basin and place under a commode; the woman is then to sit on the commode, covering the basin with her clothing.

—from *On Farming*, second century B.C.,
translated from the Latin by Andrew Dalby

Elena Molokhovets on Borscht

Elena Molokhovets, in the tradition of Le Mésnagier de Paris, *wrote* A Gift to Young Housewives *for Russian newlyweds in 1861, the year that the serfs were freed. Through political upheavals and revolutions it continued to be revised until 1917. In the years of Communism, her book went out of print, but pirated editions appeared on the streets as soon as Communism had fallen. Molokhovets wrote about the great Russian bourgeois cuisine that, like so many bourgeois things in Russia, was at its height in the nineteenth century and now has vanished.* —M.K.

Ukrainian borshch
(Borshch malorossijskij)

Prepare bouillon from 3 lbs of fatty beef or fresh pork, or from beef with smoked ham. Omit the root vegetables, but add a bay leaf and allspice. Strain the bouillon. An hour before serving add a little fresh cabbage, cut into pieces. Cook, stirring in beet brine or grain *kvass* to taste or about 2 spoons vinegar. Meanwhile thoroughly wash and boil 5 red beets, but do not peel or cut them; that is, boil them separately in water without scraping. Remove them when tender, peel, and grate. Stir 1 spoon of flour into the beets, add them to the bouillon with some salt, and bring to a boil twice. Put parsley in a soup tureen (some people add the juice of a grated raw beet) and pour in the hot borshch. Add salt to taste. Sprinkle with black pepper, if desired, and serve with the sliced beef, pork, or ham; or with fried sausages, meatballs, or mushroom buns. This borshch may also be served with fried buckwheat kasha, pancake pie with beef stuffing, or plain pancakes.

—from *A Gift to Young Housewives,* 1897,
translated from the Russian by Joyce Toomre

JAMES BEARD ON RADISHES

FROM MY EARLIEST YEARS I HAVE ADORED THE CRISPNESS, colorfulness, and spicy tang of radishes. I can recall my first feeble efforts at gardening, when I planted little rows of radishes and was so thrilled when they came up, and even more thrilled when it was time to pull them and eat them fresh from the ground. Very few things in life have ever tasted better to me.

Then I remember that on my first trip to France I was introduced to that perfect combination of good bread, sweet butter, and the firm, brilliantly red radishes the French always include on their hors d'oeuvre list in the spring, when the radishes are at their finest. I found the contrast of flavors and textures very interesting and satisfying to the taste

Willy Ronis, *Untitled* (Willy Ronis/Rapho)

buds. In England one sometimes finds radishes on the breakfast plate with toast and butter, and that's extremely good, too. I often serve a plate of early spring radishes with their leafy bright green tops still on (I like to eat the tops if they are fresh and tender—there's a lovely bite to them), accompanied by homemade bread and butter, as a first course.

As my palate and I grew more sophisticated, I went to a cocktail party where I encountered a delicious hors d'oeuvre of an anchovy fillet wrapped around a red radish, which I thought was something really extra special.

Although we are most familiar with the tiny red globe radishes or the more elongated ones we buy in the markets, radishes do vary considerably in color, shape, and size, and in flavor from mild to peppery hot. The long white icicle radishes, less strongly flavored, are wonderful eaten freshly pulled and crisp, with a sprinkling of salt. Then there are the huge black radishes which, peeled, grated, and mixed with chicken or goose fat, make a delectable spread for bread. The Japanese use an enormous white radish called *daikon* which grows 2 or 3 feet long and has a sweet and tangy flavor unlike any other. These radishes are usually served as a garnish, thinly sliced in soups, or grated and served in a tiny bowl to be eaten with or stirred into the dipping sauce for sashimi, those tender little slivers of raw fish, or tempura, batter-dipped, deep-fried vegetables and fish.

Radishes have been cultivated for thousands of years in the Far East, and they are one of the most flavorful of vegetables. As a salad material, their pungent, peppery taste gives piquancy to otherwise dull fare—and it's always nice to know that 3½ ounces of radishes are only about 17 calories.

While radishes are a familiar ingredient in a mixed green salad, recently I found an exciting new way to use them when I attended some classes in Middle Eastern cooking given on the West Coast by my great friend and co-worker, Philip Brown. He made a salad with oranges, I believe Moroccan in origin, that I have since adapted and served to many people. It's very good with lamb, and sensational with curry or other dishes that have a hot seasoning or are rather rich in butter or oil.

Nothing could be simpler and more beautiful to look at than his *Radish and Orange Salad.* Peel 4 good-sized navel oranges, and either section them or slice them very thinly, being sure to remove all the bitter white pith. Arrange these on a bed of washed and dried salad greens—I prefer the crisp leaves of romaine or iceberg lettuce. Now wash, trim, and shred 1 bunch red radishes. I use a Mouli shredder, a little gadget with a handle that cuts vegetables into lovely, long shreds, but

you could use the shredding side of a hand grater. Then kind of drape the radish shreds around the fruit, so you get a glorious color contrast of deep orange, bright green, rosy red, and snow white. Or you can make a wreath of radish shreds around the oranges, or pile them in a mound in the center—here's where you can give your artistic instincts free rein.

Although the original dressing for this salad is made with lemon juice, sugar, and salt, I like to use a vinaigrette, made with 8 tablespoons olive oil to 1 tablespoon lemon juice, 1 teaspoon salt, ½ teaspoon freshly ground black pepper, and 1 to 2 tablespoons orange juice. Taste the dressing before adding it to the salad and tossing—you may need more lemon juice, or lime juice, which is excellent with it. You'll find this vinaigrette has a quite different flavor that enhances the mixture of fruit and vegetables.

Sometimes I vary the salad by alternating sections of orange and grapefruit, or orange and grapefruit sections and avocado slices, which combine with the crisp piquancy of the radish in a most subtle way. So next time you're feeling a bit bored with your standard salad, try one of these.

—from *On Food,* 1974

KARL FRIEDRICH VON RUMOHR ON CUCUMBERS

I HARDLY DARE INCLUDE THESE STRANGE VEGETABLE fruits in the nutritious category because they are coarse textured and indigestible and held by Southerners to be fever-inducing. Despite this, their insipid sweetness makes them equally unsuitable for inclusion in either of the next two categories. Therefore, in view of their excellent juice, which clears the blood and strengthens the lungs and liver, we shall place cucumbers in this first group of nourishing vegetable plants.

Unripe cucumbers are normally peeled and sliced raw, and eaten in salads. Their juice, the only useful part of these indifferent fruit, is usually pressed out on these occasions.

A pleasant vegetable side dish can be made by peeling and chopping unripe cucumbers and then steaming them in a strong stock which has been well seasoned and acidulated. They can also be hollowed out and filled with a meat stuffing. (Prepared in the following manner, cucumbers can stand on their own as a vegetable: Peel the cucumber, remove the seeds and cut it into pieces. Place in a pot lined with a few slices of bacon or some butter and cook on the fire. As soon as the cucumber begins to brown, moisten it with a spoonful of good meat stock. Let it simmer until it is really tender and has absorbed the stock sufficiently. Season as desired, using a drop of lemon juice or vinegar, chopped fine herbs and pepper.)

Cucumbers are, however, most suited to the creation of assorted pickles. Their glasslike, spongiform cell structure renders them exceptionally receptive to the introduction of outside flavours, and to the development of flavours inherent in them. Small cucumbers are pickled in vinegar, flavoured as desired with dill, horseradish, garlic, whole Spanish peppers and Nepal pepper. The important point is to pick the cucumbers on a dry day and select good, unblemished specimens; furthermore, a strong wine vinegar should be used; lastly, the containers should be sealed thoroughly and stored in a cool, dry place.

Larger cucumbers which are still not ripe can be placed in a brine with dill and vine and cherry leaves; they should be allowed to ferment gently so that their flavour is mid-way between that of a salt pickle and a vinegar pickle, just like a tasty sauerkraut. Quantities of excellent preserves are made with these fermented cucumbers in Bohemia, Lausitz [ie around Dresden] and all over the Slavonic North. In Northern areas, fermented vegetables act as substitutes for decaying fruit. However, I believe that Dutch soured cucumbers are the best. This is partly due to the essential superiority of the long, white, bristly cucumber which the Dutch prefer to cultivate and also to the fact that they like to add a few Spanish peppers and other seasonings which improve the flavour and help to preserve the cucumbers.

Cucumbers which are almost mature and

are beginning to turn whitish yellow should be peeled and sliced lengthways. Their seeds should be removed, together with the fibres, and the hollowed cucumbers then placed in a dry container with salt, whole mustard seeds, horseradish, peppercorns and a little garlic, if there are no strong objections to it. A bay leaf and a split Spanish pepper will make welcome additions. Bring some strong vinegar to the boil and pour it, still bubbling, over the cucumbers. Over the next few days, repeat the process by pouring away the vinegar, boiling up fresh and pouring it hot over the cucumbers and seasonings. The container should finally be firmly sealed and placed in a cool, dry place until needed.

—from *The Essence of Cookery,* 1822,
translated from the German by Barbara Yeomans

JANE GRIGSON ON LAVER

The English think their food, if at all edible, is suitable for the English alone. But actually they have successfully imposed their food on other cultures and nothing marks English hegemony more clearly than breakfast. In Scotland, Wales, and even Ireland, you can find English breakfast with the national name—Irish breakfast or Welsh breakfast. But in truth, ham and bacon and eggs in the morning is English. The Scots, Welsh, and Irish are Celts, and Celtic breakfast involves oatmeal, seaweed, and usually some kind of seafood. The seaweed is almost always laver. A true Welsh breakfast is laver-bread and cockles. Like many Celtic dishes, it sounds a little off-putting, but if done right, it's a memorable experience. —M.K.

LAVER IS THE ONE SEAWEED WE CAN DECENTLY COUNT IN English or Welsh cooking as a vegetable. The coasts of the Bristol Channel are the modern laver world. Places to buy it, in the form of laver-bread, a black, almost viscous pulp, are Cardiff, Swansea, Port Talbot, Newport, also Bristol, Barnstaple and Ilfracombe (I get laver-bread by post from Howells of St Mary Street, Cardiff).

It was more widely sold and eaten in the past, in Scotland and Ireland for instance until recently. In 18th-century Bath, according to Christopher Anstey's *New Bath Guide,* 'fine potted laver' used to be cried in the streets, along with oysters and pies. It is now sold in markets and by fishmongers.

Once you have learnt to recognize laver *(Porphyra leucosticta* and *Porphyra umbilicalis)* it is more bothersome than difficult to prepare laver-bread for yourself. The seaweed is common on rocks between high and low tide, the fronds, purple-pink, wavy and fine, have to be washed free of sand and salt (with a little bicarbonate of soda to take away the bitterness) and then stewed in fresh water until they become tender 'and can be worked like spinach with broth or with milk or a pat of butter and a squeeze or two of lemon juice.'

I have lifted that quotation from *Kettner's Book of the Table* (1877), which was written not by Kettner the restaurateur but by the celebrated Victorian critic Eneas Dallas. Dallas complained that laver had lost its popularity and was no longer to be met so frequently in London clubs. If only French cooks had ruled England, he wrote, 'they would have made it as famous as the truffles of Perigord.'

Before I tasted laver—with oatmeal, bacon, roast lamb—I was intrigued by the name. Welsh? No, it was not Welsh, it was straightforward Latin, the name Pliny used for a water plant which certainly wasn't a seaweed. Our seaweed was called laver first by 17th-century botanists. The older name, as in Scotland and Ireland, was slawk or sloke.

Laver grows round the world, and is one of the favourite seaweeds in Japanese cuisine. The Japanese improve it by cultivation. It is dried in sheets—they can be bought in Japanese shops in London and elsewhere—and is used especially in combinations with rice.

Laver-Bread with Bacon

The Welsh and Irish way of eating laver. I remember years ago, having it for breakfast in one of Cardiff's main hotels. Very good.

Take about three heaped tablespoons of laver and mix them with enough oatmeal to be able to form small coherent cakes. Turn them in oatmeal, then fry them in bacon fat and serve with bacon, or with bacon, sausage and lamb chop as part of a mixed grill.

—from *Vegetable Book,* 1978

GIACOMO CASTELVETRO ON SPINACH

Giacomo Castelvetro was an Italian political refugee in England. There was much that he liked about the country that had saved him, but he felt that the people ate too much meat and sweets and not enough fruits and vegetables. In 1614 he wrote a treatise on Italian fruits and vegetables in the hope that the English would adopt some of these plants.   —M.K.

NEXT COMES SPINACH, A VERY GOOD AND WHOLESOME GARden plant, which we eat on its own or accompanied by other herbs, such as spinach beets, parsley and borage.

In Italy it is eaten especially in Lent, cooked in salted water and served with oil, pepper, a little verjuice and raisins.

Another way is to cook the spinach first in plain water, drain it, chop it very fine with a large knife, and finish cooking it on a low heat in a pan with oil or butter, seasoned with salt, pepper and raisins; this makes a really delicious dish.

We often put this spinach mixture in tarts, and in *tortelli* which are fried in oil or butter and served with honey or, better still, sugar.

—from *The Fruit, Herbs & Vegetables of Italy,* 1614,
translated from the Italian by Gillian Riley

KARL FRIEDRICH VON RUMOHR ON SPINACH

THIS PLANT, WITH ITS PRETTY COLOUR AND MILDLY ARO-
matic flavour, is very often consumed as a vegetable. Apart from its
advantages from a dietetic point of view, it manages to flourish
throughout the year, baulking only in the face of the sharpest frost or
most persistent drought.

In some areas, people have fallen into the bad habit of boiling
spinach in water, which is then poured away while the spinach is
chopped and steamed in butter or meat stock before being served as
a vegetable dish. As mentioned above, the spinach may also be given
a new and foreign flavour by the addition of onions, and other intrud-
ers such as beurre manié and breadcrumbs may be used to bind it.
This treatment of spinach is really most unsuitable.

If you like to eat your spinach finely chopped, it should, like so
many other herbs, be blanched and then chopped. It can then be
steamed very gently in water or meat stock over a moderate fire, with
butter and salt being added as necessary. Flour and breadcrumbs will
deprive spinach of a great deal of its natural freshness and flavour, but,
if people insist, the use of these two ingredients is certainly preferable
to that of chopped onions.

The Italians dig up the entire spinach plant when it is still in the
first bloom of its youth. They remove only the outermost leaves and fibrous roots and steam the little plants whole, without cutting and
chopping them. The roots of young spinach plants are indeed very
tasty, imparting a trace of aromatic bitterness to the sweeter leaves
and creating a flavour which will please even the most indulged palate
after a few samples.

The combination of spinach and sorrel, steamed as above, is first
rate.

A quantity of spinach will have a pleasant, mitigating effect upon
the strong flavour of the bitter spring herbs. These are mostly wild and
possess many beneficial properties, but many people, accustomed to
sweet flavours, find them unpleasant. A good proportion of dandelion
and watercress should be used in this herbal spinach, chervil, parsley,
lettuce and any other aromatic herbs being added in smaller quantities. The mixture is chopped and steamed as above.

It is traditional in some parts of Germany to gather all sorts of wild herbs during the Easter week. Varieties such as orache, nettles, dandelions, watercress and young caraway shoots are chopped and combined to make a most delicious vegetable dish, similar to spinach. It is known as Negenschöne in the Saxon dialect.

One particular variety of beet is cultivated only for the sake of its tender and edible leaves, which are prepared like spinach. As these leaves remain green, becoming even more tender, in the worst winter weather, the plant is often known as spinach beet. Quantities of it are grown on the barren upper slopes of the Swiss Alps, particularly in Urseren, and it has in the past been known as the Swiss beet because it spread throughout Europe from Switzerland. The juice of the true spinach has a very pleasant green colour and mild flavour so that it can be used to great advantage to give a good colour to all kinds of dishes and sauces. The pressed juice of raw spinach is indeed very unlikely to spoil any dish in which it is employed as a colouring, regardless of the amount used. It is ideal for giving an attractive shade to cold herb sauces.

To make a cold herb sauce, take one half part spinach and one quarter tarragon, the last quarter being a mixture of sorrel, purslane, parsley and chervil. Add a tiny shallot, or half of a larger one, with a few basil, marjoram and thyme leaves. Pound the mixture in a mortar made of wood or stone. Use a wooden spoon to remove the pulverized herbs and put them with boiling vinegar through a fine hair sieve into a clean earthenware pot. Put this pot on the fire and bring it just to the boil, then remove it. Salt and a pinch of saltpetre should be added at the outset to improve the colour. Allow the mixture to cool slowly, stirring it frequently so that it does not lose volume. The sauce may be thickened with olive oil, egg yolks, or a little semi-solidified white stock, as appropriate.

—from *The Essence of Cookery,* 1822,
translated from the German by Barbara Yeomans

MARJORIE KINNAN RAWLINGS ON OKRA

OKRA IS A CINDERELLA AMONG VEGETABLES. IT LIVES A lowly life, stewed stickily with tomatoes, or lost of identity in a Creole gumbo. I do not know whether the magic wand with which I wave it into something finer than mere edibility is original, but I know no other cook who serves it as I do. To bring it to its glamorous fulfillment, only the very small tender young pods must be used. These are left with the stem end uncut and are cooked exactly seven minutes in rapidly boiling salted water. I serve them arranged like the spokes of a wheel on individual small plates, with individual bowls of Hollandaise sauce set in the center. The okra is lifted by the stem end as one lifts unhulled strawberries, dipped in the Hollandaise and eaten much more daintily than is possible with asparagus. The flavor is unique. The Hollandaise, it goes without saying, must be perfect; just holding its shape; velvety in texture; properly acid. I use the yolk of one egg, the juice of half a lemon, and a quarter of a pound of Dora's butter per person. The only other place I have eaten Hollandaise as good as mine is at the Ritz-Carlton, and even theirs does not have quite enough lemon juice to suit me. And of course, for the price of one serving of broccoli or asparagus à la Hollandaise at the Ritz, I can buy a whole hamper of okra and feed Dora for a week.

—from *Cross Creek,* 1942

ANNABELLA P. HILL'S GUMBO

By 1872, Annabella P. Hill was a sixty-two-year-old widow with only one of her eleven children still alive. That daughter would die the following year. Two of her sons had been killed within three months of each other, serving the Confederacy in the Virginia campaign. Her husband, a prominent politician, had dropped dead, presumably of a stroke, in 1860, while delivering a speech opposing Georgia's secession from the Union. So, in 1872, when she published Mrs. Hill's Southern Practical Cookery and Receipt Book, *the past was very much on her mind. She was not of the Civil War generation but of the generation that gave up their sons to the war. And so while this is a Southern book from the Reconstruction period, her recipes are rooted in old food ways from a world she had known long before so many losses.* —M.K.

GUMBO.—FRY A YOUNG CHICKEN; AFTER IT GETS COLD, take out the bones. In another vessel fry one pint of young, tender, cut up ochra and two onions. Put all in a well-cleaned soup-kettle; an iron stew-pan lined with tin or porcelain is best. Add one quart of water; stew gently until done; and season with pepper and salt. Another way of preparing Gumbo, is: Cut up a fowl as if to fry; break the bones; lay it in a pot with a little lard or fresh butter. Brown it a little. When browned, pour a gallon of water on it; add a slice of lean bacon, one onion cut in slices, a pint of tomatoes skinned, two pints of young pods of ochra cut up, and a few sprigs of parsley. Cover closely, removing the cover to skim off all impurities that may rise to the top. Set the soup-kettle where the water will simmer gently at least four hours. Half an hour before the soup is put in the tureen, add a thickening, by mixing a heaping table-spoonful of sassafras leaves, dried and pounded fine, with a little soup. Stir this well into the soup. Serve with a separate dish of rice.

Gather the leaf-buds of the sassafras early in the spring; dry, pound, sift, and bottle them. Miss Leslie recommends stirring the soup with a sassafras stick, when the powdered leaves cannot be procured. The sassafras taste is very disagreable to some persons, therefore should be omitted when this is the case.

—from *Mrs. Hill's Southern Practical Cookery and Receipt Book*, 1872

GIACOMO CASTELVETRO
ON ARTICHOKES

IN ITALY OUR ARTICHOKE SEASON IS IN THE SPRING, unlike England, where you are fortunate enough to have them all the year round.

We eat them raw or cooked. When they are about the size of a walnut they are good raw, with just salt, pepper and some mature cheese to bring out the flavour. Some people do not eat artichokes with cheese; they either dislike cheese, or it gives them catarrh, or they are simply unaware of how it improves the flavour. Artichokes are not so good to eat raw when they have grown as big as apples.

We cook them in your English manner, which is not to be despised, and in other ways as well.

If you do not feel like eating artichokes raw, select some small ones and cut off the tips of the pointed outer leaves. Boil them first in fresh water to take away the bitterness, and then finish cooking them in rich beef or chicken broth. Serve them in a shallow dish on slices of bread moistened with just a little of the broth, sprinkled with grated mature cheese and pepper to bring out their goodness. We love these tasty morsels; just writing about them makes my mouth water.

Another way with these small artichokes is to give them a boil first, then bake them in little pies, with oysters and beef marrow, nicely seasoned with salt and pepper.

We usually cook the larger ones on a grid over charcoal, having cut away the top halves of the leaves, and serve them with oil or melted butter, and salt and pepper. They taste even better if you squeeze some bitter orange juice over them after roasting; they appeal enormously to everyone who eats them like this.

We cook the very big artichokes, like those you have here, in water first; then we trim off the top halves of the biggest leaves and stuff between them oysters and some of their juices, morsels of beef marrow, oil or bits of fresh butter, and salt and pepper. Then we case them in pastry, and bake them, and they are delicious beyond belief.

When artichokes start to get hard and woody, towards the end of the season, many growers cut off all the leaves and the choke and throw the hearts straight away into a bucket of water to keep them white. They sell these 'bottoms' as we call them, very cheaply—seven or eight for a Venetian *soldo*.

Artichoke hearts

The best way of cooking these 'bottoms' is to stew them in a pot with oil, salt and pepper; or fry them in oil and serve them sprinkled with salt, pepper and bitter orange juice.

These artichoke hearts can be preserved for winter use by boiling them a little in water, then draining them and putting them on a board to dry in the sun. When they are quite dry they should be stored well away from damp. Then when we come to eat them, they are reconstituted in tepid water, floured and fried, and seasoned with salt, pepper and bitter orange juice.

—from *The Fruit, Herbs & Vegetables of Italy,* 1614,
translated from the Italian by Gillian Riley

CHAPTER ELEVEN

A Hill of Beans

GALEN ON BEANS AND PEAS

BEANS HAVE A MULTIPLE USE: FROM THEM ARE MADE SOUPS, both the watery sort in a saucepan and the thick sort in a casserole. They are also an ingredient of a third recipe with pearl barley. The gladiators with me use a lot of this sort of food each day when building up the condition of their bodies not with dense and compressed flesh, as does pork, but instead rather more spongy.

But however it is made it is a flatulent food, even if it is cooked for a long time, although barley loses all its flatulence during the time that it is boiled. For anyone who pays attention and attends closely to the state of the body that follows from each food, a sensation arises throughout the whole body of stretching due to flatulent wind, especially when that person is unused to this sort of food or eats it without proper cooking.

The substance of beans is not solid and heavy, but spongy and light. They also possess a cleansing action like barley, for it can be clearly seen that their meal wipes dirt off the skin, something which slave-dealers and women have realised since they use bean meal for washing every day, just as other people use sodium carbonate, which is suitable for washing thoroughly too. They smear their face with it just like barley because it removes superficial blemishes which go by the name of burrs. By the same power, therefore, it slows nothing down in its passage through the body, which is a problem with viscous foods with thick juices that contain no purgative element, the examples we have mentioned being groats, spelt, finest wheat flour and starch.

The soup made from beans may be flatulent, but it becomes even more flatulent when the beans are used boiled whole. If they are roasted—for some people eat them like this in place of sweetmeats—they lose their flatulence, but become difficult to digest and slow to pass through the bowels, whilst for nourishment they distribute a thick juice to the body. Eaten when green, before they have been ripened and dried, they share the same attribute as all other fruits which we serve before their peak has been reached: namely that of supplying nourishment to the body that is moister and consequently more productive of waste, not only in the bowels, but throughout the whole body. So understandably such food is less nourishing and passes through the body faster.

A lot of people not only eat green beans when still raw, but also cook them with pork just like vegetables, although in the country they cook them with goat and lamb. Other people, realising that they are flatulent, mix them with onions when they are making a thick soup in a casserole. Some people even serve raw onions with this soup without cooking them together, because with all foods any tendency towards flatulence is mitigated through heating and diluting.

Peas

Peas are very much the same in composition as beans, but although they are eaten in the same way, they nonetheless differ in two respects: firstly, they are not as flatulent as beans; and secondly, they do not have a purgative power. They are therefore slower to pass through the stomach than beans.

—from *On the Powers of Foods*, A.D. 180,
translated from the Latin by Mark Grant

WAVERLEY ROOT ON CASSOULET

THE OUTSTANDING DISH OF LANGUEDOC IS CASSOULET, white beans cooked in a pot with various types of meat, which takes its name from the dish in which it is cooked, the *cassole*—an old-fashioned word no longer in current use. Originally it belonged to the family of farm-kitchen dishes, like *pot-au-feu,* which remain on the back of the stove indefinitely, serving as a sort of catch-all for anything edible that the cook may toss into the pot. Anatole France claimed in his *Histoire Comique* that the *cassoulet* he used to eat in a favorite establishment in Paris had been cooking for twenty years. It is to be doubted that any restaurant could be found today in which the stoves had not been allowed to cool off in that length of time. Modern fuels may be more convenient to handle than the farmer's wood, but they are too expensive not to be turned off between meals.

This sort of a dish is obviously likely to vary with the . . . individual cook, or even with what the individual cook happens to have at hand (my own cook makes a first-rate *cassoulet,* but the ingredients are likely to be different every time). The one thing that does not change is the beans. Nevertheless, you can work up a hot argument among *cassoulet*-fanciers at any time about the ingredients of the real *cassoulet.* It is a subject as touchy as the correct composition of a mint julep in certain regions of the American south. With the caution that this is a most variable dish, even when made on the same spot by the same person, what seems to be majority opinion on the standard varieties of the dish, which then serve as points of departure for individual fantasy, is offered here:

There are three main types of *cassoulet,* those of Castelnaudary, Carcassonne, and Toulouse, of which the first seems to have been the original dish. It is therefore, in principle at least, the simplest, combining with the beans only fresh pork, ham, a bit of pork shoulder, sausage, and fresh pork cracklings. Carcassonne starts with this, and adds hunks of leg of mutton to the mixture (in season, there may also be partridge in this *cassoulet*). Toulouse also starts out with the Castelnaudary base, but adds to it not only mutton (in this case from less expensive cuts), but also bacon, Toulouse sausage, and preserved goose. The last ingredient may sometimes be replaced by preserved duck, or there may even be samples of both.

This would seem to make everything plain—Castelnaudary, only pork; Carcassonne, distinguished by mutton; Toulouse, distinguished by goose. However, an authority I have just consulted, which lays down these distinctions very sternly, then goes on to give two recipes for *cassoulet de Castelnaudary;* one of them contains mutton and the other contains goose. The conclusion that must be drawn is that *cassoulet* is what you find it.

The only invariable rule that can be stated about *cassoulet,* with whatever name it may be ticketed on the menu, seems to be that it is a dish of white beans, preferably those of Pamiers or Cazères, cooked in a pot with some form of pork and sausage. After that it is a case of fielder's choice. Other points various forms of *cassoulet* are likely to have in common are: the use of goose fat in the cooking; seasoning that includes assorted herbs, an onion with cloves stuck into it, and garlic; and enough liquid to give it plenty of thick juice, sometimes provided by meat bouillon. The approved method is first to cook meat and beans together—they are likely to enter the process at different times, depending on their relative cooking speeds—and to finish the process by putting the whole thing into a pot, coating the surface with bread crumbs, which gives it a crunchy golden crust, and finishing the cooking very slowly, preferably in a baker's oven. There is a tradition that the crust should be broken and stirred into the whole steaming mass again seven times during the cooking.

—from *The Food of France,* 1958

JOSÉ MARIA BUSCA ISUSI ON THE SMOOTHNESS OF TOLOSA BEANS

José Maria Busca Isusi, the author of numerous books and cookbooks and director of the food history magazine Cofradia Vasca de Gastronomia, Basque Gastronomic Society, *was the leading Basque food writer and commentator from the 1950s until his death in the 1980s. This was a considerable accomplishment in a society*

*that prides itself on its food commentary. Basque food writing, in the
tradition of the Baron von Rumohr, is about documenting and preserving traditions.*

*Busca Isusi was not the first to reflect on the importance of
earthenware in making beans, though he may have investigated it
with more thoroughness than anyone else. It has long been argued
that the secret of the Boston baked bean was the earthenware Boston
bean pot, though Fannie Farmer completely dismissed this and said
beans could be made well in a metal cooking pot. Neither Basques
nor Bostonians believe this.*   —M.K.

IN THE GASTRONOMIC FIRMAMENT OF GUIPÚZCOA, THE
stars are many and bright and the beans of Tolosa are generally considered of the first magnitude. Our subject, the beans of Tolosa, particularly those grown in the soil of this town, must be bought in the
Tolosa market. Tolosa is a *carrefour*, an intersection, an extension between Goyerri and Beterri, and it is logically supposed that in its markets you can also find local products.

The bean of Tolosa is a novelty in Guipúzcoan gastronomy, like
wine from America. Before Columbus we only ate broad beans. The
red bean made such an impression on Guipúzcoans that even today
they are sometimes called *indiollar*, or Indian chicken. The Guipúzcoan Order of Jesuits had a major business importing turkeys from
America.

The fame of Tolosa beans goes beyond our borders, and the Guipúzcoan characteristic of the dish is smoothness. The unctuousness of the
sauce produced is unique, and this is not a subjec-
tive but a completely objective observation—a
thick and chocolate-colored sauce that
no other bean produces.

Analyzing in detail the Guipúzcoan
way of making Tolosan red beans, we
must take into account that the earthen
casseroles are better than metal ones, and that
metal pots are not adequate for cooking Tolosa
beans. Tolosa beans reject this kind of pot.

It is well known that the calcareous [lime]
content of water is of critical importance to
the cooking of all types of dried legumes, as

well as some green vegetables. Today the chemical action that takes place in this kind of water has been completely explained, and fortunately the waters of Guipúzcoa, in general, are not hard. The best water in which to cook beans is rain water, and for many years now homemakers in rural areas have recognized this.

For a long time I have been trying to understand what it is about our earthen casseroles that makes them cook better than metal, and only recently I had the good fortune to encounter the technical explanation in a magnificent book. The cooking of beans causes four important occurrences:

1. It dissolves films.
2. It decomposes demi-cellulose.
3. It alters cellulose.
4. It coagulates starch.

During the cooking the protopectins are partially transformed into pectins and acids, which are the products that cause thickening during cooking, and it seems Tolosa beans have an abundance of this. To understand the beans, this change in pectins is of decisive importance. The change in pectins produces something called *pectasa,* which rapidly activates at a temperature between 50 and 60 degrees centigrade. At 90 degrees it is destroyed, but logically it has already been activated.

This action of the *pectasa* at low temperatures explains why you have to soak beans for several hours. Actually, the beans are lightly cooking while they are soaking. Then, once put on the fire, the action of the pectasa continues until the temperature reaches 90 degrees. This is why the slower the heating, the greater the effect of the pectasa.

So, the casserole transmits the heat much more slowly than the old-fashioned cast-iron casseroles, which in turn are slower than the enamaled metal, and this is slower than the aluminum ones. So it is because of the way the heat travels through the casserole that beans cooked in earthenware will be smoother than those cooked in newer pots.

This also explains why Navarra housewives *asustar* the beans, which is adding cold water during the cooking so that the beans are never in boiling water. It is certain disaster to put beans in boiling water, because after having been soaked and then going immediately to boiling water leaves little time for the pectasa to act.

However, there are other things that make Tolosa beans uniquely smooth. Two American products in our fields join as brothers magnificently: corn and red beans. Beans and corn live together in a romantic embrace that protects them from the sun's rays. Furthermore, our climate is ideal for some American plants that don't like dry weather, such as tobacco, chili peppers, tomatoes, and beans. The beans of Tolosa, which do not like sun, are always grown in gentle shade.

Another factor commonly known in chemistry is that lime phosphate deteriorates the quality of dried beans. Normally, Tolosa beans are grown only with cow manure, and never with superphosphates. We understand that this is critical for the quality of the beans.

Let's finish up with another factor. Beans from siliceous earth, which has a low pH, are of a much higher quality than those grown in calcareous soil, which has a high pH. A good place to observe this is the Urola Valley. Up until Aspeitia, the left side is siliceous. The beans that grow on the side of Beloqui, which is calcareous, do not have the quality of those of Elosua, on the Irimo Mountain where the soil is siliceous.

Having written all this I have committed the sin of being pedantic, but I believe I can be forgiven for good intentions. We have to search for technical understandings into the farthest corners of our cuisine, and this article is an attempt, more or less successful, to offer the opinions of those who study Basque cooking in general, and especially Guipúzcoan cuisine.

—from *Cofradia Vasca de Gastronomia*, no. 6, San Sebastián, 1972, translated from the Spanish by Mark Kurlansky

CHAPTER TWELVE

The Fish That Didn't Get Away

ALICE B. TOKLAS MURDERS A CARP

COOK-BOOKS HAVE ALWAYS INTRIGUED AND SEDUCED ME. When I was still a dilettante in the kitchen they held my attention, even the dull ones, from cover to cover, the way crime and murder stories did Gertrude Stein.

When we first began reading Dashiell Hammett, Gertrude Stein remarked that it was his modern note to have disposed of his victims before the story commenced. Goodness knows how many were required to follow as the result of the first crime. And so it is in the kitchen. Murder and sudden death seem as unnatural there as they should be anywhere else. They can't, they can never become acceptable facts. Food is far too pleasant to combine with horror. All the same, facts, even distasteful facts, must be accepted and we shall see how, before any story of cooking begins, crime is inevitable. That is why cooking is not an entirely agreeable pastime. There is too much that must happen in advance of the actual cooking. This doesn't of course apply to food that emerges stainless from deep freeze. But the marketing and cooking I know are French and it was in France, where freezing units are unknown, that in due course I graduated at the stove.

In earlier days, memories of which are scattered among my chapters, if indulgent friends on this or that Sunday evening or party occasion said that the cooking I produced wasn't bad, it neither beguiled nor flattered me into liking or wanting to do it. The only way to learn to cook is to cook, and for me, as for so many others, it suddenly and unexpectedly became a disagreeable necessity to have to do it when war came and Occupation followed. It was in those conditions of rationing and shortage that I learned not only to cook seriously but to buy food in a restricted market and not to take too much time in doing it, since there were so many more important and more amusing things to do. It was at this time, then, that murder in the kitchen began.

The first victim was a lively carp brought to the kitchen in a covered basket from which nothing could escape. The fish man who sold me the carp said he had no time to kill, scale or clean it, nor would he tell me with which of these horrible necessities one began. It wasn't difficult to know which was the most repellent. So quickly to the murder and have it over with. On the docks of Puget Sound I had seen fishermen grasp the tail of a huge salmon and lifting it high bring it down on the dock with enough force to kill it. Obviously I was not a fisherman nor was the kitchen table a dock. Should I not dispatch my first victim with a blow on the head from a heavy mallet? After an appraising glance at the lively fish it was evident he would escape attempts aimed at his head. A heavy sharp knife came to my mind as the classic, the perfect choice, so grasping, with my left hand well covered with a dishcloth, for the teeth might be sharp, the lower jaw of the carp, and the knife in my right, I carefully, deliberately found the base of its vertebral column and plunged the knife in. I let go my grasp and looked to see what had happened. Horror of horrors. The carp was dead, killed, assassinated, murdered in the first, second and third degree. Limp, I fell into a chair, with my hands still unwashed reached for a cigarette, lighted it, and waited for the police to come and take me into custody. After a second cigarette my courage returned and I went to prepare poor Mr Carp for the table. I scraped off the scales, cut off the fins, cut open the underside and emptied out a great deal of what I did not care to look at, thoroughly washed and dried the fish and put it aside while I prepared

Carp Stuffed with Chestnuts

For a 3-lb. carp, chop a medium-sized onion and cook it gently in 3 tablespoons butter. Add a 2-inch slice of bread cut into small cubes which have previously been soaked in dry, white wine and squeezed dry, 1 tablespoon chopped parsley, 2 chopped shallots, 1 clove of pressed garlic, 1 teaspoon salt, ¼ teaspoon freshly ground pepper, ¼ teaspoon powdered mace, the same of laurel (bay) and of thyme and 12 boiled and peeled chestnuts. Mix well, allow to cool, add 1 raw egg, stuff the cavity and head of the fish, carefully snare with skewers, tie the head so that nothing will escape in cooking. Put aside for at least a couple of hours. Put 2 cups dry white wine into an earthenware dish, place the fish in the dish, salt to taste. Cook in the oven for 20 minutes at 375°. Baste, and cover the fish with a thick coating of very fine cracker crumbs, dot with 3 tablespoons melted butter and cook for 20 minutes more. Serve very hot accompanied by noodles. Serves 4. The head of a carp is enormous. Many continentals consider it the most delectable morsel.

—from *The Alice B. Toklas Cook Book,* 1954

TAILLEVENT'S OYSTER STEW

SCALD OYSTERS AND WASH THEM WELL, PARBOIL THEM A little and fry them in oil together with chopped onions; take toast, pea puree or the water in which the oysters were scalded, or any other hot, boiled water, and a generous proportion of wine and verjuice, and strain this; then add in ground cinnamon, ginger, cloves, grains of paradise, and saffron for colour, infused in vinegar, and onions fried in oil, and boil all of this together. It should be stiff and yellowish, and salted to taste. Some people do not boil the oysters in this.

—from *Le Viandier,* c. 1390,
translated from the French by Terence Scully

ROBERT MAY ON OYSTER STEW

In the seventeenth century, large defining cookbooks started to appear throughout Europe. These were books in the tradition of Taillevent but with more explanation and flowing prose. The first of these books in England came out the year the civil war ended and monarchy was re-

stored. Not surprisingly, Robert May, the author, cooked for the Catholic royalists. His book, The Accomplisht Cook, *offered one thousand well-written and detailed recipes.*   —M.K.

To stew oysters in the French Way.

Take oysters, open them and parboil them in their own liquor, the quantity of three pints or a pottle; being parboil'd, wash them in warm water clean from the dregs, beard them and put them in a pipkin with a little white wine, & some of the liquor they were parboil'd in, a whole onion, some salt, and pepper, and stew them till they be half done; then put them and their liquor into a frying-pan, fry them a pretty while, put to them a good piece of sweet butter, and fry them a therein so much longer, then have ten or twelve yolks of eggs dissolved with some vinegar, wherein you must put in some minced parsley, and some grated nutmeg, put these ingredients into the oysters, shake them in the frying-pan a warm or two, and serve them up.

To stew Oysters otherways.

Take a pottle of large great oysters, parboil them in their own liquor, then wash them in warm water from the dregs, & put them in a pipkin with a good big onion or two, and five or six blades of large mace, a little whole pepper, a slic't nutmeg, a quarter of a pint of white wine, as much wine-vinegar, a quarter of a pound of sweet butter, and a little salt, stew them finely together on a soft fire the space of half an hour, then dish them on sippets of French bread, slic't lemon on them, and barberries, run them over with beaten butter, and garnish the dish with dryed manchet grated and searsed.

—from *The Accomplisht Cook,* 1685 revision

ANTON CHEKHOV ON OYSTERS

I CAN EASILY RECALL THE RAINY TWILIGHT AUTUMN EVENING when I stood with my father in a crowded Moscow street and fell ill, strangely. I suffered no pain, but my legs gave way, my head hung on one side, and my speech failed. I felt that I should soon fall.

Had I been taken to hospital at the moment, the doctor would have written: "Fames"—a complaint uncommon in medical text-books.

Beside me on the pavement stood my father in a ragged summer overcoat and a check cap. On his feet were big, clumsy goloshes. Fearing that people might see he had neither boots nor stockings, he wrapped his legs in old gaiters.

The more tattered and dirty became that once smart summer overcoat, the greater became my love. He had come to the capital five months before to seek work as a clerk. Five months he had tramped the city, seeking employment; only to-day for the first time he had screwed up his courage to beg for alms in the street.

In front of us rose a big, three-storied house with a blue signboard "Restaurant." My head hung helplessly back, and on one side. Involuntarily I looked upward at the bright restaurant windows. Behind them glimmered human figures. To the right were an orchestrion, two oleographs, and hanging lamps. While trying to pierce the obscurity my eyes fell on a white patch. The patch was motionless; its rectangular contour stood out sharply against the universal background of dark brown. When I strained my eyes I could see that the patch was a notice on the wall, and it was plain that something was printed upon it, but what that something was I could not see.

I must have kept my eyes on the notice at least half an hour. Its whiteness beckoned to me, and, it seemed, almost hypnotised my brain. I tried to read it, and my attempts were fruitless.

But at last the strange sickness entered into its rights.

The roar of the traffic rose to thunder; in the smell of the street I could distinguish a thousand smells; and the restaurant lights and street lamps seemed to flash like lightning. And I began to make out things that I could not make out before.

"Oysters," I read on the notice.

A strange word. I had lived in the world already eight years and three months, and had never heard this word. What did it mean? Was it the proprietor's surname? No, for signboards with innkeepers' names hang outside the doors, and not on the walls inside.

"Father, what are oysters?" I asked hoarsely, trying to turn my face towards his.

My father did not hear me. He was looking at the flow of the crowd, and following every passer-by with his eyes. From his face I judged that he dearly longed to speak to the passers, but the fatal, leaden words hung on his trembling lips, and would not tear themselves off. One passer-by he even stopped and touched on the sleeve, but when the man turned to him my father stammered, "I beg your pardon," and fell back in confusion.

"Papa, what does 'oysters' mean?" I repeated.

"It is a kind of animal. . . . It lives in the sea. . . ."

And in a wink I visualised this mysterious animal. Something between a fish and a crab, it must be, I concluded; and as it came from the sea, of course it made up into delightful dishes, hot *bouillabaisse* with fragrant peppercorns and bay leaves, or sour *solianka* with gristle, crab-sauce, or cold with horseradish. . . . I vividly pictured to myself how this fish is brought from the market, cleaned, and thrust quickly into a pot . . . quickly, quickly, because every one is hungry . . . frightfully hungry. From the restaurant kitchen came the smell of boiled fish and crab soup.

This smell began to tickle my palate and nostrils; I felt it permeating my whole body. The restaurant, my father, the white notice, my sleeve, all exhaled it so strongly that I began to chew. I chewed and swallowed as if my mouth were really full of the strange animal that lives in the sea. . . .

The pleasure was too much for my strength, and to prevent myself falling I caught my father's cuff, and leaned against his wet summer overcoat. My father shuddered. He was cold. . . .

"Father, can you eat oysters on fast days?" I asked.

"You eat them alive . . ." he answered. "They are in shells . . . like tortoises, only in double shells."

The seductive smell suddenly ceased to tickle my nostrils, and the illusion faded. Now I understood!

"How horrible!" I exclaimed. "How hideous!"

So that was the meaning of oysters! However, hideous as they were, my imagination could paint them. I imagined an animal like a frog. The frog sat in the shell, looked out with big, bright eyes, and moved its disgusting jaws. What on earth could be more horrible to a boy who had lived in the world just eight years and three months? Frenchmen, they said, ate frogs. But children—never! And I saw this fish being carried from market in its shell, with claws, bright eyes, and shiny tail. . . . The children all hide themselves, and the cook, blinking squeamishly, takes the animal by the claws, puts it on a dish, and carries it to the dining-room. The grown-ups take it, and eat . . . eat it alive, eyes, teeth, claws. And it hisses, and tries to bite their lips.

I frowned disgustedly. But why did my teeth begin to chew? An animal, disgusting, detestable, frightful, but still I ate it, ate it greedily, fearing to notice its taste and smell. I ate in imagination, and my nerves seemed braced, and my heart beat stronger. . . . One animal was finished, already I saw the bright eyes of a second, a third. . . . I ate these also. At last I ate the table-napkin, the plate, my father's goloshes, the white notice. . . . I ate everything before me, because I felt that only eating would cure my complaint. The oysters glared frightfully from their bright eyes, they made me sick, I shuddered at the thought of them, but I wanted to eat. To eat!

"Give me some oysters! Give me some oysters." The cry burst from my lips, and I stretched out my hands.

"Give me a kopeck, gentlemen!" I heard suddenly my father's dulled, choked voice. "I am ashamed to ask, but, my God, I can bear it no longer!"

"Give me some oysters!" I cried, seizing my father's coat-tails.

"And so you eat oysters! Such a little whipper-snapper!" I heard a voice beside me.

Before me stood two men in silk hats, and looked at me with a laugh.

"Do you mean to say that this little manikin eats oysters? Really! This is too delightful! How does he eat them?"

I remember a strong hand dragged me into the glaring restaurant. In a minute a crowd had gathered, and looked at me with curiosity and amusement. I sat at a table, and ate something slippy, damp, and mouldy. I ate greedily, not chewing, not daring to look, not even knowing what I ate. It seemed to me that if I opened my eyes, I should see at once the bright eyes, the claws, the sharp teeth.

I began to chew something hard. There was a crunching sound.

"Good heavens, he's eating the shells!" laughed the crowd. "Donkey, who ever heard of eating oyster shells?"

After this, I remember only my terrible thirst. I lay on my bed, kept awake by repletion, and by a strange taste in my hot mouth. My father walked up and down the room and gesticulated.

"I have caught cold, I think!" he said. "I feel something queer in my head. . . . As if there is something inside it. . . . But perhaps it is only . . . because I had no food to-day. I have been strange altogether . . . stupid. I saw those gentlemen paying ten roubles for oysters; why didn't I go and ask them for something . . . in loan? I am sure they would have given it."

Towards morning I fell asleep, and dreamed of a frog sitting in a shell and twitching its eyes. At midday thirst awoke me. I sought my father; he still walked up and down the room and gesticulated.

—from "Oysters," 1884,
translated from the Russian

ELEANOR CLARK ON BELONS

Eleanor Clark, the author of several novels, won a National Book Award for her beautiful little 1959 book about the Breton village that produces the famous Belons oysters.   —M.K.

THE OUTCOME IS A LITTLE LUXURY ITEM, OF RATHER LARGE economic consequence but no great importance to the world's nourishment. It should be. The oyster is very high in nutrition value, at least as much so as milk, but that is scarcely relevant as things stand because not enough people can afford it. So the whole point is flavor, and sociologically speaking, how can you justify that? Is it worth all the pain and trouble? Should it even be allowed?

You can't define it. Music or the color of the sea are easier to describe than the taste of one of these Armoricaines, which has been lifted, turned, rebedded, taught to close its mouth while traveling, culled, sorted, kept a while in a rest home or "basin" between each change of domicile, raked, protected from its enemies and shifting sands etc. for four or five years before it gets into your mouth. It has no relation at all to the taste, if there is one, of the usual U. S. restaurant oyster, not to mention the canned or frozen one. (No Armoricaines are canned, or frozen; there is no such business.) Or rather yes, it has the relation of love to tedium, delight to the death of the soul, the best to the tolerable if tolerable, in anything. Or say of French bread, the kind anybody eats in France, to . . . well, never mind. It is briny first of all, and not in the sense of brine in a barrel, for the preservation of something; there is a shock of freshness to it. Intimations of the ages of man, some piercing intuition of the sea and all its weeds and breezes shiver you a split second from that little stimulus on the palate. You are eating the sea, that's it, only the sensation of a gulp of sea water has been wafted out of it by some sorcery, and are on the verge of remembering you don't know what, mermaids or the sudden smell of kelp on the ebb tide or a poem you read once, something connected with the flavor of life itself . . .

—from *The Oysters of Locmariaquer,* 1959

ARCHESTRATUS ON SMALL FRY, FILEFISH, AND SOWFISH

SMALL FRY [*APHUE*]. VALUE AS SHIT ALL SMALL FRY EXCEPT the Athenian kind. I'm speaking of *gonos* which the Ionians call foam. Get it when fresh and caught in the beautiful bay of Phaleron, in its sacred arms. It is also of good quality in wave-girt Rhodes, if it is local fish. And if perhaps you desire to taste it, you should buy at the same time [sea] nettles, nettles with long locks. Mix them together and bake them on a frying pan, grinding the fragrant flowers of the greens in oil.

In Aenus and the Pontus buy the sow-fish, which some mortals call the 'dug-out-from-sand.' Boil the head of this fish, adding no flavourings, but putting only in water and stirring often. Serve by it pounded hyssop, and if you want anything more, drip on it sharp vinegar. Then dip it well and hurry, even to the point of choking, to swallow it eagerly. The fin and the other parts of the fish are baked.

Selachians: now famous Miletus nurtures the best. But why talk of the file-fish or the broad-back ray? I would as soon dine on oven-baked crocodile in which the children of the Ionians take delight.

—from *The Life of Luxury,* c. 330 B.C.,
translated from the Greek by John Wikins and Shaun Hall

JOSÉ MARIA BUSCA ISUSI ON COD AND ON THE BASQUE PROBLEM

THE COD MOST FREQUENTLY EATEN TODAY IS *GADUS morhua (bacalao, makailo),* which has been gutted and cured before it reaches our markets. This species does not inhabit our coasts. Those fish called fresh cod in the markets are specimens of whiting *(Merlangus merlangus)* or pollack *(Pollachius pollachius).*

The true codfish or *bacalao* inhabits the North Atlantic, spreading throughout the European area from France to Norway. Its appearance in Cantabrian waters is rare. It prefers the deep waters of cold seas.

According to some, the term *bacalao,* as well as the Danish word *bakelau* and the Dutch *baukaelja,* is derived from the island of Bacalieu, near Newfoundland. According to others, *bacalao* comes from the Gaelic word *bachall,* a type of pole on which *bacalao* was once dried.

Whatever the etymology of the word, the fact remains that cod is of great economic importance and for centuries has played a vital role in the nutrition of European peoples. Arguments over cod and whales have spurred on numerous wars and disputes, and through the centuries diplomats have had to negotiate these constant disagreements between the fishermen of different nationalities.

Up until recently, cod was caught by hook only and prepared and cured on shore near its native waters. Today it is widely fished with nets and prepared in commercial factories.

The same thing has happened with cod as with chorizos, hams, wines, liquors, etc. Industry has ensured uniformity and economy in these products, but the quality of the more naturally prepared foodstuffs cannot be maintained. In industrial preparation of cod, heat, cold, and chemicals enter into the process. The economic results are favorable but the gastronomic ones are detestable. A well-cured *bacalao* should ideally possess white and flexible meat, dark skin, and its own unique smell which it should maintain throughout culinary preparation.

Basque fishermen have caught and consumed this fish for centuries. Today cod is considered second-rate in the majority of countries, but in our country it is prepared with a particular technique that raises its status and converts it into a dish worthy of the finest tables.

The culinary problem of converting a dried and cured fish into a succulent dish has been solved by following either of two completely different procedures.

One method—primitive and rough—is the one used in the preparation of *zurrukutuna* and *ajo arriero*. In this procedure pieces of cured cod are grilled over coals. Aided by the heat, the salt impregnates the fish and removes the little water that remains in the cells. At that moment, the pieces dampen and go soft. In this state it is easy to remove the skin and spines and at the same time break the white meat sections into pieces. The fish is rinsed with water to remove excess salt. In this way it is readied for its final preparation.

To make *ajo arriero,* the cod is soaked in an oil in which generous amounts of chopped garlic, peeled peppers, tomatoes, and red peppers have been browned. This original dish is very different from the effeminate *ajo arriero* that is served in many restaurants, where the dish is not only robbed of its flavor but also adulterated with lobster.

In the countryside, *ajo arriero*—accompanied by a wine of the quality of a Murchante and a good bread made with flour from the Bardenas—is a good culinary representative of the noble Ribera region and is a delight to the palate.

Zurrukutuna begins with the same desalting process used for *ajo arriero,* and the cod is then added to a soup along with tomato and bread. There are many recipes, all more refined than that for *ajo arriero.*

The second preparation of *bacalao* is slow, smooth, and wise. Created on the coast, it is one of the glories of Basque cooking. The cod undergoes a two-part preparation: the desalting and then the tempering or setting of the *bacalao* in hot water. The best procedure for desalting is to submerge the fish in a river or stream of clean water for about eighteen hours.

When our rivers deserved the name "river" and were not full of contaminants and sewage as they are today, they well could have accommodated such an operation. Now we must settle for immersing the fish in large vessels of cold water and changing the water every four or five hours.

After this time spent in the water, the cells—now salt-free—are in a condition to recover a lot of the water lost in the curing process.

To temper the cod, the pieces are placed in a pot with cold water and put on the heat in such a way that the temperature rises slowly. The temperature of the water should not exceed 65° C (150° F). The operation of tempering is the criterion for knowing the quality of the fish. If it is of prime quality it will become white, firm, and smooth. If it is a commercial *bacalao* in which chemicals have been introduced, we will end up with a fibrous mass, and in this case it is best not to continue with the preparation. Cod can be in the water at 60° C (140° F) for about forty-five to sixty minutes.

There is a method for rapid tempering which consists of heating the pot as rapidly as possible until a froth appears on the surface. This operation must be carefully watched. It is justified only as a time-saving measure, because if the water reaches 90° C (195° F) the precious gelatins in the skin are lost.

Now the *bacalao* is ready for the final stage of preparation. We will review the method called *a la vizcaina* first, given its excellence and popularity. This sauce essentially consists of a purée of onions and *choricero* peppers, using lard and bacon grease as fat. In general, all red sauces are referred to as *a la vizcaina,* but this is a gross error. After consulting various books and recipes I remain convinced—despite the objections of others—that in the sauce properly called *a la vizcaina,* the only red element should be that of the *choricero* pepper, not tomatoes or sweet peppers. The recipe of the old Bilbao restaurant El Amparo, in my opinion, is not only the most genuine and authentic but also the best.

The El Amparo preparation begins with onions (not sweet) that are chopped and slowly cooked in a casserole with lard. The addition of olive oil is not obligatory. A little parsley, ham, and black pepper may be added. The procedure must be gradual so that any small amount of sugar in the onion does not become caramelized.

After about three hours the mass is considerably reduced, boiling water is added, and it continues to boil for two more hours. It is then strained through a fine colander, and the pulp of *choriceros*— one pepper per slice of fish—is added. (Prior to their addition, the *choriceros* are soaked in water for about twelve hours.) Two hard-cooked egg yolks are mixed with water and a little bacon grease and then added to the mixture. The fish slices are placed in a clay casserole skin side up, without stacking; the purée is added, and the dish is set to simmer slowly until the ingredients become well integrated.

The dish improves upon this slow reheating. It seems as if, in the time lapse between preparation and reheating, the flavors of the sauce and the fish are intensified. With fresh fish the interchange of flavors is quick, but it seems as if the cells of the cured cod are a bit inert due to the tempering process.

There are at least three other great recipes in which tempered cod is used. These authentic Basque preparations are briefly described below.

Cod *al pil-pil* is boiled down by putting slices of fish in the finest olive oil and giving them a treatment similar to that used on young eels. The oil should remain transparent. Because of the simplicity of this method, the fish must be of the highest quality. There exists no sauce which can cover up any inherent defects.

Bacalao ligado, frequently confused with *bacalao al pil-pil,* is made with a sauce that is similar to that of *salsa verde,* which we mention in the section on hake. In the case of cod, some of the water in which the fish has been soaked is added to the dish because the slices of cod do not contain enough water to produce an emulsion despite prolonged soaking.

The third and, for me, the finest method for preparing cod is *bacalao al Club Ranero.* This recipe is very well described in the *Enciclopedia culinaria.* It is a *bacalao ligado* to which is added a fried mixture of green peppers, onions, and tomatoes. The mixture is fried well, but care is taken that the elements do not fall apart. The recipe is a creation of the French chef Caveriviere and, although it is not well known and of foreign origin, I have included it in the recipe section, considering it to be the finest way of preparing cod in the Basque manner.

—from *Alimentos y guisos en la Cocina Vasca,* 1983,
translated from the Spanish by Gretchen Holbert

TABITHA TICKLETOOTH
ON THE DREAD FRIED SOLE

In 1860, when Tabitha Tickletooth's The Dinner Question *was published, the title page featured a photograph of Tabitha, looking a bit grumpy in lace and frilly bonnet. Tabitha's real name was Charles Selby, a popular London comic actor and the first known cross-dressing cookbook author.* —M.K.

THIS IS THE FATAL DISH THAT HAS DRIVEN HUNDREDS OF "well-to-do" husbands to dine at their clubs, and is looked upon by the working man as analogous in its want of toothsomeness with the cold shoulder and sickly hash of washing days. Let me endeavour to show the wives of both conditions of housekeepers, who have hitherto by their want of knowledge in the preparation, and skill in the *pan*-ipulation, of this too-often spoiled homely dish, scared their liege lords from the domestic board, how, as Juliet says of her truant Romeo, to "Lure the tassel-gentles back again."

Choose your fish (if possible) *yourself;* you will easily know if it be fresh (which it *must* be, or the best of cookery will be thrown away) by the edges of the mouth being "pinky" (they are white when stale), and the *fibre,* in kitchen parlance the *flesh,* being elastic. Take care, by the way, that you *have* the identical fish you choose, for fishmongers have been known occasionally to practise sleight of hand in the skinning; beware also, if you buy a "pair," of having one fresh and the other stale—a trick too often played on the unwary.

Preparation.

After skinning, cutting off the tails and fins, and *"gutting,"* which somewhat unpleasant operations are generally performed by the fishmonger, but I would advise you to effect them yourself *about an hour before you begin your cooking,* which will have the double advantage of keeping the "flesh" crisp and preventing the aforesaid sleight of hand, wash, and wipe your fish *quite* dry, with a *dry* clean cloth; then fold them in another cloth, equally clean and dry, dividing each with a fold, and place them aside until the time arrives for putting them in the pan.

Now cut out the crumb of a stale loaf (a penny one will be

sufficient for "a pair" of moderate size),* put it in the centre of a fine
clean towel, gather the corners in one hand (as you would when tying
up a pudding), then with the other hand break up the bread and rub
the pieces together (in the bag formed by the towel) until they are
nearly reduced to powder. This you will find to be a cleaner and more
expeditious method than grating, for the grater is seldom in *working order,* and does not do its work so evenly.

Put the crumbs into a shallow dish, and proceed to the next
manœuvre, which is to beat up an egg (in the same way I have described for the veal cutlet), and the accessories are ready.

Your fire and pan being in *working order* (see cutlet directions), un-
roll the cloth from your fish, give them a *slight sprinkle* of flour from
the dredging box, to absorb any remaining moisture and form a foundation for the egg and bread crumbing, as painters size their canvas
before they commence their colouring, then draw them (you may, if
you prefer it, use a paste brush) first through the beaten-up egg,**
and then through the crumbs, taking care that every part be thoroughly covered with both. Then *half fill your pan* with the best Lucca
oil, lard, or *sweet* beef dripping, and pray attend to the next most important piece of information.

The great secret of frying soles well is to use plenty of fat, *for if you
do not have a full half inch of it above them when they are in the pan, they
will either burn, be fried too brown, or be too greasy.****

Now take them by the heads and tails, and drop them carefully

---

*Doctor Kitchener says, "When you want a great many bread crumbs, divide your loaf
(which should be two days old) into three equal parts: take the middle or crumb piece, the
top and bottom will do for table. *In the usual way of cutting the crust is wasted.*"
**Of course you will use a *fork* for beating up the egg. I think it necessary to mention
this for the benefit of *very young* housewives, many of whom I have known to use a knife or a
spoon; indeed, as may be seen by the following old country adage, such errors have often
been run into:—

"Beat with a knife
Will cause sorrow and strife;
Beat with a spoon
Will make heavy soon;
Beat with a fork
Will make light as a cork."

For "frothing," or making cream for light puddings, you must whip up the egg with a whisk.
***As frying is *boiling in oil* instead of water, the culinary student will see that *by the
fish being thoroughly covered with the fat, every portion of it is exposed at the same moment to
the same action of the heat.* The albumen is *instantly* coagulated on the surfaces, which, with
the egg and bread crumbs, forms a coating which prevents saturation. If, however, one side
be left uncovered, the fat, by bubbling up and dashing over it in *small* quantities, sinks into
the body of the fish, which is thus *gradually saturated,* and rendered so greasy that the flavour
is destroyed, and its rankness is offensive to a delicate stomach.

into the pan (you have been already told how to know if the fat is at the proper temperature), which shake to prevent sticking and burning. The *first* side will take about five minutes, and the *second* from three and a half to four; but to make sure that all is going on well, you may now and then (after giving the pan a shake) lift the fish a little with your slice, to see if it be getting brown. When it is so (mind it must be *light* brown), it is time to turn, which you must do cleverly with your slice. Proceed in the same way with the second side, and then take up; but before dishing, drain for a few minutes on a strainer, or a sheet of white blotting paper, then serve on a *hot* dish (with a strainer at the bottom). Garnish with a sprig or two of crisped parsley,* and then you have your soles *dry, crisp, well coloured, delicately flavoured, and pleasing alike to the eye and the palate.*

Plain melted butter is the *best* sauce (for which see my receipt further on); but many prefer a more expensive one, like the tea at the cockney refreshment establishments at Gravesend, *made with shrimps* (for which also see my receipt).

Anchovy, Hervey, Worcester, or Reading sauces should be on the table to suit all tastes; but I would recommend, if you wish to have the sweet flavour of the fish, nothing but plain melted butter.

When you have dished up your fish, strain the fat you have fried it in, and put it aside in a jar, as it will serve several times (of course for nothing else but fish); but if you can afford it, have *fresh* material every time.

Very large soles should be cut into three or four pieces (before the egg and bread crumbing), or "filleted," which is effected by passing a sharp knife down the centre and the *inner* edge of the fins, and tearing the "flesh" from the bones. This is a French method, pursued in clubs and large establishments; but for homely kitchens it will be found extravagant.

—from *The Dinner Question,* 1860

---

*Parsley is crisped by being taken out of cold water and thrown into the boiling fat for *half an instant,* after you have taken out your fish, which, as the old country housewives say; makes it

"As crisp as glass
And green as grass."

ALEXANDRE DUMAS PÈRE ON CRABS

When trying to understand the peculiar race stereotyping of this entry it is important to remember that Alexandre Dumas was the Haitian-born son of a mulatto general. The father was the offspring of a French aristocrat and a slave girl, and the Dumas family for a time was based in the southwestern Haitian town of Jeremie. No doubt Dumas, in his old age, remembered the popularity of land crabs in the Caribbean.   —M.K.

THERE ARE SEVERAL SPECIES OF CRAB. HOWEVER, ONLY the large crab of Brittany and the *crapelet* of the Channel are worthy to appear on our tables, despite their being difficult to digest; their eggs are better and negroes feed on them. The people of the Antilles live almost exclusively on crabs.

Crabs are cooked in salted water, like lobsters and prawns, with unsalted butter, parsley and a bunch of leeks. Let them cool in their cooking liquid. Then remove carefully the white meat. Take out with a spoon the creamy soft roe and mix it with the cleaned meat, adding watercress, coarse pepper, a little virgin olive oil and a little verjuice. Garnish your platter with the two big claws and serve it as a very elegant *rôt,* especially during Lent.

—from *Le Grand Dictionnaire de Cuisine,* 1873, translated from the French by Alan and Jane Davidson

PETER LUND SIMMONDS
ON LAND CRABS

THE FLESH OF ALL CRUSTACEOUS ANIMALS, ALTHOUGH IN great request, is rather difficult of digestion; and much of it cannot be eaten with impunity. There are classes of persons who are as averse to use shell-fish for food, as a Mahommedan or Mussulman are to partake of pork. It is therefore curious to reflect how, and where, the thousands of tons of crustacea and shell-fish taken to Billingsgate and Hungerford markets are disposed of. Lobsters, cray-fish, prawns, shrimps, oysters, mussels, periwinkles, and whelks, are there every morning in great abundance, and the high retail prices they fetch, show that this description of food must be well relished by the Londoners.

The land crabs of the West Indies are an esteemed delicacy, and the ravenous pigs feed on them with equal avidity to the great danger of their health.

I need not here advert to the migratory habits of the crabs, to their uniting at certain periods in vast numbers, and moving in the most direct course to the sea, marching in squadrons and lines, and halting twice a-day for feeding and repose. These movements may often be seen in Jamaica, and other West Indian islands, where millions on millions string themselves along the coast on progresses from the hills to the sea, and from the sea to the hills.

The reader of Bishop Heber's *Indian Journal* will remember his account of the land crabs at Poonah. 'All the grass land generally through the Deckan swarms with a small land crab, which burrows in the ground, and runs with considerable swiftness, even when encumbered with a bundle of food almost as big as itself. This food is grass or the green stalks of rice; and it is amusing to see them sitting as it were upright, to cut their hay with their sharp pincers, then waddling off with the sheaf to their holes as quietly as their side-long pace will carry them.'

This is not the same land crab of which we are speaking, but it is a graphic picture of the *Gecarcina ruricola*, in its habit of feeding.

They cut up roots and leaves, and feed on the fallen fruit of trees; but we have little more than conjecture for the cause of their occasional deleterious qualities. Impressed with the notion that the crabs owe their hurtful qualities to the fruit of the manchineel tree, Sloane

imagined that he had explained the fatal accidents which have occurred to some persons after eating them, from neglect, or inattentiveness to precaution in cleaning their interior and removing the half
digested particles of the fruit. It has been ascertained that they feed
on such dangerous vegetables of the morass as the *Anona palustris,* a
fruit exceedingly narcotic. It is well enough known that the morass
crab is always to be suspected. The land crabs, however, collect leaves
less for food than to envelop themselves in, when they moult. After
concealment for a time within their burrows, they come forth in those
thin teguments forming a red tense pellicle, similar to wet parchment,
and are more delicate in that condition, and more prized for the table.
The white crabs are the most bulky of the tribe, and are the least esteemed, and the most mistrusted.

Land-crabs, says a Jamaica paper, of March last, are to be seen on
the highways between this, Montego Bay, and Gum Island, just like
bands of soldiers, marching to a battle-point of concentration. This
bids fair to supply the epicure, at an easy rate, with this class of crustacea. It is one of the most remarkable, for it is composed of animals
breathing by means of branchiæ or gills, and yet essentially terrestrial;
so much so, indeed, that they would perish from asphyxia if submerged for any length of time.

I select Browne's account of the habits of the black or mountain
crab, because he resided many years in Jamaica, and seems to have
lost no opportunity of making personal observations; and his remarks
tally with my own experience, from three years' residence in Jamaica.

'These creatures are very numerous in some parts of Jamaica, as
well as in the neighbouring islands, and on the coast of the main continent; they are generally of a dark purple colour, but this often varies,
and you frequently find them spotted, or entirely of another hue. They
live chiefly on dry land, and at a considerable distance from the sea,
which, however, they visit once a year to wash off their spawn, and afterwards return to the woods and higher lands, where they continue
for the remaining part of the season; nor do the young ones ever fail
to follow them, as soon as they are able to crawl. The old crabs generally regain their habitations in the mountains, which are seldom within
less than a mile, and not often above three from the shore, by the latter end of June, and then provide themselves with convenient burrows,
in which they pass the greatest part of the day, going out only at night
to feed. In December and January they begin to be in spawn, and are

then very fat and delicate, but continue to grow richer until the month of May, which is the season for them to wash off their eggs. They begin to move down in February, and are very much abroad in March and April, which seems to be the time for the impregnation of their eggs, being then frequently found fixed together; but the males, about this time, begin to lose their flavour and richness of their juices. The eggs are discharged from the body through two small round holes situated at the sides, and about the middle of the under shell; these are only large enough to admit one at a time, and as they pass they are entangled in the branched capillaments, with which the under side of the apron is copiously supplied, to which they stick by the means of their proper gluten, until the creatures reach the surf, where they wash them all off, and then they begin to return back again to the mountains. It is remarkable that the bag or stomach of this creature changes its juices with the state of the body; and while poor is full of black, bitter, disagreeable fluid, which diminishes as it fattens, and at length acquires a delicate, rich flavour. About the month of July or August, the crabs fatten again and prepare for moulting, filling up their burrows with dry grass, leaves, and abundance of other materials: when the proper period comes, each retires to his hole, shuts up the passage, and remains quite inactive until he gets rid of his old shell, and is fully provided with a new one. How long they continue in this state is uncertain, but the shell is observed to burst, both at the back and sides, to give a passage to the body, and it extracts its limbs from all the other parts gradually afterwards. At this time, the fish is in the richest state, and covered only with a tender membraneous skin, variegated with a multitude of reddish veins; but this hardens gradually after, and becomes soon a perfect shell like the former; it is, however, remarkable, that during this change, there are some stony concretions always formed in the bag, which waste and dissolve gradually, as the creature forms and perfects its new crust. A wonderful mechanism! This crab runs very fast, and always endeavours to get into some hole or crevice on the approach of danger; nor does it wholly depend on its art and swiftness, for while it retreats it keeps both claws expanded, ready to catch the offender if he should come within its reach; and if it succeeds on these occasions, it commonly throws off the claw, which continues to squeeze with incredible force for near a minute after; while he, regardless of the loss, endeavours to make his escape, and to gain a more secure or more lonely covert, contented to renew his limb with

his coat at the ensuing change; nor would it grudge to lose many of
the others to preserve the trunk entire, though each comes off with
more labour and reluctance, as their numbers lessen.'

There are several varieties of land crabs, such as the large white,
the mulatto, the black, and the red. The black and red crabs are most
excellent eating: when in season, the females are full of a rich glutinous substance, called the eggs, which is perfectly delicious. Epicurean planters, in some of the West Indian Islands, have crab pens,
(after the manner of fowl coops,) for fattening these luxuries. The best
manner of dressing them is to pick out all the flesh from the shell,
making it into a stew, with plenty of cayenne pepper, dishing it up in
the shell; in this way they are little inferior to turtle. They are usually
simply boiled, or roasted in the embers, by which they are deprived of
their luscious flavour, and become not only insipid in taste but
disgusting to look at.

In Dominica, they form an ingredient in the well-known 'pepper-
pot.' The black crabs are also picked from their shell, stewed with
Indian kale and pods of chilhies, and eaten with a pudding made of
maize flour or rice; this dish is greatly esteemed by most of the inhabitants.

In the islands and cays of the Bahamas group, land crabs literally
swarm, and afford food for the inhabitants the greatest part of the
year: even the hogs are fed upon them. It is the grey or white kind of
crab, common to Cuba and the Bahamas. In the autumn they are very
fat, and equal in flavour to the black species of Jamaica. They are
found in myriads in all parts, and thought a great delicacy; but a
stranger tires of them in a few weeks.

The black crab is very fat and delicious; but the white and the mulatto crabs are sometimes dangerous, from feeding upon poisonous
leaves and berries. To prevent any evil consequences, the flesh is
washed with lime-juice and water.

Land crabs were probably plentiful in Italy, in the time of Virgil,
for in his *Fourth Georgic* he forbids the roasting of red crabs near an
apiary, the smell of them being disagreeable to the bees.

—from *The Curiosities of Food: Or the Dainties and Delicacies
of Different Nations Obtained from the Animal Kingdom,* 1859

CAROLINE SULLIVAN'S JAMAICAN LAND CRABS

In 1893, Caroline Sullivan, the mistress of a large Jamaican house-hold, wrote a book of traditional cooking. It was the first Jamaican cookbook ever written. —M.K.

Baked Black Crabs

Carefully pick the meat from all the claws and smaller bones of a dozen boiled crabs; this takes a long time and careful picking. Then open the backs and extract the eggs, throwing away the galls and putting aside the black water which is to be added again at the last minute. When all the picking is done, add two tablespoons of butter, a teaspoon of black pepper, a dessertspoon of sauce or pepper vinegar, a little cayenne and some nutmeg to the meat. Mix well, adding salt to taste, and fill as many of the backs as you can, leaving room for a dressing of breadcrumbs on which dabs of butter are placed to moisten. Before putting the meat into the backs, put one or two eggs in each shell and do not forget to mix in the black water, as that has the full black crab flavour. The twelve crabs ought to make ten good crab back fillings.

—from *The Jamaican Cookery Book,* 1893

JOSÉ MARIA BUSCA ISUSI ON EELS

Every year at the mouths of the great Basque rivers, Basques eagerly await the arrival of tiny elvers, the next generation of eel from the Saragossa Sea in the mid-Atlantic. And every year there are fewer and fewer and they are more and more expensive. They have gotten so expensive that many Basque bars offer fake ones made on Japanese machines from pressed white fish. These, of course, in no way other than size resemble the real thing.

While eels are struggling against extinction—not so much from overfishing as pollution—we are only beginning to understand anything about these creatures. As recently as the 1920s it was still

believed that Aristotle was correct in saying that eels did not repro-
duce but somehow regenerated out of mud. Only recently it was dis-
covered that eels, banned in Jewish dietary law because they do not
have scales, actually do have scales but they are imbedded in the
skin. The entire defense system of an eel is to make itself too slimy
and slippery to be grabbed.   —M.K.

THE EEL FAMILY IS A SMALL BUT INTERESTING GROUP FROM our point of view.

The eel *(Anguilla anguilla—anguilla, angira* in the adult state, and *anguilla, txitxardin* in the immature phase) is a most plentiful fish along our coasts and in our rivers. Until recently, its life cycle was unknown, and many legends circulated about it. Today, the mystery of its reproduction has been cleared up.

Immature eels, called elvers, constitute without a doubt one of the dishes most desired by Basques. It is one of the most original recipes in our cuisine. As I said before, there have been fabulous legends concerning these tender little fish, and even today uninformed people argue over whether or not they are actually the young of the eel.

Thanks to the studies of Schmidt, Gandolfi, and other investigators, we know in general the life cycle of the eels. The eels of our rivers begin a fall journey toward the sea when they have reached a certain stage in their development. The journey is of a nuptial nature and ends in the Sargasso Sea, where the birth of the young takes place. The newborn eels, having the shape of tiny laurel leaves, begin the arduous journey toward the rivers their parents abandoned.

This northward migration begins in the spring, and during the first summer they pass longitude 50°W. In the second summer they move toward the Azores. By now their initial size upon migrating (less than half an inch) has increased five times. During the third summer they reach our coasts and are ready to enter the rivers with the first autumn freshets. At this stage their shape is not flattened but rather cylindrical. This is the exact moment at which the culinary genius of our Basque fishermen takes over.

The eels and elvers are plentiful in all of Europe, with the exception of the Black Sea and its tributary rivers. Yet I believe that only in our country have people dared to prepare and consume a dish which resembles a bunch of worms. Eels have very tasty meat. They are more highly appreciated by the Basques of the Ebro basin than by the Cantabrian Basques.

Elvers constitute a very complete meal—it should be noted that the animal is eaten whole—with an agreeable physical sensation to the palate and a very mild taste. This flavor is easily perceived and quite agreeable in boiled elvers, but in the common form of preparation—*al pil-pil*—the unique taste is significantly masked by garlic, oil, and hot red pepper. In order that elvers be agreeable to the palate, they must be prepared with utmost care, and strict rules of procedure must be followed.

Elvers must be alive and then must be killed quickly. To accomplish this they are dropped in water made strongly nicotinic (by the addition of tobacco). Once dead, they are carefully cleaned until the abundant mucus which covers them is removed. This removal of mucus is essential, because upon cooking, the mucus would congeal into clots, resulting in a significant loss to the overall quality of the dish.

Once properly cleaned, they are "coagulated" in salted water at a full boil. The word "coagulate" is used because elvers are like transparent gelatin. In a few minutes, through the action of the heat, they are converted into the white or black-white animals known throughout the world. Gradations in whiteness are due to a simple increase in pigmentation as the elvers proceed upstream through the rivers.

Elvers are generally sold in the markets in this cleaned and cooked state. In the last phase of preparation, they are first submerged in salty, tepid water for a final cleansing. They are then placed on clean cloths to be drained of excess water but at the same time kept moist.

Olive oil of the finest quality is placed in a *cazuela* (clay casserole) and pieces of garlic are browned in it. The casserole is then taken off the heat. Finely chopped red pepper is added, and when the oil has lowered in temperature the elvers are added.

The clay casserole is immediately placed on the fire. The elvers cannot begin to fry yet, because the abundant liquid that the elvers emit must first evaporate. Soon a subtle, pleasant crackling begins, and when the bubbling has spread throughout the casserole the dish is ready to be served.

The *cazuela* in which the elvers are traditionally prepared and served is made of fired clay. As was mentioned earlier, this casserole retains heat better than one made of iron.

There is a difference among the various eel catches. Inhabitants along the various rivers engage in great discussions concerning the quality of elvers captured in different areas. The eels that enter our rivers are without a doubt all of a common origin and were comparable before the Basque Country was industrialized. Today each river has its own specific refuse, and perhaps as a result, the different eel populations may vary in quality.

For me, the true difference is due to distinct methods of preparation. The young eel is such a delicate organism that it cannot be handled in great quantities without harm. Success lies in not heaping them up and overcooking them, events which occur too easily when there is an excess of handling in the process.

There is an extravagant Basque recipe for hake, called *medallones de merluza euskal etxea,* in which elvers serve as a side dish. Normally, however, every Basque considers it culinary heresy to eat elvers in any way other than *al pil-pil.*

Adult eels are prepared in *salsa verde* and constitute an exquisite dish in the season of peas, asparagus, and artichokes. In the Ribera de Navarra region they are eaten with immature beans *(pochas)* and are also prepared with tomato and pepper. Eel blood contains a toxic substance called ichthyotoxin. This blood is often given mixed with wine to alcoholics to aid in their cure. It loses its toxicity through the action of heat.

The conger eel *(Conger conger, congrio, itxar)* is plentiful on our coasts and in our markets. Its meat is good, but half of its bulk is full of spines. This proves considerably inconvenient for serving it in slices. It can be used in the making of soup. Conger eel in *salsa verde* is excellent. Long ago it was eaten much more frequently.

—from *Alimentos y guisos en la cocina Vasca* 1983,
translated from the Spanish by Gretchen Holbert

ERNEST HEMINGWAY
ON FISH IN THE SEINE

I WOULD WALK ALONG THE QUAIS WHEN I HAD FINISHED work or when I was trying to think something out. It was easier to think if I was walking and doing something or seeing people doing something that they understood. At the head of the Île de la Cité below the Pont Neuf where there was the statue of Henri Quatre, the island ended in a point like the sharp bow of a ship and there was a small park at the water's edge with fine chestnut trees, huge and spreading, and in the currents and back waters that the Seine made flowing past, there were excellent places to fish. You went down a stairway to the park and watched the fishermen there and under the great bridge. The good spots to fish changed with the height of the river and the fishermen used long, jointed, cane poles but fished with very fine leaders and light gear and quill floats and expertly baited the piece of water that they fished. They always caught some fish, and often they made excellent catches of the dace-like fish that were called *goujon.* They were delicious fried whole and I could eat a plateful. They were plump and sweet-fleshed with a finer flavor than fresh sardines even, and were not at all oily, and we ate them bones and all.

One of the best places to eat them was at an open-air restaurant built out over the river at Bas Meudon where we would go when we had money for a trip away from our quarter. It was called La Pêche Miraculeuse and had a splendid white wine that was a sort of Muscadet. It was a place out of a Maupassant story with the view over the river as Sisley had painted it. You did not have to go that far to eat *goujon*. You could get a very good *friture* on the Île St.-Louis.

I knew several of the men who fished the fruitful parts of the Seine between the Île St.-Louis and the Place du Verte Galente and sometimes, if the day was bright, I would buy a liter of wine and a piece of bread and some sausage and sit in the sun and read one of the books I had bought and watch the fishing.

Travel writers wrote about the men fishing in the Seine as though they were crazy and never caught anything; but it was serious and productive fishing. Most of the fishermen were men who had small pensions, which they did not know then would become worthless with inflation, or keen fishermen who fished on their days or half-days off from work. There was better fishing at Charenton, where the Marne came into the Seine, and on either side of Paris, but there was very good fishing in Paris itself. I did not fish because I did not have the tackle and I preferred to save my money to fish in Spain. Then too I never knew when I would be through working, nor when I would have to be away, and I did not want to become involved in the fishing which had its good times and its slack times. But I followed it closely and it was interesting and good to know about, and it always made me happy that there were men fishing in the city itself, having sound, serious fishing and taking a few *fritures* home to their families.

With the fishermen and the life on the river, the beautiful barges with their own life on board, the tugs with their smokestacks that folded back to pass under the bridges, pulling a tow of barges, the great elms on the stone banks of the river, the plane trees and in some places the poplars, I could never be lonely along the river. With so many trees in the city, you could see the spring coming each day until a night of warm wind would bring it suddenly in one morning. Sometimes the heavy cold rains would beat it back so that it would seem that it would never come and that you were losing a season out of your life. This was the only truly sad time in Paris because it was unnatural. You expected to be sad in the fall. Part of you died each year when the leaves fell from the trees and their branches were bare against the wind and the cold, wintry light. But you knew there would always be the spring, as you knew the river would flow again after it was frozen.

When the cold rains kept on and killed the spring, it was as though a young person had died for no reason.

In those days, though, the spring always came finally but it was frightening that it had nearly failed.

—from *A Moveable Feast,* 1964

CHAPTER THIRTEEN

Poultry, Fowl, and Other Ill-Fated Birds

ANTHIMUS ON CHICKEN, PEACOCKS, AND OTHER DOMESTIC POULTRY

WE NOW COME TO FOWL. LOOK OUT FOR FATTENED PHEAS-ants and geese, for their breasts are agreeable because they are fed. The parts that consist of white meat only are more suitable. Do not eat their hind parts, because they burden the stomach, since they are the product not of natural but of forced feeding.

Hens and plump chickens, so long as they are not fattened, are good provided that in winter they have been killed two days before and in summer the evening before eating. Birds that are prepared while they still give off a suitable smell make for better eating, particularly their breasts and wings, because those parts nourish good humours and blood. The hind parts of all birds are suitable particularly for healthy people, and this applies to these and all the other parts. Medical writers pay attention to those parts which are most important among the different sorts of food available to people living a luxurious life and tasting of a variety of foodstuffs. It is on behalf of these people that this scheme of diet has been written, and especially for those who are weak in body. For if one item mixed among various wholesome ingredients at a meal is raw and not suitable, it ruins all the other good ingredients and prevents the stomach from digesting properly. The fowl just mentioned are suitable both if cooked well in a sauce and if steamed, provided they are cooked immediately after being killed. They are also suitable roasted, so long as they are roasted carefully at a distance from the hearth.

If you can procure peacocks, let those that are older be killed five or six days beforehand, and make sure that they are hung until they give off a good smell, because they have that sort of meat. They should be eaten after being cooked either in pieces or whole in a sauce. If you wish, you

Berenice Abbott, *Chicken Market, 55 Hester Street*, 1937

can add a little honey and pepper to the sauce after it has been cooked. Smaller or younger peacocks can be killed one or two days beforehand.

—from *On the Observance of Foods,* sixth century A.D.,
translated from the Latin by Mark Grant

CALIPH AL-MA'MUN ON CHICKEN AND PISTACHIOS

This Baghdad recipe was attributed to the household of the Caliph al-Ma'mun, who died in A.D. 833. —M.K.

BOIL CHICKENS AND CUT THEIR MEAT INTO STRIPS. WASH rice, dry it, pick it over, mill it fine, and then cook it with fresh milk, syrup, and [lamb] tail fat, moistening with each liquid until it is nearly done. Its completion is that the chicken breasts are thrown on it after their meat is pounded fine. Resume cooking and scent it with rosewater and musk and sprinkle with three ounces of pounded pistachios and take it up. The measurements: rice, a pound; syrup, three ounces; tail fat, three ounces; milk, two pounds; pistachios, three ounces; fat chickens, four.

—from *Kitab Wasf al-At'ima al-Mu'tada,*
The Description of Familiar Foods, 1373,
translated from the Arabic by Charles Perry

HANNAH GLASSE ON TURKEY

To roast a Turky.

The best Way to roast a Turky is to loosen the Skin on the Breast of the Turky, and fill it with Force-Meat made thus: Take a Quarter of a Pound of Beef Sewet, as many Crumbs of Bread, a little Lemon-peel, an Anchovy, some Nutmeg, Pepper, Parsley, and a little Thyme; chop and beat them all well together, mix them with the Yolk of an Egg, and stuff up the Breast; when you have no Sewet Butter will do: Or you may make your Force-Meat thus: Spread Bread and Butter thin, and grate some Nutmeg over it; when you have enough roll it up, and stuff the Breast of the Turky; then roast it of a fine Brown, but be sure to pin some white Paper on the Breast till it is near enough. You must have good Gravy in the Dish, and Bread-sauce made thus: Take a good Piece of Crumb, put it into a Pint of Water, with a Blade or two of Mace, two or three Cloves, and some whole Pepper; boil it up five or six Times, then with a Spoon take out the Spice, and pour off the Water (you may boil an Onion in it if you please) then beat up the Bread with a good Piece of Butter and a little Salt; or Onion Sauce made thus: Take some Onions, peel them, and cut them into thin Slices, and boil them Half an Hour in Milk and Water; then drain the Water from them, and beat them up with a good Piece of Butter; shake a little Flour in, and stir it all together with a little Cream, if you have it (or Milk will do) put the Sauce into Boats, and garnish with Lemon.

Another Way to make Sauce: Take Half a Pint of Oysters, strain the Liquor, and put the Oysters with the Liquor into a Sauce-pan, with a Blade or two of Mace; let them just plump, then pour in a Glass of White Wine, let it boil once, and thicken it with a Piece of Butter roll'd in Flour: Serve this up in a Bason by itself, with good Gravy in the Dish, for every Body don't love Oyster Sauce. This makes a pretty Side Dish for Supper, or a Corner Dish of a Table for Dinner. If you chase it in the Dish, add Half a Pint of Gravy to it, and boil it up together. This Sauce is good either with boiled or roasted Turkies or Fowls; but you may leave the Gravy out, adding as much Butter as will do for Sauce, and garnishing with Lemon.

To make Mock Oyster-Sauce, either for Turkies or Fowls boil'd.

Force the Turkies or Fowls as above, and make your Sauce thus: Take a Quarter of a Pint of Water, an Anchovy, a Blade or two of Mace, a

Piece of Lemon-peel, and five or six whole Peppercorns; boil these together, then strain them, add as much Butter with a little Flour as will do for Sauce; let it boil, and lay Sausages round the Fowl or Turky. Garnish with Lemon.

—from *The Art of Cookery, Made Plain and Easy*, 1747

WAVERLEY ROOT ON GUINEA FOWL

Food, Waverley Root's encyclopedia, was a later work after his better-known The Food of France *and* The Food of Italy. *In the tradition of Dumas's* Le Grand Dictionnaire, *it is completely arbitrary and whimsical, full of the writer's own personal prejudices, which is exactly the way good food writing should be.*   —M.K.

EVER SINCE OUR POULTRY RAISERS SUCCEEDED IN TAKING the taste out of turkey, the most flavorful bird of the barnyard has been the guinea fowl. This is perhaps because the guinea, though it lives on farms, has not resigned itself to being domesticated, and has consequently not completely lost the dark flesh of wild birds and their gamey taste; it is frequently compared with pheasant.

As everyone who has raised guineas (I have) knows, they are virtually wild animals. They like to roost on the topmost branches of the tallest trees, and display no interest in coming down to be killed for dinner or for the market. They descend when grain is offered, but remain so wary that it is difficult to approach them; one suspicious movement from the farmer, and the whole flock is off. They can get along without his grain, for guineas are perfectly capable of foraging for themselves. Their acceptance of foods is wide, ranging from ants' eggs, for which they will tear anthills open, to carrion. A French nature writer has reported seeing several guineas devouring, vulturelike, a large dead fox; and indeed guineas, with their bare unfeathered heads, do seem at times to resemble vultures; there is even an East African species called *Acryllium vulturinum*.

One way of dealing with the difficulty of killing guineas is that

which is sometimes utilized in southwestern France, shooting them down from their trees, but this is hardly practical for anyone handling guineas on a large scale; you bag one, and that is the last you see of the others for several days. Another solution is to keep them caged (in a cage the size of a small aviary, for they require space); but they will not lay in confinement, though they do so prolifically when free. Unlike many wild birds, which produce only one clutch a year, guinea hens lay continuously from May until cold weather sets in; but they do not lay in a fashion favorable to farmers. They hide their nests in hollows scratched out of the ground under bushes or other shelter where they are practically unfindable.

As though this were not enough to discourage the raising of guinea fowl, they are also irascible and noisy. They cow other barnyard birds, even turkeys, though turkeys are much larger, and keep up an incessant nerve-wracking screeching, which has been described as sounding like the noise made by a rusty windmill. This racket is said to have the advantage of making it possible to distinguish the cocks from the hens (their plumage is identical), for while one sex cries *pot-rack, pot-rack, pot-rack,* the other repeats *rack-pot, rack-pot, rack-pot;* but this means of identification has never worked for me.

One result of the guinea's self-serving savagery seems to be its freedom from disease, in striking contrast to poultry which has benefited from the tinkering of man, like chickens and turkeys, which are subject to an interminable list of diseases and sometimes seem to take positive pleasure in succumbing to them. Despite this lone advantage, the difficulties have discouraged most poultry raisers (among whom was Thomas Jefferson, who was fond of them), so that, except in France, almost nobody attempts to produce guineas for a mass market. They appear as luxuries in high-priced restaurants which buy them directly from small-scale producers who aim exclusively at such outlets. This accounts for the fact that very few new varieties have been developed by breeders, the most important being white guineas, which, like white turkeys, seem to have been created to cater to a popular delusion that whiteness, a symbol of purity, guarantees finer flavor.

In the days when Europeans were bestowing names on unfamiliar foods, any exotic product was apt to be ascribed more or less at random to any exotic locality, of which only a few, vaguely localized, were recognizable to the general public. The guinea fowl was an exception, identified correctly from the beginning as an African bird. Its origin is usually given as West Africa, which is, of course, where Guinea is located. The area is very probably the birthplace of *Numida meleagris galatea,* from which the imperfectly domesticated modern bird is supposed to have descended. Either this bird had acquired a wider range in classical times than is attributed to it now, or it was some other of the score of African species which the ancients, not given to fine nomenclatural distinctions, consumed. They had not adventured as far as Guinea, but they imported birds from North Africa. Greece, which knew them by 500 B.C., presumably received them from Egypt, the source of many of her foreign foods. Significantly, this bird is known in Italian today as *gallina faraona,* Pharaoh's hen; but the Romans, when the guinea hen became an appreciated item on upper-class menus, apparently preferred to bring them in from nearer regions of North Africa, for they called them Numidian hens or Carthaginian hens—except when the host was putting on the dog, for a wedding banquet, say, when they might appear under such fancy names as Phrygian chicken (used on one Pompeiian menu which has come down to us) or Bohemian chicken, even more impressive, since Bohemia in those days was exquisitely exotic, a place of which Romans had heard but had never seen.

The guinea fowl never got down to a common level in the ancient world, unlike the chicken, so when the Roman Empire disappeared, the guinea went with it. It does not seem to have reappeared until the sixteenth century, when merchants from Portugal, by then in control of Guinea, started selling them to France, where they were first called, *gyunettes* or *poules de Guinée* and then, incorrectly, *poules de Turquie* or *poules d'Inde,* a name transferred shortly thereafter, with equal inexactitude, to the American turkey. The French naturalist Pierre Belon wrote in 1555 that guinea fowls "had already so multiplied in the houses of the nobles that they had become quite common." This disposes of the often repeated assertion, by which, in the past, I have been taken in myself, that it was Catherine de' Medici who introduced the guinea hen to France; actually the bird reached there before the marrying Medicis did. That it was indeed the Portuguese who brought the bird to France is attested to by its name in French today, *pintade,* from the Portuguese *pintada,* "painted," or, in this case, "splotched," referring to the round spots which speckle the guinea's plumage. A Greek legend explained that the sisters of Meleager, son of the king of Calydon, were so grief-stricken when their brother died that they broke into uncontrollable weeping, which ended only when they were changed into guinea hens; the spots are their tears. Hence the ancient name *meleagris* for this bird, preserved by modern taxonomists in the scientific names given to many of its species.

The guinea hen was also appreciated in Italy in Renaissance times; from Africa and Europe it has now spread all over the world. The first to reach the Far East may have been those which Pierre Poivre took to Cochin-China when, in 1749, he was negotiating for the right to open a French trading counter there. Among the presents he gave the king of Cochin-China were some guinea fowl, which according to his account were at that time unknown there. In the New World, they seem to have appeared first in Haiti, probably imported along with slaves bought in Guinea. Live poultry was often taken aboard ships, to provide fresh food during long voyages; Africa could not have provided chickens in those days, but it could offer guineas. We may suppose that the surplus birds of the ship's stores, still alive at the end of the trip, were taken ashore.

I notice with a certain surprise that many writers describe the guinea fowl as ugly. Despite its vulturelike head, it has always struck me as a notably decorative bird. Some of its varieties are so handsomely patterned that I can imagine their having been designed by Van Gogh.

—from *Food,* 1980

F. T. Cheng on Bird's Nest

I found F. T. Cheng's little book for £5 in one of those small and dusty Charing Cross used-book shops. The title in English is Musings of a Chinese Gourmet, *which is an apt description of the book. The cover also has Chinese characters on it that mean* A Thesis on Living. *The book was published in 1954 and the author, F. T. Cheng, was the former Chinese ambassador to Britain. This insightful book is not as obscure as I at first thought. From time to time, I find quotes from this book in British food books.* —M.K.

THEREFORE, THERE IS NOTHING VERY EXTRAORDINARY in that the Chinese should like shark's fin, "Bird's Nest," and other "odd" things, which often only mean delicacies undiscovered. The shark, indeed, is a very ferocious animal, but its fin must be most harmless and the cleanest part of a fish. Well prepared, it is not only most delicious to the palate but also most wholesome to the system, because of the high percentage of calorie, protein, calcium, and phosphorus it contains, as already mentioned in the preceding chapter. It is the same with "Bird's Nest." The word "nest" is, perhaps, misleading. Some people may imagine that "Bird's Nest Soup" is soup made simply from a bird's nest pulled down from a tree grown, perhaps, in one's own garden, boiled in water with or without the bird or its young, and then served with pepper and salt! The Chinese, who have survived for thousands of years and have contributed so many fundamental discoveries and inventions to the world, should be credited with a better sense than that. The so-called "Bird's Nest" is no more and no less than predigested protein from some kind of sea weed gathered from the sea—not by the ordinary swallows as commonly believed, but by a particular specie of petrel of the *Procellariidae* family, living not on land but along the cliffs of the Pacific islands—and digested by the alkaline fluid of the mouths of these birds before using it for building their nests. As food it possesses a delicate flavour, which will be brought out by a tasty *bouillon,* and is specially rich in protein, particularly good for those who suffer from ulcerated stomach, as evidenced by Dr. Cotui's recent discovery of the use of predigested protein for the treatment of that ailment. After all, Chinese taste for rare delicacies is by no means isolated. It finds a counterpart in the menu of a no less known restaurant than the Sports Afield Club, New York City, such as:

Mexican Armadillo (for 4)	$100.00
Beaver & Beaver Tail	27.00
South American Boar	18.00
Caribou	75.00
Australian Kangaroo	50.00
Muskrat	62.00
Porcupine	55.00
Ostrich Eggs	35.00
Water Buffalo	13.00

Judged by the prices charged, these must be highly regarded as delicacies. With this observation, what are relished by the Chinese may now be discussed. . . .

"Bird's Nest."

Its real nature and nutritious properties have been noted. Its preparation is very simple. For one conventional dish use about three ounces, because it is very light. Soak it in lukewarm water for three hours. Pick out all the feathers that are found in it and wash it in cold water gently. When this is done it is clean and ready for cooking. Then cook it in one of the following ways in a *double saucepan:*

(a) Stuff it into a whole chicken and cook it with seven cups of water until the chicken becomes quite tender. Then salt it to taste and serve it with the soup and chicken.

(b) Cook it with plain but highly tasty chicken broth (enough for 10–12 persons) for two hours over a medium fire. Then salt it to taste and serve the whole thing as soup. As soon as it is dished, sprinkle over it two dessertspoonfuls of finely minced lean ham.

(c) Cook it as in *(b)*, salt it to taste, and thicken it with a little cornflour. At the same time mince finely an ounce or so of the white meat of a chicken, put this in two tablespoonfuls of cold water, beat up the white of one egg, and mix these well in a liquid form. When the soup is to be served, but not a moment before, pour the mixture into it, stirring well the whole thing. Take care that, before pouring the mixture

into the soup, the fire is turned off; otherwise the minced chicken would be overdone and the soup would taste coarse. Lastly, when the soup is actually dished, sprinkle over it two dessertspoonfuls of finely minced lean ham. In taking "Bird's nest" soup made in this way, it is recommended to add a little Chekiang vinegar, if any, which will enhance the taste.

(d) "Bird's nest" can be used as a sweet, in which case it is cooked in plain water for two hours over a medium fire and then sugared to taste. Crystal sugar should be used.

It is interesting to note that "Bird's nest" was known to the Chinese as a delicacy earlier than shark's fin. When the Imperial Palace in Peking was taken over from the last Manchu Monarch, much unused "Bird's nest" was found in the Provision Room with other food materials but practically no shark's fin.

—from *Musings of a Chinese Gourmet,* 1954

LUDWIG BEMELMANS
ON POULETS DE BRESSE

WHEN WE CAME THE NEXT DAY TO VIENNE, WE WANTED TO stop at the famous Pyramide, once, and perhaps still, one of the great temples of gastronomy. On that day the chef-proprietor of the establishment was in an off mood or else the publicity he had received had caused him to suffer from *folie de grandeur:* he had several near nervous breakdowns in our presence, screamed in his kitchen and behaved in his dining room like a police official rather than a restaurateur. It is as damaging to a low bistro as to the best of restaurants when the proprietor discovers that he is a rare and remarkable man with his pots and bottles. Upon seeing his picture in various publications and reading a description of himself he becomes obese with acquired personality.

The specialties of the house here, besides a fine dish consisting of the tails of crayfish au gratin, is the chicken from Bresse. I have followed pigs on stilts looking for truffles and I know a little about the growing of grapes and the bottling of wine and the making of brandy, but the raising of chickens of Bresse is still a remote subject to me. It must, however, be a mammoth industry in France; for while you get hams from half a dozen places and even the sardine cans bear the names of various regions, the chicken served in a good restaurant in France is always from Bresse, and it is an excellent bird, as everyone will agree.

I was able to arrest the attention of the proprietor of the Pyramide long enough to ask him about the chicken. He told me: "Of chickens I can tell you that they are never better than from September to February. Their meat then is well made and is not insipid. After February, the meat is not as tender nor as white. These we have now are young ones, four or five months old, and I am not too happy about them, for they have no character. We use them only for entrees. For the roasting chicken we must wait; it must be older. As for Bresse, I know as much about it as you do. I suppose Bresse is to chicken what Cologne is to water—some Eau de Cologne is made in Cologne, some in Paris. Some chickens come from Bresse; some people raise their own chickens of Bresse; some poulets de Bresse are raised right here in Vienne. At least those I serve are."

The chicken we were served was cooked in cream, flavored with estragon, and it was so-so. The wine, not being subject to the temper of cooks nor the season of chickens, was of the very best.

—from Ludwig Bemelmans, *La Bonne Table*, 1964

MARJORIE KINNAN RAWLINGS
ON KILLING BIRDS

I AM STILL TORN ON THE MATTER OF BIRD-SHOOTING. I dread the day when conscience shall triumph over palate. There is no more delicious food than quail or dove, the one meat white, the other dark. I dress them whole, and they must be picked, never skinned. I stuff them with buttered crumbs and pecans, dip them in flour and brown them in butter. I place them then in a casserole, pour over them the browned butter to which a little hot water has been added, add an eighth of a cup of sherry for every bird, cover and bake slowly until meltingly tender. I prefer as accompaniments a Chablis or even a Sauterne for quail, and Burgundy for doves. I like to serve with them soft-cooked grits, small crisp biscuits, wild grape or wild plum jelly, whole baby beets warmed in orange juice and butter with grated orange peel, carrot souffle, a tomato aspic salad, and tangerine sherbet for a dessert. I make the tangerine sherbet by any good orange sherbet recipe, substituting tangerine juice for orange juice, and using more lemon juice and less sugar syrup. I cannot recommend the dessert, delicate as it is, unless one has one's own tangerine trees. It takes two large water buckets of tangerines to make sherbet for eight.

In the matter of cooking ducks, I am in violent opposition to the pretendedly Epicurean school of raw bloody duck whisked through a duck press. The advice to "run your duck through a very hot oven" leaves me shuddering. I prefer my thoroughly done, moist, crumbling duck to any dripping, rubbery slices, fit only for the jaws of a dinosaur. When my flock of Mallards has an unusually successful season, so that I am fairly over-run with ducks, and the feed-bill equals that of four mules, I am sometimes obliged to decimate their numbers. My friends hint the year around that I have too many ducks. When I give in to them and announce a duck dinner, I find myself unable to eat, and must have a poached egg on the side. But on these sad occasions, I am certain of the age of the ducks, and I roast the young ones quickly. When I am uncertain, as one must be, with wild killed ducks, I take no chances, and steam them until tender, then proceed with the roasting, basting often with butter if the wild ducks have little or no fat. The rest of the menu is: claret; fried finger-strips of grits; sweet potato orange baskets; small whole white onions, braised; hot sherried grapefruit; tiny hot cornmeal muffins; a tossed salad of endive dressed with finely chopped chives, marjoram, basil, thyme and French dressing made with tarragon vinegar; for dessert, grape-juice ice cream.

—from *Cross Creek,* 1942

RAWLINGS'S BLACKBIRD PIE

THIS DISH IS ILLEGAL, SINCE THE TAKING OF RED-WINGED blackbirds is forbidden by Federal law—which I discovered probably just in time to save myself a term in the penitentiary. But I made it often in lean days at the Creek, and since it is so delicious, and since any small birds may be substituted for the red-winged blackbirds, such as ricebirds (legal in season), quail, dove, or one-pound-size chickens, I list it.

Brown the whole dressed birds in one tablespoon butter to every bird. Cover with hot water. Add one bay leaf, one teaspoon salt and a dash of pepper. Simmer until tender, tightly covered. Add one carrot cut in strips and two small whole onions to every bird. Simmer fifteen minutes. Add one small raw potato, diced, to every bird. Simmer fifteen minutes more. More hot water may be needed, as gravy should cover mixture. Thicken gravy with one tablespoon flour dissolved in two tablespoons cold water to every cup of gravy. Place mixture in casserole, add two tablespoons chopped parsley, one-quarter cup sherry to every bird, and cover with biscuit crust as for steak and kidney pie. Bake in hot oven twenty minutes or until well browned. Four birds per person are right, so that for six people, one has truly "four and twenty blackbirds baked in a pie."

—from *Cross Creek Cookery,* 1942

CHAPTER FOURTEEN

The Meat of the Matter

PLUTARCH ON EATING MEAT

CAN YOU REALLY ASK WHAT REASON PYTHAGORAS HAD FOR abstaining from flesh? For my part I rather wonder both by what accident and in what state of soul or mind the first man who did so, touched his mouth to gore and brought his lips to the flesh of a dead creature, he who set forth tables of dead, stale bodies and ventured to call food and nourishment the parts that had a little before bellowed and cried, moved and lived. How could his eyes endure the slaughter when throats were slit and hides flayed and limbs torn from limb? How could his nose endure the stench? . . .

But you who live now, what madness, what frenzy drives you to the pollution of shedding blood, you who have such a superfluity of necessities? Why slander the earth by implying that she cannot support you? Why impiously offend law-giving Demeter and bring shame upon Dionysus, lord of the cultivated vine, the gracious one, as if you did not receive enough from their hands? Are you not ashamed to mingle domestic crops with blood and gore? You call serpents and panthers and lions savage, but you yourselves, by your own foul slaughters, leave them no room to outdo you in cruelty; for their slaughter is their living, yours is a mere appetizer.

It is certainly not lions and wolves that we eat out of self-defence;

on the contrary, we ignore these and slaughter harmless, tame creatures without stings or teeth to harm us, creatures that, I swear, Nature appears to have produced for the sake of their beauty and grace. . . .

What a terrible thing it is to look on when the tables of the rich are spread, men who employ cooks and spicers to groom the dead! And it is even more terrible to look on when they are taken away, for more is left than has been eaten. So the beasts died for nothing! There are others who refuse when the dishes are already set before them and will not have them cut into or sliced. Though they bid spare the dead, they did not spare the living.

We declare, then, that it is absurd for them to say that the practice of flesh-eating is based on Nature. For that man is not naturally carnivorous is, in the first place, obvious from the structure of his body. A man's frame is in no way similar to those creatures who were made for flesh-eating: he has no hooked beak or sharp nails or jagged teeth, no strong stomach or warmth of vital fluids able to digest and assimilate a heavy diet of flesh. It is from this very fact, the evenness of our teeth, the smallness of our mouths, the softness of our tongues, our possession of vital fluids too inert to digest meat that Nature disavows our eating of flesh. If you declare that you are naturally designed for such a diet, then first kill for yourself what you want to eat. Do it, however, only through your own resources . . .

For what sort of dinner is not costly for which a living creature loses its life? Do we hold a life cheap? I do not yet go so far as to say that it may well be the life of your mother or father or some friend or child, as Empedocles declared. Yet it does, at least, possess some perception, hearing, seeing, imagination, intelligence, which last every creature receives from Nature to enable it to acquire what is proper for it and to evade what is not. Do but consider which are the philosophers who serve the better to humanize us: those who bid us eat our children and friends and fathers and wives after their death, or Pythagoras and Empedocles who try to accustom us to act justly toward other creatures also? You ridicule a man who abstains from eating mutton. But are we, they will say, to refrain from laughter when we see you slicing off portions from a dead father or mother and sending them to absent friends and inviting those who are at hand, heaping their plates with flesh.

—from *Moralia,* first century A.D.,
translated from the Greek by Harold Chermiss and William Helmbold

CLAUDE LÉVI-STRAUSS ON BOILED VS. ROASTED

BOILED FOOD IS LIFE, ROAST FOOD DEATH. FOLKLORE THE world over offers countless examples of the cauldron of immortality; but there is no indication anywhere of a spit of immortality. A rite performed by the Cree Indians of Canada conveys very clearly the cosmic totality attributed to boiled food. The Cree believed that the Creator told humans that the first berries to be picked had to be boiled. Then the bowl had to be held first towards the sun, who was asked to ripen the berries, then towards the thunder who was asked for rain, and finally towards the earth, who was asked to bring forth her fruits. For the Ojibwa too, boiled meat had a relationship to the order of the universe; although they usually cooked squirrels by spitting the carcases and roasting them in the flames, they purposely boiled them when rain was needed. In this case, the roast and the boiled are given differential functions and their combination constitutes a culinary universe, which is a miniature reflection of the cosmos. Perhaps a similar interpretation would be appropriate for the unusual Welsh recipe which involved stuffing roast goose with boiled ox-tongue and then encasing it in a layer of forcemeat, inside a pastry crust; the dish was supposed to last all through Christmas week.

—from *The Origin of Table Manners,* 1968,
translated from the French by John and Doreen Weightman

ALEXANDRE DUMAS *PÈRE* ON BEEFSTEAK

I REMEMBER SEEING THE BIRTH OF BEEFSTEAK IN FRANCE, after the 1815 campaign, when the English stayed in Paris for two or three years. Until then our cuisine and theirs had been just as separate as our points of view. It was therefore not without a certain trepidation that one saw beefsteak trying to introduce itself slyly into our kitchens. Yet, we are an eclectic people and without prejudice. So, as soon as we had realized that, in spite of 'coming from the Greeks, it was not poisoned,' before we held out our plates, and gave beefsteak its citizenship papers.

And yet, there is still something which separates English from French beefsteak. We prepare our beefsteak with a piece of fillet from the sirloin *(aloyau),* whereas our neighbours take something which we call *sous-noix* of beef, that is to say rumpsteak, for theirs. This cut of beef is always more tender there than it would be here, because the English feed their cattle better than we do, and slaughter their cattle younger than we do in France. They therefore take this cut of beef, and slice it in thick pieces of about half an inch, flatten these a little, and cook them on a cast-iron plate made expressly for the purpose, using ordinary coal instead of charcoal. Real beef fillet should be put on a thoroughly heated grill, with live coals, and should be turned only once in order to conserve its juices, which then marry up with the maître d'hôtel sauce. This part of English beef (and, to verify this, every time I go to England I eat it with renewed pleasure) is infinitely more flavourful than the part from which we take our steaks. One must eat it in an English tavern, sautéed with Madeira wine, or with anchovy butter, or on a bed of cress, well sprinkled with vinegar. I would recommend that it should be eaten with gherkins, if there were even one nation in the world which knew how to make gherkins.

As for French beefsteak, the best sauce to accompany it is maître d'hôtel, because one can sense the predominance of the flavour of the herbs and the lemon. But there is one observation which I will permit myself to make. I see our cooks flattening their steaks on the kitchen table with the flat side of the meat chopper; I think that they are committing a grave sin, and that they are causing certain nutritional elements to spurt out of the meat, elements which would play their role well in the process of mastication.

In general, ruminant animals are better in England than in France because, while living, they are treated with quite particular care. Nothing equals those quarters of beef, cooked whole, which are rolled along on little carts like railway wagons between the habitués of English taverns. Those pieces of beef, fat interlarded with lean, which one cuts for oneself as one wishes, from a portion of an animal weighing one hundred pounds! There is nothing to compare with them for exciting the appetite.

—from *Le Grand Dictionnaire de Cuisine,* 1873,
translated from the French by Alan and Jane Davidson

ANTHIMUS ON EATING RAW MEAT

PERHAPS THERE WILL BE ASKED THE QUESTION OF HOW IT is that other peoples eat raw and bloody meat and yet are healthy. The answer is that these peoples may not really be healthy, because they make themselves remedies; for when they feel ill, they burn themselves on the stomach and the belly and in other places, in the same way that untamed horses are burned. My explanation for all this is as follows: these people just like wolves eat one sort of food rather than a variety of foods, since they possess nothing but meat and milk, and whatever they have they eat, and they appear to be healthy because of the restricted nature of their diet. Sometimes they have something to drink, and sometimes they do not, and this lack of abundance seems to be responsible for their state of health.

—from *On the Observance of Foods,* sixth century A.D.,
translated from the Latin by Mark Grant

NELSON ALGREN ON NEBRASKA BUFFALO BARBECUE

A HALF CENTURY AND MORE AFTER THE LAST STRAGGLING remnants of free-ranging buffalo herds were slaughtered in western Nebraska, buffalo meat is reappearing in Nebraska on festival days.

A traveler will seldom find it on a restaurant bill-of-fare, but he may read an invitation in the newspaper to a free helping of barbecued buffalo at some community celebration. Once it was merely a matter of "catching your buffalo," now it is necessary to wait until a government herd needs thinning and a few animals are being sold.

The barbecue pit is dug the previous day and a fire started in the late evening. By midnight the bottom of the pit contains a deep bed of glowing coals free from smoke. The meat is placed on the spit, and the spit must be turned at exactly the right moment to force the juices back into the roasting meat rather than letting them trickle off into the fire. The sauce, a tangy mixture of salt, pepper, vinegar, and oil, is swabbed on at intervals.

By midmorning the meat is ready to serve. A table made of boards placed across trestles is set up near the pit. Great baskets of buns, dishes of homemade pickles, and dozens of tin cups appear. The men of the village have managed the pit, but the women are taking over now. A fire is built between two flat stones, a shining new wash boiler produced, and coffee-making is under way.

Half a dozen of the village women are ranged behind the table, which boasts neither a tablecloth nor cutlery. The men have brought great platters of sliced buffalo meat, dark and a trifle stringy on the inside, crisp and dark brown around the outer edges. The hungry crowd, though giving the impression of a stampede in the beginning, has now formed an orderly line and files past the table where each is given a paper plate containing buns and several large slices of meat and has a chance to grab a pickle or two in passing. As each person secures his share of the lunch, he marches on to the steaming coffee boiler where a couple of women are ladling the hot strong brew into tin cups. There are sugar and cream for those who must have them, but the style of the day is to drink it black.

Plates and cups once filled, it is merely a matter of finding a spot of ground free of sandburs and sitting down. There is much talk and laughter, punctuated by squeals or yelps as hot coffee splashes over or concealed sandburs are discovered. The meat is nearly always tough and, despite the greatest care, has a flavor of smoke, but the sharp yet mellow sauce, combined with open-air appetites, makes second and even third helpings inevitable.

Sometimes a program is arranged for the afternoon. A bronco is ridden by some local champ, foot races are run, an impromptu ball game staged, or a budding orator may attempt to corral an audience. Usually, however, country women take advantage of the day in town to shop and visit with seldom-seen friends, while the menfolk congregate in groups and talk crops, herds, and politics.

But whatever else is or isn't done, the festivities end in a dance, without which no sandhill celebration is complete. Weather permitting, it is held on a platform built for that purpose near the bandstand.

If the evening has turned cold, and sandhill evenings often do, a hall is usually available.

—from *America Eats,* c. 1940

SAMUEL CHAMBERLAIN ON THE SUNDAY EVENING BARBECUE

BREAKFAST AND DINNER HELD THEIR SURPRISES, BUT Clémentine did not become genuinely goggle-eyed until suppertime, when our host invited her to join in that noted American institution, the Sunday evening barbecue. With something approaching stupefaction she watched him wheel out a portable grill, complete with a glittering array of accessories, and then start a charcoal fire. The whole picture may have become slightly blurred after that. There were cocktails, which Clémentine refused with a frightened smile. Then a platter of steaks and double-thick lamb chops appeared, bordered with bacon and ready to be grilled. A triumphant shout from both Diane and Phinney announced the one gastronomic treat they had been yearning for—hot dogs! A tray of cold cans appeared, and Diane took delight in informing the bewildered Clémentine that they contained beer. And finally, great ears of yellow corn were bared (the kind that never grows in France), and were prepared for the grill. It was too much to expect any newly arrived Burgundian to take in her stride. Clémentine blushed and retired into a confused silence. But a moment later little Phinney was tugging at her elbow. *"Venez,* Clémentine! *Vous allez voir! Les chiens chauds!"* He tugged more, until she came close to the grill, where a fine specimen of the great American hot dog awaited each of them, "with both," as they say in the trade. Then the two retired to a little table and began their feast. Phinney's eyes shone with delight as he clutched his roll in one hand and his soft drink in the other. Clémentine's reserve suddenly melted. She poured her beer out of the can into a paper cup and began to consume her *"chien chaud avec moutarde et peekaleelee."* A broad smile crossed her face. The Americanization of Clémentine had begun.

—from *Clémentine in the Kitchen,* 1943

M.F.K. FISHER ON TRIPE

THE MAIN TROUBLE WITH TRIPE IS THAT IN MY PRESENT dwelling place, a small town in Northern California, I could count on one hand the people who would eat it with me. What is more, its careful slow preparation is not something I feel like doing for a meal by myself at this stage of the game, or even several stages. It is one of the things that call for a big pot and plenty of hungry people.

Not even my children really liked it, although studiously conditioned reflexes forced them to taste it in various guises and countries and to give fair judgment, which in their case was NO.

Friends tell me that they hate tripe because they, in turn, were forced to eat it when young or saw too much of it in fraternity boardinghouses as an "economy meat": reasons like that.

I could claim a childhood trauma if I needed to, and I admit that I did not face a dish of tripe from my grandmother's death until I was a good decade from it. In modern lingo, tripe-wise I lay fallow. The old lady, gastronomical dictator appointed by her own vision of Righteous Christian Living, a Nervous Stomach, and the fact that she more than generously shared the expenses of our exploding household, for some reason approved of eating the inner linings of an ox's first and second bellies.

In *Larousse Gastronomique,* where tripe is classified as "Offal," there is news for Grandmother. (She would dismiss it as foreign nonsense, of course.) "Rich in gelatine, tripe needs prolonged cooking," says the culinary scripture, "and is not easy to digest, so that it has no place in the diet of the dyspeptic [or] sufferers from gout." I sense that my dam was practicing upon herself and us a kind of sympathetic medicine to request that tripe be prepared and served (to be brave, eat a lion's heart; to remain shy and timid, eat violets in a salad, and so on . . .). Oxen are reputedly serene and docile, and she had a digestive system that ranked her among the leaders in Battle Creek's regular army of malnourished missionaries and would have honored her with a front seat at any late-Victorian spa in farther waters, like Vichy or Baden-Baden. The reasoning, perhaps: since an ox has not one but two pieces of equipment for his continuous ruminative consumption of the grains and grasses known also to be salubrious for man, why would partaking of some of his actual stomach not help Mrs. Holbrook's own unhappy organ?

Ergo.

Q.E.D.

Ecco.

Which we did and were, but apparently not enough to give me the same stubborn dislike for tripe that most of my friends claim. My grandmother unwittingly enjoyed perfect digestion, thanks to her constant attention to it, and it is no more than her due reward if she believed that her hypersensitive innards would and could assimilate this delicate honeycomb of animal muscle, with gastric gratitude if not pleasure. She did not believe in the latter anyway, as part of a true and upright life, and as for the hinted danger of gout, only gentlemen had that, in her days of rigid divisions of the sexual hazards of existence.

When I was little, there was only one way to serve tripe fit to eat, *i.e.,* fit for Grandmother to eat. It was seldom prepared when my mother was feeling fit enough herself to maintain some control over the menus, but when she was low in our private pecking order we ate it fairly often. My father, quietly and successfully determined to remain cock of the roost with dignity, always found it commendable, or at least edible. The recipe for it, if I felt sturdy enough to give it in correct form, would start with boiling the rubbery reticulum in pieces, draining it too casually, and dousing it with something called White Sauce which was and will remain in the same class as my grandmother's Boiled Dressing. The dish was at best a faintly odorous and watery challenge to one's innate sense of the fitness of things.

I recognize that such experiences can lead to cynicism, or the analyst's couch. In my own case, they seem mainly to have stiffened my wish to prove them mistaken, and I am now a happy if occasionally frustrated tripe eater.

I had a good beginning, the second time around (really a kind of ghost laying), at Crespin in Dijon. The small restaurant is gone now, but for a long time it served some of the simplest and lustiest meals I have ever eaten, especially on market days for the wine people who came in from all that part of Burgundy to talk about casks, corks, sulphates.

There were always snails at Crespin, of course, except in exceptionally hot weather, and in the cool months oysters out on the sidewalk in kelpy baskets, and all downed by the dozens. There was the classical green salad to scour the maw, and always a good plain tart of seasonal fruits if one could still face it. I remember some cheeses in the winter. And then there were sealed casseroles of *tripes à la mode de Caen véritable.*

Those casseroles, for two or six or eight people, seemed to possess the inexpressible cachet of a numbered duck at the Tour d'Argent, or a small perfect octahedral diamond from Kimberley. They were unsealed at the table. The vapor hissed out, and the whole dish seethed. Plates were too hot to touch bare-handed, to keep the sauce from turning as gluey as a good ox would need it to be (at a temperature more suited to his own digestion). It was served with soup spoons as well as knives and forks, and plenty of crusty bread lay alongside. It was a fine experience.

Crespin, with its hoary monstrous old oyster opener always there on the wintery sidewalk, his hands the most scarred I have ever seen and still perhaps the surest in the way he handled the Portugaises, the green Marennes, upon their dank beds of fresh seaweed . . . Crespin and the old man and even the ruddy marketers are gone, except on my own mind's palate.

The last time I went there, I was alone. It was a strange feeling at first. I was in Dijon late in the 1950's, to go again to the Foire Gastronomique. The town was jumping, quasi-hysterical, injected with a mysterious supercharge of medieval pomp and Madison-Avenue-via-Paris commercialism. I went to several banquets where ornate symbols were pinned and bestowed, with dignitaries several levels above me in the ferocious protocol of eating and drinking, and then I went by myself to the restaurant I wanted to be in once more.

In the small, low room there was a great hum and fume, like market day but even better, and every table but one was occupied by large, red-faced, happy, loud Burgundians. *My* table was empty, and it seemed indicated by the gods that I had come to sit at it. I had sat there many times before, and never would again. It was a little apart but not obtrusively so, up a step like the fantastic banquet boards still cluttered and heavy at the official feastings, but pleasantly enclosed on three sides, with the white window curtains at my back. If I had not come, a potted plant would have been set neatly in my place, I know. I felt pleased to be there instead, and as usual I was awed by my continuing good luck in life, especially now and then.

I think I ate a few snails, to stay in the picture. (The old scarred

oysterman was not there, it being early November and very warm. . . .)
Then, although after all the banquets I felt about as hungry as a sated
moth, I ordered a small and ritual casserole of *tripes*.

They were as good as they had ever been some decades or centuries ago on my private calendar. They hissed and sizzled with delicate authority. Nobody paid any attention to my introspective and
alcoved sensuality, and the general noise beat with provincial lustiness
in the packed room, and an accordionist I had last seen in Marseille
slid in from the frenzied streets and added to the wildness, somewhat
hopelessly. When he saw me digging into my little pot of tripe, he
nodded, recognizing me as a fellow wanderer. I asked him if he would
have a drink, as he twiddled out near-logical tunes on the instrument
he wore like a child on his belly. He looked full at me and said, "Sometime a *pastis* at the Old Port." I have not yet met him there again, but
it is almost doubtless that I shall.

I could not know that the next time I returned, lemminglike, to
the dank old town, Crespin and the white curtains and all of it would
be gone, but it is. It is too bad to explain.

The classical recipes for preparing tripe can be found in any good
cookbook, which someone who has read this far will already know and
be able to consult. I myself like the French methods, but there are excellent ones in almost every culture which permit the use of this type
of animal meat. Here is a good one which is fresh to the taste, adapted
from the "Trippa alla Petronius" served currently in a London restaurant called Tiberio:

Tripe Petronius

3 pounds tripe, previously boiled until tender	¾ cup butter
	4 tablespoons tomato puree
4 medium-sized carrots chopped very fine	1 glass (6 to 8 ounces) dry white wine
3 sticks of celery chopped very fine	½ glass olive oil
	2 cloves of garlic, minced
3 large onions chopped very fine	½ cup chopped fresh parsley
	½ cup chopped fresh basil

Drain tripe and cut into 1-inch squares. Gently brown the three vegetables in the butter. Add tomato puree and wine, and stir until sauce thickens.
Add tripe and simmer slowly for 1 hour.

In separate skillet warm olive oil, and add garlic, parsley, and basil, taking care not to overheat. Cook slowly about 5 minutes, mix quickly into tripe, and serve.

This is a comparatively quick recipe (the true *tripes à la mode de Caen* may take at least twelve hours of baking), and it is very simple, which explains why it is sought after in a posh Mayfair restaurant where the clients may feel jaded. I think that the fresh herbs give it special quality, but perhaps it could be successfully tinkered with if they proved to be unprocurable. Fortunately this is seldom the case with parsley. If dried basil had to be used, one to two tablespoonfuls should be soaked in one and a half instead of one cup of wine and then drained, and I would be tempted to go a step further and use a light dry red instead of the Tiberio's white. All this would, I fear, make the whole dish more "ordinary."

While I am about it, I might as well discuss why it is much easier to make things with tripe now than it was a hundred or so years ago, or when I myself was little. I do this in a missionary spirit, convinced that they can be very good to eat and should be less shunned in our country. In these days tripe is almost always taken through its first tedious cleansings in special rooms, at the wholesale butchers' factories. My friend Remo, "meatman and mentor," says somewhat cryptically that the stuff is subjected to enormous pressure, which I assume means with steam. It is then trimmed to a uniform niceness, wrapped in bundles rather like large pallid grape leaves, and delivered fresh or quick-frozen to the markets where there is any demand for it.

Once the cook takes over from the butcher, this modern treatment makes it possible to prepare tripe for any dish in an hour or a little more, by washing it well and then simmering it in ample water flavored to taste with carrots, onion, celery, herbs. When tender but not too soft it is drained, and then AVANTI, EN AVANT, FORWARD! Here is the older method, perhaps to shame some of us into trying our luck for a change, recommended in 1867 by the expatriate Pierre Blot, in his *Hand-Book of Practical Cookery, for Ladies and Professional Cooks. Containing the Whole Science and Art of Preparing Human Food:*

TRIPE

How to clean and prepare. Scrape and wash it well several times in boiling water, changing the water every time, then put in very cold water for about twelve hours, changing the water two or three times;

place it in a pan, cover it with cold water; season with parsley, chives, onions, one or two cloves of garlic, cloves, salt, and pepper; boil gently five hours, take out and drain.

When I was a child I felt a somewhat macabre interest in watching our cook go into this old routine. It started in a washtub, with much sloshing with big scrub brushes and whackings at the slippery ivory-white rubber. Then I am sure that baking soda was put into a couple of the several changes of water, making things foam in an evil way . . . I suppose a battle with some of the digestive juices my grandmother counted on? For the last cool soaking, handfuls of salt were thrown in, or so it now seems to me. But I am downright sure that in our house there was no fancy nonsense of herbs and suchlike in the final slow boiling. Plain fare with a good white sauce, that is what we were served. "Eat what's set before you, and be thankful for it," was the gastronomical motto that quivered always in the air above our table while Grandmother sat there, and with a certain amount of philosophical acceptance it can be a good one, the whole chancy way.

—from *With Bold Knife and Fork,* 1968

GRIMOD DE LA REYNIÈRE ON PIGS

Much like the pig, Grimod de la Reynière has a historic importance far greater than his current reputation. In France, his most often quoted, though seldom attributed, statement is "tout est bon dans un cochon," *everything is good on a pig.*   —M.K.

THE VALUE OF A PIG IS SO WIDELY RECOGNIZED, ITS USEfulness in cooking so deeply felt, that it would be superfluous to sing its praises. It is the king of animals, the one whose empire is the most universal, whose qualities are the least questioned. Without it there is no lard, and consequently no cooking, without it there are no hams,

no sausages, no andouilles, no blood sausage, and consequently no charcuteries. Doctors like to say that
the meat is indigestible, heavy, and laxative.
We will leave the doctors to their whin-
ing; they are angry that no one is listening because the pig is, as far
as indigestion is concerned,
one of the most sparkling jewels on the crown. Jews, on the
other hand, look on pork with
horror, and a lot of Christians
these days are virtually Jews,
not eating blood sausage and an-
douilles. In fact, though the pork products are much better in Lyons
and Troyes than in Paris, our charcuteries are triumphing over all ob-
stacles and their recipes and styles have emerged as leaders in the art
of making from a pig the most varied, the wisest, and the most exquisite recipes.

Nature in its perfection arranged it that everything on a pig is
good *[tout est bon dans un cochon]* and there is nothing to throw away.
The arts share with food the honor of using the bristles; and if Mr.
Corps and Mr. Jean (two of Paris's leading charcutiers) owe their for-
tune to its flesh, the bristles on its back became the tool of glory for
Raphael, nor have they been useless to Rameau.

The pig is the civilized version of the wild boar—in fact, what a
boar has been reduced to by castration and slavery. But that degrada-
tion has been to the advantage of our sensuality, and the peace-loving,
sociable qualities of the one seem, at least in the kitchen, preferable
to the wild, republican virtues of the other.

—from *Almanach des Gourmands,* 1804,
translated from the French by Mark Kurlansky

APICIUS ON SOW'S BELLY AND FIG-FED PORK LIVER

Sow's Belly

Sow's udder or belly with the paps on it is prepared in this manner: the belly boil, tie it together with reeds, sprinkle with salt and place it in the oven, or, start roasting on the gridiron. Crush pepper, lovage, with broth, pure wine, adding raisin wine to taste, thicken [the sauce] with roux and pour it over the roast.

Stuffed Sow's Belly

Full sow's belly is stuffed with crushed pepper, carraway, salt mussels; sew the belly tight and roast. Enjoy this with a brine sauce and mustard.

Wine Sauce for Fig-Fed Pork

Fig-fed pork liver (that is, liver crammed with figs) is prepared in a wine sauce with pepper, thyme, lovage, broth, a little wine and oil.

—first century A.D.,
translated from the Latin by Joseph Dommers Vehling

MRS. BEETON ON SHEEP

Isabella Beeton, popularly known for the past century and a half as Mrs. Beeton, was a woman ahead of her time. Her recipes gave exact measurements and cooking times four decades before Fannie Farmer was credited with establishing the concept. The eldest of twenty-one children, she married magazine publisher Samuel Beeton when she was nineteen. She became a true partner in his business—translating, proofreading, doing layouts, and writing a weekly column on fashion and food. In 1861 they published the first edition of Beeton's Book of Household Management, *a book in the tradition of* Le Mésnagier de Paris, *and it quickly sold sixty thousand copies. It has been a standard reference of the English-*

speaking world ever since, sometimes titled Mrs. Beeton's Cookery
Book. *Mrs. Beeton died not long after publication at the age of
twenty-eight, following the birth of her fourth child.* —M.K.

OF ALL WILD OR DOMESTICATED ANIMALS, THE SHEEP IS,
without exception, the most useful to man as a food, and the most necessary to his health and comfort; for it not only supplies him with the
lightest and most nutritious of meats, but, in the absence of the cow, its
udder yields him milk, cream, and a sound though inferior cheese;
while from its fat he obtains light, and from its fleece broadcloth,
kerseymere, blankets, gloves, and hose. Its bones when burnt make an
animal charcoal—ivory black—to polish his boots, and when powdered, a manure for the cultivation of his wheat; the skin, either split or
whole, is made into a mat for his carriage, a housing for his horse, or a
lining for his hat, and many other useful purposes besides, being extensively employed in the manufacture of parchment; and finally, when
oppressed by care and sorrow, the harmonious strains that carry such
soothing contentment to the heart, are elicited from the musical
strings, prepared almost exclusively from the intestines of the sheep.

This valuable animal, of which England is estimated to maintain an
average stock of 32,000,000, belongs to the class already indicated under the ox,—the Mammalia; to the order of Rumenantia, or cud-
chewing animal; to the tribe of Capridœ, or horned quadrupeds; and
the genus Ovis, or the "sheep." The sheep may be either with or without horns; when present, however, they have always this peculiarity, that
they spring from a triangular base, are spiral in form, and lateral, at the
side of the head, in situation. The fleece of the sheep is of two sorts, either short and harsh, or soft and woolly; the wool always preponderat-
ing in an exact ratio to the care, attention, and amount of domestication
bestowed on the animal. The generic peculiarities of the sheep are the
triangular and spiral form of the horns, always larger in the male when
present, but absent in the most cultivated species; having sinuses at the
base of all the toes of the four feet, with two rudimentary hoofs on the
fore legs, two inguinal teats to the udder, with a short tail in the wild
breed, but of varying length in the domesticated; have no incisor teeth
in the upper jaw, but in their place a hard elastic cushion along the mar-
gin of the gum, on which the animal nips and breaks the herbage on
which it feeds; in the lower jaw there are eight incisor teeth and six mo-
lars on each side of both jaws, making in all 32 teeth. The fleece consists

of two coats, one to keep the animal warm, the other to carry off the water without wetting the skin. The first is of wool, the weight and fineness of which depend on the quality of the pasture and the care bestowed on the flock; the other of hair, that pierces the wool and overlaps it, and is in excess in exact proportion to the badness of the keep and inattention with which the animal is treated.

—from *Beeton's Book of Household Management,* 1860

Alexis Soyer on the Turkish Way to Roast Sheep

In 1857, Alexis Soyer, London's most celebrated chef, decided on his own initiative and expense, to go to the battlefront in the Crimean War to see if he could improve the taste and nutrition of the food of the British army. Along the way he observed the Black Sea food traditions. —M.K.

THOUGH A PRIMITIVE METHOD, IT IS FAR FROM BEING A bad one. About a hundredweight of wood is set on fire in an open place, yard, kitchen, or elsewhere, and when burnt the ashes are piled up pyramidically to about the length of the lamb. Four stones, about a foot high, are then placed two at each end, and about eighteen inches from the fire; the lambs are spitted, head and all, upon a long piece of wood, with a rough handle similar to that of a barrel-organ. They are then put down; each one being turned by one man, who now and then moves the ashes to revive the fire, at the same time basting the lambs with a bunch of feathers dipped in oil. A pan should be placed underneath to receive the fat. This was on this occasion omitted. Each lamb took about three hours doing by that slow process; but I must repeat, they were done to perfection, and worthy of the attention of the greatest epicure.

—from *A Culinary Campaign,* 1857

Henri Cartier-Bresson, *"Little White Beds" Charity Ball*, 1952 (Magnum Photos)

LE MÉSNAGIER DE PARIS
ON FAKING GAME MEAT

IF YOU WOULD LIKE TO PASS OFF A PIECE OF BEEF AS venison—or bear meat if you live in an area where bear is found—pick a beef filet or beef leg, boil it, then lard it, then put it on a skewer for roasting. You must eat it with a sauce from boar tail. The beef should be boiled, then larded, especially lengthwise, and then cut into small pieces. Then pour the well-warmed sauce over the beef, which should first be roasted or plunged into boiling water and immediately removed because beef is more tender than deer.

To disguise beef as bear meat: With a piece of beef leg make a black sauce with ginger, cloves, black pepper, grains of paradise [melegueta pepper, a West African seed that became a medieval food craze], etc. Put two slices in each dish—the beef will have the taste of bear meat.

—from *Le Mésnagier de Paris*, 1393,
translated from the French by Mark Kurlansky

ELIZA SMITH'S FAKE VENISON

Eliza Smith, according to her own writing, was in charge of food for various wealthy households. She was British and died about 1732. That seems to be all that is known about her. Her book on food and medicine, which was published posthumously in 1758, however, was one of the influential cookbooks of the late eighteenth century. It was the first cookbook ever published in America, although the American edition had certain revisions, including a "Cure for Rattlesnake Bite," authored by a slave named Caesar who was paid for his contribution with emancipation and £100 a year for life. —M.K.

BONE A RUMP OF BEEF, OR A LARGE SHOULDER OF MUTTON; then beat it with a rolling-pin; season it with pepper and nutmeg; lay it twenty-four hours in sheep's-blood; then dry it with a cloth, and season it again with pepper, salt, and spice. Put your meat in the form of a paste, and bake it as a venison-pasty, and make a gravy with the bones, to put in when it is drawn out of the oven.

—from *The Compleat Housewife*, 1758

ELIZA SMITH ON RECOVERING VENISON WHEN IT STINKS

One of the great revolutions in nouvelle cuisine was shortening the curing time of game. Pheasants in particular used to be left to rot. Brillat-Savarin said one should hang a pheasant until the breast meat turned green. Grimod said one should hang them by the tail feathers until the carcass fell to the floor. He also said that a pheasant should be hung for "as long as it takes for a man of letters who has never learned the art of flattery to receive a pension."

It was Claude Lévi-Strauss many years later who made the point that rotten is a subjective judgment—one man's gamey is another man's rotten. But game was often cured to a point that some people found "a bit too gamey." —M.K.

TAKE AS MUCH COLD WATER IN A TUB AS WILL COVER IT A handful over, and put in good store of salt, and let it lie three or four hours; then take your venison out, and let it lie in as much hot water and salt; and let it lie as long as before; then have your crust in readiness, and take it out, and dry it very well, and season it with pepper and salt pretty high, and put it in your pasty. Do not use the bones of your venison for gravy, but get fresh beef or other bones.

—from *The Compleat Housewife,* 1758

NEAPOLITAN RECIPE TO MAKE A COW, CALF, OR STAG LOOK ALIVE

This is from a recipe collection written by a fifteenth-century Neapolitan chef whose name has been lost. —M.K.

FIRST KILL THE COW OR CALF NORMALLY, THEN SKIN IT beginning at the hooves—but keep the hooves and the horns attached to the hide; when skinned, stretch the hide; then get cumin, fennel, cloves, pepper and salt, all ground up to a powder, and sprinkle it over the inside of the hide; then cut away the shin-bone downward from the knee, and remove the tripe through the flank; if you wish, you can roast capons, pheasants or other creatures and put them into the cow's body. If you want to bake it in the oven, lay it on a grill; if you want to roast it over the fire, get a piece of wood—that is, a pole like a spit— insert it, lard it well and roast it slowly so as not to burn it. Then make iron bars large enough to hold it standing up; when it is cooked, set up the bar on a large plank and bind it [*i.e.,* the animal] so that it stands on its feet; then dress it in its hide as if it were alive; if the meat has shrunk anywhere because of the cooking, replace it with bay-laurel, sage, rosemary and myrtle; draw the hide back [in place] and sew it so the iron cannot be seen, and give it a posture as if it were alive.

The same can be done with a deer, a sow and a chicken, and with any other animal you wish. Note that preparing this sort of animal requires a cook who is neither foolish nor simple-minded, but rather he must be quite clever. And note, my lord, that if your cook is not skillful he will never prepare anything good that *is* good, no matter how hard he tries.

—Author unknown, from a fifteenth-century
Neapolitan recipe collection,
translated from the Italian by Terence Scully

JANE GRIGSON ON FAGGOTS AND PEAS

FAGGOTS ARE A GOOD-TEMPERED DISH. THEY CAN BE reheated. They can be cooked at an even lower temperature, if this suits your convenience. Should they not be nicely browned, a few minutes under the grill, very hot, will do the trick.

Faggots were popular in the past as a way of using up odd bits and pieces left over after a pig was killed. They often included the lights, heart and melt—and indeed many butchers who sell their own faggots use these parts still, rather than the belly of pork in this recipe, as well as the liver. Recipes vary in different parts of the country, just as pâté recipes do in France. Welsh faggots, for instance, may include a chopped cooking apple, and omit the egg. The rich savoury pleasure of faggots—one name given to them is savoury ducks—is very largely due to the enclosing grace of caul fat which keeps the dark lean meat well basted. For this you will need to go to a small family butcher, preferably an older man, who really understands meat.

The word faggot means a bundle, like a faggot of kindling for a fire, so do not be afraid to vary the recipe with additions and alterations of flavouring.

FOR 6

500 g (1 lb) pig's liver, minced
300 g (10 oz) belly of pork,
   minced
2 large onions, chopped
1 clove garlic, chopped
4 sage leaves, chopped, or
   1 teaspoon dried sage

½ teaspoon mace
2 medium eggs
Up to 125 g (4 oz) breadcrumbs
Salt, pepper
Piece of caul fat
150 ml (¼ pt) beef or veal
   or pork stock

Put liver, pork, onion, garlic and sage into a frying pan, and cook gently for 30 minutes without allowing the mixture to be brown. Stir occasionally.

Strain off the juices and set aside. Mix the meat, etc., with the mace, eggs and enough breadcrumbs to make a firm, easy-to-handle mixture. Taste and season. Soften the caul fat in a bowl of tepid water and cut it into roughly 12 cm (5") squares. Divide the meat into 60 g (2 oz) knobs, and wrap each one in a square of caul fat. Place side by side close together in an ovenproof dish, which is not too deep: the faggots should stick up slightly above the rim. Pour in the stock. Bake for 40–60 minutes in a moderate oven, mark 3–4, 160–180°C (325–350°F), until the tops are nicely browned. About 20 minutes after the start of cooking time, strain off the juices into the liquor that was left from the first cooking. Stand the bowl in a bowl of ice-cubes, so that the fat rises quickly to the surface and can be skimmed off. Pour the stock over the faggots about 5 minutes before the end of cooking time. Serve with garden peas in the summer time, or with a purée of dried peas in the winter.

—from *English Food,* 1974

APICIUS ON STUFFED DORMICE

The animal whose common name is "edible dormouse," known in zoology as Glis glis, *is a uniquely European creature. Romans used to fatten them with a special diet before cooking them. Seven inches long with a bushy seven-inch tail, the edible dormouse has not known much favor since Roman times, perhaps because it reminds park lovers of the thing they are trying to forget—that a squirrel is just a rat with a bushy tail.*

—M.K.

Stuffed Dormouse

Is stuffed with a forcemeat of pork and small pieces of dormouse meat trimmings, all pounded with pepper, nuts, laser, broth. Put the dormouse thus stuffed in an earthen casserole, roast it in the oven, or boil it in the stock pot.

—first century A.D.,
translated from the Latin by Joseph Dommers Vehling

———

LUDWIG BEMELMANS ON ELEPHANT CUTLET

ONCE UPON A TIME THERE WERE TWO MEN IN VIENNA WHO wanted to open a restaurant. One was a dentist who was tired of fixing teeth and always wanted to own a restaurant, and the other a famous cook by the name of Souphans.

The dentist was, however, a little afraid. "There are," he said, "already too many restaurants in Vienna, restaurants of every kind, Viennese, French, Italian, Chinese, American, American-Chinese, Portuguese, Armenian, Dietary, Vegetarian, Jewish, Wine and Beer restaurants—in short, all sorts of restaurants."

But the chef had an Idea. "There is one kind of restaurant that Vienna has not," he said.

"What kind?" said the dentist.

"A restaurant such as has never existed before, a restaurant for cutlets from every animal in the world."

The dentist was afraid, but finally he agreed, and the famous chef went out to buy a house, tables and chairs, and engaged help, pots and pans and had a sign painted with big red letters ten feet high saying: "CUTLETS FROM EVERY ANIMAL IN THE WORLD."

The first customer that entered the door was a distinguished lady, a countess. She sat down and asked for an elephant cutlet.

"How would Madame like this elephant cutlet cooked?" said the waiter.

"Oh, Milanaise, sauté in butter, with a little spaghetti over it, on that a filet of anchovy, and an olive on top," she said.

"That is very nice," said the waiter and went out to order it.

"Jessas Maria und Joseph!" said the dentist when he heard the order, and he turned to the chef and cried, "What did I tell you? Now what are we going to do?"

The chef said nothing; he put on a clean apron and walked into the dining room to the table of the lady. There he bowed, bent down to her and said, "Madame has ordered an elephant cutlet?"

"Yes," said the countess.

"With spaghetti and a filet of anchovy and an olive?"

"Yes."

"Madame is all alone?"

"Yes, yes."

"Madame expects no one else?"

"No."

"And Madame wants only one cutlet?"

"Yes," said the lady, "but why all these questions?"

"Because," said the chef, "because, Madame, I am very sorry, but for one cutlet we cannot cut up our elephant."

—from *La Bonne Table,* 1964

PETER MARTYR ON SEA TURTLES

Peter Martyr, sometimes known as Pietro Martire, published in 1555 only the second book to appear in the English language describing the Americas, The Decades of the Newe Worlde or West India. *The following passage describes a small island, which today is known as Isla Beata off the Dominican Republic.*

The European arrival in North America unleashed a series of environmental disasters. This small piece unintentionally reveals one. Europeans loved to eat sea turtles and, even worse, their eggs. Within a matter of decades sea turtles were endangered. By 1620, the Bermuda Assembly had passed a law banning the killing of these animals in their waters. —M.K.

ON THE LEFTE SYDE OF *HISPANIOLA* TOWARDE THE Southe, near unto the haven *Beata,* there lythe an Islande named *Portus Bellus.* They tell marvelous thynges of the monsters of the sea aboute this Island, and especially of the tortoyles. For they saye that they are bygger then great rounde targettes. At suche tyme as the heate of nature moveth theym too generation, they coome foorthe of the sea: And makynge a deepe pytte in the sande, they laye three or foure hudreth egges therein. When they have thus emptied their bagge of conception, they putte as much of the sande ageyne into the pytte, as maye suffyce to cover the egges: And soo resorte ageyne to the sea, nothynge carefull of their succession. At the daye appopynted of nature to the procreation of these beautes, there escapeth owte a multitude of tortoyles, as it were pissemares swarming owte of an ante hyll: And this onely by the heate of the soonne withowte any helpe of their parentes. They say that their egges are in maner as bygge as geese egges. They also compare the fleshse of these tortoyles, to be equall with veale in taste.

—from *The Decades of the Newe Worlde or West India,* 1555

ALEXIS SOYER ON COOKING MEAT FOR FIFTY MEN

Although little remembered today, Soyer was one of the heroes of the Crimean War, beloved by officers and men for having improved the food. His culinary effort was credited with saving more lives than Florence Nightingale's nursing. Among other innovations, he invented a portable field stove. But the "culinary campaign," as he called it, was rigorous, and though he was only forty-eight at the time, it ruined his health and he died soon after. —M.K.

No. 1—Soyer's Receipt to Cook Salt Meat for Fifty Men.
Headquarters, Crimea, 12th May, 1856.

1. Put 50 lbs. of meat in the boiler.
2. Fill with water, and let soak all night.
3. Next morning wash the meat well.
4. Fill with fresh water, and boil gently three hours, and serve.
Skim off the fat, which, when cold, is an excellent substitute for butter.

For salt pork proceed as above, or boil half beef and half pork—the pieces of beef may be smaller than the pork, requiring a little longer time doing.

Dumplings may be added to either pork or beef in proportion; and when pork is properly soaked, the liquor will make a very good soup. The large yellow peas as used by the navy, may be introduced; it is important to have them, as they are a great improvement. When properly soaked, French haricot beans and lentils may also be used to advantage. By the addition of 5 pounds of split peas, half a pound of brown sugar, 2 tablespoons of pepper, 10 onions; simmer gently till in pulp, remove the fat and serve; broken biscuit may be introduced. This will make an excellent mess.

—from *A Culinary Campaign,* 1857

CHAPTER FIFTEEN

Easy on the Starch

MARTINO'S SICILIAN MACARONI

Libro de arte coquinaria, Book of Culinary Art, *by Maestro Martino da Como is considered the most important Italian recipe collection of the fifteenth century. Martino came from northern Italy but made his reputation in Rome. Most Italian recipe collections of the period show his influence. Sicilians make much of the fact that Martino thought of macaroni as a Sicilian invention. Many historians doubt the story of Marco Polo introducing pasta from China, though China then, and now, abounded in flat, broad, thin, and stuffed pastas. But Marco Polo barely mentioned pasta in 1300 in his ghost-written book, and there is little record of Italians experimenting with a new "Chinese" food. The word "maccheroni," the original word for pasta, seems to be the key. The word was used in the thirteenth century before Marco Polo's return. Unfortunately for the Sicilian case, it was mentioned in Naples. There is also evidence of an earlier Greek lasagna. Nevertheless, Sicilians can argue that the great Martino called it* Maccaroni siciliani. —M.K.

MAKE A DOUGH OF THE BEST FLOUR, MIXED WITH THE
white of one egg and rosewater, blended with water. If you want to
make only two plates of it add only one or two yolks, making this a
very tough dough, and roll small round sticks a handswidth in length
and the thickness of straw. Take an iron rod a handswidth long and a
cord thick and use it to roll the sticks of dough on the table with both
hands. Then pull the metal rod out and a macaroni with a hollowed
center remains. Dry these macaronis in the sun. Once dry, they can be
kept for two to three years. Cook in water or a good meat stock and
sprinkle with grated cheese when you serve them with melted butter
and mild spices. These macaroni need to boil for an hour.

—from *Libro de arte coquinaria*, c. 1420s,
translated from the Italian by Mark Kurlansky

SHIZUO TSUJI ON RICE

*Shizuo Tsuji, a baker's son with a prestigious degree in French liter-
ature, by chance became a kind of Japanese Escoffier. Like the earlier twentieth-century French master, he defined the cuisine of his
country and his culture for several generations. Like Escoffier, his
motto was "make it simple." "Japanese culture," he pointed out,*

"was born of austerity." Unlike in China, in Japan austerity is central even to the imperial cuisine. Through his famous cooking school founded in Osaka in 1960, an institution that has outlived him, Shizuo Tsuji has explained for Japanese and Westerners not only the techniques, but also the cutlure and history that are the underpinnings of Japanese food. —M.K.

RICE IS A BEAUTIFUL FOOD. IT IS BEAUTIFUL WHEN IT grows—precision rows of sparkling green stalks shooting up to reach the hot summer sun. It is beautiful when harvested, autumn gold sheaves piled in diked, patchwork paddies. It is beautiful when, once threshed, it enters granary bins like a cataract of tiny seed-pearls. It is beautiful when cooked by a practiced hand, pure white and sweetly fragrant.

Rice is the staple of staples. Not only is it a dish in itself, rice is a necessary ingredient in many other common Japanese foods. Fermented, it is *saké,* the well-known Japanese liquor. The thick, sweet lees of *saké* are present in many dishes. Rice bran adds flavor to pickles. The grain also makes a delicate vinegar, which is just being discovered by the West and one day may be found on the staple shelf of any Western kitchen.

Historically, rice was a measure of wealth. The worth of medieval fiefs was counted in terms of a rice volume unit, the *koku,* roughly equivalent to 5 bushels (this value actually fluctuated greatly). Even after the beginning of a strong cash economy, samurai were paid their stipends in *koku* of rice. Today, when the Japanese grow all the rice they need and much more, it is hard to convince farmers to plant anything other than rice. It is not only government rice crop subsidies that lead them to single- and double-crop with modern high-yielding strains. Rice has been planted through the millennia, and the cycle of its growth and harvest is a part of the unchanging rhythm of the seasons. Just as the mountains in the background of every Japanese scene change mood depending on the time of day and whether the light is that of summer, autumn, winter, or spring, so, too, with the rice paddies in the foreground. Rice, like mountains, is part of Japan.

Regardless of how many other dishes are served, a Japanese feels he has not really eaten unless there is rice. At restaurant banquets the rice is not served until after the succession of various fish, poultry, meat, and vegetable dishes, when it completes the meal together with *miso* soup and pickles. But in ordinary homes, rice is central to the meal, and any fish, poultry, meat, or vegetable dishes are basically "luxuries"—tasty side dishes *(okazu)*. It is not uncommon in times of austerity, and in poor households, for the rice, *miso* soup, and pickles to constitute the entire meal.

The rice that tastes the best is *shinmai,* or "new rice," on the market in autumn, fresh from harvest. This first rice is moist and tender and requires less water in cooking than last year's shelf-dried stuff. Perhaps with more than a twinge of nostalgia, city residents send to their home provinces in autumn to order a few kilograms of new rice, and normally taciturn people carry on and on about which province on which sides of which mountains with how much rainfall and what sort of growing season and planted in which variety yields the very best rice in Japan. Rice can be a subject of old memories, of regional pride, and of all manner of expert knowledge.

—from *Japanese Cooking: A Simple Art,* 1980

Neapolitan Rice with Almonds

To make ten servings get a pound and a half of almonds and half a pound of rice; wash the rice three times, cook it well and drain it thoroughly; grind the almonds—so they do not make oil as they are ground, add in a little clear water or rosewater—and strain them; set the almond milk to boil in a pot with half a pound of fine sugar; as it begins to boil, add in the rice and put the pot on coals away from the fire, stirring continuously with a spoon, and let it boil for half an hour.

Similarly, you can cook the rice with goat's milk or some other milk.

Nota: To keep any similar dish from picking up smoke, take a cloth folded in three or four layers—but first, remove the preparation from the pot, without scraping the bottom, and put it into another pot; then soak the cloth in clear water, wring it out, place it thus folded over the pot and leave it there for half an hour, or for at least a quarter of an hour; then soak it again, and put it back again on the pot: this is how the smokey taste is drawn out. Proceed likewise for Spelt Porridge: there is no better way.

—Author unknown, from a fifteenth-century
Neapolitan recipe collection,
translated from the Italian by Terence Scully

MARJORIE KINNAN RAWLINGS
ON HUSH PUPPIES

HUSH-PUPPIES ARE IN A CLASS BY THEMSELVES. THEY ARE a concomitant of the hunt, above all of the fishing trip. Fresh-caught fried fish without hush-puppies are as man without woman, a beautiful woman without kindness, law without policemen. The story goes that they derived their name from old fishing and hunting expeditions, when the white folks ate to repletion, the Negro help ate beyond repletion, and the hunting dogs, already fed, smelled the delectable odors of human rations and howled for the things they scented. Negro cook or white sportsman tossed the remaining cornmeal patties to the dogs, calling, "Hush, puppies!"—and the dogs, devouring them, could ask no more of life, and hushed.

SERVES 3 TO 4

1 cup cornmeal	*1 small to medium onionminced,*
2 teaspoons baking powder	*1 egg*
½ teaspoon salt	*¼ cup milk or water*

Mix together the dry ingredients and the finely cut onion. Break in the egg and beat vigorously. Add the liquid. Form into small patties, round or finger-shaped. Drop in the deep smoking fat in which the fish has been fried, until they are a deep brown. Serve hot and at once.

I have a strange recipe from St. Simon's Island, off the coast of Georgia, that adds a little sugar and a small can of corn to hush-puppies. Sugar is anathema in any cornbread except the most delicate cornmeal muffins. It is more than inappropriate to the hearty honesty of hush-puppies. As to the canned corn, this is a free country and the experimenter may legally add it if he so wishes. He may not legally, however, then call the results hush-puppies.

From a rural correspondent I had passed on one of those flashes of genius that touch cooking at fortunate moments. His mother, he wrote, made hush-puppies in small round cakes about two inches in diameter, then with her finger poked a hole in the center, as for a doughnut. This gives twice the amount of crisp, crunchy crust, the very best part of the hush-puppy, and does away with any tendency to a heavy center. I recommend it earnestly.

I do not recommend a practice of some sportsmen, of using beer for the mixing fluid. By it, the sweet nutty flavor of the hush-puppy is a little soured, even when baking soda is used instead of baking powder. Devotees of this custom are likely to be those so unbalanced by large quantities of the mixing fluid that they are in no condition to treat hush-puppies with the respect due them.

—from *Cross Creek Cookery,* 1942

ANGELO PELLEGRINI ON POLENTA

IF THERE IS ANY ONE DISH—ASIDE FROM PASTE, WHICH IS so widely used in soups—eaten in greater quantities than any other, it is *polenta*. North of Rome, in Tuscany, in Lombardy, in Piedmont, and in the Venetian provinces, this thick, coarse, corn-meal mush is always on the table. The metropolitan American knows it as the elegant dish served in Italian restaurants in Boston, New York, and San Francisco. Or perhaps he has eaten it at the home of his Italian friends, served with casserole rabbit or chicken and mushrooms. Excellent fare, superb when served with rich, red wine; but such is not the *polenta* as eaten by the Italian peasant! Of course, the mush itself, since it is nothing more than corn meal cooked in water, is the same anywhere, though the grind and the quality of the corn make some difference; but the condiment, the fowl, the mushrooms, the rich sauce—these

the Italian has found in America, and with them a means for trans-
muting a dish which in his native land had become obnoxious to him.

The culinary inventiveness of the Italian housewife, as I well remember, was severely taxed in devising means to make such humble
fare attractive to her children. Except on rare occasions, as rare as
they were memorable, the best she could do was to smother it with
salt cod baked in tomato sauce. Everywhere she was frustrated by lack
of ingredients. And so we ate it hot with cream cheese, or with turnip
greens cooked and sprinkled with a miserly dash of olive oil, or with
hot cracklings, and a thousand other lowly auxiliaries. We ate it cold
with figs and grapes, with green onions and cheese. We buried it in
bowls of bean broth and cabbage. We sliced it and grilled or fried the
stuff with indifferent results. It was, it remained, always and forever—
polenta, a veritable plague, an evil from which no deliverance seemed
possible. We had not yet thought seriously of America.

But of all the miserable bait with which we were lured into eating
more and more of that insipid and bloating yellow nightmare, the
lowly pilchard was positively the worst. I do not know how pilchards
were cured, nor do I care. They came pressed beyond recognition in
barrels; ugly, foul, putrefied little creatures from the Mediterranean.
The perverse genius of the race, the evil inventiveness of the Borgias
and the Medicis, the hatred of the Guelfs and Ghibellines have coa-
lesced in the pilchard barrel of the Italian grocery store. When I was
dispatched to the grocer's to buy a brace of the little critters, I knew
what lay in store. On the way home I gouged out their eyes and ate
them out of sheer spite, cursing the while in a manner shockingly pre-
cocious in one so young. At home they were broiled on live coals,
sprinkled with olive oil, and placed in a platter on the center of the
table. Then each member of the family would take his turn dabbing
pieces of *polenta* on the fish—gentle little taps, just enough to soak up
the stench. When the stomach was about full, the fish was divided
among the members of the happy family, each to do with his share as
he wished. That is to say, to eat it and thank God for another bellyful.

I frequently complained, in the innocent manner of children who
have yet to learn that their misery cannot always be interpreted in
terms of parental discipline, and asked why we had to eat such awful
stuff. My grandfather, who preferred bread dunked in wine—which he
had regularly for breakfast until his eighty-eighth year, when he died
prematurely of snakebite—sought to console me on such occasions by
telling me what *he* had had to eat when *he* was a boy. The sermon was

his version of the familiar one which has left grandchildren grumbling since the first grandfather mumbled it in his beard. His fare, he assured me, had been the same *polenta*, served with the same befouled Mediterranean pilchard, but with this miserable difference: after the fish had been warmed over the coals, his mother suspended it on a string from the ceiling so that it hovered over the center of the table. Then each member of the family would tap it gaily with his piece of *polenta*, sending it with deft strokes across the way to his brother or sister who promptly returned the compliment. And thus amid peals of laughter and bacchanalian revelry, each filled his belly and concluded with a prayer for a bumper crop of yellow corn. That done, the pilchard, somewhat frayed but none the worse for wear, was ceremoniously detached from the string, wrapped securely in wax paper, and stored in the pantry to await the morrow's eager barrage of *polenta*. When completely worn out, it was replaced by another, more foul and evil-smelling. Grandfather was a grand old man.

—from *The Unprejudiced Palate*, 1948

CATHERINE E. BEECHER AND HARRIET BEECHER STOWE ON POTATOES

Catherine E. Beecher was an educator with strong views on the role of women in society and the home. Her father, Henry Ward Beecher, a staunch and puritanical Calvinist, had taught his daughters to pursue life with "a sense of mission." Catherine rebelled against her father's religion but kept the sense of mission, establishing, in 1823, a girl's school in Hartford, the purpose of which was to teach women that they must be the guardians of the world's morality and this guardianship began at home. The school failed, but she went on to numerous other educational projects and wrote a number of widely read books, including Letters on the Difficulties of Religion, Essay on Slavery, *and* The Moral Instructor. *Despite this, her fame was minor compared to that of her sister, the author of* Uncle Tom's Cabin. *And for that reason she asked her sister to coauthor* The American Woman's Home, *a book of far more than recipes, a guide to her moral philosophy and the role of woman in it, in the long tradition of* Le Mésnagier de Paris. *The other advantage to including her sister was that Harriet Beecher Stowe had raised seven children, whereas sister Catherine's betrothed had been lost at sea earlier in her life and she never married.* —M.K.

AS REGARDS THE DEPARTMENT OF VEGETABLES, THEIR NUMber and variety in America are so great that a table might almost be furnished by these alone. Generally speaking, their cooking is a more simple art, and therefore more likely to be found satisfactorily performed, than that of meats. If only they are not drenched with rancid butter, their own native excellence makes itself known in most of the ordinary modes of preparation.

There is, however, one exception. Our staunch old friend, the potato, is to other vegetables what bread is on the table. Like bread, it is held as a sort of *sine-qua-non;* like that, it may be made invariably palatable by a little care in a few plain particulars, through neglect of which it often becomes intolerable. The soggy, waxy, indigestible viand that often appears in the potato-dish is a downright sacrifice of the better nature of this vegetable.

The potato, nutritive and harmless as it appears, belongs to a family suspected of very dangerous traits. It is a family connection of the deadly-nightshade and other ill-reputed gentry, and sometimes shows strange proclivities to evil—now breaking out uproariously, as in the noted potato-rot, and now more covertly, in various evil affections. For this reason scientific directors bid us beware of the water in which potatoes are boiled—into which, it appears, the evil principle is drawn off; and they caution us not to shred them into stews without previously suffering the slices to lie for an hour or so in salt and water. These cautions are worth attention.

The most usual modes of preparing the potato for the table are by roasting or boiling. These processes are so simple that it is commonly supposed every cook understands them without special directions; and yet there is scarcely an uninstructed cook who can boil or roast a potato.

A good roasted potato is a delicacy worth a dozen compositions of the cook-book; yet when we ask for it, what burnt, shriveled abortions are presented to us! Biddy rushes to her potato-basket and pours out two dozen of different sizes, some having in them three times the amount of matter of others. These being washed, she tumbles them into her oven at a leisure interval, and there lets them lie till it is time to serve breakfast, whenever that may be. As a result, if the largest are cooked, the smallest are presented in cinders, and the intermediate sizes are withered and watery. Nothing is so utterly ruined by a few moments of overdoing. That which at the right moment was plump with mealy rich-ness, a quarter of an hour later shrivels and becomes watery—and it is in this state that roast potatoes are most frequently served.

In the same manner we have seen boiled potatoes from an un-taught cook coming upon the table like lumps of yellow wax—and the same article, under the directions of a skillful mistress, appearing in snowy balls of powdery whiteness. In the one case, they were thrown in their skins into water, and suffered to soak or boil, as the case might be, at the cook's leisure, and after they were boiled to stand in the water till she was ready to peel them. In the other case, the potatoes being first peeled were boiled as quickly as possible in salted water, which the mo-ment they were done was drained off, and then they were gently shaken for a moment or two over the fire to dry them still more thor-oughly. We have never yet seen the potato so depraved and given over to evil that it could not be reclaimed by this mode of treatment.

As to fried potatoes, who that remembers the crisp, golden slices of the French restaurant, thin as wafers and light as snow-flakes, does not speak respectfully of them? What cousinship with these have those coarse, greasy masses of sliced potato, wholly soggy and partly burnt, to which we are treated under the name of fried potatoes in America? In our cities the restaurants are introducing the French article to great accept-ance, and to the vindication of the fair fame of this queen of vegetables.

—from *The American Woman's Home,* 1869

FANNIE MERRITT FARMER
ON POTATOES

COMPOSITION.

Water 78.9%.
Starch 18%.
Proteid 2.1%.
Mineral matter .9%.
Fat .1%.

POTATOES STAND PRE-EMINENT AMONG THE VEGETABLES used for food. They are tubers belonging to the Nightshade family; their hardy growth renders them easy of cultivation in almost any soil or climate, and, resisting early frosts, they may be raised in a higher latitude than the cereals.

They give needed bulk to food rather than nutriment, and, lacking in proteid, should be used in combination with meat, fish, or eggs.

Potatoes contain an acrid juice, the greater part of which lies near the skin; it passes into the water during boiling of potatoes, and escapes with the steam from a baked potato.

Potatoes are best in the fall, and keep well through the winter. By spring the starch is partially changed to dextrin, giving the potatoes a sweetness, and when cooked a waxiness. The same change takes place when potatoes are frozen. To prevent freezing, keep a pail of cold water standing near them.

Potatoes keep best in a cool dry cellar, in barrels or piled in a bin. When sprouts appear they should be removed; receiving their nourishment from the starch, they deteriorate the potato.

New potatoes may be compared to unripe fruit, the starch grains not having reached maturity; therefore they should not be given to children or invalids.

—from *Boston Cooking-School Cook Book,* 1896

SHEILA HIBBEN ON AMERICAN POTATOES

Sheila Hibben, a food writer for The New Yorker, *was the original critic for its "Restaurants" column. Her work, both books and articles, showed a deep interest in preserving authentic American cooking.* —M.K.

Mashed Potatoes
(Emporia, Kansas)
SERVES 6

Pare, cut in quarters, and boil 6 medium-sized potatoes; drain and shake over heat to dry. Mash with a wire masher, add 2 tablespoons of butter, beat hard, and add 1½ cups of scalded milk gradually while beating. Sprinkle in 1 tablespoon of chopped chives, add salt to taste, and continue beating until as light and fluffy as a soufflé. Add a little more scalded milk if needed. Pile up lightly in an oven-proof dish and put in a hot oven (400° F.) until the peaks of the mixture just begin to color.

Scalloped Potatoes
(Maine)
SERVES 6

4 medium-sized potatoes   *salt and pepper*
3 tablespoons butter   *milk*
flour

Peel raw potatoes and slice very thin, crosswise. Butter the bottom and sides of a deep baking dish; put in a layer of potato slices, sprinkle with pepper and salt, dredge very lightly with flour, and dot with butter. Repeat twice. Pour over enough milk barely to cover. Bake, covered, in a moderate oven (350° F.) for 40 minutes. Uncover and continue baking another 20 minutes, or until the potatoes are tender and well browned on top.

Stuffed Baked Potatoes
(Illinois)

6 potatoes   *2 teaspoons chopped parsley*
4 thin bacon strips, fried   *½ cup top milk, scalded*

2 tablespoons butter

1 teaspoon finely chopped chives

salt and pepper

melted butter

Select smooth, moderately large potatoes of uniform size. Wash with vegetable brush and place in shallow pan in hot oven (425° F.). Bake for 50 to 60 minutes, or until soft. (Test by taking up with a cloth and squeezing; if soft the potato is done.) Cut a ½ inch slice off top; scoop out inside and mash with crumbled bacon, butter, chives, parsley, and milk. Season to taste with salt and pepper and stuff shells with mixture. Brush with melted butter and arrange close together, stuffed end up, in shallow baking dish. Bake in hot oven (400° F.) just long enough to brown the tops.

Potato Charlotte
(Ohio)
SERVES 6

1 medium-sized onion, chopped fine

3 tablespoons butter

3 potatoes

2 eggs, well beaten

½ cup milk

salt and pepper

Fry onion in butter until it just begins to color. Grate the raw potatoes and combine with the onion; season with 1 teaspoon salt and ¼ teaspoon pepper. Combine eggs with milk and mix well with potatoes. Grease and heat a heavy frying pan, pour potato mixture into it and bake in hot oven (450° F.) until well browned on top. With the aid of a spatula and pancake turner slide onto a hot platter and serve with pot roast.

—from *American Regional Cookery*, 1932

PABLO NERUDA ON FRENCH FRIES

Between the years 1954 and 1959, Chilean poet Pablo Neruda (1904–1973), the 1971 Nobel laureate in literature, wrote four volumes of odes to mundane everyday objects. Many of his "common things" were foods. —M.K.

Ode to French fries

What sizzles
in boiling
oil
is the world's
pleasure:
French
fries
go
into the pan
like the morning swan's
snowy
feathers
and emerge
half-golden from the olive's
crackling amber.

Garlic
lends them
its earthy aroma,
its spice,
its pollen that braved the reefs.
Then,
dressed
anew
in ivory suits, they fill our plates
with repeated abundance,
and the delicious simplicity of the soil.

—*Odes to Common Things*, 1954,
translated from the Spanish by Ken Krabbenhoft

CHAPTER SIXTEEN

A Pinch of Seasoning

PLINY THE ELDER ON THYME

THERE ARE TWO KINDS OF THYME: THE PALE AND THE dark. Thyme flowers about the period of the summer solstice, when the bees collect from it. It offers a rough guide to the yield of honey, for beekeepers hope for an abundance of honey if the thyme flowers profusely. Thyme is damaged by rain and sheds its flowers. The seed is invisible to the eye; but the seed of wild marjoram, although very small, is large enough to be seen. But what does it matter that Nature has hidden the seed of thyme?

We know that it is inside the flower itself and that a plant grows from the flower when sown. Is there anything with which men have not experimented? Attic honey has a greater reputation than that of any other kind in the whole world. And so thyme has been imported from Attica and, as I am informed, grown with difficulty from the flower. But another characteristic of Attic thyme proved a hindrance: survival depends on a sea breeze. The same view was held in olden times about all kinds of thyme, and people believed that this was the reason why thyme did not grow in Arcadia. They also thought that the olive was found only within 35 miles of the sea, whereas we know today that thyme covers

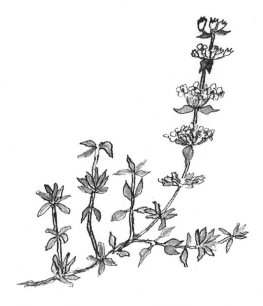

even the stony plains of the province of Gallia Narbonensis, and this is almost the only source of revenue for the inhabitants. Thousands of sheep gather there from distant places to graze on the thyme.

—from *Natural History,* first century A.D.

THE TAMLUD ON GARLIC

Five things were said of garlic:

It satisfies your hunger.
It keeps the body warm.
It makes your face bright.
It increases a man's potency.
And it kills parasites in the bowels.
Some people say that it also encourages love and removes jealousy.

—from the Babylonian Talmud, A.D. 500

PLATINA ON BASIL

WHAT THE GREEKS CALLED *OKUMON* WE ALSO CALL *ocimum* [basil], with the first syllable long, that is, in my judgment, what is commonly called "princely." It is sown in spring and is transplanted in summer because it flourishes better from a slip. It flowers at the bottom first, then at the top, as Theophrastus says, and it remains in flower a long time. The doctor Chrysippus gave basil harmful properties because it is bad for the stomach, dulls the eyes, brings on insanity, and obstructs the liver, so that a she-goat never touches this sort of herb. Especially, if it is ground and covered with stones, scorpions will be generated from it. Chewed up and placed in the sun, it makes worms and nourishes lice. Among the Africans they also think this has been established: if anyone eats basil on a day when he is struck by a scorpion, he cannot be saved.

All these stories really are found through experience to be false, since she-goats eat basil, and the minds of men who smell it are not altered. Also, it heals the bites of both land and sea scorpions when a little wine and vinegar is added. It has also been discovered by experience that, when it is flavored with vinegar, it is healthful for the faint. Galen affirms that a scorpion is wonderfully pleased by the smell of basil and therefore goes willingly toward its stalk, but it must be used sparingly because of its excessive force, which comes from its warmth and dryness.

—from *On Right Pleasure,* 1465,
translated from the Latin by Mary Ella Milham

PLATINA ON SAFFRON

I WOULD JUSTIFIABLY ADD TO THE SPICES SAFFRON [*crocus*] since it grows with their characteristics, with the color with which it is quite often adorned, and with its savor, in which there is no small amount of strength. We have wild and cultivated saffron. It has roots like an onion but is not in every way of the same productiveness and pleasantness. The first rank is ascribed to the Cilician variety, both there in the Taurus mountains and in Tmolus; the second rank, to the Lycian; and the third, to the Italian, although varieties grow everywhere.

When the best saffron is touched by a hand, if it is brittle, it rustles. Another test: if it has been conveyed from hand to mouth, it lightly stings the face and eyes. The best everywhere is that which is oiliest and instantly fragrant. It blooms at the setting of the Pleiades and for a few days is green in flower and leaf. It is gathered in winter and dried in the shade. Moderate use of saffron, whose force is warm and dry, is beneficial to the lungs, chest, liver, and heart. When drunk with wine, it creates drunkenness because it has a strong odor. The tales of poets tell that a youth named Crocus was changed into a flower of his name. There are others, though, who think that it is called *crocus* from the town of Corycus in Cilicia.

—from *On Right Pleasure,* 1465,
translated from the Latin by Mary Ella Milham

KARL FRIEDRICH VON RUMOHR
ON SORREL

SORREL LEAVES CAN ENHANCE THE FLAVOUR OF STOCKS, they can flavour a variety of sauces and can be consumed as a vegetable, either alone, or mixed with other herbs.

Sorrel is especially mild, with a pleasant bitterness, in winter and spring and it is therefore particularly important at this time of year not to deprive it of this fine acidity by blanching it before cooking. It becomes more robust in summer and the pedantic German habit of blanching it before chopping and cooking is then less damaging to it.

Some people, being unable to stand any assertive flavour, like to add sugar to their sorrel dishes. I have reason to believe that sweetened sorrel actually engenders acids whilst the unsweetened version eliminates them.

It is quite appropriate to thicken steamed sorrel with an egg yolk mixed in a little stock.

A sauce can be made by boiling freshly chopped sorrel in meat stock and a variation is made by steaming tender sorrel leaves in meat stock, diluting this a little and then thickening it with a few egg yolks.

—from *The Essence of Cookery*, 1822,
translated from the German by Barbara Yeomans

THE AOBO TU
ON SALT MAKING

The Aobo Tu was written between 1333 and 1335 by a man named Chen Chun from Yuan, who served in the Chinese government salt administration, the yansi, at the salt works of Xiasha in a marshy area along a tributary of the Yangtze. His stated goal was to inform the government of the latest in salt-producing technology so that the government could improve the life of salt workers. At times highly technical, at other times poetic, this book was intended by Chen Chun to be the definitive government guide on salt production. —M.K.

Through the bamboo tube the brine is released and begins to flow into the pan.
Today the fire is started in the whole unit.
Daily boiling and refining month after month, no rest can be taken, fearing that the fire is too fierce and that the pan would easily get [too] dry.
The blazing fire vault is more than three *chi* [high] from the ground [and is so hot that] the sea's waves are instantly boiled down to salt.
During the boiling nobody cares about cold or hot [weather], because the hearth workers [*zaoding*] are sweating [their own] rain. . . .

When the firing term (*huofu*) is one of high quality, then the salt will easily crystallize.
As the sun is burning and the winds strongly blowing, [this period] is superior to other months.
[Salt] which is about to be formed, but is [still] wet and not yet dry is removed and loaded on the "bed for removing [salt]" where it will become [like] snow.
When the brine in the pan [is about to] dry up, [brine] is added again and again,

[because] it is important that there is no interruption in [the operation of] the pan.
The workers' faces are ash-gray and their sweat is like blood.
During the whole day and from sunset to dawn no rest may be
taken. . . .

The huge pan has not yet cooled down and the fire has just extinguished, [the salt] in the pan is being lightly shovelled, because the
iron should not be scraped.
There are [salt grains] resembling the not yet full moon of last
night,
which has been eaten and harmed by the magic toad and whose
roundness thus has [some] deficiency.
There are also [grains] resembling triangular crystals
or steamed bread with cracks in the form of a cross.
There is some anxiety that the weather is often cold and misty,
but [also] happiness about the salty snow [produced] at the sea
shore. . . .

Dead ashes (*sihui*) do not burn again,
while living ashes (*shenghui*) are not yet dead.
Yesterday morning they were still in the burning [hearth] vault,
today they are as cold as water.
Nobody objects to the heavy weight of the ash loads.
Heaping up the ashes, how could they be wasted.
Exposed to dryness and then leached,
they are [like] ghosts returning to life. . . .

How much is boiled within one day,
and how much is collected daily?
One is only afraid that [the quota] cannot be reached,
thus not only meeting with [the superiors'] sneering and scolding
[but also with beating].
The daily levies (*ke*) have their working schedule,
and for official affairs no wasting of time is [allowed].
Month after month, no false reports are presented,
and one does not dare to cause delays to the salt supervising
officials. . . .

The loose salt resembles heaped up snow,
and hundreds of heaps are spread on the ground.
The guarding might be somewhat lax,
or the doors of the unit may sometimes be open in the night.
[Therefore] a lot of buffaloes and ships are provided,
and also manpower is used for carrying.
The head storehouse has all under control,
it does not have to call for [the boats], they come by themselves.

—from *The Aobo Tu,* 1333–1335,
translated from the Chinese by Hans Ulrich Vogel

CHAPTER SEVENTEEN

Just a Salad

PLATINA ON LETTUCE

APULEIUS THINKS LETTUCE [*LACTUCA*] IS NAMED FROM AN abundance of milk [*lac*], that is, of humor, or because it fills nursing women with milk. There are several varieties of this vegetable, but broad-stemmed, low-growing, and curly and are really praised before all others. They are planted all year in fertile, well-watered and fertilized places; it is therefore all right to scatter seed at the winter solstice, transplant or sow seed with the west wind and transplant at the vernal equinox. The white varieties tolerate the winter best. There is a chilling nature in all these, for they are considered cold and damp, and for this reason they take squeamishness away from the stomach in summer and stimulate the appetite for food.

They say the divine Augustus was preserved in a time of ill health by the use of lettuce, and no wonder, because it aids digestion and generates better blood than other vegetables. It is eaten cooked or raw. You season raw lettuce this way if it does not need washing, for that is more healthful than what has been washed in water; put it in a dish, sprinkle with ground salt, pour in a little oil and more vinegar and eat at once. Some add a little mint and parsley to it for seasoning so that it does not seem entirely bland and the excessive chill of the lettuce does not harm the stomach. Put cooked lettuce, with the water pressed out, in a pan and serve to your guests seasoned with salt, oil and vinegar. Some sprinkle a bit of well-ground and sifted cinnamon or pepper on it. This food induces sleep, soothes a cough generated by a warm humor, moves the urine, slows passion and moves the bowels. Its frequent use, though, especially dulls the keenness of vigorous eyes.

There is another sort of lettuce which is called goat-lettuce. If this is ground and thrown into the sea, the fish which are nearest are killed immediately, and river fish do the same. There is *serralia* lettuce, a wild kind which is named for a so-called saw [*serra*], which they think it has on its back. This is perhaps endive.

—from *On Right Pleasure*, 1465,
translated from the Latin by Mary Ella Milham

FRANÇOIS RABELAIS ON EATING PILGRIMS IN SALAD

François Rabelais was a sixteenth-century cleric and writer born in Chinon, France, from whose writing has evolved two adjectives in English: gargantuan and Rabelaisian. Gargantuan means gigantic, from his five-volume story of a giant named Gargantua and his son Pantagruel. Rabelaisian means possessing the qualities of both wild imagination and crude language. Rabelais's writing, of course, was Rabelaisian. Gargantuan appetites are a frequent theme. Rabelais was not only Rabelaisian but hedonistic, funny, ironic, and so deeply intellectual that it is almost impossible to find all the thoughts, references, and subtexts that are jammed into his work. —M.K.

THE STORY REQUIRES US TO RELATE WHAT HAPPENED TO SIX pilgrims coming from Saint-Sébastien, near Nantes, who, to get lodging that night, for fear of the enemy had hidden in the garden upon the pea-straw, between the cabbages and the lettuce.

Gargantua found himself a bit thirsty, and asked if someone could find him some lettuce to make a salad, and, hearing that there was some of the finest and biggest in the country, for the heads were as big as plum trees or walnut trees, decided to go there himself, and carried off in his hand what seemed good to him. With it he carried off the six pilgrims, who were so afraid that they dared neither speak nor cough.

So, as he was washing it in the fountain, the pilgrims were whispering to one another: "What's to be done? We're drowning here, amid the lettuce. Shall we speak? But if we speak, he'll kill us as spies."

And as they were deliberating thus, Gargantua put them with the lettuce on one of the dishes of the house, as big as the cask of Cisteaux, and, with oil and vinegar and salt, was eating them as a pick-me-up before supper, and had already swallowed five of the pilgrims. The sixth was in the dish, hidden under a lettuce leaf, except for his staff, which showed above it. Seeing it, Grandgousier said to Gargantua:

"That's a snail's horn there; don't eat it."

"Why not?" said Gargantua. "They're all good all this month."

And, pulling out his staff, he picked up the pilgrim with it, and was eating him nicely; then he drank a horrific draft of *pineau,* and they waited for supper to be ready.

The pilgrims, eaten thus, pulled themselves as best they could out away from the grinders of his teeth, and thought they had been put in some deep dungeon in the prisons, and, when Gargantua drank the great draft, thought they would drown in his mouth, and the torrent nearly carried them off into the gulf of his stomach; however, jumping with the help of their staffs as the Michelots do, they got to safety in the shelter of his teeth. But by bad luck one of them, feeling the surroundings with his staff to find out if they were in safety, landed it roughly in the cavity of a hollow tooth and struck a nerve in the jawbone, by which he caused Gargantua very sharp pain, and he started to cry out with the torment he endured.

So, to relieve himself of the pain, he had his toothpick brought, and, going out toward the young walnut tree, he dislodged milords the pilgrims. For he caught one by the legs, another by the shoulders, another by the knapsack, another by the pouch, another by the scarf; and the poor wretch who had hit him with the staff he hooked by the codpiece; however, this was a great piece of luck for him, for he pierced open for him a cancerous tumor that had been tormenting him since they had passed Ancenis.

So the dislodged pilgrims fled through the vineyard at a fine trot, and the pain subsided. At which time he was called to supper by Eudémon, for everything was ready.

—from *Gargantua and Pantagruel,* 1534,
translated from the French by Donald M. Frame

GIACOMO CASTELVETRO ON SALAD

IT TAKES MORE THAN GOOD HERBS TO MAKE A GOOD salad, for success depends on how they are prepared. So, before going any further, I think I should explain exactly how to do this.

It is important to know how to wash your herbs, and then how to season them. Too many housewives and foreign cooks get their greenstuff all ready to wash and put it in a bucket of water, or some other pot, and slosh it about a little, and then, instead of taking it out with their hands, as they ought to do, they tip the leaves and water out together, so that all the sand and grit is poured out with them. Distinctly unpleasant to chew on . . .

So, you must first wash your hands, then put the leaves in a bowl of water, and stir them round and round, then lift them out carefully. Do this at least three or four times, until you can see that all the sand and rubbish has fallen to the bottom of the pot.

Next, you must dry the salad properly and season it correctly. Some cooks put their badly washed, barely shaken salad into a dish, with the leaves still so drenched with water that they will not take the oil, which they should to taste right. So I insist that first you must shake your salad really well and then dry it thoroughly with a clean linen cloth so that the oil will adhere properly. Then put it into a bowl in which you have previously put some salt and stir them together, and then add the oil with a generous hand, and stir the salad again with clean fingers or a knife and fork, which is more seemly, so that each leaf is properly coated with oil.

Never do as the Germans and other uncouth nations do—pile the badly washed leaves, neither shaken nor dried, up in a mound like a pyramid, then throw on a little salt, not much oil and far too much vinegar, without even stirring. And all this done to produce a decorative effect, where we Italians would much rather feast the palate than the eye.

You English are even worse; after washing the salad heaven knows how, you put the vinegar in the dish first, and enough of that for a footbath for Morgante, and serve it up, unstirred, with neither oil nor salt, which you are supposed to add at table. By this time some of the leaves are so saturated with vinegar that they cannot take the oil, while the rest are quite naked and fit only for chicken food.

So, to make a good salad the proper way, you should put the oil in first of all, stir it into the salad, then add the vinegar and stir again. And if you do not enjoy this, complain to me.

The secret of a good salad is plenty of salt, generous oil and little vinegar, hence the text of the Sacred Law of Salads:

Insalata ben salata,
poco aceto e ben oliata.

Salt the salad quite a lot,
then generous oil put in the pot,
and vinegar, but just a jot.

And whosoever transgresses this benign commandment is condemned never to enjoy a decent salad in their life, a fate which I fear lies in store for most of the inhabitants of this kingdom.

—from *The Fruit, Herbs & Vegetables of Italy*, 1614,
translated from the Italian by Gillian Riley

MARGARET DODS JOHNSTONE ON SALADS

Margaret Dods Johnstone established England's first cooking club, the Cleikum Club. Unusual for British cookbooks of the early nineteenth century, hers includes not only French and

*English recipes but also recipes from Germany and Spain and
even Asia.*   —M.K.

Of Salads.

Salad herbs are cooling and refreshing. They correct the prutrescent
tendency of animal food, and are antiscorbutic. Salads are at any rate
a harmless luxury where they agree with the stomach; and though they
afford little nourishment of themselves, they make a pleasant addition
to other aliments, and a graceful appearance on the dinner-table. *Lettuce,* of the different sorts, or *salad* as it is often called, is the principal
ingredient in those vegetable messes. It should be carefully blanched
and eat young; when old, its juices become acrimonious and hurtful.
Lettuce possesses soporific qualities, and is recommended as a
supper-article to bad sleepers. *Radishes,* when young, are juicy and
cooling, but a very few days change their nature, and they become
woody and acrid; when not very young, they ought to be scraped. *Cress*
and *mustard* are cordial and grateful, and of an agreeable pungency;
and *celery,* when young and properly blanched, by its peculiar nutty
flavour, contributes much to what EVYLYN calls "harmony in the com-
posure of a sallet." A variety of other herbs mingle in full well-selected
salads, such as sorrel, young onions, cucumbers, tomatas, endive,
radish-leaflets, &c. Many wild herbs were formerly employed, and are
still used on the continent and in America, as saladings. As this is
quite a delicate, *jaunty* branch of the culinary art, we would recommend that young ladies residing in the country should gather their
own salad herbs, and dress salads for their families, which will give a
better chance of a duty being well done, which, in the hurry of the
stew-pan, the spit, and the stove, the poor distracted cook must often
perform with haste and slovenliness. Never make a salad till near the
dinner-hour, as it will flatten and lose its light appearance by standing.
Foreigners call many things salads we would merely reckon cold, little,
dressed dishes. As this may produce a confusion of ideas in the young
housekeeper we notice it here. Our ancestors had the same notion of
what *sallets* were that the French still retain.

An English Salad and Salad-Sauce.

Let the herbs be fresh gathered, nicely trimmed and picked, and re-
peatedly washed in salt and water. Drain and cut them. Just before dinner is served, rub the yolks of two hard-boiled eggs very smooth on a

soup-plate, with a little very rich cream. When well mixed, add a tea-spoonful of made mustard and a little salt, a spoonful of olive-oil, one of oiled butter, or two of sour cream may be substituted, and when this is mixed smooth, put in as much vinegar as will give the proper degree of acidity to the sauce,—about two large spoonfuls; add a little pounded lump-sugar if the flavour is liked. Put this sauce in the dish, and lay the cut herbs lightly over it; or mix them well with it, and garnish with beet-root sliced and marked, rings of the white of the eggs, young radishes, &c. Onions may be served separately on a small dish. Some *knowing* persons like grated Parmesan put to their salad and sauce.

—from *Cook and Housewife Manual,* 1829

Mrs. Beeton on Endive

This vegetable, so beautiful in appearance, makes an excellent addition to winter salad, when lettuces and other salad herbs are not obtainable. It is usually placed in the centre of the dish, and looks remarkably pretty with slices of beetroot, hard-boiled eggs, and curled celery placed round it, so that the colours contrast nicely. In preparing it, carefully wash and cleanse it free from insects, which are generally found near the heart; remove any decayed or dead leaves, and dry it thoroughly by shaking in a cloth. This vegetable may also be served hot, stewed in cream, brown gravy, or butter, but when dressed thus, the sauce it is stewed in should not be very highly seasoned, as that would destroy and overpower the flavour of the vegetable.

Average cost, 1*d.* per head.
Sufficient,—1 head for a salad for 4 persons.
Seasonable from November to March.

ENDIVE.—This is the *C. endivium* of science, and is much used as
a salad. It belongs to the family of the *Composite,* with Chicory, common Goats-beard, and others of the same genus. Withering states,
that before the stems of the common Goats-beard shoot up, the roots,
boiled like asparagus, have the same flavour, and are nearly as nutritious. We are also informed by Villars that the children in Dauphiné
universally eat the stems and leaves of the young plant before the flowers appear, with great avidity. The fresh juice of these tender herbs is
said to be the best solvent of bile.

Stewed Endive

INGREDIENTS.—6 heads of endive, salt and water, 1 pint of broth,
thickening of butter and flour, 1 tablespoonful of lemon-juice, a small
lump of sugar.
    Mode.—Wash and free the endive thoroughly from insects, re-
move the green part of the leaves, and put it into boiling water,
slightly salted. Let it remain for 10 minutes; then take it out, drain it
till there is no water remaining, and chop it very fine. Put it into a
stewpan with the broth; add a little salt and a lump of sugar, and boil
until the endive is perfectly tender. When done, which may be ascertained by squeezing a piece between the thumb and finger, add a
thickening of butter and flour and the lemon-juice: let the sauce boil
up, and serve.

Time.—10 minutes to boil, 5 minutes to simmer in the broth.
Average cost, 1*d.* per head.
Sufficient for 3 or 4 persons.
Seasonable from November to March.

Endive a la Francaise.

INGREDIENTS.—6 heads of endive, 1 pint of broth, 3 oz. of fresh butter; salt, pepper and grated nutmeg to taste.
    Mode.—Wash and boil the endive as in the preceding recipe; chop
it rather fine, and put into a stewpan with the broth; boil over a brisk
fire until the sauce is all reduced; then put in the butter, pepper, salt,

and grated nutmeg (the latter must be very sparingly used); mix all well together, bring it to the boiling point, and serve very hot.

Time.—10 minutes to boil, 5 minutes to simmer in the broth.
Average cost, 1*d.* per head.
Sufficient for 3 or 4 persons.
Seasonable from November to March.

—from *Beeton's Book of Household Management*, 1860

GRIMOD DE LA REYNIÈRE'S WARNING ON CELERY

THE MOST IMPORTANT USE FOR CELERY IS IN SALAD, OR better yet rémoulade with an excellent mustard from Maille or Bordin. Well-seasoned in a good purée it can garnish major dishes, such as braised leg of lamb, a mouton roast, etc. For home cooking it serves as a low-cost side dish, but the best way to serve it is a cream: A well-made celery cream is the test of a good cook and presents fairly daunting problems.

Celery, once it is cooked, loses some of its medicinal qualities; however, it is still clearly an aromatic plant, good for the stomach, warming, and consequently a fairly powerful aphrodisiac. Our conscience forces us to warn shy people that considering this last quality of celery, they might abstain from eating it or use it with caution. Suffice it to say that it is in no way a salad for bachelors.

—from *Almanach des Gourmands,* 1804,
translated from the French by Mark Kurlansky

CHAPTER EIGHTEEN

The Thing About Truffles

What did Grimod mean when he said that a truffle was a "foretaste of paradise"? Brillat-Savarin wrote, "Nobody dares admit that he has been present at a meal where there was not at least one dish with truffles." What is it about this underground fungus? Is it the fact that it is underground, hidden from sight, hard to find? For more than a century agronomists have dreamed of farming it, but many think that if they succeeded, if it became readily available, it would lose its mystique. At a dollar a basket, the bumpy fungus might find itself abandoned like the kiwi, a Chinese gooseberry whose tree produces too many fruit to maintain exotic status. Waverley Root thought it was the price: Truffles were so valuable that nobody dared eat a big enough piece to understand what it really tasted like. Surely, if you just took a bite, like from an apple, it would be a disappointment.

But then one day he did. —M.K.

WAVERLEY ROOT ON TRUFFLES

"LYBIANS, UNYOKE YOUR OXEN!" JUVENAL CRIED. "KEEP your grain, but send us your truffles!"

Truffles were already an old story by Juvenal's time. They were being eaten in Mesopotamia at least by 1800 B.C., although I do not know that we are obliged to believe the contemporary French author who tells us that a certain Queen Shibtu of Babylon was fond of truffles wrapped in papyrus and roasted in the ashes of the hearth, the ancient precursor of the French *truffes sous les cendres.* The Romans had truffles from Greece, where they seem to have been appreciated, but less so than by themselves; Coelius Apicius concocted six truffle recipes, but we do not know what kind of truffles they were: one description suggests that they were gray truffles, a sort which has little flavor. The ancient Romans also ate, from their own territory, the truffles of Spoleto, in Umbria, highly thought of still; but whether they discovered them before or after Juvenal appealed to the Libyans I do not know. Apparently they never discovered that in what is now the Piedmont they possessed the tubercle most exclusively associated with Italy today, the white truffle.

Pliny agreed with Juvenal that the best truffles came from Africa; the latter prized them so highly that he advised the well-to-do to prepare them with their own hands, for they were too precious to trust to servants. Yet he did not rank them above what he evidently felt was Italy's best MUSHROOM, putting them only on the same level as *boleti,* while Martial even ranked them a degree lower. *Boleti* did not mean what we might expect it to today—the boletus—but Caesar's mushroom, *Amanita caesarea.* This species does indeed make excellent eating, but today it would generally be considered inferior to the truffle: Is it possible that the ancients did not know our best truffle, probably a native of France, not of Italy, nor of Libya either? Indeed we may wonder whether Martial was talking about truffles at all when, in a burst of unbridled empathy, he cast himself as a truffle and wrote: "We truffles, who burst through the nurturing soil with our soft heads, are of earth's apples second only to *boleti.*" The peculiarity of truffles is precisely that they do not burst through the nurturing soil with heads soft or otherwise, but remain buried snugly underground.

Truffles disappear from history after the collapse of the Roman Empire, though they must still have been there, allowed to stay underground by a society which was not characterized by gastronomic finesse. The reference books tell us that they returned about the middle of the fourteenth century, but without offering any specific examples; they are not mentioned in the anonymous *Le Ménagier de Paris* at the end of that century. The first trustworthy reference I have found dates from the fifteenth century, when Platina wrote of truffles that "they must be eaten as the last course, for they help greatly to make meat descend through the opening of the stomach." It is at this period also that we first hear of truffles being sought in France with the aid of pigs carefully muzzled to prevent them from eating the truffles before their masters had time to lay hands on them. They seem at that time almost always to have been pickled, which must have deprived them of much of their natural flavor. The celebrated chef Pierre François de la Varenne rescued them from pickling in the seventeenth century, using them in cooking like other mushrooms. In the eighteenth, truffles were still rare and expensive. "A truffled turkey," Brillat-Savarin wrote, "was a luxury, found only on the tables of the greatest lords and of kept women."

It was in the nineteenth century that truffles reached their apogee. They cannot be said, however, to have penetrated deep into the less privileged layers of society in 1848, when the mob which pillaged the pantries of Louis Philippe's Tuileries palace of its fine foodstuffs left his stock of truffles untouched because nobody knew if they were safe to eat. Yet in 1825 Brillat-Savarin had written, "Nobody dares admit that he has been present at a meal where there was not at least one dish with truffles. However good it may be in itself, an entrée does not appear to advantage unless it has been enriched with truffles." The demand for them trebled, and so did the price. "The Bourbons governed with truffles," Alexandre Dumas wrote, and of the two reigning theatrical queens of the time he ranked Mlle. George above Mlle. Mars because the former served truffles to her guests and the latter did not. Balzac, who mentions truffles often in his works, said of the Comte de Fontaine, one of the characters in his *Le bal de Sceaux,* that "the luxury of his table at his dinners, perfumed with truffles, rivaled the celebrated feasts by which the ministers of the times assured themselves of the votes of their warriors in parliament."

FROM THE BEGINNING THE TRUFFLE WAS A MYSTERY, AND to a certain extent it still is. Some of the ancients held that it was produced by spontaneous generation, and others improved on that by adding that truffles were formed where lightning had struck. Theophrastus recognized them correctly as plants, but Pliny found it difficult to believe that a plant could grow without roots. "We know for a fact," he wrote, "that when Lartius Licinius, an official of praetorian rank, was serving as Minister of Justice at Cartagena in Spain a few years ago, he happened when biting on a truffle to come on a denarius contained inside it which bent his front teeth. This clearly shows that truffles are lumps of earthy substance balled together." To this day there are Spaniards who believe that the truffle is a product of the Devil, partly perhaps because the ground where it is found often presents a devastated appearance, as though it had been scorched by infernal fires. They are "the jewels of poor soils," Colette put it, absolving the Devil. Yet even in this century a malignant power has been attributed to these mushrooms, which, it is held, becomes more potent at night. A French writer advised anyone who discovered that he was traversing truffle territory at night to cross himself quickly three times for protection.

THE ORIGIN OF THE TRUFFLE IS UNKNOWN [WROTE BRILLAT-Savarin]. We find it, but we do not know how it is born nor how it grows. The most skillful men have busied themselves with it, they have believed that they had identified its seeds, they have promised that they would sow it at will. Vain efforts! Lying promises! Their plantings have never been followed by crops.

THE ATTEMPT TO GROW TRUFFLES GOES BACK AT LEAST 175 years, during which time triumphant claims of success have been uttered from time to time—followed, invariably, by silence. One of the first came from a French peasant who, early in the nineteenth century, planted acorns from "truffle oaks" (the scrub oaks around which truffles are oftenest found) in truffle territory and attributed truffles found there ten or fifteen years later to his acorns; but nobody else has succeeded in achieving this result since. Strenuous efforts to cultivate truffles were made about 1870, when phylloxera devastated the vineyards of Périgord and the Quercy, forcing landholders to seek other sources of revenue; but an increase of the harvest at this time seems to have been the result of more intensive truffle hunting rather than of any increase in the number of truffles. Seedling oaks have been planted in the hope that they would encourage the development of satellite truffles, without significant success; and pieces of truffles or truffles themselves have been buried in what seemed propitious soil, and the ground has been soaked with water in which truffles had been steeped. "Wasted effort," wrote *Le Monde* in January 1978. "The truffle is a wild and fantastic vegetable, whose underground growth escapes all observation and defies all prediction."

One month after this pessimistic conclusion, the French National

Institute for Agronomics announced that it had produced twenty cultivated truffles which had taken three and a half years to grow after a seeding of truffle spores accompanied by the planting of oak saplings. The first, it was reported, weighed 170 grams, nearly six ounces, a good size, quality undescribed. But at the time of writing it is still not possible, and will not be possible for several years, to assert that the problem of cultivating truffles has been solved. The planting, in 1974, had been a large one—150,000 oak seedlings, covering an area of about 7500 acres in a number of plantations on land chosen because it seemed suitable for truffles: who can say that this much land might not have developed twenty truffles in three and a half years even if the oaks had never been planted and the spores never sown?—and three and a half years should theoretically have been too little time to permit a truffle to reach this size and too little time also to permit an oak sapling to contribute to its growth.

THE TRUFFLE HAS FOR CENTURIES BEEN CELEBRATED WITH extravagant praise. The most common epithet for it is "black diamond," perhaps originated by Brillat-Savarin, who called it "the black diamond of the kitchen"; it has also been called the "black pearl." George Sand, in a kittenish moment, referred to the truffle as "the fairy apple." Alexandre Dumas, who said that it "holds the first place among mushrooms," called it, in bad Latin, the *"sacro sanctorum"* of gourmets. For the Marquis de Cussy it was "the underground empress," for James de Coquet "a fragrant nugget," and for Fulbert-Dumonteil "the divine tuber."

I did not go overboard about the truffle myself in *The Food of France*, where I wrote that "on those rare occasions when truffles are served relatively alone, their own taste can be detected as a rather faint licorice flavor." The fact is that I had not then ever tasted a really first-class truffle, but I didn't know it; and besides, I had been subjected to an experience which should have put me off truffles forever. In an unwary moment I had consented to be filmed eating *truffes sous les cendres* for a television short on Paris restaurants, a process which I had assumed would take about half an hour. I ate truffles-cooked-in-the-ashes for five hours without a break—the same truffles, which by the end of the session had become thoroughly tired, and so had I. I felt that I never wanted to see a truffle again.

Several years later I was invited to the opening of a new Parisian restaurant owned by a man who was a specialist in the foods of the

French southwest—truffle country. Truffles were present, beautiful truffles which should have been painted by Van Gogh—as large as tangerines, almost black, with a suggestion of purple, attractively pebbled, and glistening as though they had just been oiled. They were there to admire, not to eat: they were too precious to be lavished, free, on guests. But it happened that I was standing between the Admiral de Toulouse-Lautrec and the restaurant owner when he steeled himself to make the supreme sacrifice. I did not rate such magnificent treatment, but the admiral did—not because he was an admiral, not because he was an authentic member of the famous painter's family, but because his wife was Mapie de Toulouse-Lautrec, the Mary Margaret McBride of France (I purposely avoid comparison with present practitioners of public gastronomy out of cowardice), who was not present. Our host unlocked one of the glass cases behind which his truffles beamed at us, removed one, and handed it to the admiral, who regarded it with misgiving. "Here," he said, thrusting it at me. "*You're the food expert.*" I bit full into it and my mouth was flooded with what was probably the most delicious taste I have ever encountered in my entire life, simultaneously rich, subtle and undescribable. I ate it all, while the other guests regarded me with loathing.

"Rather faint licorice flavor" indeed! There was no suggestion of licorice, nor of any other fragrance I could recollect. I find it quite impossible to pass on any idea of its taste. If I say it was as sturdy as meat, I will start you off on a completely wrong track as to its savor. If I say it was as unctuous and aromatic as chocolate, I will do the same. Truffles taste like truffles, and like nothing else whatsoever; and it is a rare, rare privilege to be able to taste a fresh truffle of this quality. I never have since, though I have occasionally come across truffles which redeemed those I had reduced to chewing gum for the television camera—at Rocamadour and Sarlat, in the heart of French truffle country, and in Perugia, in the heart of Umbrian truffle country.

The Umbrian truffles seemed to me quite rich, but they did not match the French samplings, which I assume were Périgord truffles, reputed since the end of the fifteenth century to be the best of the forty-two botanically recognized species. Périgord truffles are not restricted to the Périgord; indeed, almost none of them come from there today, for the truffle fields of that area became exhausted many years ago and were almost unanimously abandoned, as yielding too few truffles to be worth hunting for; but after its long resting period, the Périgord country seems now to be recuperating. Meanwhile the most important truffle region of France has become the Quercy, capital Cahors, just south of Périgord. (Quercy comes from the Latin *quercus,* "oak," the tree with which the truffle is most frequently associated.) The truffles of this province and also of the Vaucluse, good truffle country too, as well as of one or two other minor truffle centers, are authentic Périgord truffles, for this is not a place name, but the popular equivalent of a species name. The Périgord truffle is *Tuber melanosperm,* also called the black truffle—in the Périgord dialect, the *truffaïro* (*negro soumo l'amò d'un domna,* "black as a damned soul"). It is indeed black or a very dark brown on the outside; inside, the flesh (technically the gleba) is whitish to begin with, but as it ripens passes through gray to brown. The mature truffle is a dark brown inside, but not uniformly so; it gives a marbled appearance, and is threaded with very fine white veins.

The second best truffle, in common opinion, is *T. magnatum,* the white truffle of northern Italy, which grows especially in the region of Alba (the Umbrian truffle mentioned above was black, not white). Its flesh is described poetically in the Italian Rinaldi-Tyndalo mushroom encyclopedia as "rosy white, then silver amethystine," and, like the Périgord truffle, it appears to be marbled. The odor is described as like a mixture of garlic and cheese, and almost everybody agrees that it has a faint taste of garlic (there is a good deal of sulfur in truffles, including Périgord truffles, which is principally what accounts for the flavor of garlic). I did not myself note a garlic taste on the only occasion when I have eaten white truffles, and though it is usually reported that their taste is stronger than that of black truffles, it seemed to me to be rather too thin to justify the praise lavished on that species; but after having so badly underestimated the black truffle on the basis of insufficient experience, I am not going to base any opinion on the strength of a single sampling. I shall assume that the white truffles I met were not the best representatives of their type. White truffles, unlike black truffles, are never cooked. They are usually sliced thin and sprinkled over whatever dish they are to adorn; if it is a hot dish, they are added to it at the last moment, after the cooking is over.

In France, where there are between fifteen and twenty thousand professional truffle gatherers, all small operators, there are, besides the Périgord truffle, other black, brown, gray, violet and white truffles of several species, ranging in flavor from "extreme succulence to pale banality"—most of them closer to the banal side. One rarely hears specific mention of the other kinds. I have come across references to an Italian variety, black outside and white inside, described as "without much flavor." Of the gray truffle, Dumas wrote that it was "almost as delicate as the white truffle" of northern Italy, but Colette described it as "almost insipid." I do not know the species of Alsatian truffles, of which there are in any case not many, but an eighteenth-century historian of cooking wrote that though they were inferior to Périgord truffles, "they have nevertheless their own special perfume and their own charm."

The truffle is pretty much unsung in English literature, for it seems to have short-changed English-speaking countries. The only edible variety in the British Isles is *T. aestivus,* the summer truffle, dark brown or black, with an aromatic odor but not much taste. Found oftener in association with beeches than with oaks, it is the best Britain can do. (There is also a winter truffle, *T. brumale,* dark and fragrant, which I suspect may be the kind I encountered in Umbria.) The situation is even sadder in the United States, where there are perhaps as many as thirty varieties of truffles, none of which make particularly good eating. Every once in a while somebody discovers truffles there and glimpses fortune ahead, only to suffer disappointment. This happens oftenest in Oregon and California, but the truffles there are neither numerous enough nor good enough to be worth gathering; they have also appeared occasionally in Tennessee, North Carolina and Vermont.

A number of writers nowadays think Juvenal went overboard in his praise of Libyan truffles. According to Brillat-Savarin, those tubers had whitish or reddish flesh, in contrast to the brownish flesh of all the best truffles of today, with the exception of the Italian white truffle. Was the tuber he was talking about really a truffle? The truffle is normally a mushroom of the temperate zone; there seem to be no truffles in Africa today (there is reported to be a white truffle in Morocco, but I have not been able to pin it down). What does appear in Africa, and specifically in Libya, is a tuber of the genus *Terfezia,* hence not a truffle, though for want of a better name it is sometimes called "truffle" in English, and sometimes the "desert truffle" in French, but usually *terfas.* It looks something like a truffle, and exists in black and red varieties. I suspect that this may also be the "truffle" found in the Kalahari Desert of Botswana. If there is a real truffle in Africa, the United Nations Food and Agricultural Organization has not heard about it.

"HOW DO YOU PREFER YOUR TRUFFLES?" AN ANXIOUS hostess who was preparing to take the risk of inviting him to dinner asked the famous gourmet Curnonsky. "In great quantity, madame," he replied. "In great quantity." This may have taken her aback, but it was the right answer. If you want to be able really to taste a truffle, you need enough of it to provide a fair sample. "Truffles are a luxury," James de Coquet wrote, "and the first requirement of luxury is that you should not have to economize. A capon with no truffles at all is better than one which has been truffled, but not enough." A character in a book of the nineteenth-century gastronomic writer Charles Monselet cried, "I don't want truffles cut into little pieces, so scarce that you have to scrape the insides of your chicken to find a few shavings; no, I want avalanches of truffles, *I want too much of them.*"

Robert J. Courtine, a contemporary French gastronomic writer, inveighs perhaps a little too vehemently against the use of bits and snippets of truffle to ornament various dishes, in which their taste is often imperceptible. He admits the use of small pieces of truffle only for Périgueux sauce, a marvelous confection as made by my mother-in-law, a native of the Périgord, but you are not likely to find its equal in restaurants—she takes two days to produce it. On one occasion Courtine conceded grudgingly that pieces of truffle might be permissible in the classic Lyons specialty, chicken in half-mourning, where the mourning note is provided by black truffles, or in pheasant Suvarov, where they are an essential ingredient of the dish, not a mere decoration; but he continued to object to the classic combination of truffle in foie gras. It may have been his influence which caused a Paris restaurant to serve a slab of pure untruffled foie gras, with a whole fresh truffle on the side, a dish for kings—wealthy kings. In the days of the truffle's glory, the proportion of truffles to foie gras was such that it was remarked that instead of truffled foie gras this preparation should have been called "foie-gras'd truffles." Nowadays such a lavish use of truffles would price this marriage off the menu, for expensive as foie gras may be, truffles, volume for volume or weight for weight, are much more so. Another dish I have not seen on a menu for a long time, even in the most expensive restaurants, is the one Charles Chaplin used as a symbol of snobbery in *A Woman of Paris*—truffles cooked in champagne.

Truffles are never likely to descend to a price within reach of the average consumer, for the demand increases and the supply diminishes each year. In 1892, described as "the year of grace" by Périgord truffle gatherers, 2000 tons of truffles were harvested in France. Just before World War I the figure had dropped to 300 tons, by the 1950s to 100, in 1971 to 85, and it now varies between 25 and 150 tons annually, depending chiefly on the weather. France is the world's most important producer of truffles, and enjoys a virtual monopoly of them, for it buys most of the surplus truffles of Italy and Spain, the only other truffle-exporting countries. The French demand alone is greater than the French supply; but France exports about one-third of her superior truffles, making do herself with the less prestigious varieties she buys from the others. Even if the present attempts at the artificial planting of truffles succeed, their price is not likely to drop very much, for what has always made truffles expensive is the cost of gathering them. It is a hit-or-miss affair at best: "Truffles is not farming, it's luck," one producer told John Hess. Since the truffle grows underground, the first problem is to find it, and the second to ease it up gently in order not to disturb the mycelium and prevent it from giving birth to more truffles. This means expenditure of care and time in an era when time is becoming more and more costly, and the employment of hand labor in an era when hand labor also is becoming more and more costly.

For the detection of the tubers, truffle hunters have used sows, dogs, goats (in Sardinia), bear cubs (in Russia, or so I am told), the water-witch's wand (with indifferent success) and the know-how of the skilled observer. Under the last heading, it is not difficult to recognize probable truffle ground because of its scorched-earth appearance, but as this may cover a circle with a radius of 150 feet or more around the nourishing tree, trying to locate the exact spots at which the tubers, walnut-sized or larger, are hiding remains a puzzle. However, though most truffles grow well below the surface, often as deep as a foot, a large one buried less deeply sometimes cracks the soil, where a trained eye can detect its presence. An easier sign for the experienced truffle hunter to read is the presence of flies, of which several species try to lay their eggs in truffles—particularly one which looks like a small wasp, and another which is blue. If a swarm of them hovers over a certain spot, there is probably a truffle beneath it. Some truffle hunters claim to have a sense of smell sufficiently acute to locate truffles, but it is more common to have recourse to animals better endowed olfactorily by nature; even if a man were their equal he would be handicapped over pigs and dogs by wearing his nose higher from the ground, unless he elected to crawl over the terrain on hands and knees.

Truffles are often sought at night, especially in Italy. It is usually explained that this is because the odor of truffles is stronger then, but it may be suspected that there is another reason: to make it difficult for spies to spot the exact location where a truffle has been found. Another tuber may be expected to form in the same location, and if someone else knows where that is, the landowner may arrive to gather his next truffle only to find that someone has been there before him. Night truffle digging is done with the aid of a small flashlight, which does not illuminate a sufficient area to help a truffle thief to find the right place. Poachers are one of the banes of the truffle-land owner; during the season, about November through February, Sunday promenaders, especially if they are accompanied by dogs, are regarded with suspicion.

As is usually the case with expensive foods, fraud is rampant in the truffle market. At the level of the first sale, by the truffle digger to the wholesaler, tunnels bored into truffles by insects are frequently filled skillfully with clay or even with lead, the latter less commonly, for much of this metal would make the truffle too heavy and the buyer suspicious. For foreign markets, where there is little familiarity with this tuber, gray truffles are often dyed black to make them look like the prized Périgord variety. The limit has been reached in Holland and the United States, where traders offer what they refer to disarmingly as "fantasy truffles"—black balls of blood, starch and egg yolk treated with synthetic truffle flavoring. When truffles enter into other foods—such as foie gras—they may be replaced by the mushrooms which the French have named "death trumpets," possibly to discourage others from finding out how good they are. This is not a very serious fraud, for you do get a substitute of excellent flavor, but you pay truffle prices for it.

Truffles are often credited with aphrodisiac virtues, and though one is tempted to ask what isn't, the report in this case is more insistent than in most others. True or not, Mme. de Pompadour believed it, and stuffed herself with truffles, among other things, to maintain an ardor which was not natural to her, for the benefit of the king. No less an authority than Brillat-Savarin (but he was only relaying what others had said) wrote that eating truffles "permitted the stuttering and underpowered Emperor Claudius not to lose face before his young and impetuous wife, Messalina"; but if Juvenal was right, Messalina had slight need of Claudius, being bountifully busied elsewhere, and when she herself fed him mushrooms, it was not truffles, to invigorate him, but a type of fungus selected to do quite the opposite. I have read in a magazine article that it was to truffles "that Henry IV owed his prowess in the bedroom," but most accounts agree that the gallant French monarch required no other stimulant than the presence of an attractive woman. We are told also that one of Napoleon's generals advised him to eat truffles to increase his potency, but not whether Napoleon took his advice, and I have read also, authority unstated, that Louis XIV ate a pound of them a day. No doubt he did: he was a glutton.

Brillat-Savarin devoted exhaustive research to this question, and while he remarked that truffles provoked dreaming, like many mildly exciting foods, he concluded cautiously that "the truffle is not at all a positive aphrodisiac; but it can, on certain occasions, make women more tender and men more amiable."

Truffles might very well act as a general stimulant to the system, for they contain a not inconsiderable dosage of invigorating mineral salts—iron, for instance. Balzac testified to the help this food gave him in his work of creation. "If one truffle falls on my plate," he wrote, "that will suffice: it is the egg which immediately hatches ten characters for my *Comédie Humaine.*"

The worst gastronomic use ever made of the truffle was probably that committed by Delmonico's, the famous New York restaurant, which, attempting to outdo itself for a gala dinner, created ice cream (flavor unspecified) with truffles—"strange to say, very good," said Ward McAllister, who was strange too.

—from *Food,* 1980

GIACOMO CASTELVETRO
ON TRUFFLES

BOTANISTS TELL US THAT THIS NOBLE FRUIT IS A KIND OF mushroom, which grows hidden underground and never sees the light of day. Some people go hunting truffles out of gluttony, and some are greedy for money, and they have two ways of searching for them. When the ground is covered in snow, there sometimes appears on the surface a tiny, bright yellow plant which peasants know conceals truffles, hidden about five or six inches underground.

Our poet Petrarch, comparing the eyes of his beloved to the rays of the sun, said in his nineteenth sonnet, which begins '*Quando il pianeta che . . .*':

> Nor that glow which lights up
> Hills and dales with little flowers,
> But cannot penetrate the earth,
> Which, pregnant by itself alone,
> Produces this fruit so rare . . .

'This fruit so rare' has been interpreted as a dish of truffles the poet was intending to send to a friend.

The other way of finding truffles is by means of that dirty animal, the pig, who loves them more than anything else, and whose acute sense of smell leads it to where they are hidden. The aroma of truffles is rather like that of mushrooms, but much stronger, so the pig can find them however deep the snow is. It digs with its snout into the earth under the snow, and would devour the truffles straight away, but for the wily peasant, who keeps a sharp eye on the pig and when it finds some, drives it away with his spade and grabs the truffles for himself.

The biggest truffles are about the size of an egg; but some are as big as a quince. Truffles are not as spongy as mushrooms. There are two kinds; one has black flesh, like charcoal, and the other is pale. Both of them have a rough, black skin. The black truffles are the best and the most expensive. They sell for more than half a golden *scudo* the pound. They are mainly found around Rome. The pale ones cost less, and large quantities are to be had in Lombardy.

TRUFFLES SHOULD BE WRAPPED IN DAMP PAPER AND cooked in the ashes for about a quarter of an hour. Then peel them just as you would a baked apple or pear, cut them up very small, and finish cooking them in a pan with oil, salt and pepper. When they are nice and hot the truffles are ready to eat, and they are good to eat as they are, with just some lemon or bitter orange juice.

Truffles will keep for a whole year. This is how it is done: after roasting them in the ashes, peel your truffles and cut them into small pieces. Put them in a little pot of olive oil, so that all the pieces are completely covered, and then close it tightly. Store the pot in a dry place. When you need some, take out as many as you want, and heat them in a pan with fresh oil, salt and pepper. Don't forget to serve them with a squeeze of lemon or bitter orange juice—they need nothing else.

With truffles I come to the end of my description of the fruit, herbs, and vegetables of Italy. It would be appropriate for me to finish with an amusing little incident concerning truffles that occurred during my first journey away from home.

IN THE YEAR OF OUR LORD 1572 I FOUND MYSELF IN Germany, studying the somewhat cumbersome language of that noble nation. I was living in the village of Rotteln in Baden Baden, about three miles outside the beautiful city of Basle, which was so full of students from Italy, France and Spain that I had been unable to find lodgings there.

One day I was invited to dine with the lord of that village and the surrounding countryside. The company consisted of a group of gentlemen, one of whom, a charming young baron, had just returned from a visit to Italy. When he heard where I was from, he said, 'Can you tell me, my friend, since you are Italian, why it is that the noblemen of the most civilized nation in the world perambulate their estates in the company of pigs?'

I assumed that he must have seen someone out hunting truffles, in the way I have just described, and could not help laughing at his bewilderment. He took this in bad part, as if I had been calling him a liar or making fun of him. 'Well,' he said crossly, 'is it true, or isn't it?' So to placate him I quickly replied, 'You are absolutely right, you may well have seen quite a few of these gentlemen walking along behind a pig, tied to one of its back legs with a piece of string. But you must also have noticed that the gentleman was followed by a peasant with a spade or shovel over his shoulder.' 'Well, yes, that's true,' he said, 'but there they all were, out walking with pigs.'

'What you saw,' I went on, 'was not an Italian nobleman leading his pig to pasture, but a gentleman following his pig on a treasure hunt. And great fun it is, too. The pig has a keen sense of smell, without which it would never be able to find the treasure, which is hidden deep in the ground under the snow. If you had waited long enough you would have seen the animal rootling in the ground with its snout, and the gentleman pulling the pig back, while the peasant dug away with his spade.'

The young nobleman replied, 'Now that I understand what was

going on, I am no longer scandalized by such behaviour, and am very much obliged to you. But I still cannot imagine what on earth it was that they could have been searching for. If you do not mind, I should be vastly obliged to you for an explanation.'

'Well,' I replied, 'the treasure is not a lump of earth, as some people think, but a sort of mushroom that grows in the ground and never shows above it, called *tartufo.*'

When he heard its name, so like the German *der Teufel* (which means 'devil'), he said, 'Good heavens, how can you bear to eat that sort of monster!' At which I could not prevent myself from laughing out loud, and said, 'I wish to God we had some of these little devils here today, for I am sure that you and all the present company would enjoy them enormously.'

'Well, I must confess,' he said, 'I can well believe that, for I remember how I used to refuse to eat frogs and snails, when I was in your country. I thought they were quite repellent, and now I enjoy them so much I eat them the way other people do chickens or partridges.'

He then went on to talk of other things, and our conversation came to an end. Later he very courteously invited me to visit him. I was entertained on several occasions in his beautiful castle, delightfully situated on a nearby hilltop. There he would offer me exquisitely prepared frogs, and we would both laugh heartily at our little misunderstanding.

—from *The Fruit, Herbs & Vegetables of Italy,* 1614,
translated from the Italian by Gillian Riley

Karl Friedrich von Rumohr on Edible Fungi

THE TRUFFLE IS BY FAR THE BEST OF THE EDIBLE FUNGI. No-one will dispute that it is the jewel in the crown of any lavishly dressed table. Not all truffles are equally fragrant and tasty, however.

The best come from the Périgord area and the Etsch valley, near Trento. The truffle should also be fully mature, without being over-ripe. Truffles which are beginning to decompose should be thrown away, even if they do retain a certain amount of goodness.

Any attached soil is normally removed from truffles by immersing them in simmering wine. Some like to peel them but their rather woody skin actually has the best flavour.

Truffles can be simmered in a mixture of wine and meat stock with whole peppercorns. They are then drained thoroughly, spread out on a cloth and served with fresh butter as a starter.

An Italian method is to heat slivers of truffles on a plate with oil, salt and pepper. Lemon juice is squeezed over them before serving or they may be sprinkled with parmesan cheese. The mixture can be served on slices of toast.

The entire civilised world is familiar with the truffle's power to flavour sauces, pies and stuffings. Once people realised what an effect foods can have upon human emotions, they started to make extensive use of delectable meals on ambassadorial missions. The channels of diplomacy have thus become a fine means of disseminating knowl-edge of special and rare flavours. Any ambassador who represents his master in words only is hardly regarded as doing his job properly. Re-grettably this has led to an increase in the price of this ambiguous nat-ural product at its very source, with the result that the pleasure of the quiet truffle gourmets is somewhat curtailed.

I have encountered one small variety of woody fungus, the prun-joli, only in Italy. This fungus is the equal of the truffle in terms of aroma and strength of flavour but is much less substantial. It may be added to all sorts of chopped mixtures and may, for example, be served on toast, combined with some sort of animal product.

Cultivated fungi, or mushrooms [champignons], are grown in spe-cial beds or can be found wild in horse pastures. Of all the fungi found in Germany, mushrooms have the most tender flesh and the best flavour. The English make a very spicy ketchup from old mushrooms and this has been confused with the Indian soya in our German cook-ery books.

There are many varieties of edible fungi. It is, however, easy to make a mistake and pick a similar, poisonous variety instead of an ed-ible specimen. This explains why many people who value their lives re-frain from consuming any sort of fungus at all.

There are some excellent books on the subject of fungi in general

Ernest Bloch, *The Mushroom Lady,* 1912

and in detail, and householders and cooks should be able to learn from these. Nature delights, however, in cloaking deadly poison and magical flavour in identical garb. There are various suggestions for testing whether fungi are poisonous. These include using onions and dipping in silver spoons. Some believe that they can tell from the smell of a fungus whether it is edible.

—from *The Essence of Cookery,* 1822,
translated from the German by Barbara Yeomans

LUDWIG BEMELMANS ON PIGS AND TRUFFLES

THE NEXT DAY THE VOYAGE BEGAN IN EARNEST AND, AS IT should be, the car was newly washed and in order. Denise was properly dressed, the baggage was in its right place, and I had the route in my head. I set the clock on *"temps de marche"*—an early start is best; it was eight-seventeen. The run would be to Brive la Gaillarde. Normally, in a car like this, I made Cannes in two easy stages, and it could be done in one day, but now I went slowly to look at France. The fields were fresh in the green of spring, it was all orderly, the birds were singing, and nature was celebrating with red, yellow and blue and white flowers and pink blossoms. The day passed and we stopped at the Hôtel de la Truffe Noire in time for dinner.

The hotel itself is nothing extra, but still it is worth a visit. In the kitchen is a chef of the first order, and his specialty is truffles. By way of decoration there is a truffle on all the china.

We arrived there about eight, and I ordered *Truffes sous la cendre*— a manner of cooking them in a jacket of dough under ashes, and when Denise ate them, she looked as if she were eating the ashes. She held a truffle on her fork and she asked, *"Vous aimez ça?"*

I said, "Yes, I like it very much, don't you?"

"Oh, these truffles, *je ne les aime pas trop,*" she said, making a face. "They taste blah blah—I don't know how to say it."

"They are a great delicacy."

"Where do they grow?"

"In the ground, and they are very hard to find. Pigs, special truffle pigs, are used to find them."

"Ah." She said "Ah" the way other people say "Oh" when something unpleasant is told them.

"You don't have to eat them."

"Ah, but if they are so expensive . . ."

"Give them to me and I will order you a *saucisson chaud.*"

"*Merci beaucoup.*"

The next morning we took a walk around the town and Denise said, "Last night in my room, I thought about the pigs."

"What pigs?"

"The pigs with the truffles. How do they know that they are truffles?"

I had no answer to that, and then she asked how it was that people liked them when they tasted so "blah."

I said that it was an acquired taste.

"What is an acquired taste? To eat things that you don't like?"

"Yes, the first cup of coffee tastes awful, the first oyster is hard to swallow, the first snail, the first dish of tripe, kidney, brains, and also other things. The first cigarette and pipe. . . ."

"But the pigs like the truffles?"

"Yes, they are found mostly in soggy earth. A man on stilts follows the pig, and when the pig has uprooted the truffle, then the man, who has a pole with a nail at the end of it, sticks the pig and the pig cries 'Ouch' and drops the truffle. Every tenth truffle the pig is allowed to keep."

"Poor pig! Are all things that are costly gotten with pain?"

"Yes, most. Diamonds are mined deep underground, pearls are obtained with danger, animals are trapped for fur, and the money to buy things is sometimes as hard to get as the things it buys."

"It is terrible for God to lend you life and then take it away, and make the time between hard for people."

"But just now we are happy."

"We are very happy." Then we rolled on.

—from *La Bonne Table,* 1964

Pellegrino Artusi on Truffled Potatoes

THINLY SLICE BLANCHED, PEELED POTATOES AND LAY THEM in a frying pan, interspersed with thinly sliced truffles and grated Parmigiano. Add a few chunks of butter, salt, and pepper, and when the potatoes start to crackle, dampen them with broth or meat sauce and simmer them until done. Before removing the potatoes from the fire, sprinkle them with lemon juice; serve them hot.

—from *The Art of Eating Well,* 1891,
translated from the Italian by Kyle M. Phillips III

Galen on Truffles

THESE SHOULD BE CLASSIFIED AMONG THE ROOTS OR bulbs, since they have no pronounced quality. Chefs use them as a vehicle for seasonings, just as they do with all the other foods that are called flavourless, harmless and watery in taste. What all these foods have in common is that the nutrition they distribute to the body holds no particular power, but is rather cold, whilst in terms of thickness—of whatever sort is present in what has been eaten—it is thicker from truffles, but moister and thinner from large gourds, and in proportion from the other foods.

—from *On the Powers of Foods,* A.D.180,
translated from the Latin by Mark Grant

CHAPTER NINETEEN

Loving Fat

Zola and Lu Wenfu distrusted fat people, and Balzac, Brillat-Savarin, and Grimod were suspicious of the thin. But my skepticism is only aroused by people of any girth who claim that they do not like fat. We all love fat. It is what makes a dish—makes it "fat." A friend in Budapest recently told me of a luncheon she attended. That great fat-loving society is now trying to eat more modern, lighter, healthier, and for lunch, a group of friends made vegetable sandwiches on whole-grain bread. But first they spread the bread with goose fat. When my friend expressed surprise, she was told in an offhand way, "Well, you have to give the sandwich some flavor." —M.K.

ANTHIMUS ON BACON

AT THIS POINT I WILL EXPLAIN HOW BACON MAY BE EATEN to the best effect, for there is no way that I can pass over this Frankish delicacy. If it has been simply roasted in the same way as a joint of meat, the fat drains into the fire and the bacon becomes dry, and whoever eats it is harmed and is not benefitted; it also produces bad humours and causes indigestion. But if bacon that has been boiled and cooled is eaten, it is more beneficial, regulating constipated bowels and being well digested. But it should be boiled well; and if of course it is from a ham, it should be cooked more. None of the rind should be eaten, because it is not digested. Bacon fat which is poured over some foods and vegetables when oil is not available is not harmful. But frying brings absolutely no benefit.

—from *On the Observance of Foods*, sixth century A.D., translated from the Latin by Mark Grant

---

Newfies on Scrunchions

Scrunchion is a Newfoundland word for the fatback of pork cut into cubes and then fried. In Newfoundland and Labrador, scrunchions and also the cooked-off fat are used in everything from fish, to chowder, to biscuits, to cakes. Traveling farther south, down the Canadian Maritime coast and that of New England, the use of scrunchions diminishes. But historically they are part of cooking in this entire area.

The same is true of cod tongues, a food of cod-fishing communities. They are not actually tongues but the gelatinous white meat from the throat of the fish. —M.K.

CAREFULLY WASH FRESH COD TONGUES AND DRY IN A PAper towel. Allow seven or eight per person. Put 1½ cups flour, 1 teaspoon salt, ½ teaspoon pepper together in a plastic bag. Put tongues in and shake them until evenly floured. Cut up ½ pound salt pork and fry until golden brown. Remove pork cubes and fry tongues until golden brown on both sides.

Served with mashed potatoes and green peas.

—Recipe from Margaret Freake of Joe Batt's Arm, collected by the family of Rev. Ivan F. Jesperson, from *Fat-Back & Molasses: A Collection of Favourite Old Recipes from Newfoundland and Labrador,* 1974

PLATINA ON OLIVE OIL

THE ORDER OF COURSES NOW DEMANDS THAT A PLAN BE offered for preparing and cooking dishes. Since almost all are mixed foods, one must speak first about certain simple ingredients for this category and first about the olive and olive oil. There are several kinds of olives: the preserving kind, the *pausia,* the long olive, the oblong olive, which is best preserved of all olives, as Varro says, the Salentine and the Spanish. The preserving kind are larger and best to eat, as are now the Bolognese and Picene. Bitter ones should be split on both sides with a small knife and soaked for a while in cold water until the bitterness goes away with the fat. When they have been put in a large jar or wooden container covered with water, with salt and fennel, and when they are cooked down, they will last a long time. They are eaten with fish and roasted meats so as either to dispel squeamishness or induce appetite. The olive is difficult to digest, of little nutriment, and generates crass and sticky humors. Eaten outside the regular meal, it represses vapors to the head.

Oil is more easily made from the other kinds of olives, as is customary for some with an olive press, or with a mill, which is more useful, or with a special oil press, which is more difficult. The olives are put in baskets, put under presses, and pressed until nothing more than dry pulp appears. That part of the oil which comes first is more pleasant to eat if it is not from olives which are rotting or overripe or too warm. Pliny calls this *omphacinum,* for the Greeks call an unripe olive *omphax.* This sort of oil tends toward coldness and dryness.

You can keep olives green to make oil whenever you wish in this way: immerse in honey olives which have been picked from the tree and take them out whenever you want as if they were recently plucked from the tree. From these you may make fresh oil if you wish. But what is pressed from ripe olives, even if it is fattier or heavier in odor, is nevertheless considered more useful than oil from unripe olives because of its temperate qualities, for it tends toward heat and dampness. Oil spread with salt can be rescued from too much fattiness, and this is done better if the scum is taken from the bottom of the jar, for all dregs of oil and wine move toward the bottom, as toward the top of honey. Hence oil is better at the top because it likes vapors, wine is better in the middle, and honey is best at the bottom, far from all dregs.

The property of oil is to warm the body. Since this was known, when

Hannibal was about to lead his lines against the Romans at the Trebia in the dead of winter, he smeared the bodies of the soldiers with oil for smoothness and strength, and won. Oil helps wonderfully against cold. Drunk on an empty stomach, it either kills worms or drives them from the stomach. It is considered an antidote, especially against poison, for drunk with warm water it brings up the poison with vomit. There are even several kinds of simulated olive oil, which are being passed over deliberately because they contribute nothing to our discussion.

—from *On Right Pleasure and Good Health,* 1465, translated from the Latin by Mary Ella Milham

---

MARION HARRIS NEIL TELLS THE STORY OF CRISCO

In 1912, in an age when "science" was the magic word for all that was new and exciting, even in food, at a time when industry was revolutionizing American food with its packaged products, and when many of the dried cereals and soft drinks that are household names today were launched, the Procter & Gamble Company of Cincinnati, famed for its Ivory soap, claimed to have invented something to revolutionize American life. It was hydrogenated vegetable shortening, solid vegetable fat, and they called it Crisco.

The goal was to get Americans to give up pork fat, scrunchions, and lard, and instead to use Crisco. Crisco was advertised as a way to get children to eat more fat. Calories was a newly disseminated idea and the belief was that children needed them in order to grow. And there was nothing with a greater concentration of calories than fat. Children should eat as much fat as possible, it was pointed out in The Story of Crisco, the 1913 book produced by Procter & Gamble to promote the new fat. It argued that girls in particular were a problem because they exhibited a tendency to reject fat. The booklet said, "It therefore is necessary that the fat which supplies their growing bodies with energy should be in the purest and most inviting form and should be one that their digestions welcome, rather than repel." And what could be more inviting than a can of white grease? —M.K.

Brief, Interesting Facts

Crisco is being used in an increasing number of the better class hotels, clubs, restaurants, dining cars, ocean liners.

Crisco has been demonstrated and explained upon the Chautauqua platform by Domestic Science experts, these lectures being a part of the regular course.

Domestic Science teachers recommend Crisco to their pupils and use it in their classes and lecture demonstrations. Many High Schools having Domestic Science departments use Crisco.

Crisco has taken the place of butter and lard in a number of hospitals, where purity and digestibility are of *vital* importance.

Crisco is Kosher. Rabbi Margolies of New York, said that the Hebrew Race had been waiting 4,000 years for Crisco. It conforms to the strict Dietary Laws of the Jews. It is what is known in the Hebrew language as a "parava," or neutral fat. Crisco can be used with both "milchig" and "fleichig" (milk and flesh) foods. Special Kosher packages, bearing the seals of Rabbi Margolies of New York, and Rabbi Lifsitz of Cincinnati, are sold the Jewish trade. But all Crisco is Kosher and all of the same purity.

Campers find Crisco helpful in many ways. Hot climates have little effect upon its wholesomeness.

Baked Shad

1 shad weighing 4 lbs.	*1 egg*
¼ lb. mushrooms	*Salt and white pepper*
½ cupful Crisco	*Salt pork*
2 tablespoonfuls chopped parsley	*1 cupful cream*
2 tablespoonfuls chopped chives	*1 teaspoonful cornstarch*
1 cupful breadcrumbs	

Clean, wipe and dry the shad. Melt Crisco, add breadcrumbs, chopped mushrooms, parsley, chives, egg well beaten, salt and pepper. Stuff fish with this forcemeat, then lay it in a greased pan, put thin strips of salt pork over it and bake in hot oven for forty minutes. Lay the fish on a hot platter. Pour cream into baking pan, add cornstarch and stir till boiling. Serve with the fish.

—from *The Story of Crisco,* 1913

FANNIE MERRITT FARMER
ON BUTTER

COMPOSITION.

Fat, 93%.
Water, 5.34%.
Mineral matter, .95%.
Casein, .71%.
Pratt Institute.

BUTTER OF COMMERCE IS MADE FROM CREAM OF COW'S milk. The quality depends upon the breed of cow, manner of, and care in feeding. Milk from Jersey and Guernsey cows yields the largest amount of butter.

Butter should be kept in a cool place, and well covered, otherwise it is liable to become rancid; this is due to the albuminous constituents of the milk, acting as a ferment, setting free the fatty acids. First-quality butter should be used; this does not include pat butter or fancy grades. Poor butter has not been as thoroughly worked during manufacture, consequently more casein remains; therefore it is more apt to become rancid. Fresh butter spoils quickly; salt acts as a preservative. Butter which has become rancid by too long keeping may be greatly improved by melting, heating, and quickly chilling with ice-water. The butter will rise to the top, and may be easily removed.

Where butter cannot be afforded, there are several products on the market which have the same chemical composition as butter, and are equally wholesome. Examples: Butterine and oleomargarine.

Buttermilk is liquid remaining after butter "has come." When taken fresh, it makes a wholesome beverage.

—from *Boston Cooking-School Cook Book,* 1896

LUDWIG BEMELMANS ON THE BUTTERMACHINE

THERE ARE TWO DOYLES HERE—ONE A SERGEANT, THE other a lieutenant. The sergeant is efficient and thin; the lieutenant is fat, with the face of an old lady and little eyes that easily turn hard with offense. He always looks past my face when he speaks to me. The soldiers have invented a very right and beautiful name for him—his trousers have given them this idea—they call him "Satchel Ass." A "satchel" is a portmanteau and "ass" is a donkey but in this case it is the Army word for *derrière*—it fits well. When he walks, it looks as if this portmanteau were constantly opened and closed, and when he sits down it flows over the chair. When he has been around, they do not say, "Lieutenant Doyle was here"; they say, "Doyle was here." Question: "Which one?" Answer: "Satchel Ass Doyle."

Lieutenant Doyle is the glee-club leader and mess officer. He complains all day long about the flies, looks into the ice machine and the ice-boxes, and his pet is the buttermachine. He looks at it twice a day with affection. He bought it himself and he shows all the other officers or some friends of his that come visiting how it works. "That's a great little piece of machinery there," he says to them.

The buttermachine has been here ten days. Before that we cut the butter with a small square frame over which a row of thin sharp wires were stretched, making about sixteen squares. These wires run from left to right and up and down. One man and a tub of water with ice is all that is needed to cut all the butter for the men, the patients and even the officers' mess; and all this takes is at the most ten minutes.

Now we have to first rinse the buttermachine with hot water, fill it with ice, then trim the blocks of butter, because as they are they do not fit the round cylinder inside the ice. The cylinder is long and round; the blocks of butter are square and short. One and a half of them, after they are trimmed, fit into the machine. When they are in there, a tight cover is attached, the heavy lid clamped down, and then the work begins.

A man has to stand in front of the machine and work a little lever from left to right and back again to the left; and every time these two motions are completed, one little square of butter falls out of the machine.

I have told Lieutenant Doyle that it is a waste of time, that the butter was cut in ten minutes before and now it takes two hours to do it, and twice a day; it is ridiculuous. But he says, "That buttermachine is all right."

I have detailed Mulvey, who is the laziest of the K.P.s, to this work, and he is now in the dining room and sings his awful song in there and makes these little butterpieces. Mulvey soon finds out that, with making a little fuss, he can stretch his work so that he has nothing else to do, and when Lieutenant Doyle comes in and sees him cleaning the machine very carefully, he stops and smiles and he tells me, "Mulvey is a good man." But I will fix that.

We have one mess table that has a broken leg. After midday meal, when the dishes are washed, would be a good time to do this, but then there are too many people and I think such things should always be done alone with no one around for confusion when somebody asks questions later on.

Sunday is the best day; then all is very quiet, everyone is out. On the next Sunday, when I am not invited out until late in the evening, I move the table with the broken leg over to the door and change it for the one on which the buttermachine sits. This one has good legs. There is a corner of the table which meets the door when it is opened—soldiers rush into rooms—and on that corner is the machine. It is very heavy, about one hundred and fifty pounds.

After this is arranged, I go up to my quarters. There was a crash as soon as I got up there, but I dressed and left, because it was time to meet Doris's car.

THE NEXT DAY WHEN I AM BACK IN THE MESS HALL, THE cook says, "Somebody busted the buttermachine. Lieutenant Doyle is wild and wants to see everybody who works here."

The best thing is to go right over to headquarters and look surprised and make a face that asks, "Who could have done this? Let me think."

Mulvey is there already answering questions. The buttermachine is also there, but I am afraid that it can be repaired; one of the pig-iron legs is broken off, and the machinery under the cylinder, where the lever goes back and forth and the butter comes out, seems mangled, but it looks good otherwise.

Lieutenant Doyle has no suspicions; he points at the machine and says, "What do you think of that?" but he asks no more. Mulvey has told him when he saw the machine last and another man how he found it. Whoever opened the door and broke it is not to be determined because he would not report himself and no one has seen anybody else.

All questions and answers are filled out on a long printed statement which the Army issues for all things that break or are lost or worn out. Mulvey is back washing dishes and we cut the butter the old way for some weeks. Then Lieutenant Doyle comes and takes Mulvey away from the dishwashing. He comes back with a small table with very strong legs. Lieutenant Doyle has picked out a corner where to put it; near this corner are no doors. Outside is a truck, with a new buttermachine.

—from *La Bonne Table*, 1964

WILLIAM VERRALL'S
VERY FAT PEAS

William Verrall managed the White Hart Inn in Lewes, Sussex, England. The inn was a center of political activity for the Duke of Newcastle, whose French cook, St. Clouet, profoundly influenced Verrall's cooking. Whether this recipe is French or English, surely no one has ever gotten more fat into a plate of peas, considering that cream is unchurned butter. —M.K.

Pease with Cream
Des petits pois a la creme

Let your pease be very young, put them into a stewpan with a bit of bacon with some cloves stuck in, pour in a ladle of broth, a bunch of onions and parsley, pepper, and a little salt if it is required, stew them gently until almost dry, take out the bacon and herbs, and put about a gill of cream, a bit of butter and flour mixt, let it go gently on about ten minutes, squeeze in the juice of lemon or orange, and dish them up very hot. Sometimes I have Mr. Clouet put in a bit of fine sugar, and in the English way of stewing pease I have never seen it done without.

—from *The Cookery Book,* 1759

CHAPTER TWENTY

Bearing Fruit

ROARING LION ON "BANANAS"

Though Calypsonians usually come from poor families and spend their entire lives impoverished, they are the most famous stars in their small island nation of Trinidad, eclipsing even sports figures. Calypso is a Trinidadian music form with both African and European roots. A Calypsonian is a writer and performer and always writes and sings his own songs, debuting them at the annual lenten carnival. Roaring Lion, who was born Rafael de Leon in 1909, was one of the pioneers in taking Calypso outside of Trinidad, which is why his Calypsos are among the best known internationally, especially "Ugly Woman (Never make a pretty woman your wife)" and "Mary Ann (Down by the sea side she sifting sand)." A good Calypso should have double and triple meanings, sexual, political, and social implications. A simple song about bananas is never simply about bananas. —M.K.

Bananas

I know a little dame she's beautiful and named Rosy
She's charming, very attractive and lovely
She is fussy and wouldn't eat a potato
No cauliflowers, no macaroni, or beans and tomatoes

(Chorus A)
But she fancies banana, just give me banana
Those lovely bananas
That's the food for me

Now Rosy, she never partakes of mussels
She hates winkles and strongly objects to cockles
She thinks kippers awful, and oughtn't to be tolerated
Fish and chips dreadful, highly tasteless and over-rated

(Chorus B)
But she says bananas
I love bananas
Big ripe bananas
That's the food for me

Now Rosy, never indulges in drinking
She talks very little, but does a great deal of thinking
She hates champagne, and a dry martini and ginger
As well as a whiskey, creme de menthe and brandy and soda

(Repeat Chorus B)

—c. 1936

ANTHIMUS ON APPLES

SWEET APPLES THAT HAVE BEEN PROPERLY RIPENED ON
the tree are good, but those that are sour are not suitable. For
healthy and sick people sweet apples are good, as well as pears

well ripened on the tree, for hard and sour fruit is extremely harmful.

—from *On the Observance of Foods*, sixth century A.D.,
translated from the Latin by Mark Grant

ALEXANDRE DUMAS *PÈRE* ON APPLES

APPLES ARE EATEN RAW OR STEWED, IN JAMS AND *MARmelades*. An agreeable cider, which is of good quality and keeps well, is also made from them. Sour apples, mixed with about a third of sweet apples, are mainly used for this.

The French provinces which are the most abundant in apples are Normandy, Auvergne and the Vexin français. Brittany also supplies a fairly considerable quantity.

The best apples to be eaten in winter are the *reinettes*, the *court-pendu*, the *pomme d'api* and the *calville*. There are three varieties of *calville*: the white, the red and the yellow. The red *calville* is the best of the three, this being the one which has red skin and flesh which is partly reddish. It contains a sweet juice and suits those who have acidity of the stomach, always assuming that only a few are eaten. *Reinettes* are particularly suitable for the bilious. But of all the apples the *court-pendu* is the best; its flavour is very agreeable, its flesh delicate and its aroma very sweet.

The *pomme d'api*, which is always eaten raw, is the smallest and the hardest of all the apples. It contains a juice which is full of flavour and very suitable for refreshing the mouth and quenching thirst; but its flesh is heavy and difficult to digest.

Bernardin de Saint-Pierre, one of

the most famous of the sons of Normandy, gives in the following in-genious bit of fiction an account of the origin of apple trees in his province:

'The beautiful Thetis,' says he, 'having seen Venus carry off from under her very eyes the apple which was the prize for beauty, without herself being allowed to take part in the competition, resolved to seek revenge. So, one day when Venus had descended to part of the coast belonging to the Gauls and was searching there for pearls with which to adorn herself, and shellfish for her son, a Triton robbed her of her apple, which she had left on a rock. He then took it to the goddess of the sea; and Thetis immediately sowed its seeds throughout the neigh-bouring countryside to immortalize the memory of her revenge and of her triumph. This, say the Celtic Gauls, is the reason for the very large number of apple trees which grow in our land, and for the particular beauty of our girls.'

To avoid the expense incurred in weddings, Solon ordered the newly married to eat only one apple before going to bed on the first night of the marriage. This was hardly very substantial or very cheer-ing for the poor newly-weds.

Pommes au beurre • **Apples cooked with butter**

With a corer remove the cores of about twenty beautiful apples. Peel nine or ten of these, as you would for making a compote, simmer them in lightly sugared water until they are three quarters cooked, and drain them. Cook the remaining apples in a casserole with a little butter, cinnamon and a glass of wa-ter until they have melted into a purée. Spread a part of this *marmelade* on a platter with a little apricot compote. Arrange the whole apples on this, fill the hole in the middle of each with butter and garnish the spaces in between the apples with the rest of the *marmelade*. Glaze with powdered sugar, and cook in the oven until they have turned a good colour. Plug the holes in the apples with cherries, or jam, and serve hot.

Charlottes de pommes • **Apple charlotte**

Peel and quarter about twenty beautiful French *reinette* apples. Remove the cores, and put the apple slices in a casserole with a little butter, cinnamon, lemon and a glass of water. Put a lid on the casserole, put it on a gentle fire and let the apples cook without stirring them. Let them stick very gently to the pan, to give them a slightly grilled taste. Add some sugar and some first-class butter. Let all this reduce, and keep stirring, until the *marmelade* thickens; then remove the cinnamon and the lemon. Cut some slices of soft bread, about the width of two fingers. Arrange these on the bottom and around the sides of a mould; in the middle of the mould put the apple *marmelade,* having mixed it with some apricot *marmelade* in order to make the dish more refined. Then, when the mould is filled, cover it with slices of bread and cook for about twenty minutes in an oven or on glowing coals. Let the charlotte take colour, turn the mould out on to a platter and serve. Don't forget to use clarified butter for buttering your bread.

—from *Le Grand Dictionnaire de Cuisine,* 1873,
translated from the French by Alan and Jane Davidson

Apicius on Preserving Fruit

To Preserve Fresh Figs, Apples, Plums, Pears and Cherries

Select them all very carefully with the stems on and place them in honey so they do not touch each other.

—first century A.D.,
translated from the Latin by Joseph Dommers Vehling

Platina on Figs

THE FIG ALONE, OF ALL TREES, DOES NOT BEAR FLOWERS but produces its fruit from its milk. It has several varieties. The white fig is from trees of good omen, but the black from those of bad omen.

The trees of good omen are considered to be the oak, the Italian oak, the holm-oak, the cork-oak, the beech, the hazel, the service-tree, the pear, the apple, the grape, the plum, the cornel cherry, and the lotus.

Some figs are called Chian from a place, taking the name from a city in Syria. I think the African fig is so-called from that province. The anxious Cato brought its fruit into the Senate when he was seeking a third Punic War and badgering the senators, especially those who did not think it at all the stuff of Roman virtue that Carthage be destroyed. As soon as he said, "How long do you think this fruit has been picked from its own tree? Since all agree that it is fresh, know that it was picked not three days ago at Carthage, so close is our enemy," at once the Third Punic War was launched, by which Carthage, once the rival of the Roman Empire, was destroyed. There are also names taken from discoverers, such as Livian, Calpurnian, Pompeian. There are also late-ripening figs, early-ripening figs, two-crop figs, and tough-skinned figs, which ripen either slowly or quite fast, because they produce figs twice a year and because they are enveloped in a tough skin. There are Numidian and Mariscan and Carian figs too. According to Macrobius, figs which do not ripen at all are called *grossuli,* for Albinus, speaking about Brutus, said, "He eats *grossuli* with honey like a fool."

Fresh figs, especially ripe ones, do not do much harm, since they incline toward warmth and moisture, although all fruits generate bad humors. Dry figs affect the epileptic, soothe the lungs, chest and throat exacerbated by catarrh, open obstructions of liver and spleen, cast gross humors out of the kidneys and bladder, and drive bad blood out to the skin. Frequent use generates lice, though. Early-ripening figs abound in dangerous moisture and for this reason cannot be dried, while two-crop figs, the type of which Augustus was exceptionally fond, produce this fruit, as it were, from the dregs of their own nature. Pompey the Great, after he had conquered Mithridates, found a recipe in Mithridates' writing desk written in his own hand in which he maintained that he was safe and secure against all poisonings for the whole day if he took one walnut, two dried figs (the most potent antidote), twenty leaves of rue and a grain of salt, all ground together and eaten on an empty stomach. There is also a goat-fig of a wild kind which never ripens. Fresh figs, though, will last a long time if they are picked with stems as long and unbruised as possible and put in honey.

—from *On Right Pleasure and Good Health,* 1465, translated from the Latin by Mary Ella Milham

Henry David Thoreau on European Cranberries

August 23, 1854. *Vaccinium oxycoccus* has a small, now purplish-dotted fruit, flat on the sphagnum, some turned partly scarlet, on terminal peduncles, with slender thread-like stems, and small leaves, strongly resolute on the edges—of which Emerson says, the "Common cranberry of the north of Europe," cranberry of commerce there.

October 17, 1859. These interesting little cranberries are quite scarce, the vine bearing (this year at least) only amid the higher and drier sphagnum mountains amid the lowest bushes about the edge of the open swamp. There the dark red berries (quite ripe, only a few spotted still) now rest on the shelves and in the recesses of the red sphagnum. There is only enough of these berries for sauce to a botanist's Thanksgiving dinner.

I have come out this afternoon a-cranberrying, chiefly to gather some of the small cranberry, *Vaccinium oxycoccus*. This was a small object, yet not to be postponed, on account of imminent frosts—that is, if I would know this year the flavor of the European cranberry as compared with our larger kind. I thought I should like to have a dish of this sauce on the table at Thanksgiving of my own gathering. I could hardly make up my mind to come this way, it seemed so poor an object to spend the afternoon on. I kept foreseeing a lame conclusion—how I should cross the Great Fields, look into Beck Stow's Swamp, and then retrace my steps no richer than before. In fact, I expected little of this walk, yet it did pass through the side of my mind that somehow, on this very account (my small expectation), it would turn out well, as also the advantage of having some purpose, however small, to be accomplished—of letting your deliberate wisdom and foresight in the house to some extent direct and control your steps. If you would really take a position outside the street and daily life of men, you must have deliberately planned your course, you must have business which is not your neighbors' business, which they cannot understand. For only absorbing employment prevails, succeeds, takes up space, occupies territory, determines the future of individuals and states, drives Kansas out of your head, and actually and permanently occupies the only desirable and free Kansas against all border ruffians. The attitude of resistance is one of weakness, inasmuch as it only faces an enemy; it has its back to all that is truly attractive. You shall have your affairs, I will have mine. You will spend this afternoon in setting up your neighbor's stove, and be paid for it; I will spend it in gathering the few berries of the *Vaccinium oxycoccus* which Nature produces here, before it is too late, and be paid for it also, after another fashion. I have always reaped unexpected and incalculable advantages from carrying out at last, however tardily, any little enterprise which my genius suggested to me long ago as a thing to be done, some step to be taken, however slight, out of the usual course.

How many schools I have thought of which I might go to but did not go to! expecting foolishly that some greater advantage (or schooling) would come to me! It is these comparatively cheap and private expeditions that substantiate our existence and batten our lives—as, where a vine touches the earth in its undulating course, it puts forth roots and thickens its stock. Our employment generally is tinkering, mending the old worn-out teapot of society.

Our stock in trade is solder. Better for me, says my genius, to go cranberry-ing this afternoon for the *Vaccinium oxycoccus* in Gowing's Swamp, to get but a pocketful and learn its peculiar flavor—aye, and the flavor of Gowing's Swamp and of *life* in New England—than to go consul to Liverpool and get I don't know how many thousand dollars for it, with no such flavor. Many of our days should be spent, not in vain expectations and lying on our oars, but in carrying out deliberately and faithfully the hundred little purposes which every man's genius must have suggested to him. Let not your life be wholly without an object, though it be only to ascertain the flavor of a cranberry, for it will not be only the quality of an insignificant berry that you will have tasted, but the flavor of your life to that extent, and it will be such a sauce as no wealth can buy.

Both a conscious and an unconscious life are good; neither is good exclusively, for both have the same source. The wisely conscious life springs out of an unconscious suggestion. I have found my account in travelling in having prepared beforehand a list of questions which I would get answered, not trusting to my interest at the moment, and can then travel with the most profit. Indeed, it is by obeying the suggestions of a higher light within you that you escape from yourself and, in the transit, as it were see with the unworn sides of your eye, travel totally new paths. What is that pretended life that does not take up a claim, that does not occupy ground, that cannot build a causeway to its objects? that sits on a bank looking over a bog, singing its desires?

However, it was not with such blasting expectations as these that I entered the swamp. I saw bags of cranberries, just gathered and tied up, on the banks of Beck Stow's Swamp. They must have been raked out of the water, now so high, before they should rot. I left my shoes and stockings on the bank far off and waded barelegged through rigid andromeda and other bushes a long way, to the soft open sphagnous center of the swamp.

I found these cunning little cranberries lying high and dry on the firm uneven tops of the sphagnum—their weak vine considerably on one side—sparsely scattered about the drier edges of the swamp, or sometimes more thickly occupying some little valley a foot or two over, between two mountains of sphagnum. They were of two varieties, judging from the fruit. *The one,* apparently *the ripest,* colored most like the common cranberry but more scarlet—that is, yellowish-green, blotched, or checked with dark scarlet-red, commonly pear-shaped. *The other,* also pear-shaped, or more bulged out in the middle, thickly and finely dark-spotted or peppered on yellowish-green or straw-colored or pearly ground—almost exactly like the *Smilacina* and *Convallaria* berries now, except that they are a little larger and not so spherical, with a tinge of purple. A singular difference. They both lay very snug in the moss, often the whole of the long (one and a half inch or more) peduncle buried, their vines very inobvious, projecting only one to three inches, so that it was not easy to tell what vine they belonged to, and you were obliged to open the moss carefully with your fingers to ascertain it; while the common large cranberry there, with its stiff, erect vine, was commonly lifted above the sphagnum. The grayish-speckled variety was particularly novel and pretty, though not easy to detect. It lay here and there snugly sunk in the sphagnum, whose drier parts it exactly resembled in color, just like some kind of swamp-sparrow's eggs in their nest. I was obliged with my finger carefully to trace the slender pedicel through the moss to its vine, where I would pluck the whole together, like jewels worn on or set in these sphagnous breasts of the swamp— swamp pearls, call them—one or two to a vine and, on an average three-eighths of an inch in diameter. They are so remote from their vines, on their long thread-like peduncles, that they remind you the more forcibly of eggs, and in May I might mistake them for such. These plants are almost parasitic, resting wholly on the sphagnum, in water instead of air. The sphagnum is a living soil for it. It rests on and amid this, on an acre of sponges. They are evidently earlier than the common. A few are quite soft and red-purple. I waded quite round the swamp for an hour, my bare feet in the cold water beneath, and it was a relief to place them on the warmer surface of the sphagnum. I filled one pocket with each variety, but sometimes, being confused, crossed hands and put them into the wrong pocket.

I enjoyed this cranberrying very much, notwithstanding the wet and cold, and the swamp seemed to be yielding its crop to me alone, for there are none else to pluck it or to value it. I told the proprietor once that they grew here, but he, learning that they were not abundant enough to be gathered for the market, has probably never thought of them since. I am the only person in the township who regards them or knows of them, and I do not regard them in the light of their pecuniary value. I have no doubt I felt richer wading there with my two pockets full, treading on wonders at every step, than any farmer going to market with a hundred bushels which he has raked, or hired to be raked. I got further and further away from the town every moment, and my good genius seemed to have smiled on me, leading me hither, and then the sun suddenly came out clear and bright, but it did not warm my feet. I would gladly share my gains, take one or twenty into partnership and get this swamp with them, but I do not know an individual whom this berry cheers and nourishes as it does me. When I exhibit it to them I perceive that they take but a momentary interest in it and commonly dismiss it from their thoughts with the consideration that it cannot be profitably cultivated. You could not get a pint at one haul of a rake, and Slocum would not give you much for them. But I love it the better partly for that reason even. I fill a basket with them and keep it several days by my side. If anybody else—any farmer, at least—should spend an hour thus wading about here in this secluded swamp, bare-legged, intent on the sphagnum, filling his pocket only, with no rake in his hand and no bag or bushel on the bank, he would be pronounced insane and have a guardian put over him; but if he'll spend his time skimming and watering his milk and selling his small potatoes for large ones, or generally in skinning flints, he will probably be made guardian of somebody else. I have not garnered any rye or oats, but I gathered the wild vine of the Assabet.

—from *Wild Fruits*, 1859

HENRY DAVID THOREAU
ON WATERMELONS

WATERMELONS. THE FIRST ARE RIPE FROM AUGUST SEVENTH to twenty-eighth (though the last is late), and they continue to ripen till they freeze; are in their prime in September.

John Josselyn, an old resident in New England, speaks of the watermelon as one of the plants "proper to the country." He says that it is "of a sad grass-green color, or more rightly sap green; with some yellowness admixed when ripe."

September is come with its profusion of large fruits. Melons and apples seem at once to feed my brain.

How differently we fare now from what we did in winter! We give the butcher no encouragement now, but invite him to take a walk in our garden.

I have no respect for those who cannot raise melons or who avoid them as unwholesome. They should be spending their third winter with Parry in the arctic regions. They seem to have taken in their provisions at the commencement of the cruise, I know now how many years ago, and they deserve to have a monument erected to them of the empty cans which held their preserved meats.

Our diet, like that of the birds, must answer to the season. This is the season of west-looking, watery fruits. In the dog-days we come near to sustaining our lives on watermelon juice alone, like those who have fevers. I know of no more agreeable and nutritious food at this season than bread and butter and melons, and you need not be afraid of eating too much of the latter.

When I am going a-berrying in my boat or other carriage, I frequently carry watermelons for drink. It is the most agreeable and refreshing wine in a convenient cask, and most easily kept cool. Carry these green bottles of wine. When you get to the field you put them in the shade or in water till you want them.

When at home, if you would cool a watermelon which has been lying in the sun, do not put it in water, which keeps the heat in, but cut it open and place it on a cellar bottom or in a draught of air in the shade.

There are various ways in which you can tell if a watermelon is ripe. If you have had your eye on the patch much from the first, and so know the history of each one and which was formed first, you may presume that those will ripen soonest. Or else you may incline to those which lie nearest to the center of the hill or root, as the oldest.

Next, the dull, dead color and want of bloom are as good signs as any. Some *look* green and livid, and have a very fog of bloom on them, like a mildew. These are as green as a leek through and through, and you'll find yourself in a pickle if you open one. Others have a dead dark-greenness, the circulations coming less rapid in their cuticles and their blooming period passed, and these you may safely bet on.

If the vine is quite lively, the death of the quirl at the root of the stem is almost a sure sign. Lest we should not discern it before, this is placed for a sign that there is redness and ripeness within. Of two, otherwise similar, take that which yields the lowest tone when struck with your knuckles, that is, which is hollowest. The old or ripe ones ring bass; the young, tenor or falsetto. Some use the violent method of pressing to hear if they crack within, but this is not to be allowed. Above all no tapping on the vine is to be tolerated, suggestive of a greediness which defeats its own purpose. It is very childish.

One man told me that he couldn't raise melons because his children *would cut them all up.* I think that he convicted himself out of his own mouth. It was evident that he could not raise children in the way they should go and was not fit to be the ruler of a country, according to Confucius's standard. I once, looking by a special providence through the blinds, saw one of his boys astride of my earliest watermelon, which grew near a broken paling, and brandishing a case-knife over it, but I instantly blowed him off with my voice before serious damage was done—and I made such an ado about it as convinced him that he was not in his father's dominions, at any rate. This melon, though it lost some of its bloom then, grew to be a remarkably large and sweet one, though it bore, to the last, a triangular scar of the tap which the thief had designed on it.

The farmer is obliged to hide his melon patch far away in the midst of his corn or potatoes. I sometimes stumble on it in my rambles. I see one today where the watermelons are intermixed with carrots in a carrot bed and so concealed by the general resemblance of the leaves at a little distance.

It is an old saying that you cannot carry two melons under one arm. Indeed, it is difficult to carry one far, it is so slippery. I remember hearing of a lady who had been to visit her friends in Lincoln, and when she was ready to return on foot, they made her the rather onerous present of a watermelon. With this under her arm she tript it glibly through the Walden Woods, which had a rather bad reputation for goblins and so on in those days. While the wood grew thicker and thicker, and the imaginary dangers greater, the melon did not grow any lighter, though frequently shifted from arm to arm; and at length, it may have been through the agency of one of those mischievous goblins, it slipt from under her arm, and in a moment lay in a dozen pieces in the middle of the Walden road. Quick as thought the trembling traveller gathered up the most luscious and lightest fragments with her handkerchief, and flew rather than ran with them to the peaceful streets of Concord.

If you have any watermelons left when the frosts come, you may put them into your cellar and keep them till Thanksgiving time. I have seen a large patch in the woods frozen quite hard, and when cracked open they had a very handsome crystalline look.

Watermelons, said to be unknown to the Greeks and Romans. It is said to be one of those fruits of Egypt which the Jewish people regretted in the desert under the name of *abbattichim*.

The English botanists may be said to know nothing about watermelons. The nearest that Gerarde gets to our watermelon is in his chapter on "Citrull Cucumbers," where he says, "The meat or pulp of Cucumber Citrill which is next unto the bark is eaten."

In Spence's *Anecdotes* it is said that Galileo used to compare Ariosto's *Orlando* to a melon field. "You may meet with a very good thing here and there in it, but the whole is of very little value." Montaigne says, quoting Aurelius Victor, "The emperor Dioclesian, having resigned his crown and retired to 'private life,' was some time after solicited to resume his charge, but he announced, 'You would not offer to persuade me to this, had you seen the fine condition of the trees I have planted in my orchard, and the fair melons I have sowed in my garden.' " Gosse, in his *Letters from Alabama,* says of the watermelon, "I am not aware that it is known in England; I have never seen it exposed in the London markets," but it is abundant all over the United States; and in the South:

> The very negroes have their own melon "patches," as well as their peach orchards, and it is no small object of their ambition to raise earlier or finer specimens than their masters. . . . [It] may be considered as the best realization of the French princess's idea of "ice with the chill taken off." . . . A cart-load is brought home from the field nearly every evening, to supply the demand of the family for the next day; for during this torrid weather, very little business but the eating of water-

melons is transacted. If a guest call, the first offering of friendship is a glass of cold water as soon as seated; then there is an immediate shout for watermelons, and each taking his own, several are destroyed before the knife is laid down. The ladies cut the hard part, near the rind, into stars, and other pretty shapes, which they candy as a conserve for winter.

—from *Wild Fruits*, 1859

FERDINAND HÉDIARD ON MANGOES

In 1854, Ferdinand Hédiard opened a shop in Paris that provided the French with their first look and taste of exotic fruits. He had them shipped green from Spain, North Africa, Black Africa, the Caribbean, South America, and Asia. He particularly delighted in demonstrating at his counter the proper way to peel a banana. Among the fruits he introduced was the mango. —M.K.

A FRUIT THAT IS HIGHLY VALUED IN THE TROPICS, THE mango, especially the "greffé" mango, is very fragile and hard to transport. However, we received some in 1889, in November and December. The skin is a yellowish green color, sometimes with a red blush; the meat is the color of apricot flesh. In Réunion they make excellent preserves: The mangoes are presented quartered in a sugar syrup. It is a very pretty and delicious dessert.

—from *The Notebook of Ferdinand Hédiard*, 1890,
translated from the French by Mark Kurlansky

CHRISTOPHER COLUMBUS
ON PINEAPPLES

*Ferdinand Colon, the son of Christopher Columbus, reproduced
passages from his father's journal of the second voyage in 1493, and
since the original journals have now been lost, these transcriptions
are all that remain. At the time Columbus arrived on the island of
Guadeloupe, the Caribs from South America were in the process of
conquering the islands and had introduced South American plants
to the Caribbean, including the pineapple.   —M.K.*

THEY FOUND IN THE HOUSES MANY PARROTS, GREEN AND
blue and white and red, big as a common rooster; they also found
pumpkins, and a certain kind of fruit that seemed as green pinecones,
like ours, only larger, and inside full of a substantial pulp as in a melon,
and of much sweeter and delightful aroma and flavor, which grow in
plants that are similar to the lily or aloe.

—from the journal of Christopher Columbus, 1493,
according to his son, Ferdinand Colon,
translated from the Spanish by Mark Kurlansky

LIONEL WAFER ON PINEAPPLES

Born about 1660, Lionel Wafer wrote of great adventures in Panama and the Caribbean, where he appeared to have known many of the legendary pirates of the day—he may even have been one of them. When Wafer returned to England, possibly after spending time in a colonial prison, he published his book New Voyage and Description of the Isthmus of America, *which was much valued for its descriptions.*   —M.K.

ON THE *ISTHMUS* GROWS THAT DELICIOUS FRUIT WHICH we call the Pine-Apple, in shape not much unlike an Artichoke, and as big as a Mans Head. It grows like a Crown on the top of a Stalk about as big as ones Arm, and a Foot and a half high. The Fruit is ordinarily about six Pound weight; and is inclos'd with short prickly Leaves like an Artichoke. They do not strip, but pare off these Leaves to get at the Fruit; which hath no Stone or kernel in it. 'Tis very juicy; and some fancy it to resemble the Tast of all the most delicious Fruits one can imagine mix'd together. It ripens at all times of the Year, and is rais'd from new Plants. The Leaves of the Plant are broad, about a Foot long, and grow from the Root.

—from *New Voyage and Description of the Isthmus of America,* 1699

CHAPTER TWENTY-ONE

The Dark Side of Chocolate

FRANCISCO DE QUEVEDO ON THE CURSE OF TOBACCO AND CHOCOLATE

Chocolate is a food, like bananas or anchovies, that lives a different existence in its producing nations than in the lands to which it is exported. Just as banana growers eat their fruit as a green vegetable, and anchovy fishermen eat their little fish fresh, chocolate is known in the Caribbean and Africa, where it is produced, as a juicy fruit.

It is an odd-looking offspring, a bumpy pod that shoots out of the trunk of a tree on a hoselike stem and looks like it was stuck there by mistake. In these hot countries, children split the pods open and refresh themselves on the milky-white, bland but juicy pulp inside, spitting out the bitter seeds. But it is those seeds, or beans, that the world craves. They are crushed and their natural blend of solid matter and fat are ground into a paste.

There has always been a suspicion of something dark, powerful, hallucinogenic, and addictive in chocolate. The Aztecs, Mayans, and other Mexican and Central American people introduced the beans to Europeans, claiming they had been made by gods. The bitter substance seemed to be used in ways that produced somewhat al-

tered states, especially in Aztec religious ceremonies during which it was served mixed with hallucinogenic mushrooms.

Here is the great difference between Columbus and Cortés: Columbus first ran across this xocoatl in 1502 as a drink on an island off present-day Nicaragua. The fact that the gods had made these small hard beans in the "Garden of Life" in no way impressed him, but, in the name of thoroughness, he took a few back in Spain. The Castillian court thought these beans were interesting and unusual, but useless.

Seventeen years later, Cortés ran across the same hard, bitter beans in the Yucatán. He asked for recipes and returned to Spain with formula for a soup, a drink, and a paste. He also ensured the interest of the Castillian court by pointing out that the locals had sometimes used the beans as money.

The soup, actually a sauce, has never been popular in Europe. In Mexico it is known as a mole, and as Mexico added to its cultural heritages, the number of ingredients ground into paste to be used as a mole sauce continued to grow. Pre-Spanish moles may have been predominantly chocolate, chiles, tomatoes, and dried, crumbled corn tortillas—all indigenous products. Later, Spanish and Arab foods such as almonds, raisins, garlic, pepper, cloves, and cinnamon were added. A Mexican mole, true to Mexico's hybrid culture, can have dozens of ingredients. But the European idea of mixing sugar with chocolate was never part of this. Chocolate was a bitter flavoring. Only a few Europeans adopted the sauce—it is used in Tuscany with boar and in the Basque country with hare.

The drink made an impression on Europe. Some Europeans seemed overwhelmed by the chocolate-drinking craze, and the European reputation of chocolate was in no way helped by such chocolate delinquents as Louis XIV's wife, Maria Theresa, who could not stop drinking it. She had it every day, which was thought to be the reason all her teeth fell out.

But when the Castillians tried out the paste recipe, they thought they had found something of commercial value. It was the monks in Guajaca who introduced sugar to the paste, and once they had this paste of chocolate and sugar, the Spanish crown attempted to keep the formula secret. They sold it in blocks mixed with other exotic American ingredients such as vanilla and hot chili peppers. The chocolate was usually redbrick colored from the addition of annatto, the Caribbean seed Columbus had seen rubbed on the bodies of tribesmen, giving them the label "redskins."

The Spanish kept their monopoly until the sixteenth century, when

*the Portuguese learned the secret in Brazil. At the time, Portugal had
a significant population of Jews who had been expelled from Spain,
and once these Jews were driven farther into Europe, starting with the
French Basque port of Bayonne, the secret of the paste was out.*

*But while its commercial reputation grew, chocolate kept its
slightly sinister image. In the seventeenth century a Spanish poet
denounced it.*   —M.K.

THERE CAME THE DEVIL OF TOBACCO AND THE DEVIL OF
chocolate, who avenged the Indies against Spain, for they have done
more harm by introducing among us those powders and smoke and
chocolate cups and chocolate beaters than the King had ever done
through Columbus and Cortés and Almagreo and Pizarro. For it was
better and cleaner and more honorable to be killed by a musket ball
or a lance then by snuffing and belching and dizziness and fever.

—from *El Entometido y la Dueña y el Soplon,* 1628

EDWARD KIDDER
ON CHOCOLATE CREAM

*Edward Kidder, a celebrated seventeenth- and early-eighteenth-
century London pastry maker, had loyal students who recorded
his recipes in leather-bound notebooks. A number of these notebooks
are still available. This recipe comes from one such handwritten
book.*   —M.K.

TAKE A PT. OF CREAM WITH A SPOONFULL OF SCRAPT
chocolate boyle them well together

Mix with it the yolks of 2 eggs & thicken & mill it on the fier then
pour it into your chocolate cups

—c. 1730

BRILLAT-SAVARIN ON CHOCOLATE

Brillat-Savarin liked ideas. He wrote about few specific foods extensively. One notable exception was chocolate. The Paris chocolate maker he mentions, Debauve, was also singled out for excellence by Grimod de la Reynière. Debauve's store, as with those of most chocolate makers at the time, was a pharmacy. When Brillat-Savarin was writing The Physiology of Taste, *the shop was at 26, rue de Saints-Pères, a shady street off the Boulevard Saint-Germain. Sometime not long after Brillat-Savarin's book was published, the chocolate-making pharmacy seemed to have taken on a partner, Gallais, and moved two doors down to number 30, where it has been ever since. Today, the semicircular wooden pharmacist counter offers a variety of filled chocolates to please those blessed with both a discerning sweet tooth and a sense of history. The store still makes thin disks of chocolate—the same health remedy sampled by Brillat-Savarin and Grimod.* —M.K.

Chocolate and Its Origins

The men who first assaulted the frontiers of America were driven there by the hunger for gold. At that time, almost all the known values were in terms of minerals; agriculture and commerce were in their infancy, and political economy had not yet been born. The Spaniards, therefore, hunted in the New World for precious metals, since found to be almost sterile in that they depreciate as they multiply, and in that we have discovered many other more active means of adding to the main body of wealth.

But those far countries, where sunshine of every degree makes the fields burst with richness, were found perfect for the cultivation of sugar and coffee; they also hid, it was disclosed, the first potatoes, indigo plants, vanilla, quinine, cocoa, and so forth; and it is these which were the true treasures.

If these discoveries have taken place in spite of the barriers erected by a suspicious nation, it is reasonable to hope they will be multiplied in the years to come, and that the researches carried on by the scholars of old Europe will enrich the Three Powers with a multitude of substances which will give us entirely new sensations, just as vanilla has already done, or which will add to our alimentary resources, like cocoa.

Sylvia Plachy, *Chocolate Cake*, 1991

We have come to think of *chocolate* as the mixture which results from roasting together the cacao bean with sugar and cinnamon: such is the classic definition. Sugar is an integral part of it; for with cacao alone we can only make a cocoa paste and not chocolate. And when we add the delicious perfume of vanilla to this mixture of sugar, cacao, and cinnamon, we achieve the *ne plus ultra* of perfection to which such a concoction may be carried.

It is thus to a small number of ingredients that taste and experience have reduced the things which have been mixed with cacao, such as pepper, pimento, anis, ginger, and so on, each of which has been tried out successively.

The cacao plant is native to South America; it is found both on the islands and on the continent; but by now it is agreed that the trees which give the best fruit are those which flourish along the shores near Maracaibo, in the valleys of Caracas, and in the rich province of Soconusco. There the pod is larger, the sugar less bitter, and the aroma more refined. Since the time when these lands became less inaccessible, such comparisons have been made whenever wished, and skilled palates have not been misled by them.

The Spanish ladies of the New World are madly addicted to chocolate, to such a point that, not content to drink it several times each day, they even have it served to them in church. This sensuality has often brought down upon them the wrath of their bishops; but the latter have ended by closing their eyes to the sin, and the Reverend Father Escobar, whose spiritual reasoning was as subtle as his moral doctrine was accommodating, issued a formal declaration that chocolate made with water was not contrary to the rules of fast days, even evoking (to the profit of his penitents), the time-worn adage. *Liquidum non frangit jejunium.*

Chocolate was brought into Spain during the seventeenth century, and it immediately became popular because of its extremely strong flavor, which was appreciated by women and especially by monks. Fashion has not changed in this respect; and even today, on the Peninsula, chocolate is served whenever there is any reason for offering refreshments.

It was carried over the mountain frontiers with Anne of Austria, daughter of Philip III and wife of Louis XIII. Spanish monks, too, made it known by the presents which they sent to their French brothers. The various ambassadors from Spain to Paris also helped make chocolate fashionable, and at the beginning of the Regency it was more commonly known than coffee, since it was drunk as a pleasant aliment, while coffee was still thought of as a luxurious and rare beverage.

It is common knowledge that Linnaeus called cocoa *cacao theobroma* (drink of the gods). It has always been wondered why he gave it such a strong title: some people have attributed it to his own passionate love for the drink; others to his wish to please his confessor; still others to his gallantry, since it was his queen who was the first to introduce it to common usage.

Properties of Chocolate

Chocolate has given rise to profound dissertations whose purpose was to determine its nature and its properties and to place it properly in the category of hot, cold, or temperate foods; and it must be admitted that these written documents have done little to set forth the truth.

But with time and experience, those two sublime teachers, it has been shown as proof positive that carefully prepared chocolate is as healthful a food as it is pleasant; that it is nourishing and easily digested; that it does not cause the same harmful effects to feminine beauty which are blamed on coffee, but is on the contrary a remedy for them; that it is above all helpful to people who must do a great deal of mental work, to those who labor in the pulpit or the courtroom, and especially to travellers; that it has produced good results in cases of chronic illness, and that it has even been used as the last resource in diseases of the pylorus.

Chocolate owes these different properties to the fact that, being in truth no more than *eleosaccharum,* there are few substances that contain more nourishing particles for a like weight: all of which makes it almost completely assimilable.

During the last war cacao was scarce, and above all very expensive: we busied ourselves in finding a substitute for it; but all our efforts were fruitless, and one of the blessings of peace has been to rid us of the various brews which we were forced to taste out of politeness, and which had no more to do with chocolate than chicory has to do with real mocha coffee.

Some people complain that they cannot digest chocolate; some, on the other hand, insist that it does not satisfy them and that it digests too quickly.

It is quite possible that the first have only themselves to blame, and that the chocolate they use is either of inferior quality or badly prepared; for good well-made chocolate can be assimilated by any stomach which can still digest even feebly.

As to the others, the remedy is easy: they should fortify themselves at breakfast with a little meat pie, a cutlet, or a skewered kidney; then they should drink down a good bowl of the best Soconusco chocolate, and they would find themselves thanking God for their supraperfect digestive systems.

This gives me a chance here to put down an observation the correctness of which may be counted on:

When you have breakfasted well and fully, if you will

drink a big cup of chocolate at the end you will have digested the whole perfectly three hours later, and you will still be able to dine. . . . Because of my scientific enthusiasm and the sheer force of my eloquence I have persuaded a number of ladies to try this, although they were convinced it would kill them; they have always found themselves in fine shape indeed, and have not forgotten to give the Professor his rightful due.

People who habitually drink chocolate enjoy unvarying health, and are least attacked by a host of little illnesses which can destroy the true joy of living; their physical weight is almost stationary: these are two advantages which anyone can verify among his acquaintanceship and especially among his friends who follow this diet.

Here is the proper place to speak of the properties of chocolate drunk with amber, which I myself have checked over a long period of time, and the result of which experiments I am proud to offer to my readers.

Very well then: if any man has drunk a little too deeply from the cup of physical pleasure; if he has spent too much time at his desk that should have been spent asleep; if his fine spirits have temporarily become dulled; if he finds the air too damp, the minutes too slow, and the atmosphere too heavy to withstand; if he is obsessed by a fixed idea which bars him from any freedom of thought: if he is any of these poor creatures, we say, let him be given a good pint of amber-flavored chocolate, in the proportions of sixty to seventy-two grains of amber to a pound, and marvels will be performed.

In my own particular way of designating things I call ambered chocolate *chocolate of the unhappy,* since, in each one of the various physical or mental states which I have outlined, there is a common but indefinable ground of suffering, which is like unhappiness.

Difficulties in Making Good Chocolate

In Spain, chocolate is excellently made; but we have almost given up importing it because it is not uniform in quality and when inferior material is imported we are forced to use it as it comes to us.

Italian chocolates are not at all to the French taste; in general the cacao is over-roasted, which makes the beverage bitter and without nourishment, since a part of the nut itself has been turned into ash.

Since chocolate has come into common usage in France, everyone has been taught how to make it; but few people have really mastered the art, which is far from an easy one.

First of all it is necessary to be able to tell good cacao from bad, and to be *determined* to use it in its purest form, for there are inferior samples in even the best boxes of it, and a careless merchant often lets bruised kernels slip by, which his conscience should make him reject. Then the roasting of the cacao is still another delicate operation; it demands a certain feeling for it which must border on inspiration. There are roasters who are born with this instinct, and are infallible.

Then a special talent is needed for the proper regulation of the amount of sugar which must enter into the mixture; it cannot be fixed in routine and inflexible proportions, but varies according to the intensity of flavor of each lot of cacao beans and the point at which the roasting is stopped.

Pounding and mixing both demand special care, as well, since upon them depends the digestibility of the chocolate.

Other considerations must govern the choice and amount of flavoring, which cannot be the same for chocolates meant to be used as food and those meant to be eaten as delicacies. This flavoring must also be adjusted to whether or not vanilla has been added to the mixture. The net result is that, in order to make a truly exquisite chocolate, countless subtle equations must be solved, from which we benefit without even having been conscious of them.

For some time now machines have been used for the making of chocolate; we do not feel that this method adds anything to the quality of the product, but certainly it lessens the handwork, and those manufacturers who have adopted it should be able to sell their product at much lower prices. Nevertheless they manage to dispose of it at even higher ones, a fact which makes it only too clear that the true commercial spirit has not yet appeared in France; for, rightly applied, the facility of production realized by machinery ought to prove profitable to both merchant and buyer.

As a lover of chocolate I have fairly well run the gamut of local purveyors, and have finally chosen M. Debauve, Rue des Saints-Pères 26, chocolatemaker to the king, thanking heaven meanwhile that such regal favor has fallen so rightly.

It is not too astonishing: M. Debauve, a highly distinguished pharmacist, brings to the manufacture of his chocolates the skills which he acquired through long study in a much wider sphere.

People who have not worked at a certain subject, no matter what it may be, have no conception of the difficulties which must be overcome to attain perfection in it, nor how much attention, instinct, and experience are necessary to produce, for instance, a chocolate which is sweet without being insipid, strong but not bitter, aromatic but not unwholesome, and thick but not grainy.

Such are the chocolates of M. Debauve: they owe their supremacy to a good choice of materials, to a stern vow that nothing inferior ever come from his factory, and to the master's eye which sees to every detail in production.

M. Debauve, moreover, as an enlightened pharmacist, has succeeded in offering to his numerous clients some pleasant remedies for certain sickly tendencies.

Thus, to those who are too thin he suggests the use of a restorative chocolate with salep; to highly nervous people, antispasmodic chocolate flavored with orange-flower water; to irritable souls, chocolate with milk of almond; to which list he will undoubtedly add my *chocolate of the unhappy,* well prepared with amber *secundum artem.*

But his main merit is to offer to us, at a moderate price, an excellent average-priced chocolate, from which we can make a good breakfast; which will delight us, at dinner, in custards; and which will still please us, at the end of the evening, in the ices and little cakes and other delicacies of the drawing room, without even mentioning the amusing distraction of pastilles and crackers, with or without mottoes.

We know M. Debauve only by his products; we have never seen him; but we do know that he helps mightily to free France from the tribute which she used to pay to Spain, in that he provides both Paris and the provinces with a chocolate whose reputation does not cease to grow. We also know that every day he receives more orders from beyond our borders; it is therefore because of this fact, and as a charter member of the Society for the Encouragement of National Industry, that we make here this mention and this recommendation of him, of which it will soon be seen that we are not too generous.

Official Way of Making Chocolate

Americans make their chocolate without sugar. When they wish to drink it, they have boiling water brought to them; then each person grates into his cup the amount of cacao he wishes, pours the hot water over it, and adds sugar and flavoring according to his own tastes.

This method appeals neither to our manners nor to our preferences, and here in France we like to have chocolate served to us all prepared.

Transcendental chemistry has taught us that it should neither be grated with a scraper nor ground with a pestle, since the dry friction which results in either case turns part of the sugar into starch, and makes the beverage less flavorsome.

Therefore, to make chocolate, that is to say to make it ready for immediate use, about an ounce and a half should be taken for each cup, and then dissolved slowly in water as it heats, stirring the whole meanwhile with a wooden spatula; it should boil then for fifteen minutes, so that the solution takes on a certain thickness, and then be served very hot.

"Monsieur," Madame d'Arestel, Superior of the convent of the Visitation at Belley, once said to me more than fifty years ago, "whenever you want to have a really good cup of chocolate, make it the day before, in a porcelain coffeepot, and let it set. The night's rest will concentrate it and give it a velvety quality which will make it better. Our good God cannot possibly take offense at this little refinement, since he himself is everything that is most perfect."

—from *The Physiology of Taste*, 1825,
translated from the French by M.F.K. Fisher

ALICE B. TOKLAS ON
HOT CHOCOLATE

THE LUXURY HOTEL AT NÎMES WAS IN A SAD WAY. THE proprietor had been killed at the war, the *chef* was mobilised, the food was poor and monotonous. Aunt Pauline had been militarised and so could be requisitioned for any use connected with the wounded. Gertrude Stein evacuated the wounded who came into Nîmes on the ambulance trains. Material from our unit organised and supplied a small first-aid operating room. The Red Cross nuns in the best French manner served in large bowls to the wounded piping

Hot Chocolate

3 ozs. melted chocolate to 1 quart hot milk. Bring to a boil and simmer for ½ hour. Then beat for 5 minutes. The nuns made huge quantities in copper cauldrons, so that the whisk they used was huge and heavy. We all took turns in beating.

—from *The Alice B. Toklas Cook Book*, 1954

JAMES BEARD ON HOT CHOCOLATE

A STEAMING CUP OF HOT CHOCOLATE WITH BUTTERED TOAST is surely one of the most heart-warming, body-warming, and taste-satisfying combinations known to man. When I was growing up in Portland, Oregon, my friends and I used to go to a great place called Swetland's where we would sit and sip some of the most luscious thick hot chocolate I have ever tasted.

Later on, when I visited France for the first time as a young man, I found the French breakfasting on enormous cups of hot chocolate with buttery croissants or good rolls and butter, an enchanting marriage of flavors. It wasn't only the taste of the chocolate but also the way it was served in the old days that was so nice—I remember that at Maillard's, on Madison Avenue in New York, you drank it from delightful white porcelain cups that had "hot chocolate" lettered on the sides. Some of those old chocolate cups and mugs were really works of art.

All that seems to have faded away, and it is just too bad. Chocolate now has become something that is tipped out of a little paper bag into a cup, dissolved with hot water, and served with artificial whipped cream or a marshmallow stuck on top. This is not hot chocolate, and it really pains me to think that a whole generation is growing up never knowing the glories of a truly well made cup of hot chocolate.

Chocolate, as you undoubtedly know, was one of the greatest gifts of the New World to the Old. When the Spanish conquistadors arrived in Mexico, they found some of Montezuma's courtiers drinking as many as fifty cups of chocolate a day. In fact, it has been surmised that Montezuma's love of chocolate occasioned the first chocolate ice cream—runners were sent to the mountains to bring back snow over which the whipped chocolate was poured. Personally, I think that is stretching history a bit, but it is an amusing, if apocryphal, story.

Since those days, chocolate has always been popular in Europe, and it is still drunk a lot in France and Vienna and throughout Central Europe, although the British tend to favor its less elegant relative, cocoa. Cocoa and chocolate often get confused, probably because both come from the cacao bean. Chocolate is made from the dried, roasted, and crushed "nibs" of the bean, which yield a thick liquid very high in cocoa fat. This is partially defatted, cooled, and solidified into a block of unsweetened chocolate, the type used for baking (semisweet baking chocolate has some sugar added).

Cocoa is a powdered form of chocolate with practically all the fat removed, so it is much lower in calories.

Hot chocolate can be made with either sweet chocolate, unsweetened chocolate, or semisweet chocolate. The French use sweet chocolate, the Spanish unsweetened chocolate, and the Mexicans and Puerto Ricans a packaged sweetened chocolate flavored with cinnamon and sometimes blended with finely ground almonds that is combined with milk to make a very rich drink. If you are using unsweetened chocolate, I think that honey, rather than sugar, makes a very pleasant sweetening.

For each cup of *Hot Chocolate,* melt a 1-ounce square of unsweetened chocolate in a heavy saucepan (less of a problem if you melt it in a warm oven rather than over direct heat), then mix in 1 cup cold water and honey to taste. Heat over medium heat, beating with a whisk or rotary beater, until it reaches the boiling point and is good and foamy. Serve with a dusting of cinnamon on top, or whipped cream if you like.

The rotary beater is our modern equivalent of the traditional Mexican *molinillo,* a little wooden stick with a roughly carved end that is twirled between the palms to beat the chocolate to a froth. The old chocolate pots had rounded bottoms and a *molinillo* that stuck through a hole in the top, and they made a beautifully foamy chocolate. You can still buy *molinillos,* and they are rather fun to use.

To make chocolate with the Mexican cinnamon-flavored sweet chocolate, use 1 ounce per cup and heat with cold water or, for a richer result, warm milk or light cream, beating as before. With semisweet chocolate, melt 1 ounce per cup, then stir in warm milk and a bit of cinnamon, vanilla, or vanilla bean, and heat until it comes to a boil. It is unlikely that you will need further sweetening, but taste and see.

FOR ANOTHER DELICIOUS CHOCOLATE DRINK, EQUALLY good hot or chilled, for every 4 cups melt 4 ounces semisweet chocolate, then add sugar to taste and 1 cup hot coffee. Blend the coffee with the melted chocolate, and then gradually stir in 3 cups warm milk, beating until it reaches the boiling point and is foamy. Pour into heated cups and serve with whipped cream dusted with cocoa or cinnamon.

If you let the chocolate cool and then pour it over ice cubes in a tall glass and top it with whipped cream, you'll have iced mocha, as refreshing and welcome on a hot day as hot chocolate on a cold day. Try it either way, and I think you'll agree that chocolate drinking is a delightful habit well worth reviving.

—from *Beard on Food,* 1974

CHAPTER TWENTY-TWO

Their Just Desserts

Dessert is a relatively new concept. Sweetness, of course, is a very old one, and the ancients used it, as the Chinese still do, as a flavor to counteract other flavors. Apicius believed sweet dishes were a pleasant counterpoint to salty ones. But few of his dishes were truly sweet. The blending would be within the single dish. Apicius's dishes that might seem to us like a dessert, such as a berry pie or a rose custard, were invariably mixed with salts such as a broth, and with pepper.

Pliny wrote, "Salt corrects our aversion when we find something oversweet." Throughout Medieval Europe, sweet, usually honey, was used as a countermeasure to ham, salt cod, and other salty dishes.

Sometimes sweet would be added to a dish, but other times a salty dish would be followed by a sweet one. The word "dessert" first appeared in eighteenth-century France, from a verb meaning "to clear the plates." After the dishes were cleared, the dessert would be served. Originally, this was the ending of each course in the meal. The English kept to the main point by continuing to use the word "sweet," but French desserts started to become more than just something sweet. They became elaborate, architectural showpieces—eventually so extravagant that they came only after the meal.
　　　　　　　　　　　　　　　　　　　　　　　　　　　　　—M.K.

PLINY THE ELDER ON BEES AND HONEY

BEES AND APIARIES ARE PARTICULARLY ASSOCIATED WITH gardens and flowers. In favourable conditions, beekeeping offers large returns for minimal outlay. So, for the sake of the bees, you should plant thyme, wild parsley, roses, violets, lilacs and many other flowers.

What I have discovered about bees' food is amazing and worth recording. Hostilia is a village on the River Padus. When their food-supply fails in this region, the local people put the hives on boats and carry them 5 miles up river by night. At dawn the bees come out, feed and return every day to the boats, whose position alters until such time as they have settled low in the water under the very weight of honey—an indication that the hives are full. They are then taken back to Hostilia and the honey is extracted.

In Spain the locals transport the hives about on mules for a similar reason. The food that the bees eat is of such great importance that even their honey may become poisonous. At Heraclea, in Pontus, the honey is extremely harmful in certain years, even though it comes from the same bees. The authorities for this have not said from what flowers this honey is obtained but I will record the findings. There is a plant called 'goat's bane' from its fatal effect on cattle, especially goats. When the flower of this plant withers in a rainy spring, the bees take from it a harmful poison. Consequently the ill-effects are not experienced in all years. The signs of poisonous honey are that it fails to thicken, causes sneezing and is heavier than pure honey. Cattle that have eaten poisonous honey throw themselves to the ground, seeking to cool their bodies which are running with sweat.

—from *Natural History,* first century A.D.,
translated from the Latin by John F. Healy

GALEN ON PASTRY

NOW IS THE OPPORTUNE MOMENT TO ELABORATE ON THE other sorts of pastries that are made with wheat flour. What are called griddle cakes by the Athenians, but girdle cakes by Greeks like me from Asia, are cooked in olive oil. The olive oil is poured into a frying pan which is placed over a smokeless flame. When the oil is hot, wheat flour kneaded with lots of water is spread on top. Fried quickly in the oil, this mixture becomes as firm and thick as the soft cheese that sets in wicker-work baskets. Then the cooks turn it, making what was the top the bottom, so that it comes into contact with the frying pan. When it has been sufficiently fried, they turn it so that the underside is now upperside, and when this has set they turn it two or three times more, until it is certain that the whole cake has been evenly cooked.

This food is, of course, full of thick juices, blocks the bowels and produces undigested fluids. So some people mix in honey with the dough, others sea salt. This is one sort or type (whatever term you want to use) of flat cake which, along with lots of other flat cakes, those living both in the country and the city make in a rough and ready way. All thin cakes that contain no yeast and which are baked in an oven, should be taken out and dipped at once in hot honey so as to saturate them. These are one sort of flat cake, as are all the honey cakes made with wafer biscuits.

—from *On the Powers of Food*, A.D. 180,
translated from the Latin by Mark Grant

APICIUS ON ROSE PATINA

TAKE ROSES FRESH FROM THE FLOWER BED, STRIP OFF THE leaves, remove the white [from the petals and] put them in the mortar; pour over some broth [and] rub fine. Add a glass of broth and strain the juice through the colander. [This done] take 4 [cooked calf's] brains, skin them and remove the nerves; crush 8 scruples of pepper moistened with the juice and rub [with the brains]; thereupon break 8 eggs, add 1 glass of wine, 1 glass of raisin wine and a little oil. Meanwhile grease a pan, place it on the hot ashes [or in the hot bath] in which pour the above described material; when the mixture is cooked in the *bain maris* sprinkle it with pulverized pepper and serve.

—first century A.D.,
translated from the Latin by
Joseph Dommers Vehling

A BAGHDAD RECIPE FOR MEAT, SWEETS, AND BANANAS

This dish, known in Arabic as mauziyya, from the word "mauz," meaning banana, is not a dessert in the modern sense but an example from the fourteenth century of the use of sweets.   —M.K.

TAKE LEAN MEAT OF FAT LAMB AND THE SAME AMOUNT OF fresh tail, and put them in a pot, and with them are a little Chinese cinnamon and mastic and one jug of water, so that it covers it. Then cook it and take away its scum. When it starts to be done, you transfer the water from it and the meat fries in the fat. You will have pounded one part pistachios, one part toasted hazelnuts, two parts sugar, and a little saffron rubbed with rosewater. Then take half of this and throw it on the meat in the pot. Cut fine yellow bananas onto it after it is taken from the fire and heat diminishes. Then cover it with the rest [of the nuts and sugar] and sprinkle it with a little rosewater and use it, and it is good.

—from *Kitab Wasf al-At'ima al-Mu'tada*, The Description of Familiar Foods, 1373, translated from the Arabic by Charles Perry

AMELIA SIMMONS'S
INDEPENDENCE CAKE

This is one of my favorite recipes, and it leaves a great deal to the imagination. I would like to try it one day if I ever found cake pans large enough. I think the independence cake would work out better than her "election cake," which only calls for three dozen eggs, ten pounds of butter, and fourteen pounds of sugar, but mixes them with thirty pounds of flour.

Little is known of Amelia Simmons other than that she called herself "an American orphan" and makes reference to having worked in kitchens. Her complaints about badly copied recipes by her publisher has led some to believe that she was not literate. Her book, published at her own expense in 1796, first in Hartford and later in Albany, holds an important place in history because it was the first cookbook written by an American in the United States for Americans, though the style of cooking is clearly British. —M.K.

TWENTY POUND FLOUR, 15 POUND SUGAR, 10 POUND BUTter, 4 dozen eggs, one quart wine, 1 quart brandy, 1 ounce nutmeg, cinnamon, cloves, mace, of each 3 ounces, two pound citron, currants and raisins 5 pound each, 1 quart yeast; when baked, frost with loaf sugar; dress with box and gold leaf.

—from *American Cookery*, 1796

GIUSEPPE TOMASI DI LAMPEDUSA
ON RUM JELLY

AT THE END OF THE MEAL APPEARED A RUM JELLY. THIS was the Prince's favourite pudding, and the Princess had been careful to order it early that morning in gratitude for favours granted. It was rather threatening at first sight, shaped like a tower with bastions and battlements and smooth slippery walls impossible to scale, garrisoned by red and green cherries and pistachio nuts; but into its transparent and quivering flanks a spoon plunged with astounding ease. By the time the amber-coloured fortress reached Francesco Paolo, the sixteen-year-old son who was served last, it consisted only of shattered walls and hunks of wobbly rubble. Exhilarated by the aroma of rum and the delicate flavour of the multi-coloured garrison, the Prince enjoyed watching the rapid demolishing of the fortress beneath the assault of his family's appetite. One of his glasses was still half-full of Marsala. He raised it, glanced round the family, gazed for a second into Concetta's blue eyes, then said: 'To the health of our Tancredi.' He drained his wine in a single gulp. The initials F.D., which before had stood out clearly on the golden colour of the full glass, were no longer visible.

—from *The Leopard,* 1958

Gelatin Hints from Knox

The first patented gelatin dessert in America was in 1845 by Peter Cooper, who was too far ahead of his time and unable to sell prepackaged desserts. Orator Woodward, on the other hand, was a man who understood his times when, in 1902, he came out with a product called Jell-O. The contents were sugar, gelatin, adipic acid, disodium phosphate, fumaric acid, artificial color, natural flavor with BHA, and artificial flavor. That ought to work. It did, and traditional gelatin companies, selling simply a gelatin to mix with fruit juice or other flavorings, had to become more aggressive. Knox Gelatine began publishing booklets on using its product. —M.K.

ALWAYS USE A REAL ORANGE AND LEMON IN MAKING YOUR Desserts and Salads, and take advantage of the pure health-giving vitamins that fresh fruits contain.

Electric Refrigerators—Ices and sherbets may be chilled or frozen more satisfactorily in the trays with the addition of Knox Sparkling Gelatine.

When there are odds and ends of food left over use them up in combinations with gelatine dishes and show real economy in the household. Our book, "Food Economy," directs you in their use.

Gelatine will harden much quicker if put in several small molds than in one large one. Jellies will take less time to cool and set if the soaked gelatine is melted over hot water and the remaining liquid added cold—instead of using hot liquid to dissolve it.

If you wish to combine fresh pineapple with gelatine, always first scald the pineapple, both fruit and juice. When using canned pineapple, this is not necessary, as the pineapple has already been cooked.

Jellied desserts and salads are a great help to the busy housekeeper, as they may be prepared hours before needed, or even the day before, and when guests arrive there is no last-minute hurrying.

Flowers or flags may be molded in jelly for table decorations for special occasions. Pour liquid jelly into a plain wet mold to make a thin layer. Very carefully arrange flowers and leaves on this when it has stiffened, remembering that the mold will be turned upside down, and the more attractive side must be down. Allow the remaining jelly to stiffen slightly and carefully place about the flowers by spoonfuls, and fill mold.

Instead of making fruit jellies during the hot summer months, can the juice, with or without sugar. Then during the winter months, make gelatine jellies as you need them. The gelatine jellies are much more easily prepared.

To make currant, grape or other jelly firm: If a fruit jelly does not "jell" after being boiled a sufficient length of time, add to each pint a level tablespoonful Knox Sparkling Gelatine that has been softened five minutes in one-fourth cup cold water. Heat to the boiling point, skim and strain into the glasses.

Melted ice cream should never be thrown away. Stiffen it with gelatine, using a level tablespoonful of gelatine to a pint of cream. Chocolate, Strawberry, Coffee and Pistachio are especially delicious. Chopped raisins, dates, nuts, cherries or marshmallows make an excellent combination.

Use left-over coffee for a Coffee Jelly, Coffee Spanish Cream or Mocha Sponge.

Cream puffs and eclairs may be filled with Bavarian Cream. Filling should be put in just before serving that the crust may remain crisp. These are very effective when filled with Strawberry Bavarian Cream and garnished with a few whole berries.

The jellied salads and meats are especially pretty when served in dainty baskets. These may be made with timbale irons, or line little fluted gem pans with a savory short crust and bake in oven. Baskets may also be made of halves of lemon, orange or grapefruit skins, or serve in an apple, tomato or pepper shell.

When making croquettes, try the following: Soften a teaspoonful of gelatine in a little cold water and dissolve over hot water (using as little water as possible to reduce the gelatine to a liquid). Stir into the croquette mixture and set aside until gelatine has had time to stiffen it. Croquettes may then be shaped very easily, and the heat of the frying will dissolve the gelatine again, making the inside of the croquettes soft and creamy.

—from *Dainty Desserts for Dainty People,* 1929

PELLEGRINO ARTUSI ON ICE CREAM

ACCORDING TO AN ARTICLE I ONCE READ IN AN ITALIAN newspaper, the art of chilling is strictly Italian, and ancient; apparently, the first ice creams to be served in Paris were those served at the court of Caterina de'Medici, in 1533. Reading on, I discovered that among the French the secret remained at the Louvre [*the royal palace*] because the Florentine chefs, pastrymen, and chillers in service at court jealously guarded their secrets. Thus, the people of Paris had to wait for more than a century to taste ice cream.

Despite devoting considerable effort to trying to confirm this information, I've been unable to do so. The following, however, is certain: The use of drinks chilled with the aid of stored ice or snow comes from the Orient and dates to remotest antiquity, while ice creams were introduced to France around 1660 by one Procopio Coltelli, from Palermo, who opened a café under his own name—the Café Procope—in Paris, directly in front of the theater of the Comedie Française; it became a favorite meeting place for well-to-do Parisians. The rapid success of the café, where the ice cream was modeled to look like eggs and served in egg cups, convinced those who sold lemonade or other drinks to follow Mr. Coltelli's example. One who did was named Tortoni; thanks to the popularity of his delicious ice creams, he was able to open a café that became renowned throughout Europe and made him rich.

According to Athenaus and Seneca, the ancients made icehouses to keep snow and ice, much as we do now, by digging deeply into the earth and covering the ice and snow, after thoroughly packing it down, with oak boughs and straw. They hadn't learned, however, that salt, added to the ice, greatly enhances its ability to transform any type of liquid into sherbet.

You'll almost certainly score a success with all your guests if you serve them sherbet or ice cream at the end of the dinner, especially during the summer months. Ice cream, in addition to tasting good, draws the heat of the body to the stomach, thereby aiding in the digestion. Now that American ice cream machines with triple-action mechanisms that don't require the use of a plunger have become available, making ice cream is quicker, and the ingredients are less likely to separate. Given this improvement, it would be a pity not to indulge frequently in the voluptuous pleasure ice cream provides.

To save money, the salt can be recovered from the ice water used to freeze the ice cream, by evaporating the water over the fire.

Gelato al Limone
Lemon Sherbet

1½ cups sugar   3 lemons
2 cups water

If at all possible, use garden lemons. They taste better and are more fragrant than lemons from elsewhere, which frequently have an "off" flavor.

Boil the sugar in the water with a few strips of lemon zest, uncovered, for 10 minutes. Let the syrup cool, then squeeze the lemons into it one at a time, tasting to make sure the mixture isn't too tart. Strain it, and pour it into an ice cream machine.

This will produce enough for six.

—from *The Art of Eating Well*, 1891,
translated from the Italian by Kyle M. Phillips III

M.F.K. FISHER ON GINGERBREAD

WE KNEW A WOMAN WHO SOLD REAL ESTATE IN A SMALL beach colony. She had a face like a brick wall, and a desire, some sixty years old and still undaunted, to play ingenue rôles on Broadway. Her past was cautiously shaded.

We said we were going to live in France.

She said, "Where?"

We said, "Here, there—maybe Dijon—"

Suddenly her face was blasted. "Oh, Dijon!"

She put her hands up to her eyes and wept, and then cried fiercely: "The smell of it! The smell of Dijon gingerbread! When you are there smell it for me!"

So we did.

We smelled Dijon mustard, especially at the corner where Grey-Poupon flaunts little pots of it. We smelled Dijon cassis in the autumn, and stained our mouths with its metallic purple. But all year and everywhere we smelled the Dijon gingerbread, that *pain d'épice* which came perhaps from Asia with a tired Crusader.

Its flat strange odour, honey, cow dung, clove, something unnamable but unmistakable, blew over all the town. Into the theatre sometimes would swim a little cloud of it, or quickly through a café grey with smoke. In churches it went for one triumphant minute far above the incense.

At art school, where tiny Yencesse tried to convince the hungriest students that medal-making was a great career, and fed them secretly whether they agreed or not, altar smoke crept through from the cathedral on one side, and from the other the smell of *pain d'épice* baking in a little factory. It was a smell as thick as a flannel curtain.

This is the Dijon recipe, without, of course, the mysterious quality that makes each little gingerbread shop bake loaves quite different from any others:

> Take two pounds of old black honey, the older and blacker the better, and heat it gently. When it has become a thin liquid, stir it very slowly and thoroughly into two pounds of the finest bread flour, of which about one-third is rye.
>
> Put this hot paste away in a cold place. It must stay there for at least eight days, but in Dijon, where *pain d'épice* is best, it ripens in the cold for several months or even years!
>
> Wait as long as you can, anyway. Then put it in a bowl and add six egg yolks, one level teaspoon of carbonate of soda, and three teaspoons of bicarbonate of soda.
>
> Next comes the seasoning—and it is there, I think, that lies the magic. Try these the first time, before you begin your own experimenting: some pinches of anise, a teaspoon of dry mustard, and the zest of a large lemon.
>
> Now beat it for a painfully long time. Put it in a buttered mould or pan and bake in a moderate oven for one hour—or less if you have divided this measure into more than one pan.

In Dijon little gingerbread orange slices are stuffed with marmalade and glazed, or great square loaves are sliced several times and spread with apricot jam before they are put together again. Or currants and candied fruits are baked in the loaves. Or they are left plain, to be sliced very thin and be spread with sweet butter for tea.

Whatever you do with your *pain d'épice*, you should put it away in waxed paper and an air-tight box. It will taste even better in two months or three.

—from *Serve It Forth,* 1937

JANE GRIGSON ON
ENGLISH PUDDINGS

ENGLISH PUDDINGS HAVE HAD A GREAT REPUTATION SINCE the seventeenth century—perhaps earlier—and they deserve it.

One French visitor, the protestant exile François Maximilien Misson, who came to England at the end of the seventeenth century, was lyrical in his *Mémoires et Observations faites par un voyageur en Angleterre* (published 1698, translated into English by John Ozell, 1719) about the unexpectedness and variety of English puddings. 'They bake them in an oven, they boil them with meat, they make them fifty several ways: BLESSED BE HE THAT INVENTED PUDDING, for it is a manna that hits the palates of all sorts of people.' He had in mind puddings both sweet and plain, mentioning as the most common ingredients flour, milk, eggs, butter, suet, sugar, marrow and raisins. It's rather sad that 'pudding,' among ourselves, inclines to become a work of abuse. It's true that an addiction to puddings hasn't been exactly in favour of English teeth and waistlines, but these wonderful things are some of the most subtle and imaginative combinations, relying on simple and natural ingredients.

Misson has described the heftier puddings including the kind eaten with gravy, or with sugar and butter. Filling, decidedly. But there's much to be said, and more than is usually said nowadays, for a national cooking that has invented Queen of Puddings, summer pudding, syllabubs, gooseberry fool, Bakewell Pudding and that sweet concoction we now insist on calling crème brulée as if it were French and not the Burnt Cream of English cooks of the eighteenth century.

A generous hand with the cream—not to mention butter and eggs—has been the making of many of the best English puddings. Equally their downfall has been stinginess with cream and the illusion that nobody notices if you use margarine or vegetable fat instead of butter or lard.

Another blow has been the commercialization of puddings, premixed in packets, with skimmed milk powder, chemical flavour, chemical colour and chemical preservatives. Custard powder made in this way has been one of our minor national tragedies, also the commercial use of cornflour as a thickening substitute for eggs. It's cornflour that has made people loathe the idea of blancmange, turning an ancient and courtly delicacy into those cold shapes derided as 'baby's bottom' ('dead man's leg,' 'dead baby,' according to shape, are school names I recall for some of the less appetizing suet puddings).

Puddings unquestionably were some of the first victims of mass catering and manufacture. But they survive, though in their huge number they are barely explored nowadays. For instance, how many families have sat down to Sussex Pond Pudding (sometimes called Sussex Well Pudding), for which I give the recipe? Yet it is one of the best of our suet puddings. That is a slightly complicated affair, but many of the best puddings are also the simplest. There's nothing simpler than junket flavoured with brandy, sprinkled with nutmeg and spread with clotted cream, and there's nothing simpler than adding a quince, if you can get one, to an apple pie.

People used to talk, still do talk occasionally, of the roast beef of old England, along with the revolting image in their minds of an overfed John Bull. My English family scenario would be candles on the dining-room table, clotted cream in a large triangular Coalport bowl patterned with blue and white flowers about to be added in large helpings to cold apple pie left over from Sunday lunch. The thought of it has buoyed children—and adults too, no doubt—through the tedium of Evensong.

—from *English Food*, 1974

WILLIAM ELLIS ON APPLE PIE

William Ellis was an eighteenth-century Cato, a writer principally interested in agriculture who periodically wandered into the related topic of food. His books on farming, country living, and country food were extremely popular in England at the time. —M.K.

Of Apple-Pyes, and Apple-Pasties, for Harvest and other Times.

Apple pyes and pasties are a main part of a prudent, frugal farmer's family-food, because the meal and apples that make them are commonly the produce of his land, and are ready at all times to be made use of in pyes or pasties, for giving his family an agreeable palatable repast; a covered or turn-over pasty for the field, and the round pye for the house; the first being of a make and size that better suits the hand and pocket than the round pye, and therefore are more commonly made in farmers families; for one, or a piece of one, being carried in the plowman's and plowboy's pocket, sustains their hunger till they come home to dinner, and oftentimes pleases them beyond some sort of more costly eatables; nor is it less wholesome than pleasant, for that the ingredients of the apple-pye are rather antidotes against, than promoters of the scurvy. In short, it is the apple pye and pasty, and apples made use of in some other shapes (particularly the famous Parsnip apple) that I take to be some of the cheapest and most agreeable food a farmer's family can make use of; but for displaying their value in a more elegant manner, I hope the following poem will not be unacceptable to my reader.

Of Apple-Pyes: A poem, by Mr. Welsted.

OF all the delicates which *Britons* try,
To please the palate, or delight the eye;
Of all the several kinds of sumptuous fare,
There's none that can with apple-pye compare,
For costly flavour, or substantial paste,
For outward beauty, or for inward taste.
　　WHEN first this infant dish in fashion came,
Th' ingredients were but coarse, and rude the frame;
As yet, unpolish'd in the modern arts,
Our fathers eat brown bread instead of tarts:
Pyes were but indigested lumps of dough,
'Till time and just expence improv'd them so.
　　KING *Coll* (as ancient annals tell)
Renown'd for fiddling and for eating well,
Pippins in homely cakes with honey stew'd,
Just as he bak'd (the proverb says) he brew'd.
　　THEIR greater art succeeding princes shew'd,
And model'd paste into a nearer mode;
Invention now grew lively, palate nice,
And sugar pointed out the way to spice.
　　BUT here for ages unimprov'd we stood,

And apple-pyes were still but homely food;
When god-like *Edgar,* of the *Saxon* line,
Polite of taste, and studious to refine,
In the dessert perfuming quinces cast,
And perfected with cream the rich repast:
Hence we proceed the outward parts to trim,
with crinkumcranks adorn the polish'd rim,
And each fresh pye the pleas'd spectator greets
With virgin fancies and with new conceits.

    DEAR *Nelly,* learn with care the pastry art,
And mind the easy precepts I impart;
Draw out your dough elaborately thin,
And cease not to fatigue your rolling-pin:
Of eggs and butter, see you mix enough;
For then the paste will swell into a puff,
Which will in crumbling sound your praise report,
And eat, as housewives speak, exceeding short:
Rang'd in thick order let your quincies lie;
They give a charming relish to the pye:
If you are wise, you'll not brown sugar slight,
The browner (if I form my judgment right)
A tincture of a bright vermil' will shed
And stain the pippin, like the quince, with red.

    WHEN this is done, there will be wanting still
The just reserve of cloves, and candy'd peel;
Nor can I blame you, if a drop you take
Of orange water, for perfuming sake;
But here the nicety of art is such,
There must not be too little, nor too much;
If with discretion you these costs employ,
They quicken appetite, if not they cloy.

    NEXT in your mind this maxim firmly root,
Never o'er-charge your pye with costly fruit:
Oft let your bodkin thro' the lid be sent,
To give the kind imprison'd treasure vent;
Lest the fermenting liquors, mounting high
Within their brittle bounds, disdain to lie;
Insensibly by constant fretting waste,
And over-run the tenement of paste.

To chuse your baker, think and think again,
You'll scarce one honest baker find in ten:
Adust and bruis'd, I've often seen a pye
In rich disguise and costly ruin lie;
While the rent crust beheld its form o'erthrown,
Th' exhausted apples griev'd their moisture flown,
And syrup from their sides run trickling down.
O be not, be not tempted, lovely *Nell,*
While the hot piping odours strongly swell,
While the delicious fume creates a gust,
To lick th' o'erflowing juice, or bite the crust:
You'll rather stay (if my advice may rule)
Until the hot is temper'd by the cool;
Oh! first infuse the luscious store of cream,
And change the purple to a silver stream;
That smooth balsamick viand first produce,
To give a softness to the tarter juice.

—from *The Country Housewife's Family Companion*, 1750

Hannah Glasse's Apple Pie

Make a good Puff-paste Crust, lay some round the Sides of the Dish, pare and quarter your Apples, and take out the Cores, lay a Row of Apples thick, throw in half your Sugar you design for your Pye, mince a little Lemon-peel fine, throw over and squeeze a little Lemon over them, then a few Cloves, here and there one, then the rest of your Apples, and the rest of your Sugar. You must sweeten to your Palate, and squeeze a little more Lemon; boil the Peeling of the Apples, and the Cores in some fair Water, with a Blade of Mace, till it is very good; strain it and boil the Syrup with a little Sugar, till there is but very little and good, pour it into your Pye, and put on your Upper-crust, and bake it. You may put in a little Quince and Marmalate, if you please.

Thus make a Pear-pye; but don't put in any Quince. You may

butter them when they come out of the Oven; or beat up the Yolks of two Eggs, and half a Pint of Cream, with a little Nutmeg, sweetened with Sugar, and take off the Lid, and pour in the Cream. Cut the Crust in little three-corner Pieces, and stick about the Pye, and send it to Table.

—from *The Art of Cookery, Made Plain and Easy, 1747*

CHAPTER TWENTY-THREE

A Good Drink

ALEXANDRE DUMAS *PÈRE* ON COFFEE

THE PLANT WHICH PRODUCES COFFEE IS A VERY LOW, SMALL shrub which bears fragrant flowers. Coffee comes originally from the Yemen, in Arabia Felix. At present it is cultivated in several countries. The Arab historian, Ahmet-Effendi, thinks that it was a dervish who discovered coffee, in about the fifteenth century, or in the year 650 of the Hegira.

The first European to refer to the coffee plant was Prosper Alpin, of Padua. In 1580 he accompanied a Venetian consul to Egypt. The work of which we are speaking was written in Latin, and addressed to Jean Morazini.

I have seen this tree in Cairo, in the gardens of Ali Bey. It is called *bon* or *boun*. With the berry which it produces, the Egyptians produce a drink which Arabs call *Kawa*. The taste for coffee grew to such an extent at Constantinople that the Imams complained that the mosques were deserted whereas the cafés were always full. Amurat III then permitted coffee to be consumed in private houses, as long as the doors were shut.

Coffee was unknown in France until 1657, when the Venetians first brought it to Europe. It was introduced to France through Marseilles. It became universally used, and the doctors were alarmed about it. But their sinister predictions were treated as unreal, and the result was that, despite the arguments, the cafés were no less frequented.

In 1669, the Ambassador from Mahomet II brought a large quantity to France and we are assured that coffee was being sold in Paris at that time for up to 40 crowns a pound.

Posée-Oblé, in his *Histoire des plantes de la Guyane,* written during the reign of Louis XIII, says that in Paris, near Petit-Châtelet, the decoction made of coffee and known as *cahuet* was being sold. In 1676, an Armenian named Pascale established at the market of Saint-Germain a café which he later moved to the quai de l'Ecole. He made quite a fortune out of it. But it was only at the beginning of the following century that a Sicilian called Procope re-established the coffee market at Saint-Germain. He attracted the best people in Paris, because he only provided good merchandise. Later, he set up his business in quarters opposite the Comédie Française; this new café became both a rendez-vous for theatre enthusiasts, and a battleground for literary disputes. It was in this café that Voltaire spent two hours every day. In London, during the same period, more than three thousand coffee houses were established. Mme. de Sévigné fought against the new fashion as hard as she could and predicted that Racine and the café would pass out of fashion simultaneously.

There are five principal sorts of coffee in commerce, without counting chicory, which our cooks are bent on mixing in. The best comes from *Moka* in Arabia Felix, and it alone is also divided into three varieties: *baouri,* which is reserved for the use of the great lords, *saki* and *salabi.*

Coffee from Réunion is highly esteemed in the trade but, even so, that from Martinique or Guadeloupe is preferred. That from Santo Domingo (Dominican Republic), which also includes Puerto Rico and other Islands of the Leeward group, is of inferior quality.

Coffee had come into general usage in France when, in 1808, Napoleon published his decree concerning the 'continental system' [blockade], which was to deprive France of sugar and coffee at the same time. Beet sugar was substituted for cane sugar, and coffee was eked out by mixing it half and half with chicory. This was completely to the advantage of the grocers and cooks who took to chicory with passion and maintained that chicory mixed with coffee tasted better and was healthier. The misfortune is that even today, when the continental decree has fallen into disuse, chicory remains a part of our cooks' repertoire and they have continued mixing a certain quantity of it with the coffee (which they buy ready ground) under the pretext of refreshing their masters. The masters responded to this situation by ordering coffee to be bought in the bean. But, in moulds made especially for this purpose, chicory paste has been made into the shape of coffee beans; and, whether one will or no, chicory has remained wedded to coffee.

It is usual for coffee made with water, and served after a meal, to be accompanied by a small pitcher of milk which has not been boiled, or cream. This can then be added to the coffee if one likes it this way.

—from *Le Grand Dictionnaire de Cuisine,* 1873,
translated from the French by Alan and Jane Davidson

———

SARAH JOSEPHA HALE ON DRINKING

WHAT SHALL WE DRINK?—WHY, WATER—THAT IS A SAFE drink for all constitutions and all ages,—provided persons only use it when they are naturally thirsty. But do not drink heartily of cold water when heated or greatly fatigued. A cup of warm tea will better allay the thirst, and give a feeling of comfort to the stomach, which water will not.

Toast and water, common beer, soda water, and other liquids of a similar kind, if they agree with the stomach, may be used freely without danger.

Fermented liquors, such as porter, ale, and wine, if used at all as a drink, should be very sparingly taken.

Distilled spirituous liquors should never be considered drinkable—they may be necessary, sometimes, as a medicine, but never, never consider them a necessary item in house-keeping. So important does it appear to me to dispense entirely with distilled spirits, as an article of domestic use, that I have not allowed a drop to enter into any of the recipes contained in this book.

As the primary effect of fermented liquors, cider, wine, &c., is to stimulate the nervous system, and quicken the circulation, these should be utterly prohibited to children and persons of a quick temperament. In truth, unless prescribed by the physician, it would be best to abstain entirely from their use.

Most people drink too much, because they drink too fast. A wine-glass of water, sipped slowly, will quench the thirst as effectually as a pint swallowed at a draught. When too much is taken at meals, especially at dinner, it hinders digestion. Better drink little during the meal, and then, if thirsty an hour or two afterwards, more. The practice of taking a cup of tea or coffee soon after dinner is a good one, if the beverage be not drank too strong or too hot.

—from *The Good Housekeeper,* 1841

ALEXIS SOYER ON SODA WATER

"Do you know, monsieur, that our horses have not had a drop of water today?"

"Colonel," said I, "I am not at all surprised at that; and more, you must put up with it."

"Why?" he asked.

"Simply because you can't get it, unless you like to do as I did yesterday—give them soda-water."

"Do you mean to say there is no water at all in this grand vessel?"

"None, except soda-water."

"Eh bien," said another, "give de soda-water alors."

"What, for the horses?"

"Oui, for the chevals!"

"Here, my man," said I to one of the crew, "tell the steward to bring a dozen of soda-water for the colonel's horse. Mind, colonel, it costs a shilling a bottle; but, as you are a good customer, and take a dozen, no doubt he will let you have it cheaper."

"I will not pay a sou for this bubbling water. I know what you mean. It fizzes like champagne, but it is not good to drink. The horses will never touch it. I thought it was spring-water that you called soda-water."

At all events, the soda-water was brought, to the great annoyance of the colonel, who thought he should have to pay for it; but I sent for some sherry and a few glasses, and we drank a bottle or two, instead of giving it to the horses, to the great gratification of the colonel, who, after partaking of it, said he liked it much better with sherry than brandy. About twenty banabaks soon after arrived with water in skins and leathern horse-buckets. The horses were properly watered; and thus ended the Sardinian revolt in the harbour of Balaklava, on the 14th of May, in the year 1855, beneath the ruins of the Genoese Tower and fortifications built by their ancestors.

—from *A Culinary Campaign*, 1857

BRILLAT-SAVARIN ON WATER

WATER IS THE ONLY LIQUID WHICH TRULY APPEASES THIRST, and it is for this reason that only a small quantity of it is drunk. The main body of other liquids which man consumes are no more than palliatives, and if he were limited to water, it would never have been said of him that one of his privileges was to drink without being thirsty.

—from *The Physiology of Taste*, 1825,
translated from the French by M.F.K. Fisher

ALEXANDRE DUMAS PÈRE
ON WATER

*Unique among the legions of self-declared French gourmets, Dumas
never in his life drank a glass of wine.*   —M.K.

PEOPLE WHO HABITUALLY DRINK WATER BECOME JUST AS
good gourmets about water as wine drinkers about wine.

For fifty or sixty years of my life, I have drunk only water, and no
lover of wine has ever felt the same delight in some Grand-Laffite or
Chambertin as I have in a glass of cool spring water whose purity has
not been tainted by any earthy salts.

Very cold water, even when it has been artificially cooled with
ice, acts as an excellent tonic to the stomach, without provoking
any irritation and indeed calming any which might already have existed.

But this is not the case with water coming from melted snow or
ice, which are heavy because they contain no air. Stir these waters
well before drinking, and they will lose their injurious qualities.

Formerly all of Paris slaked its thirst from the river which
traverses it. Nowadays the water comes from Grenelle; pipes bring it to
the mountain of Sainte-Geneviève, whence it is distributed throughout
Paris. For the last five or six years, water from the Dhuys has been
competing with this; it comes from the other side, that is to say from
Belleville, Montmartre and the Buttes Chaumont.

The water from the Seine was the object of so many calumnies
for such a long time, particularly by people from the provinces coming to pass a few days in Paris, that it grew weary of slaking the thirst
of two million ungrateful persons. But when the waters of the Seine
were well purified and when it was drawn from above the zoological
gardens, and from the middle of the stream, no other water was
comparable to it for limpidity, lightness and sapidity. Above all, it was
abundantly saturated with oxygen, having been turned over and over
by the multiple meanderings which, over a distance of nearly two
hundred leagues (eight hundred kilometres), subjected it to the action of the atmosphere's air. Moreover, it flows along a bed of sand
all the way from its source until it reaches Paris. Gourmands attrib-

ute to this circumstance the superior quality of fish from the Seine to those from other rivers.

Everyone knows that monks have never really liked water very much; here is one more incident which proves their antipathy for this 'dreary liquid.' A Franciscan friar used to visit a bishop's kitchen fairly assiduously, the latter having told his people to look after the good brother. One day, when the prelate was holding a big dinner, the monk happened to be at the bishopric. The monseigneur was talking about the holy man, and recommending him to the assembled company. Right away, several of the ladies exclaimed;

'Monseigneur, you must amuse us by playing a trick on the monk. Summon him, and we will give him a beautiful glass of clear water which we will present to him as a glass of excellent white wine.'

'But you're not seriously thinking of such a thing, ladies!' said the bishop.

'Oh, but it would amuse us, let us do it, Monseigneur.'

So they summoned a manservant, and had him prepare a bottle of water on the spot. This was fastened up properly, and correctly labelled. Then they had the mendicant friar summoned.

'Brother,' said the ladies, 'you must drink to the health of his Grace and to ours.'

The monk was congratulating himself on his good fortune, and prepared himself to receive it well. The bottle was uncorked and a bumper drink was poured out. However, the crafty monk, who immediately saw through the deceit, did not lose his head at all, and said in the most woeful and humble tone to the bishop: 'Monseigneur, I will not drink as you have not given your holy blessing to this nectar.'

'This is quite unnecessary, my brother.'

'But in the name of all the saints of Paradise, I implore you to do so, Monseigneur.'

The ladies joined in the discussion, and implored the prelate to have the good nature to do this for them. The bishop finally bowed to their wishes, and blessed the water. The Franciscan then called a lackey and said to him, smiling: 'Champagne, take that into the church, a Franciscan has never drunk holy water.'

He was really quite right, wasn't he?

—from *Le Grand Dictionnaire de Cuisine,* 1873,
translated from the French by Alan and Jane Davidson

THE TALMUD ON THE RIGHT AMOUNT OF WINE

THERE ARE EIGHT THINGS THAT TAKEN IN LARGE QUANTITIES are bad but in small quantities are helpful:
Travel, sex, wealth, work, wine, sleep, hot baths and bloodletting.

—from the Babylonian Talmud, A.D. 500

MAIMONIDES ON THE BENEFITS OF WINE

Moses Maimonides (1136–1204) was born in Spain but lived in Egypt. He was not only a leading doctor but one of the most respected Jewish philosophers of all time. —M.K.

THE BENEFITS OF WINE ARE MANY IF IT IS TAKEN IN THE proper amount, as it keeps the body in a healthy condition and cures many illnesses.

But the knowledge of its consumption is hidden from the masses. What they want is to get drunk, and inebriety causes harm. . . .

The small amount that is useful must be taken after the food leaves the stomach. Young children should not come close to it because it hurts them and causes harm to their body and soul. . . .

The older a man is, the more beneficial the wine is for him. Old people need it most.

—from *The Preservation of Youth,* twelfth century

A. J. Liebling on Rosé Wine

In 1926, there were in all France only two well-known wines that were neither red nor white. One was Tavel, and the other Arbois, from the Jura—and Arbois is not a rose-colored but an "onion-peel" wine, with russet and purple glints. In the late thirties, the *rosés* began to proliferate in wine regions where they had never been known before, as growers discovered how marketable they were, and to this day they continue to pop up like measles on the wine map. Most often *rosés* are made from red wine grapes, but the process is abbreviated by removing the liquid prematurely from contact with the grape skins. This saves time and trouble. The product is a semi-aborted red wine. Any normally white wine can be converted into a *rosé* simply by adding a dosage of red wine or cochineal.

In 1926 and 1927, for example, I never heard of Anjou *rosé* wine, although I read wine cards every day and spent a week of purposeful drinking in Angers, a glorious white-wine city. Alsace is another famous white-wine country that now lends its name to countless cases of a pinkish cross between No-Cal and vinegar; if, in 1926, I had crossed the sacred threshold of Valentin Sorg's restaurant in Strasbourg and asked the sommelier for a *rosé d'Alsace,* he would have, quite properly, kicked me into Germany. The list is endless now; flipping the coated-paper pages of any dealer's brochure, you see *rosés* from Bordeaux, Burgundy, all the South of France, California, Chile, Algeria, and heaven knows where else. Pink champagne, colored by the same procedure, has existed for a century and was invented for the

African and Anglo-Saxon trade. The "discovery" of the demand for pink wine approximately coincided with the repeal of prohibition in the United States. (The American housewife is susceptible to eye and color appeal.) In England, too, in the same period, a new class of wine buyer was rising with the social revolution. Pink worked its miracle there, and also in France itself, where many families previously limited to the cheapest kind of bulk wine were beginning to graduate to "nice things."

Logically, there is no reason any good white- or red-wine region should not produce equally good *rosé*, but in practice the proprietors of the good vineyards have no cause to change the nature of their wines; they can sell every drop they make. It is impossible to imagine a proprietor at Montrachet, or Chablis, or Pouilly, for example, tinting his wine to make a Bourgogne *rosé*. It is almost as hard to imagine it of a producer of first-rate Alsatian or Angevin wines. The wines converted to *rosé* in the great-wine provinces are therefore, I suspect, the worst ones—a suspicion confirmed by almost every experience I have had of them. As for the *rosés* from the cheap-wine provinces they are as bad as their coarse progenitors, but are presented in fancy bottles of untraditional form—a trick learned from the perfume industry. The bottles are generally decorated with art labels in the style of Robida's illustrations for Rabelais, and the wines are peddled at a price out of all proportion to their inconsiderable merits. There is also behind their gruesome spread the push of a report, put out by some French adman, that while white wine is to be served only with certain aliments, and red wine only with certain others, *rosé* "goes with everything," and so can be served without embarrassment by the inexperienced hostess. The truth is, of course, that if a wine isn't good it doesn't "go" with anything, and if it is it can go in any company. Tavel though, is the good, the old, and, as far as I am concerned, still the only worthy *rosé*.

—from *Between Meals,* 1959

GEORGE SAND ON EAU-DE-VIE

Amandine-Aurore-Lucile Dupin was born in France in 1804. Despite her wealth of female names she published a considerable body of writing—novels, plays, stories—under the name George Sand. Unlike the other noted women novelists of her day, George Sand was not a spinster. She had an active life and famous lovers. Though her reputation has faded in the twentieth century, and some of her writing has never been translated into English, at the time of her death in 1876 she was considered one of the greatest writers of her generation. —M.K.

CADOCHE, THE BEGGAR, HAVING BEEN CRASHED INTO BY A carriage, was brought back to the mill by the miller and cared for.

When they laid the old man on the miller's own bed, he fainted. They gave him vinegar to inhale.

"I'd rather sniff eau-de-vie," he said when he started to come to. "It's healthier."

He was brought some.

"I'd rather drink it than breathe it," he said. "It gives you more strength."

Lémor wanted to stop this. After such an accident this strong liquor could and would cause a terrible high fever. The beggar insisted. The miller tried to talk him out of it. But the lawyer, who had spent too much time studying his own health problems not to have certain medical opinions, declared that at such a moment water could be fatal to a man who has not had a drop of it in the last fifty years, that alcohol, being his customary drink, could only help him, and that since he really had nothing wrong with him other than being shaken up, the stimulation of a little snort could resuscitate him. The miller's wife and Jeannie, who, like all peasants, had a deep belief in the infallible virtues of wine and its alcohols for all problems, agreed with the lawyer that they should do as the poor man wished. The majority opinion prevailed and while they were looking for a glass, Cadoche, who felt completely consumed with the kind of thirst that consumes the long-suffering, lifted the bottle to his lips and swallowed in one gulp about half of it.

"Oh, that's too much! Too much!" said the miller, trying to stop him.

"How's that, nephew?" answered the beggar with all the dignity of a head of the family assuming his rightful authority. "You are measuring out how much I can have under your roof? You want to quibble over how much first aid I deserve?"

This entirely unjust reproach defeated the common sense of the humble and honest miller. He left the bottle at the beggar's side and told him, "Keep it for later, but for now, that's enough."

"You are a good kinsman and a great nephew," said Cadoche, who suddenly appeared revived by the eau-de-vie. "And if I have to die, I want to die under your roof, because you will bury me well. I've always admired that, a good burial. Listen, my nephew, mill workers, Mr. Lawyer! . . . You are all my witnesses. I am charging my nephew and my heir, Grand-Louis d'Angibault, with the responsibility of laying me to rest in a style no better or worse than in the manner that the old Bricolin de Blanchemont will go, no doubt quite soon . . . though barely outlasting me . . . even though he is considerably younger . . . but he took off. . . . Ah, tell me, all of you, isn't it a fool who gets his drumsticks grilled for the sake of your savings. Though its true he had some in the cast-iron pot. . . ."

"What is he saying?" the lawyer wanted to know, sitting in front of a table and not at all displeased to see the miller's wife preparing tea for the patient, since he hoped to have a nice hot cup himself to guard him against the night mist on the banks of the Vauvre.

"What is he babbling on about, his grilled drumstick and the cast-iron pot?"

"I think he's raving," said the miller. "In any case, when he is not drunk or ill, he is still old enough to babble, and he thinks more about his yesterdays than his todays. That's what old men are like. How do you feel, uncle?"

"I feel much better since that nice little drop, though your eau-de-vie has no damn flavor. Did you play a little trick and try to save some money by watering it down?"

—from *The Miller of Angibault,* 1845,
translated from the French by Mark Kurlansky

ANTON CHEKHOV'S MENU
FOR JOURNALISTS

In one of Anton Chekhov's youthful sketches, he suggested this eight-course menu for journalists.   —M.K.

(1) a glass of vodka
(2) daily shchi [cabbage soup] and yesterday's kasha
(3) two glasses of vodka
(4) suckling pig with horseradish
(5) 3 glasses of vodka
(6) horse radish, cayenne pepper, and soy sauce
(7) 4 glasses of vodka
(8) 7 bottles of beer

—from "Alarm-clock's Calendar," c. 1880

FRANCES CALDERÓN DE LA
BARCA ON PULQUE

In Mexico, pulque is infamous. The sour, milky liquid—fermented but undistilled cactus juice—is low in alcohol. It is almost exclusively a drink of indigenous Mexicans and they manage to get seriously inebriated on it, though most people of European origin are more likely to get an upset stomach, which might have to do with the fact that the fermentation process is begun with spit.   —M.K.

AT LA VENTILLA, HOWEVER, WE DESCENDED WITH A GOOD appetite, and found several authorities waiting to give C—n a welcome. Here they gave us delicious chirimoyas, a natural custard, which we liked even upon a first trial, also granaditas, bananas, sapotes, etc. Here also I first tasted *pulque;* and on a first impression it appears to me, that as nectar was the drink in Olympus, we may fairly conjecture that Pluto cultivated the maguey in his dominions. The taste and smell combined took me so completely by surprise, that I am afraid my look of horror must have given mortal offence to the worthy alcalde who considers it the most delicious beverage in the world; and in fact, it is said, that when one gets over the first shock, it is very agreeable. The difficulty must consist in getting over it.

—from *Life in Mexico,* 1840

Malcolm Lowry on Mescal

Malcolm Lowry's novel Under the Volcano *is the story of a former British consul in Mexico and his wife's attempt to rescue him and their marriage from a debilitating alcoholism.* —M.K.

"Mescal," said the Consul.

The main barroom of the Farolito was deserted. From a mirror behind the bar, that also reflected the door open to the square, his face silently glared at him, with stern, familiar foreboding.

Yet the place was not silent. It was filled by that ticking: the ticking of his watch, his heart, his conscience, a clock somewhere. There was a remote sound too, from far below, of rushing water, of subterranean collapse; and moreover he could still hear them, the bitter wounding accusations he had flung at his own misery, the voices as in argument, his own louder than the rest, mingling now with those other voices that seemed to be wailing from a distance distressfully: "Borracho, Borrachón, Borraaaacho!"

But one of these voices was like Yvonne's, pleading. He still felt her look, their look in the Salón Ofélia, behind him. Deliberately he shut out all thought of Yvonne. He drank two swift mescals: the voices ceased.

Sucking a lemon he took stock of his surroundings. The mescal, while it assuaged, slowed his mind; each object demanded some moments to impinge upon him. In one corner of the room sat a white rabbit eating an ear of Indian corn. It nibbled at the purple and black stops with an air of detachment, as though playing a musical instrument. Behind the bar hung, by a clamped swivel, a beautiful Oaxaqueñan gourd of mescal de olla, from which his drink had been measured. Ranged on either side stood bottles of Tenampa, Berreteaga, Tequila Añejo, Anís doble de Mallorca, a violet decanter of Henry Mallet's "delicioso licor," a flask of peppermint cordial, a tall voluted bottle of Anís del Mono, on the label of which a devil brandished a pitchfork. On the wide counter before him were saucers of toothpicks, chiles, lemons, a tumblerful of straws, crossed long spoons in a glass tankard. At one end large bulbous jars of many-colored aguardiente were set, raw alcohol with different flavours, in which citrus fruit rinds floated. An advertisement tacked by the mirror for last night's ball in Quauhnahuac caught his eye: *Hotel Bella Vista Gran Baile a Beneficio de la Cruz Roja. Los Mejores Artistas del radio en acción. No falte Vd.* A scorpion clung to the advertisement. The Consul noted all these things carefully. Drawing long signs of icy relief, he even counted the toothpicks. He was safe here; this was the place he loved—sanctuary, the paradise of his despair.

—from *Under the Volcano*, 1947

Robert Rose-Rosette on Martinique Punch

In 1987, I had the good fortune of having a Ti punch with Robert Rose-Rosette, Martinique's then octogenarian scholar, folklorist, and guardian of local culture. In the French Caribbean, the drink known as Ti punch in Creole, or in French, Le punch, not to be confused with various fruit drinks in the region such as planter's punch, is always made at the table. An empty glass, a spoon or stirrer known in Creole as a lélé, a wedge of lime, a carafe of cane syrup, and a bottle of "agricole" rum, local white rum distilled directly from cane juice and not from molasses, are served. As we mixed our drinks, an act Rose-Rosette considered an essential social function of his culture, my host waxed Martiniquaise in both French and Creole. "It is something voluptuous to drink a punch, a good punch," he said. These are some of his writings on the subject. —M.K.

The word "punch" is English. According to the dictionary, it came from the Hindustani or Sanskrit word *"panch,"* which means five—the number of ingredients in a drink said to be Indian: tea, lime, cinnamon, sugar, and alcohol. A French version of punch has three ingredients—a slice of lemon, sugar, and cognac or rum. No doubt this is the origin of Martinique punch.

Punch is mentioned in the second half of the seventeenth century. Père Labat, chronicler of the period, listing numerous common island drinks, mentioned *ponche,* a favorite English drink made up of two parts alcohol for one part water. He said it was the same ingredients as *sangris* except that egg yolks were used and not lemons.

The terms *"guildive"* and *"tafia,"* synonyms, appeared at the same period as did the word "rum." *Tafia* is a Creole word that even Père Labat used. There is also the expression *ratafia*, from *tafia*, which means "to your health," and one could guess the occasion [for toasts]. It comes from the two-word expression in Latin *"rata fiat,"* which meant that a bargain had been reached.

Here the expressions *tafia* and rum were interchangeable for a long time. Not so long ago a drinker was called a *tafiateur.*

Rum, according to *le Petit Robert* [dictionary], comes from English. It is an abbreviation of a word that has vanished from the language, the word *"rumbullion,"* a variation of rumbustion, meaning the condition of being muddled by alcohol, which led to the name for the alcohol that caused the condition.

Paul Baudot, the Guadeloupean lyric poet, captured the subtle beauty of punch in a memorable stanza:

Quand moin valé la bête,
Moin ka senti dans tête
Ion joli le tempête,
Ou sé dit ion jou fête.
Quand moin prend ion bon dose
Moin ka vouê tout en rose
Cé ion bien belle chose.

[Translation from the Creole: When I swallow the beast, I feel in my head, a nice little storm, on holidays. If I take a stiff shot, everything seems beautiful, it is the effect of the cause and a very nice thing.]

—from "Le Punch Martiniquais," 1986,
translated from the French and Creole by Mark Kurlansky

MARTIAL ON DRINKING MATES

Last night, after five pints of wine,
I said, 'Procillus, come and dine
Tomorrow.' You assumed I meant
What I said (a dangerous precedent)
And slyly jotted down a note
Of my drunk offer. Let me quote
A proverb from the Greek: 'I hate
An unforgetful drinking mate.'

—from *Epigrams,* first century A.D.,
translated from the Latin by James Michie

CHAPTER TWENTY-FOUR

Bugs

When I was living in Mexico City, I befriended an affable man in the bug trade. His tiny, dark, stand-up restaurant in the downtown area near the Zocalo served almost nothing but bugs. The grill in the front always had two kinds of hot fresh crunchy worms. He would invite me in for a plate or hand me a few as I walked by. Though both worms were found on the same cactus, they looked and tasted considerably different. The small reddish ones had a much stronger, almost a gamey, flavor in comparison to the large white one. He also had crunchy grasshoppers, and ant eggs, and feathery little grass fleas.

Once I couldn't finish my bugs and he offered me what Americans call "a doggie bag," though that may be inappropriate for this, especially the fleas. But this bag contained mostly grilled worms and I took them to the British embassy, where I had friends, and convinced them that the worms were a local delicacy and they all had to try them. My plan was that after they ate a few I would say that it was just a joke and nobody really eats grilled worms. But they all munched on them with such poetic resolve, such earnest faces, something in British genes from all those generations trudging across battlefields, that I did not have the heart to do it.   —M.K.

Frances Calderón de la Barca on Mosquito Eggs

Count C——a has promised to send me to-morrow a box of mosquitoes' eggs, of which tortillas are made, which are considered a great delicacy. Considering mosquitoes as small winged *cannibals*, I was rather shocked at the idea, but they pretend that these which are from the Laguna, are a superior race of creatures, which do not sting. In fact the Spanish historians mention that the Indians used to eat bread made of the eggs which the fly called *agayacatl* laid on the rushes of the lakes, and which they (the Spaniards) found very palatable.

—from *Life in Mexico,* 1840

Peter Lund Simmonds on Edible Spiders

What will be said to spiders as food? But these form an article in the list of the Bushman's dainties in South Africa, according to Sparrman; and the inhabitants of New Caledonia, Labillardiere tells us, seek for, and eat with avidity, large quantities of a spider nearly an inch long, which they roast over the fire. Even individuals amongst the more polished nations of Europe are recorded as having a similar taste; so that if you could rise above vulgar prejudices, you would in all probability find them a most delicate morsel. If you require precedents, Reaumur tells us of a young lady, who, when she walked in her grounds, never saw a spider that she did not take and crunch upon the spot. Another female, the celebrated Anna Maria Schurman, used to eat them like nuts, which she affirmed they much resembled in taste, excusing her propensity by saying that she was born under the sign *Scorpio.*

If you wish for the authority of the learned: Lalande, the celebrated French astronomer, was equally fond of these delicacies, according to Latreille. And if, not content with eating spiders seriatim, you should feel desirous of eating them by handfuls, you may shelter yourself under the authority of the German immortalized by Rosel, who used to spread them upon bread like butter, observing that he found them very useful.

These edible spiders, and such like, are all sufficiently disgusting, but we feel our nausea quite turned into horror when we read in Humboldt, that he has seen the Indian children drag out of the earth centipedes 18 inches long, and more than half an inch broad, and devour them.

—from *The Curiosities of Food: Or the Dainties and Delicacies of Different Nations Obtained from the Animal Kingdom*, 1859

Vincent M. Holt on Eating Insects

Why not eat insects? This is the kind of question that doesn't seem to require an answer. But in 1885 the question was the title of a small book by Vincent M. Holt with an introduction by Laurence Mound, the keeper of entomology at the British Museum of Natural History. Holt began by pleading, "In entering upon this work, I am fully conscious of the difficulty of battling against a long-existing and deep-rooted public prejudice." —M.K.

FRENCH

MENU

Potage aux Limaces à la Chinoise.

Morue bouillie à l'Anglaise, Sauce aux Limaçons.

Larves de Guêpes frites au Rayon.

Phalènes à l'Hottentot.

Bœuf aux Chenilles.

Petites Carottes, Sauce blanche aux Rougets.

Crême de Groseilles aux Nemates.

Larves de Hanneton Grillées.

Cerfs Volants à la Gru Gru.

ENGLISH

MENU

Slug Soup.

Boiled Cod with Snail Sauce.

Wasp Grubs fried in the Comb.

Moths sautéd in Butter.

Braized Beef with Caterpillars.

New Carrots with Wireworm Sauce.

Gooseberry Cream with Sawflies.

Devilled Chafer Grubs.

Stag Beetle Larvæ on Toast.

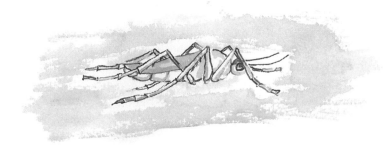

"These ye may eat; the locust after his kind, and the bald locust after his kind, and the beetle after his kind, and the grasshopper after his kind."

—LEV. xi. 22.

Why not eat insects? Why not, indeed! What are the objections that can be brought forward to insects as food? In the word "insects" I here include other creatures such as some small mollusks and crustaceans which, though not technically coming under the head of insects, still may be so called for the sake of brevity and convenience. "Ugh! I would not touch the loathsome things, much less eat one!" is the reply. But why on earth should these creatures be called loathsome, which, as a matter of fact, are not loathsome in any way, and, indeed, are in every way more fitted for human food than many of the so-called delicacies now highly prized? From chemical analysis it appears that the flesh of insects is composed of the same substances as are found in that of the higher animals. Again, if we look at the food they themselves live upon, which is one of the commonest criterions as to whether an animal is, or is not, fit for human food, we find that the great majority of insects live entirely upon vegetable matter in one form or another; and, in fact, all those I shall hereafter propose to my readers as food are strict vegetarians. Carnivorous animals, such as the dog, cat, fox, etc., are held unworthy of the questionable dignity of being edible by civilized man. In the same manner I shall not ask my readers to consider for a moment the propriety or advisability of tasting such unclean-feeding insects as the common fly, the carrion beetle, or *Blaps mortisaga* (the churchyard beetle). But how can any one who has ever gulped down the luscious oyster alive at three-and-six-pence per dozen, turn up his nose and shudder at the clean-feeding and less repulsive-looking snail? The lobster, a creature consumed in incredible quantities at all the highest tables in the land, is such a foul feeder that, for its sure capture, the experienced fisherman will bait his lobster-pot with putrid flesh or fish which is too far gone even to attract a crab. And yet, if at one of those tables there appeared a well-cooked dish of clean-feeding slugs, the hardiest of the guests would shrink from tasting it. Again, the eel is universally eaten, fried, stewed, or in pies, though it is the very scavenger of the water—there being no filth it will not swallow—like its equally relished fellow-scavenger the pig, the "unclean animal" of Scripture. There was once an equally strong objection to the pig, as there is at present against insects. What would the poor do without the bacon-pig now?

It is hard, very hard, to overcome the feelings that have been instilled into us from our youth upwards; but still I foresee the day when the slug will be as popular in England as its luscious namesake the Trepang, or sea-slug, is in China, and a dish of grasshoppers fried in butter as much relished by the English peasant as a similarly treated dish of locusts is by an Arab or Hottentot. There are many reasons why this is to be hoped for. Firstly, philosophy bids us neglect no wholesome source of food. Secondly, what a pleasant change from the labourer's unvarying meal of bread, lard, and bacon, or bread and lard without bacon, or bread without lard or bacon, would be a good dish of fried cockchafers or grasshoppers. "How the poor live!" Badly, I know; but they neglect wholesome foods, from a foolish prejudice which it should be the task of their betters, by their example, to overcome. One of the constant questions of the day is, How can the farmer most successfully battle with the insect devourers of his crops? I suggest that these insect devourers should be collected by the poor as food. Why not? I do not mean to pretend that the poor could live upon insects; but I do say that they might thus pleasantly and wholesomely vary their present diet while, at the same time, conferring a great benefit upon the agricultural world. Not only would their children then be rewarded by the farmers for hand-picking the destructive insects, but they would be doubly rewarded by partaking of toothsome and nourishing insect dishes at home.

After all, there is not such a very strong prejudice among the poorer classes against the swallowing of insects, as is shown by the survival in some districts of such old-fashioned medicines as wood-lice pills, and snails and slugs as a cure for consumption. I myself also knew a labourer, some years ago, in the west of England, who was regularly in the habit of picking up and eating any small white slugs which he happened to see, as tidbits, just as he would have picked wild strawberries.

It may require a strong effort of will to reason ourselves out of the stupid prejudices that have stood in our way for ages; but what is the good of the advanced state of the times if we cannot thus cast aside these prejudices, just as we have caused to vanish before the ever-advancing tide of knowledge the worn-out theories of spontaneous generation and barnacle geese?

Cheese-mites, the grubs of a small fly, are freely eaten by many persons, whom I have often heard say "they are only cheese." There is certainly some ground for this assertion; as these grubs live entirely upon cheese; but what would one of these epicures say if I served up to him a cabbage boiled with its own grubs? Yet my argument that "they are only cabbage" would be fully as good as his. As a matter of fact, I see every reason why cabbages should be thus served up, surrounded with a delicately flavoured fringe of the caterpillars which feed upon them. As things are now, the chance caterpillar which, having escaped the careful eye of the scullery-maid, is boiled among the close folds of the cabbage, quite spoils the dinner appetite of the person who happens to receive it with his helping of vegetable, and its loathsome (?) form is carefully hidden at the side of his plate or sent straight out of the room, so that its unwonted presence may no further nauseate the diners. Yet probably these same diners have, at the commencement of the meal, hailed with inward satisfaction the presence on the board of dozens of much more loathsome-looking oysters, and have actually swallowed perhaps a dozen of them raw and living as quite an appetizer for their dinner! At a table of gourmands, he who by chance thus gets the well-boiled larva served up in its own natural, clean food should, instead of being pitied for having his dinner spoilt, be, on the contrary, almost an object of envy, as he who gets the liver-wing. I am quite aware of the horror with which this opinion will be read by many at first sight, but when it is carefully thought over I fail to see that any one capable of correct reasoning can deny its practical truth, even if he himself, though a frequent swallower of the raw oyster and a relisher of the scavenging lobster, continues to turn up his delicate nose at my suggestion to put it to a practical proof.

The general abhorrence of insects seems almost to have increased of late years, rather than diminished, owing, no doubt, to the fact of their being no longer familiar as medicines. At one time the fact of their being prescribed as remedies by village quacks and wise men made people, at any rate, familiar with the idea of swallowing them. Wood-lice, which conveniently roll themselves up into the semblance of black pills, were taken as an aperient; centipedes were an invaluable specific for jaundice; cockchafers for the plague; ladybirds for colic and measles. The advance of medical science and the suppression of wise folk have swept away this belief in the medicinal qualities of insects, except from out-of-the-way country corners, where a stray wise woman occasionally holds a divided sway with the parish doctor. As these theories die away, why should not the useful practice of using insects as food be introduced with advantage? From time to time letters appear in the papers inquiring as to the best method of getting rid of such insect pests as the wireworm, leather-jacket, chafer-grub, etc., and I have seen one method especially recommended. This is to set traps for the insect vermin by burying slices of turnip or potato stuck upon the ends of small sticks, whose other ends project from the ground to mark the spot. The slices, in the morning, will be covered with the mischievous ravagers, which, one answer went on to say, "may then be dealt with at pleasure." I say, then, collect them for the table. Man will often, in his universal selfishness, take the trouble to do acts, if they directly affect him or his stomach, which he would not do for their mere utility; and if these wireworms, etc., were esteemed as articles of food, there would be a double incentive to the gathering of them. We have only to glance through the pages of Miss Eleanor Ormerod's excellent work on "Injurious Insects" to see what a power for harm lies in the myriads of the insect world, even if we do not know it from sad personal experience.

There cannot be said to be any really strong objection, among the upper classes, to making any new departure in the direction of foods, if it once becomes the fashion to do so. On page [388] is the *menu* of a dinner at the Chinese Restaurant at the late Health Exhibition, whose quaint delicacies were eaten and well appreciated by crowds of fashionable people, who turn up their noses at the neglected supply of new delicacies at home.

Let us look into some of the items which these professedly most refined eaters partook of with relish—though it is only fair to state that some of the ladies could not sufficiently overcome their prejudices to enjoy their meal.

The "Bird's Nest Soup" was, I believe, universally appreciated, and, personally, I thought that it was perhaps the most delicious soup I had ever tasted. Yet, from what is it made, ye dainty feeders? The nest of a small swallow, constructed by that bird principally by the means of threads of a viscid fluid secreted from its mouth. Does not that sound nasty enough? Yet what excellent soup is made therefrom, being not only delicious to the taste, but said also to possess great strengthening qualities, and to be an excellent specific for indigestion. The annual value of these nests imported into China and Japan exceeds £200,000. Surely, considering the general approbation expressed of this soup at the Health Exhibition, it would pay some enterprising London merchant to import nests into England.

The "Visigo à la Tortue" was also an excellent soup, a kind of imitation turtle, made from the octopus or cuttle-fish.—The cuttle-fish! Go to any aquarium; look on those hideous creatures and tell me, are not they loathsome? Do they look nice to eat?

"Biche de Mer à la Matelote Chinoise."—This was the dish which frightened the more delicate ladies. Why? Merely because its common English name is the "sea slug." There cannot be a particle of doubt that, if it had always previously been known only by its less common name of sea cucumber or Trepang, it would have been refused by none. What's in a name? The Trepang by any other name would taste as sweet! Those who partook of this dish all pronounced it to be excellent eating, although its ingredients did resemble in looks pieces of old shoe leather or large black slugs. Not that there could be any valid objection if it actually were made of either. Half the delicious calves' foot jelly in the world is made from old parchment and leather clippings, and slugs are no worse than oysters.

We have thus recently had an opportunity of tasting some of the varieties of a usual Chinese *menu,* and our verdict upon them was proved to be favourable by "the Chinese dinner at the Healtheries" becoming one of the fashionable entertainments of the season. There one had opportunities of watching, with wonder, the most refined ladies and gentlemen, in correct evening costume, sitting down to partake of a dinner, whose most attractive items, as shown in the *menu,* were such objects as bird's nest soup, cuttle-fish, sea slugs, and shark's fins, for no other reason than that it was the fashion to do so. I will venture to say that if it had been previously suggested to those people to have such items included in the *menu* at a country house, they would have expressed disgust at the idea. Fashion is the most powerful motive in the world. Why does not some one in a high place set the common-sense fashion of adding insect dishes to our tables? The flock would not be long in following.

After eating of those unaccustomed dishes at the Health Exhibition, and discovering how good they were, is it not a wonder that people do not look around them for the many new gastronomic treasures lying neglected at their feet? Prejudice, prejudice, thy strength is

CHINESE RESTAURANT

MENU, II SEPT., 1884.

Hors D'œuvre.

Pullulas à l'Huile.   Saucisson de Frankfort.

Olives.

Bird's Nest Soup.

Visigo à la Tortue.

Souchée de Turbot au Varech Violet.

Biche de Mer à la Matelote Chinoise.

Shaohsing Wine.

Petit Caisse à la Marquis Tsing.

Roulade de Pigeon farcie au Pistache.

Copeau de Veau à la Jardinière au Muscus.

Sharks' Fins à la Bagration.

Boule de Riz.

Shaohsing Wine.

Noisettes de Lotus à l'Olea Fragrance.

Pommes pralinée. Compôte de Leechée.

Persdeaux Salade Romain.

Vermicelli Chinoise à la Milanaise.

Beignet Soufflé à la Vanille.

Gelée aux Fruits.

Biscuit Glace aux Amande pralinée.

Glace à la Crême de Café.

Dessert.

Persimmons, Pommes Confit, Pêches,

Amands Vert, Grapes.

Thé Imperial.

enormous! People will dilate upon the delicate flavour of one fungus, under the name of mushroom, while they stamp upon, or cast from them, the disappointing young puff-ball and a dozen other common kinds of fungi, all equally nice and wholesome, if people would only recognize it, as the one they gloat over. People will, in like manner, enjoy oysters and cockles, while they abominate snails; they will make themselves ill with indigestible and foul-feeding lobsters while they look with horror upon pretty clean-feeding caterpillars. All this would not be so absurd if it were only the rich that were concerned, for they can afford to be dainty. But while we, in these days of agricultural depression, do all we can to alleviate the sufferings of our starving labourers, ought we not to exert our influence towards pointing out to them a neglected food supply?

—from *Why Not Eat Insects?*, 1885

CHAPTER TWENTY-FIVE

The French

JÉRÔME LIPPOMANO
ON HOW PARISIANS EAT

Jérôme Lippomano (1538–1591) was the Venetian ambassador to Paris. —M.K.

PARIS HAS AN ABUNDANCE OF EVERYTHING THAT COULD BE wanted. Goods from every region and tributary are carried there by the Seine—from Picardy, the Auvergne, Champagne, Burgundy, Normandy. So that even though the population is huge, they lack nothing; it all seems to fall from heaven. However, food prices, to be honest, are a little high, because Frenchmen will spend for nothing as gladly as they will spend to eat or on what they consider premium. That is why the butchers, the meat sellers, the roasters, the retailers, the cake makers, the innkeepers, are so numerous that there is utter confusion. There is no street, no matter how insignificant, that does not play its part. You want to buy an animal at the market? Or you want meat? You can do it any time, any place. Would you like prepared foods—raw or cooked? The rotisseries, the pastry makers. In less than an hour can you order dinner, a supper, for ten? for twenty? for one hundred?

You can. The rotisserie will give you the meat, the pastry maker the pâtés, the meat pie makers the pies, the main courses, the desserts: The cooks provide the jellies, the sauces, the stews.

—from *Journey to France*, 1577,
translated from the Italian by Mark Kurlansky

GEORGE ORWELL ON BEING HUNGRY IN PARIS

YOU DISCOVER WHAT IT IS LIKE TO BE HUNGRY. WITH bread and margarine in your belly, you go out and look into the shop windows. Everywhere there is food insulting you in huge, wasteful piles; whole dead pigs, baskets of hot loaves, great yellow blocks of butter, strings of sausages, mountains of potatoes, vast Gruyère cheeses like grindstones. A snivelling self-pity comes over you at the sight of so much food. You plan to grab a loaf and run, swallowing it before they catch you and you refrain, from pure funk.

—from *Down and Out in Paris and London*, 1933

VIRGINIA WOOLF ON FRENCH COOKING

"WE DID THIS, WE DID THAT." THEY'LL SAY THAT ALL THEIR lives, she thought, and an exquisite scent of olives and oil and juice rose from the great brown dish as Marthe, with a little flourish, took the cover off. The cook had spent three days over that dish. And she must take great care, Mrs. Ramsay thought, diving into the soft mass, to choose a specially tender piece for William Bankes. And she peered into the dish, with its shiny walls and its confusion of savoury brown and yellow meats and its bay leaves and its wine, and thought. This will celebrate the occasion—a curious sense rising in her, at once freakish and tender, of celebrating a festival, as if two emotions were called up in her, one profound—for what could be more serious than the love of man for woman, what more commanding, more impressive, hearing in its bosom the seeds of death; at the same time these lovers, these people entering into illusion glittering eyed, must be danced round with mockery, decorated with garlands.

"It is a triumph," said Mr. Bankes, laying his knife down for a moment. He had eaten attentively. It was rich; it was tender. It was perfectly cooked. How did she manage these things in the depths of the country? he asked her. She was a wonderful woman. All his love, all his reverence, had returned; and she knew it.

"It is a French recipe of my grandmother's," said Mrs. Ramsay, speaking with a ring of great pleasure in her voice. Of course it was French. What passes for cookery in England is an abomination (they agreed). It is putting cabbages in water. It is roasting meat till it is like leather. It is cutting off the delicious skins of vegetables. "In which," said Mr. Bankes, "all the virtue of the vegetable is contained." And the waste, said Mrs. Ramsay. A whole French family could live on what an English cook throws away.

—from *To the Lighthouse,* 1927

ALICE B. TOKLAS
ON FRENCH COOKING

THE FRENCH APPROACH TO FOOD IS CHARACTERISTIC; they bring to their consideration of the table the same appreciation, respect, intelligence and lively interest that they have for the other arts, for painting, for literature and for the theatre. By French I mean French men as well as French women, for the men in France play a very active part in everything that pertains to the kitchen. I have heard working men in Paris discuss the way their wives prepare a beef stew as it is cooked in Burgundy or the way a cabbage is cooked with salt pork and browned in the oven. A woman in the country can be known for kilometres about for the manner in which she prepares those sublimated dumplings known as *Quenelles,* and a very complicated dish they are. Conversation even in a literary or political *salon* can turn to the subject of menus, food or wine.

The French like to say that their food stems from their culture and that it has developed over the centuries. It has its universal reputation for these reasons and on account of the mild climate and fertile soil.

We foreigners living in France respect and appreciate this point of view but deplore their too strict observance of a tradition which will not admit the slightest deviation in a seasoning or the suppression of a single ingredient. For example, a dish as simple as a potato salad must be served surrounded by chicory. To serve it with any other green is inconceivable. Still, this strict conservative attitude over the years has resulted in a number of essential principles that have made the renown of the French kitchen.

French markets without deep freezing are limited to seasonal produce which is however of excellent quality with the exception of beef, milk and a few fruits. Even the common root vegetables, carrots, turnips, parsnips and leeks (the asparagus of the poor), are tender and savoury, olive oil and butter are abundant and of a high grade and bread is nourishing and delicious.

Wars change the way of life, habits, markets and so eventually cooking. For five years and more the French were deprived of most of their foodstuffs and were obliged to use inferior substitutes when they could be found. After the Liberation the markets very slowly were supplied with a limited amount of material. The population had been hungry too long, they had lost their old disciplined appreciation of food and had forgotten or were ignoring their former critical judgment. So that even now French food has not yet returned to its old standard.

—from *The Alice B. Toklas Cook Book,* 1954

THOMAS JEFFERSON ON FRENCH PRODUCE

To James Madison

Dear Sir
Fontainebleau. Oct. 28. 1785

. . . After descending the hill again I saw a man cutting fern. I went to him under the pretence of asking the shortest road to the town, and afterwards asked for what use he was cutting fern. He told me that this part of the country furnished a great deal of fruit to Paris. That when packed in straw it acquired an ill taste, but that dry fern preserved it perfectly without communicating any taste at all. I treasured this observation for the preservation of my apples on my return to my own country. They have no apples here to compare with our Newtown pipping. They have nothing which deserves the name of a peach; there being not sun enough to ripen the plumbpeach and the best of their soft peaches being like our autumn peaches. Their cherries and strawberries are fair, but I think less flavoured. Their plumbs I think are better; so also the gooseberries, and the pears infinitely beyond any thing we possess. They have no grape better than our sweet-water. But they have a succession of as good from very early in the summer till frost.

I am tomorrow to go to Mr. Malsherbes [an uncle of the Chevalr. Luzerne's] about 7. leagues from hence, who is the most curious man in France as to his trees. He is making for me a collection of the vines from which the Burgundy, Champagne, Bourdeaux, Frontignac, and other the most valuable wines of the country are made. Another gentleman is collecting for me the best eating grapes, including what we call the raisin. I propose also to endeavor to colonize their hare, rabbet, red and grey partridge, pheasants of different kinds, and some other birds. But I find that I am wandering beyond the limits of my walk and will therefore bid you Adieu.

Yours affectionately,
Th: Jefferson

—from *The Papers of Thomas Jefferson*, Julian P. Boyd, ed., 1950

HANNAH GLASSE
ON FRENCH COOKING

A FRENCHMAN, IN HIS OWN COUNTRY, WOULD DRESS A FINE Dinner of twenty Dishes, and all genteel and pretty, for the Expence he will put an *English* Lord to for dressing one Dish. But then there is the little petty Profit. I have heard of a Cook that used six Pounds of Butter to fry twelve Eggs; when every Body knows, that understands Cooking, that Half a Pound is full enough, or more than need be used: But then it would not be *French*. So much is the blind Folly of this Age, that they would rather be impos'd on by a *French* Booby, than give Encouragement to a good *English* Cook!

—from *The Art of Cookery, Made Plain and Easy*, 1747

M.F.K. FISHER
ON LEAVING FRANCE

THE NEXT TIME WE PUT TO SEA, IN 1932, WAS NOT SO MUCH later, about a year . . . but I was more than a year older. I don't know why; I simply matured in a spurt, so that suddenly I knew a lot about myself and what I wanted and what I had to do. It made me soberer, and I was much less shy.

It was hard to leave Europe. But I knew that even if we stayed, our young days there were gone. The first insouciant spell was broken, and not by the act of buying tickets, as Al seemed to believe. Nor could it ever be recaptured; that would be monstrous, like a man turned child again but still caught in his worn big body.

We ate lunch before the boat sailed at a restaurant on the Old Port in Marseille. Al and I had often been there before, and Norah, who was unusually acute about flavors, almost like a French child, was excited at the prospect of one final orgy of real *bouillabaisse*. We almost didn't get it, though.

It was the first time I had ever been turned away from a

restaurant, and it left me strangely shaken; we walked in the door and a waiter came hurrying toward us through the crowded room and before we knew it we were out on the street again . . . shoo, shoo, as if we were impudent chickens on a lawn.

Then the proprietor rushed out. He recognized Al and me. He screamed at the officious waiter. We all laughed and laughed . . . the waiter had seen my accordion, which Al carried under his arm because we couldn't find a safe parking place for it before the boat sailed, and had thought we were hungry street-singers planning to cadge a meal.

We bowed and grinned and blushed, and there Norah and Al and I were, sitting at the best table on the balcony, looking down on the Old Port in the full spring sunlight, drinking several different kinds of the proprietor's private stock of wines and trying not to wonder how we could bear to leave this land.

The *bouillabaisse* sent up its own potent saffrony steam. We mopped and dunked at its juices, and sucked a hundred strange dead creatures from their shells. We toasted many things, and often, but ourselves most of all.

And then it was time to go. I played the proprietor and several waiters my best tune, still feeling, through the good wine and food, a sense of shock that I or anyone else in the world could be turned away from a door. We all had a final drink, in a *marc du Midi* that would jar Jupiter, and then we left France.

—from *Sea Change,* 1932

CHAPTER TWENTY-SIX

The English

GEORGE ORWELL ON ENGLISH FOOD

ON THE JOURNEY I FELL IN WITH A COUPLE OF ROUMANIANS, mere children, who were going to England on their honeymoon trip. They asked innumerable questions about England, and I told them some startling lies. I was so pleased to be getting home, after being hard up for months in a foreign city, that England seemed to me a sort of Paradise. There are, indeed, many things in England that make you glad to get home; bathrooms, armchairs, mint sauce, new potatoes properly cooked, brown bread, marmalade, beer made with veritable hops—they are all splendid, if you can pay for them. England is a very good country when you are not poor; and, of course, with a tame imbecile to look after, I was not going to be poor. The thought of not being poor made me very patriotic. The more questions the Roumanians asked, the more I praised England; the climate, the scenery, the art, the literature, the laws—everything in England was perfect.

—from *Down and Out in Paris and London*, 1933

JANE GRIGSON ON ENGLISH FOOD

SINCE FINISHING THE FIRST EDITION OF THIS BOOK [*English Food*] in 1974, I have come to understand the weakness of the domestic tradition that was once our glory, and to a certain extent—in some homes—still is.

The weakness is a lack of professionalism, the lack in each of us, of a solid grounding in skill and knowledge about food, where it comes from, how it should be prepared. Somehow we do not manage in shops and restaurants to keep high standards that constantly remind the cook at home of what food can be. You have only to spend a day visiting Fauchon or Le Nôtre in Paris, or some of the supermarkets of German and Italian towns, and then spend the next visiting the groceries of Piccadilly to see what I mean. How often when you go to a restaurant for a meal are you delighted to eat something far better than you can make yourself? To enjoy some aspect of skill that makes you long to get into the kitchen next day, and see if you can come anywhere near it?

The thing is that if you have a solid basis of skill, and can constantly refer to the highest standards, you have a better chance of adapting to the changes of life than if you merely look in magazines and books for new 'recipes.' The English, like the Americans, are always demanding 'recipes.' And cookery writers like myself provide them. I am lucky in working mainly for a paper that allows me enough space to hint at the fact that words such as apple, cheese, bread are meaningless: that for good food one needs to understand that a Cox's Orange Pippin in a pie will give you a quite different result from a Bramley; that for a good cheese sauce Parmesan must be used because English hard cheeses will put too much fat into the sauce before they can achieve the same intensity of flavour; that sliced bread and frozen poultry are not worth buying—ever. I suspect, from my reading, that mass circulation women's magazines are directed by entirely populist points of view—that one should never suggest that one variety of a fruit will give you something better, because half their readers think they cannot afford it. In a country that spends the amount ours does on hard liquor, gambling, ice cream of a worthless kind, sweets, cakes, biscuits, this is nonsense. If people choose to spend it that way, fair enough. But let them not plead poverty as an excuse for bad food. And let people who provide the awful food not shrug off responsibility by saying, 'Well, it's what *they* want.'

This really is *trahison des clercs.* 'Let them have trash' seems a far worse attitude than 'Let them eat brioche.' The latter came from a complete lack of understanding; the former comes from a conniving complicity in lower standards by people who would not accept them for themselves and their families at home. To provide worthless things, or things that are worse than they should be, shows what you think of your fellow human beings. In the past food was often adulterated by unscrupulous purveyors—sand in the sugar, dried hawthorn leaves in the tea, water in the milk—but at least this was recognized as a vicious thing to do. Now our food is adulterated and spoilt in ways that are entirely legal, even encouraged. Have you managed to buy farm butter recently? Or a farmyard chicken that has run free?

And these crimes against good food are encouraged by domestic science teachers who think it is fine to teach pupils to make pies with pastry-mix and ready-prepared pie fillings. When criticized, they answer, 'We have no time; anyway at least they enable us to teach children the "manipulative skills."' What skills? The skill to turn on the tap and mix the mix to a dough? The skill to operate a tin-opener? The skill to read instructions on the packet or tin? The skill to spoon the filling into a dish? The skill to turn on the oven, a foolproof oven, to the correct temperature? Such 'manipulative skills' are usually mastered at home before school begins, or at the latest in the infant school. The development of taste and true knowledge should be the business of secondary school home economics teachers. And if they are not able to do this through bad organization of the curriculum, they should be seeking to change the system, not conniving in it and excusing themselves. I think it is ironic that the countries of Europe where you get the better food are the countries where such a subject is not taught at the usual state secondary school.

In 1974 I finished *English Food* full of hope. In discovering at least something of our tradition for myself, I began to see that we did have a treasury to be exploited, perhaps exploited into a new cookery of our own. This revision of *English Food*, in 1979, has been completed in a spirit of pessimism. It is France with its strong professional basis of skill that has produced a *nouvelle cuisine.* Oh yes, we buy the books, we have taken it to our hearts—for the moment. This means we are debasing it as fast as we can. One top-circulation women's magazine published an article adapting—sinister word—these new ideas for 'family meals.' The adaptation consisted in suggesting the use of tinned peas and carrots; it completely balked the problem of chicken. Yet the whole point of the *nouvelle cuisine,* and especially that branch known as the *cuisine minceur*, is that ingredients must be first of all of the highest quality and freshness. If they are not, many of the dishes taste as dull as any reconstituted dehydrated convenience pack. The absolutely essential lessons of the style are lost. It has been reduced to a lot of new 'recipes' that will dominate nomenclature for a year or two until the next craze hits these shores. Will Michel Guérard's best-selling books mean we can buy really young fresh peas at the greengrocery next summer? Or better-hung beef at the supermarket counter? Or that shoppers will become more resistant? I suspect it will not.

Or am I wrong? Somehow I can never quite suppress a naive optimism; an optimism that is buffeted every time I visit my local shops, but yet refuses quite to lie down even when confronted with perceived realities. Sometimes I hear from people who live in some pocket of good food that has escaped the attentions of commerce in hastening 'that sad process which Max Weber described as "the disenchantment of the world."'

—from *English Food,* 1979

ELIZABETH DAVID ON THE ONWARD (AND DOWNWARD) MARCH OF THE ENGLISH PIZZA

ALTHOUGH ANGLICIZED AND ONLY REMOTELY RELATED TO the original, mass-market versions of the Neapolitan pizza have been with us since the 1950s. Although it was, I think, the Charles Forte snack bars of that period which first listed a substance under the name of pizza on a popular and cheap menu, it is only since the early seventies that the pizza has grown into big business for the English catering world. The time when the English pizza manufacturers were obliged to explain their product by describing it as Italian Welsh Rabbit were by that time long gone. So was the period of the late Mario Zampi, the film director who imported an Italian brick-built pizza oven, installed it in a Soho restaurant, turned it over to his brother and sister-in-law to run as a pizzeria—and failed to attract custom. There was nothing wrong with the pizzas served in the Zampi establishment. They were delicious and cheap, and indeed much superior to anything offered in today's pizza houses. But Mario Zampi's good idea was ahead of his time. In an Italian restaurant of those days the customers still wanted veal escalopes and spaghetti bolognese. A pizza and a glass or two of wine as a good midday or supper-time meal had little appeal for Londoners. In the days following the end of rationing,[1] people wanted to eat meat when they went out to a restaurant, and at that time they could afford to pay for it.

In the ten to fifteen years since Mario Zampi's venture—I think that it was the first of its kind—a generation of young people has taken to the hamburger heaven, the Golden Egg Bar and the pizza house, just as that of the 1950s took to the espresso coffee bar, and that of the 1960s to the steak house. In the pizza houses you may well get a pizza just as good as in many a native Neapolitan pizzeria—although that is not exactly an extravagant compliment—and all things considered the value provided in these establishments is fair. At the take-away counters and from the deep freeze cabinets a rather different deal is offered, and increasingly, the evidence shows, accepted.

The following extracts from magazines, newspapers and publicity handouts of the past five years show, briefly, the remarkable rise in popularity and price, although not necessarily in lightness and authenticity, of the English pizza.

'Alvaro's Pizza and Pasta, 39 Charing Cross Road, is open till 3 a.m., with a license till 1 a.m. every night . . . the place is dominated by the traditional kiln-shaped pizza oven. A pizza, or helping of pasta, a glass of wine and coffee cost around 10/—.'

Queen Magazine, June 1970

'Pizza Range Ltd, who started business some 10 months ago in a kitchen off Cricklewood Broadway, have moved into a fully modernised 4,700 sq. ft. kitchen at Lyon Industrial Estate, Watford. The firm provide a full range of pizzas, either individual or for caterers.'

Caterer and Hotel Keeper, 19 November 1970

[1] Officially, this was in 1954.

'Pizza Range, Watford, Herts, is introducing its complete Pizza service . . . the pizzas are available in 7 ins. and 10 ins. rounds with five variations on a cheese and tomato topping. Recommended retail prices range from 13p up to luxury pizzas at 37p, with a colourful topping of mushrooms or mortadella, mozzarella, tomato, olives and pimiento.'

The Grocer, 24 April 1971

'In the words of Cook-Inn's managing director: "A whole new industry now in its infancy is about to expand rapidly." The menu should appeal to all palates ranging as it does from such national favourites as cottage pie and cod in batter to exotica like pizza and spare-ribs.'

Derek Cooper in the *Guardian,* 8 December 1971

'Selling about 20,000 pizzas a week, Peter Boizot is probably London's No. 1 pizza restaurateur. Now he tells me that besides new restaurants which he hopes to open whenever suitable sites are available, there are also facilities for franchising.

'And the cost? You can pay a maximum price of 68p, but one of the most popular types—there is a choice of 14—with mozzarella and tomato, costs just 30p.'

What's On, 23 February 1973

'It's so easy . . . You just warm it up and it's ready to eat . . . with salad, with chips, or on its own . . .

'And to introduce you to Pizza Pie WE ARE GIVING YOU 10p OFF.'

Leaflet distributed by Eden Vale, valid until 30 April 1973.

Ingredients were listed as flour, cheddar cheese, Spanish peeled plum tomatoes, vegetable oil, Spanish onions, tomato puree, edible starch, baking powder, salt, skimmed milk powder, sugar, garlic, monosodium glutamate, herbs and spices.

Net weight 6 oz. Price in my local shop was 20p.

'Pizza squares are supplied by Pizza Range and measure 10 × 18 inches, costing 49p. In the takeaway each square divides into six portions and sells at 25p a portion plus chips.'

Photograph caption, *Caterer and Hotel Keeper,* 20 September 1973

'A Pizza Bar with a canopy simulating the ramparts of a castle is the focal point of the Argyle and Sutherland Highlander Inn, a new £70,000 luxury pub and restaurant opened . . . on a new housing estate at Eastham, Wirral, Cheshire.'

Caterer and Hotel Keeper, 6 December 1973

'*11th Pizza Express*
'Pizza Express, a private company formed in 1965, established a foothold in fashionable Chelsea, last week, when Mr Peter I. Boizot, prospective Liberal parliamentary candidate for Peterborough, opened his eleventh Pizza Express at 234 Kings Road, London.'

Caterer and Hotel Keeper, 30 May 1974

'The pizza, like the hamburger, has become part of our popular culture—an instant food which can be elevated, by a chef's invention, into a memorable treat.'

Peter Straub in an article entitled 'The Great British Pizza,'
Nova, September 1974

'Scots-American Mr. Bob Hamilton has converted the former Mascotte Restaurant, Brighton, into a pizzeria . . . Mr. Hamilton officially launched his pizzeria in Britain, using slogans like "I'm a pizza lover," "Peace and pizza," and "This country is going to pizzas."'

Caterer and Hotel Keeper, 6 February 1975

'Ten years ago today Peter Boizot, a salesman, opened a Pizza Express in Wardour Street against the advice of the sceptics. "I was doing everything, including making the pizzas. I stayed open till 5 a.m. and took £27."
'Now he shuts at midnight and lives in Belgravia. He employs 150 people in a chain of 11 pizzerias . . . he was manning the oven again the other day trying out a new, very palatable pizza made from wholemeal.'

Peterborough in the *Daily Telegraph,* 27 March 1975

'In England pizzas . . . could claim even to be a serious rival to the dreaded cellophane-wrapped steak pie of motorway fame.'

Delia Smith in the *Evening Standard*, 11 April 1975

'LONDON'S NEW FOOD, SO CRISP, SO LIGHT
'2 giant slices of pizza with jacket potatoes 49p'

From the menu of the Pizzaland chain of restaurants, July 1975

The take-away pizza
'*Meal:* Pizza "Special." *From:* Pizzaland, Fleet Street, London, *Price:* 70p. *Weight:* 11 oz.

'The "Special" pizza—the most expensive—consisted of a bread dough base with a filling of bits and pieces of mushroom, bacon, onion, cheese, two olives, tomato and green pepper. It contained no seasoning at all, and the dough base stretched (and tasted) like rubber. The onions were raw, the bacon bits crisped almost beyond recognition and the whole mixture was sloppy.

'*Verdict:* Unappetising, and barely a meal for two even if they were hungry enough to eat it.'

Mary Collins in a report on take-away food shops,
Daily Express, 13 September 1975

—from *English Bread and Yeast Cookery*, 1977

E. M. FORSTER ON PRUNES AND ENGLISH FOOD

PORRIDGE OR PRUNES, SIR? THESE ARE GRIM WORDS, AND they fell grimly on my ear that bleak October morning. I was returning to England, my country, by one of her boat trains. We had landed at Tilbury at an unearthly hour, and the pale ferrety-faced Customs Officials had given us their usual welcome home. To their attentions succeeded the inattentiveness of the Restaurant Car. We

sat in a vacuum waiting, waiting for breakfast. The carriage was stuffy, yet cold, the table cloths drooped as if they too had lain awake half the night, and now and then a passenger fidgeted, but in vain. Breakfast could not be served until the train started. More passengers, more porters, more luggage with chalk scriggles on it loomed in the murk outside, faint variants in the eternal monotone. I opened my book and tried to read—it was a novel by François Mauriac; the Customs Officer had not liked the look of it at all. But I could not attend to the exquisite prose; the fever, the loveliness, the tenderness in hatred, the light and the scents of the south, would none of them come through. Breakfast, oh for breakfast! Mauriac cannot stay an empty stomach. At last the engine gave a jerk, the knives and forks slid sideways and sang against one another sadly, the cups said 'cheap, cheap' to the saucers, as well they might, the door swung open and the attendants came in crying 'Porridge or Prunes, sir? Porridge or Prunes?' Breakfast had begun.

That cry still rings in my memory. It is an epitome—not, indeed, of English food, but of the forces which drag it into the dirt. It voices the true spirit of gastronomic joylessness. Porridge fills the Englishman up, prunes clear him out, so their functions are opposed. But their spirit is the same: they eschew pleasure and consider delicacy immoral. That morning they looked as like one another as they could. Everything was grey. The porridge was in pallid grey lumps, the prunes swam in grey juice like the wrinkled skulls of old men, grey mist pressed against the grey windows. 'Tea or coffee, sir?' rang out next, and then I had a haddock. It was covered with a sort of hard yellow oilskin, as if it had been out in a lifeboat, and its inside gushed salt water when pricked. Sausages and bacon followed this disgusting fish. They, too, had been up all night. Toast like steel, marmalade a scented jelly. And the bill, which I paid dumbly, wondering again why such things have to be.

They have to be because this is England, and we are English. We often eat well in our homes or in clubs or in small restaurants which have not yet been spoiled, but we do not demand good food in public, and when we eat upon an object that moves, such as a train or a boat, we expect, and generally get, absolute muck. Some people go in for complaining, cursing the waiters, calling for the manager, writing to the head office and so on, but complaints seem to me the wrong end of the stick. It is no use scorning a system which can't understand how you feel. One of my friends, who does complain, was travelling recently upon a patriotic and pretentious liner. He laid about him at meals until one of his fellow passengers said acidly: 'You seem somewhat hard to please.' He replied: 'I am not hard to please. I am merely trying to find some dish which a working-class boy would not throw in his mother's face.' This made all concerned sit up, but the menus continued as before. If you do not need prunes there is porridge; if you cannot manage the bottled coffee there is the stewy tea.

Well, I drink to the cuisine of my country in the glass of warm beer which was recently served me in a smart railway buffet at Birmingham. On that occasion I did complain. The barmaid turned pert and said: 'Something warm ought to be just right for this cold day.' Then she softened and said, yes, other customers had complained, too, but the only place she was given to keep the beer was over the hot water pipes. I drink in the beer which had to be kept over the hot water. I drink in the soup which stood in the draught. May they mingle with the porridge and the prunes, and bring oblivion!

—from *We Shall Eat and Drink Again,*
eds. Louis Golding and André L. Simon, 1944

GIACOMO CASTELVETRO
ON PRUNES IN ENGLAND

PLUMS START TO BE GOOD ABOUT THIS TIME, BUT SINCE they are known everywhere I don't need to say much about them, except that they are healthy to eat and better fresh than dried. They should only be eaten when fully ripe and during meals; not afterwards as you do in this country.

—from *The Fruit, Herbs & Vegetables of Italy,* 1614, translated from the Italian by Gillian Riley

CHAPTER TWENTY-SEVEN

The Americans

LOUIS PRIMA ON THE PIZZERIA

I eat Ziti Parmegon
So that I can gaze upon
Angelina,
Angelina,
The waitress at the Pizzeria.

I keep zooping Minestrone
Just to be with her alone,
Angelina,
Angelina,
The waitress at the Pizzeria.

Ti volglio bene;
Angelina, I adore you;
E volglio, bene;
Angelina, I live for you.

E un passione
You have set my heart on fire;

But Angelina,
never listens to my song.

I eat antipasto twice
Just because she is so nice,
Angelina,
Angelina,
The waitress at the Pizzeria.

If she'll be-a
My Cara mia;
I'll be dining at the Ritz
with the waitress from the Pizzeria.

—"Angelina, the Waitress at the Pizzeria," lyrics
by Allan Roberts and Doris Fisher, 1944

LAROUSSE GASTRONOMIQUE
ON AMERICAN FOOD

*In 1938, the French gastronomic authorities went to America and
decided it was not so bad. Somehow, American cuisine, seen
through French eyes, looked exotic and a little different from what
most Americans knew.*   —M.K.

MANY ARE THE PEOPLE, HERE IN FRANCE, WHO THINK,
even write, that American cooking is barbaric and that, in general,
Americans do not know how to eat or drink.

This judgment seems unjust to those among us who have been
there and taken the occasion to experience the American table in all
its variety. It is completely different from ours, but that does not necessarily mean that it is bad.

We criticize Americans, as we do all Anglo-Saxon people, for
their habit of mixing salt and sugar. We disapprove of the association
of so many food substances in a single preparation. The use of sugar
or sugared fruit in so many American dishes seems excessive, and
with too much severity and perhaps too much irony—irony directed

at our American hosts—we have judged American cooking as barbaric.

The foundation of a cuisine, whatever it be, is the quality of its products. For the most part, American products seem fine—and judging from what we have seen in American markets, we have to admit that America is considerably more blessed than France. In that country the raising of livestock has been developed to the point of perfection, for example the poultry. The gardeners and fruit growers cultivate to perfection, and thanks to the skilled care they are given, American fruits and vegetables are magnificent.

Some claim, it is true, that American fruits and vegetables are beautiful to look at but without taste. This judgment is a bit off. The Americans have more opportunity to treat themselves to good and beautiful fruit, and the lesser products are sold considerably more cheaply than here.

So the American table has perhaps given up on foods that in general are the same quality as those found here, and if the American homemaker is not exactly guided by a knowledge of cuisine, we cannot state after spending a long time in the United States that American cooking—which, we repeat, is different from ours—could be considered fundamentally bad.

Besides, in New York, and in all the major cities, the kitchens in most of the better hotels are directed by French chefs, and if in these places a large part of the menu is focused on local dishes, which is only natural, thanks to French practitioners exercising their craftsmanship, French gastronomic doctrine prevails.

Of course, it behooves us to say that America has been these last years under dry laws and had nothing available but the so-called wine furnished by bootleggers, and this has led to a diminution in the cuisine because good food can only be appreciated accompanied by good wine. But Prohibition has ended, and things have been put back in their right place, and with the help of French wine (not to mention the wine of California!), the better places in America, managed, we repeat, by our craftsmen, will bring back, and in many cases have already brought back, the brilliance of pre-Prohibition.

But if in the quality houses of America, the great restaurants and hotels, French cooking is dominant, in private homes it is a different story, and there you can find the national and local dishes. It is of these dishes that we wish to speak. In general, though very different from what we are used to—which are dishes Americans don't like—these dishes are delicious. In the order in which they are served, we are pointing out the most typical, the most specifically American dishes.

Of the clear turtle soup, a soup that comes from England but which American gourmets like very much, we can only speak from memory. We should also mention mock turtle soup, which is very much liked. The popular soups of North America include okra consommé, chicken gumbo, oyster gumbo, soft-shell crab gumbo (Americans love soft-shell crab), chicken rice soup, beef broth, black bean soup, cream of green corn, the land turtle (a small American turtle found in swamplands near bays and gulfs), *la crème aux clams,* American oyster soup, clam chowder, which is a variation on the national soup, fish chowder, a fish soup very well liked in the United States, and finally, a whole series of soups of English origin, which for a very long time have conquered American taste.

Fish, both saltwater and freshwater, are an important part of the American diet. They also eat a lot of crustaceans and mollusks. The fish are generally enjoyed in the same way as in Europe, especially in the English ways.

These are the fish, crustaceans, and mollusks typical of North America: boiled halibut with special sauces for poached fishes; striped bass, an excellent fish sometimes known as American bass, which is served poached with lobster sauce or hollandaise sauce, and with a cucumber salad and parsleyed potatoes; red snapper, a fish caught in the Gulf of Mexico and Florida coast (braised and served with various garnishes); shad roe; weakfish, grilled or baked and served with a cucumber salad; bluefish, a fish with bluish flesh served poached or grilled; pompano, a fish similar to the saint-pierre found along our coasts, and which Americans prepare in the same way; the sheep's head, so named because its head resembles that of a sheep (it is either poached or braised); kingfish, a fish like our *merlan* [whiting, which is considerably different] and prepared in the same way; redfish of New Orleans, which is cooked in a bouillabaisse; butterfish, found on both the Atlantic and Gulf coasts and usually cooked meunière; whitefish, fish that grow as large as thirty pounds and is found in the Northwest; black bass, which is one of the better freshwater fish.

Americans are very partial to oysters, and in general to all shellfish. The most famous oysters in the United States are from Cotuit, Buzzards Bay, Cape Cod, and Smith Island. American gourmets like their oysters hot or cold. They prepare them in cocktails, grilled on skewers, grilled, fried, in pastry, creamed, sautéed, gratinée, or fritters.

Americans are great lovers of scallops, but also clams, both soft- and hard-shelled; hard- and soft-shell crabs; oyster crabs, those minuscule crustaceans found trapped inside the oysters caught in the American South along the Atlantic. These last with an edible shell are eaten fried. It is a luxury dish served in better restaurants. Soft-shell crabs are cooked meunière, grilled, fried, creole style, stuffed au gratin, in cream, curried. Hard-shell crabs are served the same way as in France.

Lobster fished off the coasts are excellent. It must be said that the delicious crustaceans are not prepared in America à l'américaine, a style that belongs to our own Paris cuisine, but grilled, cooked in broth, or Newburg.

Even though it doesn't belong to the family of fish, we should mention the small land turtle, which is one of the rarities unique to American cooking. This reptile is much in demand and is sold at high prices. There are several types. The most desired one is called the diamondback because of the pattern on its shell. In Baltimore, the turtle is prepared in cream, in Philadelphia in a casserole with browned butter. What a delicious dish!

There are many dishes of meat, game, and poultry from uniquely American recipes. Butchers have excellent meat in America. All the usual dishes for meat in England and France are also done in America.

American pork is, or really American porks are, because there are many breeds, excellent. Virginia ham, made from a race called razorbacks, is especially famous. We should point out, among the fresh pork dishes in America: pig's head. Filet of pork roasted à l'américaine, boiled corned beef, and boiled pork with a pudding of beans [pork and beans].

American poultry is of good quality. No doubt it is not on a level with *poulet de Bresse,* but American poultry farming produces good roasts and some excellent dishes. Among the most loved poultry dishes in the United States are boiled turkey; wild roasted turkey; Turkey with oyster stuffing; turkey stuffed with clams; capons; American-style chicken; American-style goose; Rhode Island duckling; and chicken pâté.

Various game, both birds and mammals, are prepared as in England and France. The woodcock, similar to a European *becasse* but with a smaller tail, is very highly thought of. Grouses are also well liked in America. There are several types: the ruffed grouse, the heath grouse, the sage grouse, the prairie chicken. All these birds are roasted and served with a bread-crumb sauce and red currant jelly.

Wild ducks are plentiful in America and the meat is delicious. The most famous is the canvasback: It is roasted and stuffed inside with a sort of celery that is removed just before serving. It is accompanied by a celery salad, sometimes with pineapple, and hominy croquettes, and red currant jelly.

Vegetables in the United States are much more interesting than supposed by French people who think Americans only eat vegetables cooked in salt water, drained, and served with fresh butter.

The ways of eating vegetables in this country are many and varied. To just mention the principal ones used in household cooking: hash-brown potatoes; creamed lima beans; sweet corn with butter, creamed, or au gratin; white corn fritters; corn croquettes; cole slaw; sauteed tomatoes; American-style zucchini; American-style red beets; parsnips; potatoes au gratin, grilled, fried; bananas in butter; American-style okra.

The Americans are also great salad enthusiasts. The salads, which they often dress with cream, sometimes have very strange composition. Thus you find celery salad with pineapple, grapefruit, and avocado (the avocado is a tropical fruit also known under the name *beurre végétal*); melon, white cabbage, etc.

There are very many both hot and cold appetizers and pastries of purely American origin. In addition to these native preparations some are imported from England, notably all the puddings and cakes of the British repertoire. Among the best-loved American sweets we list: fig pudding; bread pudding; pancakes, a sort of crepe that is eaten topped with maple syrup; corn griddle cake; American waffles; crullers; squash and potato puddings; tipsy cake; nut cake; sponge cake (the special thing about this cake, which is always eaten with a family, is that it is not cut with a knife but with a cake cutter): cupcakes; ginger cakes; New York cookies [*les cookies New-Yorkais*]; coconut macaroons, etc.

—from *Larousse Gastronomique,* 1938,
translated from the French by Mark Kurlansky

LOUIS DIAT'S OYSTER CRABS

I was curious about Larousse's assertion in 1938 that Americans like fried oyster crabs, the tiny crustaceans occasionally found in an oyster. The only American use I had ever heard of for these tiny crabs was in a New Orleans soup. But then I remembered that to Larousse, the bastion of American cuisine were the French chefs at the leading hotels. So I looked at the cooking of Louis Diat, New York's most celebrated chef of the period, a Frenchman at New York's Ritz-Carlton. Voilà. —M.K.

Whitebait and Oyster Crabs

These are in season with oysters. In the East, whitebaits come from Long Island. At times I have received some so fresh that when I immersed them in water they were revived.

It is best to fry them. Dip in milk and flour and fry in deep hot fat or oil for 2 or 3 minutes.

Fry oyster crabs with the whitebaits and serve with lemon and Tartar Sauce.

Oyster crabs are also served with Newburgh Sauce or Cream Sauce or Curry Sauce. Poach in a little butter and a glass of sherry.

—from *Cooking à la Ritz*, 1941

ANGELO PELLEGRINI ON THE ABUNDANCE OF AMERICA

FED ON THIS MEAGER AND MONOTONOUS FARE, HUNGRY for white bread, coffee, and sugar, flesh and fowl, I came to America. Against the background of pilchards and *polenta*, what I found here, in this land of refugees from hunger and oppression, remains for me a dramatic and ever fascinating story. I found, first of all, the meaning, the consumable, edible meaning, of a simple word, lost in the dictionary among thousands of others—the meaning of the word *abundance*. I had known scarcity, had lived on intimate terms with its agonizing reality; and the discovery of its opposite, its annihilator, was an experience so maddening with joy, so awful and bewildering, that I am not yet fully recovered from the initial shock. Give man bread, woolens against the cold, labor that he enjoys, and you may open wide the doors to the futile agitator of riots and revolutions. While it may be no longer true that an army marches on its stomach, it is everlastingly true that a social order endures so long as the pantries of its citizens are stocked with good food. Thus food, bread and meat in sinful profusion, was my first discovery; and after that I came to know what I can best describe as the naturalization of Italian cuisine.

When I arrived in America, I recalled and immediately understood a saying I had frequently heard in Italy. When one had met with a bit of good fortune, such as an unusual yield from the vine or perhaps a meager inheritance, his friends would say to him, *"Eh, l'hai trovata l'America!"* Ha, you have found your America. This expression, in various dialectical versions, is current among Italian immigrants in America even today.

I was not immediately impressed by the skyscrapers, the automobiles, and the roaring trains of the metropolitan centers along the eastern seaboard. The only emotion they stirred within me was fear— fear of being lost, engulfed, annihilated. What *was* immediately impressive were the food stalls; the huge displays of pastries and confections, the mountains of fish, flesh, and fowl; the crowded cafés, where the aristocrat—or so he seemed—sat beside the drayman in overalls, gulping coffee drawn from huge urns and soberly eating ham and eggs; eating such fare without any visible display of joy, as if in obedience to some distasteful duty—as if it were yesterday's *polenta*! Ham and eggs! (Come to your senses, ye brave Americans, and spare your noble dish the corrupting catsup! Amend your constitution—you did it once against misguided gourmets—that you may enjoin forever such culinary adultery.) Ham and eggs with fried potatoes, stacks of buttered toast and coffee—that was my first acquaintance with American food. It remains to this day my favorite American dish. I would pay dearly for a gulp-to-gulp moving picture of myself, seated in a New York restaurant, a hungry immigrant urchin to the core, trying to counterfeit nonchalance as I wolfed my culinary cares away. And as I remembered the boot of earth across the water, where eggs had been too precious to be served with any regularity, and where coffee had been hoarded against the bellyache—its curative value somehow mysteriously related to its scarcity—I said to myself, *"L'America é buona."* America is good.

Several years later I heard those identical words spoken by an Italian grocer to whom I had gone for provisions. It was in one of those intimate shops, none too tidy, crowded with sacks of beans, peas, lentils, *ceci,* barrels of olives, huge wheels of cheese and stacks of *salami* and dry cod, where the opulent and inefficient operator is more ready to chat than to sell. He took me into his dingy office, rolled back the top of some late executive's desk, as if he were about to show me his ledger or perhaps a recent issue of *Practical Merchandising,* and revealed loaves of bread, slabs of cheese, and several *salami.* He then pulled out a drawer, which in any sensible establishment would have catapulted a typewriter into view, and several bottles of wine emerged from the darkness. He locked the door to the establishment, sliced the *salame,* uncorked a bottle, and opened a can of olives. As he sat down and reached for the cheese, he mumbled, in his own version of the English language, "America ees gude. Today, leet the *paesani* spend the mawney in the safetyway store."

I left New York for the West Coast during the harvest season. As the train raced westward, the prodigality of America unfolded in a series of beatific visions, marred, alas! by bewildering disappointments. Somewhere along the way, the train skirted an apple orchard. Apples were heaped upon the ground in veritable mountains—or so it appeared at the time to my eager fancy. Perhaps there had been an unusual storm; perhaps they had been shaken down to be carted away to the cider mill. Or were they actually abandoned to rot on the ground? I had no way of knowing. Whatever the reason, there they were, in unguarded profusion and apparently available to anyone. There were no farmers lurking with clubs and pruning hooks among the trees, as I had seen them in Italy, ready to ward off sugar-hungry lads who might be tempted by the ripe fruit. As we continued our journey, I added apples to my blessings.

There were, as I have said, disappointments. The food distributed to immigrants on the train and at railway stations was awful. It was sold in box lunches that contained sandwiches of *salame* and cheese. There were also oranges, bananas, and apples. The bread was suspiciously white, moist, tasteless, and it stuck to the teeth. The *salame* was completely phony. It was a dry, rancid, foul-smelling substance parading under an honorable name. The cheese, a sickly-yellow mess, was positively revolting. The oranges were sour, the apples large, mealy, and without flavor. The bananas were so totally unfamiliar, both in appearance and taste, that I approached them with misgivings. I learned to like them, but it took a little time. Ham and eggs I never saw again until I reached the West Coast. Somewhere along the way I found enough French bread to take care of my needs for the remainder of the journey. I had grave doubts about the quality of such American food as bread, *salame,* and cheese, but I reserved final judgment. There is no need to hold back any longer. The bread is worse now than it was then, since the great baking trusts have become more adept at perverting wheat flour. American salami is still a stinker in disguise. The yellow counterfeit for cheese is still extant, though one may now find cheeses of excellent quality manufactured according to European formulas. American fruit would be comparable to any other if it were left on the tree long enough to ripen. I suspect that it would have more flavor if the Burbanks had plied their trade with a little less zeal and if water were used more sparingly in the orchards.

When I arrived at what was to be my future home in Washington, I realized the full meaning of America in terms of food, clothing, and shelter. Everyone ate quantities of meat, pastries, and fruit. Everyone was well-dressed. Everyone bought wood for the cook-stove though he lived in the midst of a forest where wood was rotting on the ground. To a lad who had combed the countryside in Italy in search of sticks and corncobs for fuel, this latter fact was shocking and unintelligible. Even to this day the forests of the Pacific Coast have an immediate significance for me of which the natives are totally unaware. When I drive to the hills for an outing I cannot resist the ancient urge. So I never leave the woods without first filling the trunk with wood for the fireplace.

During the first few months in America I went to the forest every day and returned home laden with its precious fruit. There were nuts and berries in profusion. With my father I hunted grouse, pheasant, quail, and rabbit. Here and there were abandoned homesteads with pear, plum, and apple orchards. The reality was more fantastic than the dream. What the returned natives had reported about America proved to be entirely accurate. It seemed possible to live on the prodigal yield of the surrounding hills. Although we all worked hard in our eagerness to take advantage of new opportunities, we did not neglect what was to be had for no more effort than was required in gathering it. We never bought a bit of fuel. A variety of game from the forest provided much of our meat for the dinner table. The cellar was always well stocked with jams, jellies, nuts, and fruit gathered in the woods and abandoned orchards. And while we were gradually becoming naturalized and eagerly looking forward to citizenship, we were also naturalizing our cuisine. We were realizing its potentialities in a land where we were no longer frustrated by scarcity and lack of variety.

The sinful waste among the native population left me amazed and horrified. On the school grounds, and later in the mills and lumber camps, I discovered the American's disrespect for food. Old and young alike drew from their lunch buckets huge sandwiches of homemade bread filled with meats, jams, and precious butter. They took large bites from the centers and threw irreverently upon the ground "the fringe of crust." The slabs of apple and raisin pie, prepared with so much care by Grandmother—grandmothers always make the best pies—were seldom entirely eaten. Only a few ate the neatly folded flaky crust at the edge.

In view of what I later heard women say about making piecrust, this fact convinced me that the ways of the American, as of the Almighty, are inscrutable. Women either apologize for, or take inordinate pride in, their pies. The only reason which makes any sense at all, why Grandmother's pie is so universally acclaimed, is that pie-making is a process which requires a lifetime to perfect. Since anyone can slice apples, the secret must lie in making the crust. I have never heard women discussing new techniques for slicing apples, though I have heard them a thousand times inquiring of each other how to make a good crust. Tell me, then, why even Grandmother's crust, perfected af-

ter three score years of study, toil, and kitchen gossip, should be igno-
miniously thrown into the slop pail!

THE ACCOUNT OF MY DISCOVERY OF ABUNDANCE SUM-
marizes an experience in which millions of immigrants to America have
shared. The overwhelming majority of them, from northern and southern Europe, from the Balkans and the Near East, have found a new felicity here basically explainable in terms of bread. They have brought to
this prodigal land a profound respect for everything that the native
takes for granted. Their frugal habits, their willingness to work, their re-
sourcefulness in meeting adversity, explain why their names appear so
infrequently on relief roles. Their culinary aptitudes, evolved in scarcity
and a bleak environment as a means of turning nothing into something,
when applied even to the most modest ingredients available to them
here, yields a consistently distinguished cuisine. Man for man and dollar for dollar, the immigrants' daily fare is several degrees of excellence
higher than that of the natives. They have evolved what can be defined
only as a naturalized cuisine. In all the population of America, they are
the most satisfied, the most gay, and the least neurotic.

—from *The Unprejudiced Palate,* 1948

JOSEPH WECHSBERG ON COOKING FOR AMERICANS

SOMETIMES I WOULD GO DOWNSTAIRS TO VISIT THE GREAT
chef in his large, stainless-steel kitchen empire where he ruled over a
hundred *toques blanches:* assistant chefs, *rôtisseurs, poissoniers, entremet-
teurs, potagiers, sauciers, hors-d'œuvriers, grilladiers, buffet-froid* men,
pastry cooks, butchers, helpers, dishwashers. He was always near the
sauce department, sticking his forefinger into sauces and tasting.
When he tasted a sauce, his blue eyes took on the cold fire of a sap-
phire, and his forehead was wrinkled in concentration. Many a time
when I came down he would be on the verge of breaking into tears.

"All day long those passengers come here asking me how I make this and what I put into that!" he would say. *"Allez, allez!* Cooking at sea isn't like cooking in a big hotel. On the Atlantic you can't send out to the market because you've forgotten something. My clients are French *and* Americans. The French love liver, tripe, *cervelle au beurre noir,* kidneys, and sweetbread. Americans may eat calf's liver, but they wouldn't touch the other things. They want grillades—steak, sirloin, *châteaubriant,* lamb chops. Their doctors have told them that grilled red meat is healthy for them. *Allez, allez!* There is more to cooking than steaks. Here we are trying our best and they complain!"

The chef looked grim. The *saucier* quickly stepped in front of his pots. It was whispered that under the angry stare of the great chef a *sauce béarnaise* would sometimes curdle.

"Yesterday," he said, "a passenger ordered braised pork loin with tomatoes, spread with tuna fish, served with macaroni." He paused a little to let the horror sink in. "He was from Ohio."

—from *Blue Trout and Black Truffles,* 1948

ALICE B. TOKLAS ON GERTRUDE STEIN'S RETURN TO AMERICA

WHEN DURING THE SUMMER OF 1934 GERTRUDE STEIN could not decide whether she did or did not want to go to the United States, one of the things that troubled her was the question of the food she would be eating there. Would it be to her taste? A young man from the Bugey had lately returned from a brief visit to the United States and had reported that the food was more foreign to him than the people, their homes or the way they lived in them. He said the food was good but very strange indeed—tinned vegetable cocktails and tinned fruit salads, for example. Surely, said I, you weren't required to eat them. You could have substituted other dishes. Not, said he, when you were a guest.

At this time there was staying with us at Bilignin an American friend who said he would send us a menu from the restaurant of the hotel we would be staying at when Gertrude Stein lectured in his home town, which he did promptly on his return there. The variety of dishes was a pleasant surprise even if the tinned vegetable cocktails and fruit salads occupied a preponderant position. Consolingly, there were honey-dew melons, soft-shell crabs and prime roasts of beef. We would undertake the great adventure.

Crossing on the *Champlain* we had the best French food. It made me think of a college song popular in my youth, Home Will Never Be Like This. If the food that awaited us at the Algonquin Hotel did not resemble the food on the French Line it was very good in its way, unrivalled T-steaks and soft-shell crabs and ineffable ice creams.

Mr. Alfred Harcourt, Gertrude Stein's editor, had asked us to spend Thanksgiving weekend with Mrs. Harcourt and himself in their Connecticut home, and there we ate for the first time, with suppressed excitement and curiosity, wild rice. It has never become a commonplace to me. Carl Van Vechten sends it to me. To the delight of my French friends I serve

Wild Rice Salad

steam ½ lb. wild rice

½ lb. coarsely chopped mushrooms cooked for 10 minutes in 3 tablespoons oil and 2 tablespoons lemon juice, 2 hard-boiled eggs coarsely chopped, 1 green pepper finely chopped, 1½ cups shelled shrimps, all lightly mixed and served with aïoli or aïlloli sauce.

Press into a mortar 4 cloves of garlic, add a pinch of salt, of white pepper and the yolk of an egg. With the pestle reduce these ingredients to an emulsion. Add the yolk of an egg. You may continue to make the sauce with the pestle or discard it for a wooden fork or a wooden spoon or a wire whisk. Real Provençal *Aïoli* makers use the pestle to the end. With whatever instrument you will have chosen you will commence to incorporate drop by drop an excellent olive oil. When the egg has absorbed about 3 tablespoons of the oil, add ½ tablespoon lemon juice. Continuing to stir, now add oil more briskly. When it soon becomes firm again add 1 dessertspoon tepid water (I repeat, tepid water). Continue to add oil, lemon juice and tepid water. The yolk of 1 egg will absorb 1 cup and 2 tablespoons oil, 1½ tablespoons lemon juice and 2 dessertspoons tepid water.

—from *The Alice B. Toklas Cook Book,* 1954

CHAPTER TWENTY-EIGHT

The Germans

TACITUS ON GERMANS

Cornelius Tacitus was born in A.D. *56 or 57 and held numerous high offices in the Roman government. While pursuing a political career he also produced many important works as a historian, the first of which was his portrait of his father-in-law, Tacitus, the most famous Roman governor of Briton, and* The Germania, *a portrait of the warlike German people.* —M.K.

THEIR DRINK IS A LIQUOR MADE FROM BARLEY OR OTHER grain, which is fermented to produce a certain resemblance to wine. Those who dwell nearest the Rhine or the Danube also buy wine. Their food is plain—wild fruit, fresh game, and curdled milk. They satisfy their hunger without any elaborate cuisine or appetizers. But they do not show the same self-control in slaking their thirst. If you indulge their intemperance by plying them with as much drink as they desire, they will be as easily conquered by this besetting weakness as by force of arms.

—from *The Germania*, A.D. 98,
translated from the Latin by H. Mattingly

JOSEPH WECHSBERG
ON AUSTRIANS

IT WAS CUSTOMARY TO HAVE FIVE MEALS A DAY. BREAKFAST was at half past seven in the morning. At ten o'clock, children had their *déjeuner à la fourchette,* sandwiches, sausages, hard-boiled eggs, fruit. Many men would go for half an hour to a beerhouse for a goulash or a dish of calf's lungs, and a glass of beer. Between ten and ten thirty little work was done in offices and shops; everybody was out eating. Two hours later, people were having lunch—at home, since eating lunch in a restaurant was unknown—and afterward they had a nap. Then to the coffeehouse for a demitasse and a game of whist or bridge, and back to the salt mines for an hour's work.

It was a strenuous life and around four thirty in the afternoon most people were hungry again and had to have their *Jause.* A genuine, central-European *Jause* consists of several large cups of coffee, topped off with whipped cream, of bread and butter, *Torte* or *Guglhupf* (the bizarre Viennese variation of a pound cake shaped like a derby on which several people have been sitting), and assorted patisserie. It is a feminine institution; my mother didn't mind skipping lunch and dinner but she had to have her *Jause.* She would often complain that she gained weight "practically from nothing," but it couldn't be the *Jause,* she said; you didn't gain weight from the *Jause.*

What with appetizers and hors-d'œuvres and a sumptuous dinner, many people had to go to Karlsbad once a year to take the cure, lose fifteen pounds, and get in shape again for another year of arduous eating.

—from *Blue Trout and Black Truffles,* 1948

KARL FRIEDRICH VON RUMOHR ON TEACHING GERMANS TO COOK

THE ART OF COOKERY ITSELF PRESENTS NO PROBLEMS WHEN people are learning to cook. This is amply demonstrated by my book. The basic rule could not be easier to grasp: make the very best of every edible substance. No other sphere of man's knowledge and activity contains so many connections and logical progressions. Even if he is not very experienced, a cook can easily progress from one step to the next. The difficulty does not therefore lie with the art itself, but in our ability, or rather inability to learn it properly.

Many boys and girls who set out to learn the art of cookery are not truly dedicated to it. Their thoughts are on the respectable financial reward when they should at first be concentrating on the skill they are learning. Once mastered, the skill will soon bring its rewards, as a tree bears fruit. No-one is likely to do well in a subject if he did not have a basic feel for it in the first place.

Infected with an excessively servile veneration of his master, a young cook will often lose himself in the maze of unnecessary complications left over from outdated styles of cookery. He will not be receptive to new views and will be unable to learn from his own experience and thoughts. I have actually seen young cooks spending entire days practising the art of sprinkling salt over dishes but I very much doubt whether the food would have tasted any better.

Then we come to the real spanners in the works: the pushy upstarts and young know-it-alls. There is nothing to be done about these. At the age when I was still cheerfully washing dishes and basins, picking over spinach and undertaking other elementary duties, no kitchen boy today can be seen for dust. He wants to be at the front line, bungling the skilled jobs and pushing ahead of his master before he has even a basic grounding in hygiene and orderliness, before he has learnt the basic principles by watching and listening. This situation should not be tolerated any longer. Nature has turned on her head and history gone into reverse.

Female cooks are totally lacking in basic training. Their minds are so full of cleaning, fashions and other idle notions that there is no room for a proper understanding of principles. Their hearts are rarely in their cooking. This makes them all the more obstinate—they will not be diverted from their familiar path. I have tried in vain to improve the ways of hundreds of German cooking women. Whenever I have poked my nose into a German kitchen run by women, the early morning scene has resembled a washhouse, despite my attempts to enlighten them by my words and deeds. Here would be a basin of pot herbs, swimming in water, there would be the day's salad, similarly inundated; here the soup meat would be steeping in cold, or even lukewarm, water, there the roasting meat and fish in the same state. I am amazed at the power of German pedantry, its lack of sexual bias, even if it does stem from our old tradition of integrity. Cooking women seem to believe themselves entitled to dispense with all such traditions, however. Unfortunately the order of the day is cheating over the shopping because housewives have grown too lazy, too ignorant and too falsely refined to keep proper storecupboards. This means that every day of the year brings its necessary expenditure, and the women will always think of themselves when spending money, resulting in chaotic penny-pinching in bourgeois households. The high drama and domestic battles are causing unprecedented restlessness among the kitchenmaids in our German towns.

I should like to contrast these tales of abrupt proceedings and garish scenes with a pleasant picture of peaceful, resigned domesticity. Excellent serving women and good housewives do exist and I hope that some of them will read these pages. The numbers of these fine serving women would be greatly increased if only they were properly paid for their work and were treated with more justice and less caprice. There are still only a few people who follow the advice of the aforementioned Rumpolt, who begins:

'The master should be in command of his servants but should be able to handle them in a friendly and amicable way. His words of command should not be proud, inflated, overbearing, immodest, violent. He should not rant and rave but should behave with great gentleness, sweetness, friendliness and modesty so that his running of the household takes the form of amicable requests and demands rather than a series of harsh orders. A lot of violent ranting and raving will confuse people, making them more stubborn and unwilling, and little will be achieved.'

Anyone who wishes to devote himself to cookery should grasp the concepts of orderliness, hygiene and punctuality early in life. He should not be allowed to read novels; if he wishes to develop his intellect he should study the natural sciences, history and mathematics; these will exercise his intelligence, improve his memory and give him knowledge which he can later apply to cookery. He should also read my book and no other.

—from *The Essence of Cooking,* 1822,
translated from the German by Barbara Yeomans

CHAPTER TWENTY-NINE

The Politics of Food

HONORÉ DE BALZAC ON EATING

Honoré de Balzac, chronicler and critic of bourgeois values in almost one hundred novels, contributed articles to Grimod de la Reynière's Almanach. *In 1828 he published his food essays as* Le Gastronome français. —M.K.

THE PREJUDICED HAVE SUCH INFLUENCE OVER THE FEEBLE-minded, they have established such errors to the ruin of truth, that it is perhaps not useless to seriously examine if the viewpoint of temperate people toward food is founded on anything other than a bad stomach.

Just as the first advocates of abstinence were undoubtedly maladjusted, the first enthusiasts of moderation were surely people lacking in appetite.

Aristippe observed that philosophers who distrust wealth are penniless. Diogenes was broke when he was a cynic. . . . That is the way it is with detractors of appetite, of the tendency that is inherent in well-born men of happy constitution. It is not the first time that charlatans, misguided and well spoken, have come to consider a virtue, that which is a well-organized vice.

However, there is an obligation to challenge those of the empty stomach, be they young or aged. No one questions the advantage of someone well satisfied over the most spiritual sickly person. An empty stomach makes an empty mind. Our reason, completely independent from our beliefs, respects the laws of digestion; and it could be said, perhaps as accurately as La Rochefoucauld said it, that good thoughts come from the stomach.

This leaves unresolved the question of whether the spirit is stronger before or after a meal. Many a writer had inspiration only when eating. There are some people who cannot take on serious questions until they have had something to drink. Ministers have often been seen coming alive only in the evening, because their head, restored, while sleeping, from the fumes of a generous wine, was clearer and conceived more lucid ideas. This was the technique of the honorable M. Pitt.

But the real triumph of the gourmet is in the field of morality. Candor is virtually synonymous with the title bon vivant. Ever since the banquet of the seven wise men and the knights of the round table, dinner is the meeting place of the most crisp minds, the most heroic hearts, and the most independent spirits.

The dinner table is a place of gathering, of delight, of brotherhood; it brings together the pleasure of peace, the ardor of courage, and warrior virtues. The most fearless soldier loses his worth when he is hungry; warriors are fed before battle; and whoever trembled with fear before eating will fear nothing afterward.

—from *Le Gastronome français*, 1828,
translated from the French by Mark Kurlansky

CURNONSKY ON POLITICAL CATEGORIES FOR GOURMETS

Curnonsky was born Maurice-Edmond Sailland in Anges, France, in 1872. He was one of the most influential food critics of the early twentieth century, although A. J. Liebling once wrote of him, "So many mediocre witticisms are attributed to him that he could not have had much time for eating." Nevertheless, for several decades, Curnonsky, the author of numerous books and articles, was to many people the man to quote for the last word on anything gastronomic. —M.K.

TO THE UNINITIATED, A GOURMET IS AN OBESE SEXAGEnarian, with gout, hobbling along, living only to eat and always overeating—and doing little work between meals.

That is not exactly right, and once again, you must distrust hasty generalizations. There are gourmets of all ages. They are even of both sexes, and I know some "gourmettes" who could put the men to shame.

Among all gourmets, there is really only one trait in common: a good sense of humor. Their guileless passion requires a good stomach and perfect organic equilibrium—and each understands the influence of health on character. No doubt the greatest orators have proclaimed, "A great soul is always master of the body it keeps." But between eloquence and reality there is space for a few qualifications. If you are suffering from kidney problems, or even a simple toothache, your concept of the universe can alter to such an extent that you find yourself questioning the four truths of the Creator.

But that is not to say that gourmets all have the same point of view, especially about cuisine. For as long as I have been around them—and that did not begin yesterday, having grown up with a father and two grandfathers who loved the good life—I have been convinced that they can be classified into the same groups as politicians.

Anyone who spends five minutes thinking about it will see that in gastronomy, too, there is an extreme right, a right, a center, a left, and an extreme left.

Extreme right—These are the passionate followers of "*grande cuisine*," an educated cuisine, well researched, a bit complicated, that demands a great chef and the best products, what one could call diplomatic cuisine, that of embassies, of grand banquets, of palaces— a cuisine that the real palaces usually can only parody.

Right—The advocates of "traditional cooking," which only accepts wood-burning fires and dishes that simmer very slowly, predicated on the belief that the only good food is home cooking, with no more than six or eight people, prepared by an elderly women who has been in the employ of the family for thirty years, with a wine cellar stocked with bottles from "before the phylloxera" [in the mid–nineteenth century, European vineyards were decimated by an American aphid and wine producers were forced to replace their root stock with American plants that were resistant to the American insect] and alcohols selected by a great grandfather, with a vegetable garden and hen house on the premises.

Center—The lovers of bourgeois cuisine and regional cuisine: Those who concede that you still can eat well at restaurants and that all over France good inns and fine hotels remain where prepared sauce bases are never used and where butter is butter. The centros keep a taste for the traditional French dishes, and our regional wines. They insist that things "have the taste of what they are" and are never altered or overdone.

Left—Partisans of cooking without affectations or complications and, since they are fond of snacking, a cuisine that can be made in a minimum of time with modest means. These people are pleased with a well-made omelette, a medium steak, a rabbit fricassee, or, indeed, a slice of ham or a cold cut. They do not reject canned food and insist on the charm of a good canned sardine in oil and that a certain brand of canned green beans is at least as good as fresh ones.

They unearth the little hole-in-the-wall where the owner does the cooking. They love to discover, for example, a simple restaurant run by a man from the provinces who gets products shipped from his native region. He praises country cooking and enjoys little local wines. They are the nomads of gastronomy and it is for them that I invented the word "*gastronomade*" [Curnonsky's word for practitioners of gastronomic tourism].

Extreme left—The dreamers, the restless, the innovators who Napoleon had called ideologues; always in search of new sensations and unproven pleasures. Curious about all foreign food, and all the foreign and colonial specialties, they wish they could taste every dish from every climate and country.

But what is most characteristic of them is a fondness for newly invented dishes. Among this group are some very worthwhile people but also some who are a little unsettling, free spirits—but with the difference that here the anarchists have a horror of *bombes*, a dessert that for them is too classic, an old-fashioned dish. In other words, these are the people on the side of saints and martyrs. Thirty years ago, a gourmet of this type declared that peas were a far too banal shade of green and he decided to produce peas that were grass green. He first treated them in hydrogen peroxide, followed by a strong shot of green malachite with a few flakes of iron. Then, satisfied with the result, and made hungry by hours of work, he ate about a pound of these house specialty green peas. . . . When I went to see him, eight days later in the hospital, his condition slightly improved, he began to understand that he should have eaten some grass—by the roots.

Do not take this example as the general stereotype. Good cooking, as in other fields, only survives by adapting to changes. I would be mistaken to reject all new dishes and innovations, since for the last thirty years, famous chefs have honored me by naming a dozen new dishes after me.

—from *Almanach des gourmands*, c. 1950,
translated from the French by Mark Kurlansky

ÉMILE ZOLA ON FAT AND THIN PEOPLE AT LES HALLES

Émile Zola's novel The Belly of Paris *was written in 1873 when he was thirty-three years old, an early work that preceded his more famous novels. The book opens on a road into central Paris. Wagons filled with food are making their way into Les Halles, Paris's newly built central market. While driving her wagon, Madame François, a vegetable vendor, sees "a black lump, lying blocking the road, nearly under a horse's hoof." She slows down and a man sorting turnips yells at her. But realizing that the lump is a man, she gets out of her cart to help him off the road. The man, Florent, nearly run over by the caravan of food entering the city, has returned from the infamous penal colony of French Guiana, so weak from starvation that he cannot stand. Despite annoying coworkers, Madame François manages to get him out of the way so that the food can pass without running him over.*

This entire novel is a food allegory. Set amid the vendors of Les Halles, against a backdrop of endless food, it is a story about the fat and the skinny, the rebels and the complacent, about who eats

*and who goes hungry. A character called La Belle Lisa is described,
"She was so beautiful, so large, so round, that she made him feel
good. Before her, he felt contented, as though he had eaten or drunk
something wonderful."*

*But plump Lisa was small-minded, as were the many fat char-
acters of the market. Her high-minded brother-in-law, Florent, was
distrusted because he was skinny. People question why he was so
skinny. One day, walking back after a refreshing day in the country, away from Paris and its "sickening smell of food," Florent's
friend Claude explained the following.*   *—M.K.*

AS THOUGH SUDDENLY WAKING FROM A DREAM, HE ASKED,
"Do you know 'the Battle of the Fat and the Thin'?"

Florent, caught by surprise, answered no. Claude excitedly praised
this series of prints, pointing out favorite parts: The Fat, bursting from
their enormity, preparing the evening glut, while the Thin, doubled
over from hunger, looked in from the street, stick figures filled with
envy, and then the Fat, seated at the table, cheeks overflowing, drive
away a Thin who had the audacity to humbly approach, looking like a
bowling pin among the bowling balls.

Claude saw in these drawings the entire drama of mankind. He
could classify all people into the Thin and the Fat, two opposing
groups, one devouring the other to grow plump and jolly. "You can
bet," he said, "that Cain was a Fat and Abel a Thin. And since that
first killing, there have always been hungry Fats sucking the blood out
of scanty eaters. It is a constant preying of the stronger on the weaker,
each swallowing his neighbor and then finding himself swallowed in
turn. . . . So you see, my friend, watch out for the Fat."

He fell silent for a moment, following their two shadows as the
setting sun stretched them ever longer. Then he murmured, "You and
I, we belong to the Thin, you see. Tell me if people with flat stomachs
like ours take up much sunlight."

Florent looked at the two shadows and smiled. But Claude became angry. "If you think this is funny, you're wrong. I suffer a lot because I am a Thin. If I were a Fat, I could paint when I felt like it, I
would have a beautiful studio, I could sell my paintings for their
weight in gold. Instead, I am a Thin. I pour my soul out to produce
things that only make the Fats shrug their shoulders. I am sure that I
will end up dying of it, my skin sticking to my bones and so flat that

they could bury me between the covers of a book. And you! You are a Thin, a perfect example, The King of Thins. Remember your argument with the fish sellers. It was spectacular, all those giant bosoms flying at your spindly chest. They were acting out of instinct, hunting the Thin the way a cat chases a mouse. You see, Fats have such a distaste for Thins, they have to drive them out of their sight, either by biting or kicking. That's why, if I were you, I'd be careful. The Quenus are Fats, and the Méhudins, too. The fact is you are completely surrounded by Fats. That would worry me."

"And what about Gavard, and Miss Saget, and your friend Marjolin?" Florent asked, still smiling.

"If you want, we can classify everyone we know for you," answered Claude. "I've been keeping a file on them in my studio for a long time with notations on which group to which each belongs. It's a whole chapter of natural history. Gavard is the kind of Fat who pretends to be a Thin. Not at all a rare species. Miss Saget and Mrs. Lecoeurare are a variety of Thin who should be feared—desperate Thins, capable of anything to fatten themselves. My friend Marjolin, Little Cadine, and La Sarriette are three Fats, still innocent with nothing more than the lovable hunger of youth. I've noticed that the Fat, when they are not old, can be charming creatures. Mr. Lebigre, he's a Fat, isn't he. Then there're your political friends, who are mostly Thins, Charvet, Clémence, Logre, Lecailles. But I make an exception for that fat slob, Alexandre, and for the enormous Robine, who has caused me a lot of trouble."

The painter continued in this vein from the Pont de Neuilly to the Arc de Triomphe. He returned to some of the people to complete their portraits with a few shared defining brush strokes. Logre was a Thin who carried his belly between his shoulders. Beautiful Lisa was all stomach, and the beautiful Norman, all bosom. Miss Saget had surely missed an opportunity sometime in her life to become fat, for she loathed the Fats while still disdaining the Thins. As for Gavard, he was compromising his role as a Fat, and would end up as flat as a bug.

"And Mrs. François?" asked Florent.

Claude was embarrassed. He struggled for an answer and finally stuttered, "Mrs. François. Mrs. François. I don't know. I never had the urge to classify her. She's a fine woman, that's all. She's not a Fat and she's not a Thin."

They both laughed. They were now in front of the Arc de Triomphe. The sun, on the crest of the hills of Suresnes, was so low on the horizon that their shadows darkened the whiteness of the monument very high up, even higher than the group of statues, like two black marks sketched in charcoal. This made Claude even more amused and he waved his arms and bent his body. And then, as he started to walk again he said, "Did you notice, just as the sun set, our two heads flew up to the sky."

But Florent stopped laughing. Paris started to overtake him again—Paris that cost him so many tears in Guiana and still frightened him. He lowered his head as he returned to that nightmare of mountains of food, but carrying with him the sweet and sad memories of this day in fresh air, scented with thyme.

—from *The Belly of Paris*, 1873,
translated from the French by Mark Kurlansky

Lu Wenfu on
Revolutionary Cuisine

Lu Wenfu was born in a small village on the north bank of the Yangtze in 1928. In 1944 he first ventured to Suzhou, a southern city famous for its cuisine and the setting for his novella The Gourmet. *It tells the story of a fat gourmet and a lean revolutionary. The revolutionary has been made manager of the most celebrated restaurant in Suzhou and is disheartened to discover that after he reorganizes it along revolutionary principles, even good revolutionaries don't want to eat there.*   —M.K.

GOURMETS! WHEN YOU WERE POOR YOU WOULD HAVE HAD these classy restaurants torn down, but as soon as you get a little money you all pile in, worried you won't get a seat, and you want high-class meals too.

The spring of 1957 was a troubled time. The restaurant employees began to write big-character posters saying what they thought of me and hung them in the corridor. Their objections to the food and the drop in business didn't upset me, but one, signed "our employee," and accusing me of seeking personal glory at the expense of the restaurant and its employees, made me furious. The adjectives used in the poster and its tone meant it could only have been written by that scoundrel Bao! Of course I had to accept all the criticisms even if they had only the minutest grain of truth in them.

Just while I was so troubled and bewildered by all that was happening, my old schoolmate Bighead Ding, on his way to a conference in Beijing, stopped off in Suzhou to see me. It was eight years since we'd met and I was overjoyed. "You must come out to dinner, we can go to our restaurant," I said, a little surprised at myself wanting to take people out to dinner as soon as I saw them. It wasn't like me.

He shook his head. "Thanks, but I've been there and I've read the posters. Tell me what you have been doing all these years."

"What have I been doing? Well, just hold on a bit and I'll tell you all about it." I called my wife in and introduced Ding to her.

Ding bowed. "I'm Ding Zhen, Bighead was my nickname. . . . But don't tell anybody else. I'm a manager just like you."

My wife smiled, scrutinizing his head as if trying to determine whether or not it was really bigger than average.

"Don't stand there gaping! Why don't you go and buy some food?" Ding had already been to my restaurant and I didn't want to become a laughing stock by taking him to another one. I'd better ask my wife to make something at home.

During the two years we'd been married my wife hadn't cooked very much. All she could do was give him tea and cigarettes and say, "You two chat for a while. Mother has gone to a neighbourhood committee meeting. She'll get you something when she comes home."

The neighbourhood meetings were always marathons. The food market would be closed by the time she finished. "Why don't you cook something today? You can't depend on Mother all the time."

"Have you forgotten?" she retorted. "You always say young people mustn't spend time on cooking if they want to get ahead. This ambitious young woman doesn't know where the oil is."

Ding burst out laughing. "I'll bet that's exactly what he said, so let him take the consequences."

"All right, then go and tell Mother we have a guest and ask her to come back."

After she went out I began to unburden myself, starting right at the beginning. "You've read those posters. One of them was a personal attack by a young man. The rest were about my work. Where have I gone wrong in these reforms? You know what it was like in the old days. I have been working to eliminate that kind of wrong. Now those posters are attacking me for doing just that. But I haven't done anything bad."

Ding fell silent, inhaling deeply on his cigarette. He was probably very troubled too.

"Well say something! You're well read, you've been working in a bookstore all these years. Pick up a book and give me a thump on the head. You'd better choose a hardcover one and give me a really good whack."

Ding laughed. "That's no good, it'll spill your brains out. I would, however, like to draw your attention to a strange physiological phenomenon. It seems that the palate of the bourgeoisie is similar to that of the proletariat. The capitalists prefer shrimp to shredded meat and cabbage, and once they've tasted them, so do the proletariat. So when they've got the money they order shrimp, but you keep pushing shredded meat and cabbage at them. I'm surprised they haven't come after you with a hammer!"

I blew up. "You can't live on shrimp."

"Of course you can't; who can afford to do that?" he retorted.

"But we get so many people, you mustn't underestimate bad tendencies, comrade."

"It's you who've underestimated them. They've got money now. If one out of a hundred wants shrimp, that's enough to fill your restaurant to bursting. You keep rattling on about liberating the working people, but then you think they're not up to your expectations. People want to eat shrimp now and again and are quite happy to let you make a little profit, but this grates on you."

"It certainly does not! I don't have anything against them."

"I know you don't like that Zhu character, but what can you do about him when he shuts himself away?"

"He doesn't hide himself away entirely."

"Of course, a lot of people other than the working masses will be eating shrimp. I'll tell you: even when the landlords and capitalists have been eliminated, you'll still have hooligans and thieves among your customers, even escaped murderers."

I believed him. You needed an official letter and an ID card to get a room in a hotel, but only money to go to a restaurant. "You're right," I sighed. "But I still think frugality is one of our national virtues. Why should we place so much emphasis on food?"

"I know, and from your personal point of view it's a fine thing. I hope you'll keep on being frugal. But you're a restaurant manager and you can't bring all your personal feelings into your work. Suzhou cuisine is famous; it's something created by labouring people over a long period of time. If you destroy it history will hold you responsible."

I went cold. My schooling had taught me the importance of history. I would get nowhere if I resisted historical trends. Anyway I doubted that this cuisine was something created by labourers; it was obviously invented by people like Zhu and Kong.

On top of that, my mother shouldn't have given us such a lavish supper, five dishes and a delicious soup.

Ding was all smiles. "Look, this trend is sneaking into your home! You'd better watch out!"

—from *The Gourmet,* 1982,
translated from the Chinese by Readers International

CHAPTER THIRTY

What Does It Mean?

CLAUDE LÉVI-STRAUSS ON
THE IDEA OF ROTTEN

WHAT EACH SOCIETY UNDERSTANDS BY "RAW," "COOKED" and "rotten" can only be determined through ethnographical observation, and there is no reason why they should all be in agreement about the definitions. The recent increase in the number of Italian restaurants in France has given French people a taste for raw food in a much "rawer" state than was traditional with us: the vegetables are simply washed and cut up, without being prepared with an oil and vinegar dressing, according to the usual French custom—except for radishes, which, however, are significantly felt to require a generous accompaniment of butter and salt. Through Italian influence we have, then, extended our category of the raw. Certain incidents which occurred after the Allied landings in 1944 show that American soldiers had a broader conception of the category of the rotten than the French; under the impression that the Normandy cheese dairies stank of corpses, they sometimes destroyed the buildings.

—from *The Origin of Table Manners,* 1968,
translated from the French by John and Doreen Weightman

MARGARET MEAD ON
THE MEANING OF FOOD

WE LIVE IN A WORLD TODAY WHERE THE STATE OF NUTRI-
tion in each country is relevant and important to each other country,
and where the state of nutrition in the wealthy industrialized countries
like the United States has profound significance for the role that such
countries can play in eliminating famine and providing for adequate
nutrition throughout the world. In a world in which each half knows
what the other half does, we cannot live with hunger and malnutrition
in one part of the world while people in another part are not only well
nourished, but over-nourished. Any talk of one world, of brotherhood,
rings hollow to those who have come face to face on the television
screen with the emaciation of starving children and to the people
whose children are starving as they pore over month-old issues of
glossy American and European magazines, where full color prints
show people glowing with health, their plates piled high with food that
glistens to match the shining textures of their clothes. Peoples who
have resolutely tightened their belts and put up with going to bed hungry, peoples who have seen their children die because they did not
have the strength to resist disease, and called it fate or the will of God,
can no longer do so, in the vivid visual realization of the amount and
quality of food eaten—and wasted—by others.

Through human history there have been many stringent taboos on
watching other people eat, or on eating in the presence of others.
There have been attempts to explain this as a relationship between
those who are involved and those who are not simultaneously involved
in the satisfaction of a bodily need, and the inappropriateness of the
already satiated watching others who appear—to the satisfied—to be
shamelessly gorging. There is undoubtedly such an element in the
taboos, but it seems more likely that they go back to the days when
food was so scarce and the onlookers so hungry that not to offer them
half of the little food one had was unthinkable, and every glance was
a plea for at least a bite.

In the rural schools of America when my grandmother was a child,
the better-off children took apples to school and, before they began to
eat them, promised the poor children who had no apples that they
might have the cores. The spectacle of the poor in rags at the rich
man's gate and of hungry children pressing their noses against the

glass window of the rich man's restaurant have long been invoked to arouse human compassion. But until the advent of the mass media and travel, the sensitive and sympathetic could protect themselves by shutting themselves away from the sight of the starving, by gifts of food to the poor on religious holidays, or perpetual bequests for the distribution of a piece of meat "the size of a child's head" annually. The starving in India and China saw only a few feasting foreigners and could not know how well or ill the poor were in countries from which they came. The proud poor hid their hunger behind a facade that often included insistent hospitality to the occasional visitor; the beggars flaunted their hunger and so, to a degree, discredited the hunger of their respectable compatriots.

But today the articulate cries of the hungry fill the air channels and there is no escape from the knowledge of the hundreds of millions who are seriously malnourished, of the periodic famines that beset whole populations, or of the looming danger of famine in many other parts of the world. The age-old divisions between one part of the world and another, between one class and another, between the rich and the poor everywhere, have been broken down, and the tolerances and insensitivities of the past are no longer possible.

But it is not only the media of communication which can take a man sitting at an overloaded breakfast table straight into a household where some of the children are too weak to stand. Something else, something even more significant, has happened. Today, for the first time in the history of mankind, we have the productive capacity to feed everyone in the world, and the technical knowledge to see that their stomachs are not only filled but that their bodies are properly nourished with the essential ingredients for growth and health. The progress of agriculture—in all its complexities of improved seed, methods of cultivation, fertilizers and pesticides, methods of storage, preservation, and transportation—now make it possible for the food that is needed for the whole world to be produced by fewer and fewer farmers, with greater and greater certainty. Drought and flood still threaten, but we have the means to prepare for and deal with even mammoth shortages—if we will. The progress of nutritional science has matched the progress of agriculture; we have finer and finer-grained knowledge of just which substances—vitamins, minerals, proteins—are essential, especially to growth and full development, and increasing ability to synthesize many of them on a massive scale.

These new twentieth-century potentialities have altered the ethical position of the rich all over the world. In the past, there were so few who lived well, and so many who lived on the edge of starvation, that the well-to-do had a rationale and indeed almost a necessity to harden their hearts and turn their eyes away. The jewels of the richest rajah could not have purchased enough food to feed his hungry subjects for more than a few days; the food did not exist, and the knowledge of how to use it was missing also. At the same time, however real the inability of a war-torn and submarine-ringed Britain to respond to the famine in Bengal, this inability was made bearable in Britain only by the extent to which the British were learning how to share what food they had among all the citizens, old and young. "You do not know," the American consul, who had come to Manchester from Spain, said to me: "you do not know what it means to live in a country where no child has to cry itself to sleep with hunger." But this was only achieved in Britain in the early 1940s. Before the well-fed turned away their eyes, in the feeling that they were powerless to alleviate the perennial poverty and hunger of most of their own people and the peoples in their far-flung commonwealth. And such turning away the eyes, in Britain and in the United States and elsewhere, was accompanied by the rationalizations, not only of the inability of the well-to-do—had they given all their wealth—to feed the poor, but of the undeservingness of the poor, who had they only been industrious and saving would have had enough, although of course of a lower quality, to keep "body and soul together."

When differences in race and in cultural levels complicated the situation, it was only too easy to insist that lesser breeds somehow, in some divinely correct scheme, would necessarily be less well fed, their alleged idleness and lack of frugality combining with such matters as sacred cows roaming over the landscapes—in India—or nights spent in the pub or the saloon—at home in Britain or America—while fathers drank up their meager pay checks and their children starved. So righteous was the assumed association between industriousness and food that, during the Irish famine, soup kitchens were set up out of town so that the starving could have the moral advantage of a long walk to receive the ration that stood between them and death. (The modern version of such ethical acrobatics can be found in the United States, in the mid-1960s, where food stamps were so expensive, since they had to be bought in large amounts, that only those who have been extraordinary frugal, saving, and lucky could afford to buy them and obtain the benefits they were designed to give.)

The particular ways in which the well-to-do of different great civilizations have rationalized the contrast between rich and poor have differed dramatically, but ever since the agricultural revolution, we have been running a race between our capacity to produce enough food to make it possible to assemble great urban centers, outfit huge armies and armadas, and build and elaborate the institutions of civilization and our ability to feed and care for the burgeoning population which has always kept a little, often a great deal, ahead of the food supply.

In this, those societies which practiced agriculture contrasted with the earlier simpler societies in which the entire population was engaged in subsistence activities. Primitive peoples may be well or poorly fed, feasting seldom, or blessed with ample supplies of fish or fruit, but the relations between the haves and the have-nots were in many ways simpler. Methods by which men could obtain permanent supplies of food and withhold them from their fellows hardly existed. The sour, barely edible breadfruit mash which was stored in breadfruit pits against the ravages of hurricanes and famines in Polynesia was not a diet for the table of chiefs but a stern measure against the needs of entire communities. The chief might have a right to the first fruits, or to half the crop, but after he had claimed it, it was redistributed to his people. The germs of the kinds of inequities that later entered the world were present: there was occasional conspicuous destruction of food, piled up for prestige, oil poured on the flames of self-glorifying feasts, food left to rot after it was offered to the gods. People with very meager food resources might use phrases that made it seem that each man was the recipient of great generosity on the part of his fellow, or on the other hand always to be giving away a whole animal, and always receiving only small bits.

The fear of cannibalism that hovered over northern peoples might be elaborated into cults of fear, or simply add to the concern that each member of a group had for all, against the terrible background that extremity might become so great that one of the group might in the end be sacrificed. But cannibalism could also be elaborated into a rite of vengeance or the celebration of victories in war, or even be used to provision an army in the field. Man's capacity to elaborate man's inhumanity to man existed before the beginning of civilization, which was made possible by the application of an increasingly productive technology to the production of food.

With the rise of civilizations, we also witness the growth of the great religions that made the brotherhood of all men part of their doctrine and the gift of alms or the life of voluntary poverty accepted religious practices. But the alms were never enough, and the life of individual poverty and abstinence was more efficacious for the individual's salvation than for the well-being of the poor and hungry, although both kept alive an ethic, as yet impossible of fulfillment, that it was right that all should be fed. The vision preceded the capability.

But today we have the capability. Whether that capability will be used or not becomes not a technical but an ethical question. It depends, in enormous measure, on the way in which the rich, industrialized countries handle the problems of distribution, or malnutrition and hunger, within their own borders. Failure to feed their own, with such high capabilities and such fully enunciated statements of responsibility and brotherhood, means that feeding the people of other countries is almost ruled out, except for sporadic escapist pieces of behavior where people who close their eyes to hunger in Mississippi can work hard to send food to a "Biafra." The development of the international instruments to meet food emergencies and to steadily improve the nutrition of the poorer countries will fail, unless there is greater consistency between ideal and practice at home.

—from "The Changing Significance of Food,"
American Scientist, 58, March–April 1970

PLATO ON THE ART OF COOKING

POLUS So answer me this, Socrates: since you think that Gorgias is at a loss about rhetoric, what is your own account of it?

SOCRATES Are you asking what art I call it?

POL. Yes.

SOC. None at all, I consider, Polus, if you would have the honest truth.

POL. But what do you consider rhetoric to be?

SOC. A thing which you say—in the treatise which I read of late— "made art."

POL. What thing do you mean?

SOC. I mean a certain habitude.

POL. Then do you take rhetoric to be a habitude?

SOC. I do, if you have no other suggestion.

POL. Habitude of what?

SOC. Of producing a kind of gratification and pleasure.

POL. Then you take rhetoric to be something fine—an ability to gratify people?

SOC. How now, Polus? Have you as yet heard me tell you what I say it is, that you ask what should follow that—whether I do not take it to be fine?

POL. Why, did I not hear you call it a certain habitude?

SOC. Then please—since you value "gratification"—be so good as to gratify me in a small matter.

POL. I will.

SOC. Ask me now what art I take cookery to be.

POL. Then I ask you, what art is cookery?

SOC. None at all, Polus.

POL. Well, what is it? Tell me.

SOC. Then I reply, a certain habitude.

POL. Of what? Tell me.

SOC. Then I reply, of production of gratification and pleasure, Polus.

POL. So cookery and rhetoric are the same thing?

SOC. Not at all, only parts of the same practice.

POL. What practice do you mean?

SOC. I fear it may be too rude to tell the truth; for I shrink from saying it on Gorgias' account, lest he suppose I am making satirical fun of his own pursuit. Yet indeed I do not know whether this is the rhetoric which Gorgias practises, for from our argument just now we got no very clear view as to how he conceives it; but what I call rhetoric is a part of a certain business which has nothing fine about it.

GORGIAS What is that, Socrates? Tell us, without scruple on my account.

SOC. It seems to me then, Gorgias, to be a pursuit that is not a matter of art, but showing a shrewd, gallant spirit which has a natural bent for clever dealing with mankind, and I sum up its substance in the name *flattery*. This practice, as I view it, has many branches, and one of them is cookery; which appears indeed to be an art but, by my account of it, is not an art but a habitude or knack. I call rhetoric another branch of it, as also personal adornment and sophistry—four branches of it for four kinds of affairs. So if Polus would inquire, let him inquire: he has not yet been informed to what sort of branch of flattery I assign rhetoric; but without noticing that I have not yet answered that, he proceeds to ask whether I do not consider it a fine thing. But I am not going to reply to the question whether I consider rhetoric a fine or a base thing, until I have first answered what it is; for it would not be fair, Polus: but if you want the information, ask me what sort of branch of flattery I assert rhetoric to be.

POL. I ask you then; so answer, what sort of branch it is.

SOC. Now, will you understand when I answer? Rhetoric, by my account, is a semblance of a branch of politics.

POL. Well then, do you call it a fine or a base thing?

SOC. A base one, I call it—for all that is bad I call base—since I am to answer you as one who already understands my meaning.

GORG. But I myself, upon my word, Socrates, do not grasp your meaning either.

SOC. And no wonder, Gorgias, for as yet my statement is not at all clear; but Polus here is so young and fresh!

GORG. Ah, do not mind him; but tell me what you mean by rhetoric being a semblance of a branch of politics.

SOC. Well, I will try to express what rhetoric appears to me to be: if it is not in fact what I say, Polus here will refute me. There are things, I suppose, that you call body and soul?

GORG. Of course.

SOC. And each of these again you believe to have a good condition?

GORG. I do.

SOC. And again, a good condition that may seem so, but is not? As an example, let me give the following: many people seem to be in good bodily condition when it would not be easy for anyone but a doctor, or one of the athletic trainers, to perceive that they are not so.

GORG. You are right.

SOC. Something of this sort I say there is in body and in soul, which makes the body or the soul seem to be in good condition, though it is none the more so in fact.

GORG. Quite so.

SOC. Now let me see if I can explain my meaning to you more clearly. There are two different affairs to which I assign two different arts: the one, which has to do with the soul, I call politics; the other, which concerns the body, though I cannot give you a single name for it offhand, is all one business, the tendance of the body, which I can designate in two branches as gymnastic and medicine. Under politics I set legislation in the place of gymnastic, and justice to match medicine. In each of these pairs, of course—medicine and gymnastic, justice and legislation—there is some intercommunication, as both deal with the same thing; at the same time they have certain differences. Now these four, which always bestow their care for the best advantage respectively of the body and the soul, are noticed by the art of flattery which, I do not say with knowledge, but by speculation, divides herself into four parts, and then, insinuating herself into each of those branches, pretends to be that into which she has crept, and cares nothing for what is the best, but dangles what is most pleasant for the moment as a bait for folly, and deceives it into thinking that she is of the highest value. Thus cookery assumes the form of medicine, and pretends to know what foods are best for the body; so that if a cook and a doctor had to contend before boys, or before men as foolish as boys, as to which of the two, the doctor or the cook, understands the question of sound and noxious foods, the doctor would starve to death. Flattery, however, is what I call it, and I say that this sort of thing is a disgrace, Polus—for here I address you—because it aims at the pleasant and ignores the best; and I say it is not an art, but a habitude, since it has no account to give of the real nature of the things it applies, and so cannot tell the cause of any of them. I refuse to give the name of art to anything that is irrational: if you dispute my views, I am ready to give my reasons. However, as I put it, cookery is flattery disguised as medicine; and in just the same manner self-adornment personates gymnastic: with its rascally, deceitful, ignoble, and illiberal nature it deceives men by forms and colours, polish and dress, so as to make them, in the effort of assuming an extraneous beauty, neglect the native sort that comes through gymnastic. Well, to avoid prolixity, I am willing to put it to you like a geometer—for by this time I expect you can follow me: as self-adornment is to gymnastic, so is sophistry to legislation; and as cookery is to medicine, so is rhetoric to justice. But although, as I say, there is this natural distinction between them, they are so nearly related that sophists and orators are jumbled up as having the same field and dealing with the same subjects, and neither can they tell what to make of each other, nor the world at large what to make of them. For indeed, if the soul were not in command of the body, but the latter had charge of itself, and so cookery and medicine were not surveyed and distinguished by the soul, but the body itself were the judge, forming its own estimate of them by the gratifications they gave it, we should have a fine instance of what Anaxagoras described, my dear Polus,—for you are versed in these matters: everything would be jumbled together, without distinction as between medicinal and healthful and tasty concoctions. Well now, you have heard what I state rhetoric to be—the counterpart of cookery in the soul, acting here as that does on the body.

—from *Gorgias,* 387 B.C.,
translated from the Greek by W.R.M. Lamb

MARCEL PROUST ON MADELEINES

MANY YEARS HAD ELAPSED DURING WHICH NOTHING OF Combray, save what was comprised in the theatre and the drama of my going to bed there, had any existence for me, when one day in winter, on my return home, my mother, seeing that I was cold, offered me some tea, a thing I did not ordinarily take. I declined at first, and then, for no particular reason, changed my mind. She sent for one of those squat, plump little cakes called "petites madeleines," which look as though they had been moulded in the fluted valve of a scallop shell. And soon, mechanically, dispirited after a dreary day with the prospect of a depressing morrow, I raised to my lips a spoonful of the tea in which I had soaked a morsel of the cake. No sooner had the warm liquid mixed with the crumbs touched my palate than a shudder ran through me and I stopped, intent upon the extraordinary thing that was happening to me. An exquisite pleasure had invaded my senses, something isolated, detached, with no suggestion of its origin. And at once the vicissitudes of life had become indifferent to me, its disasters innocuous, its brevity illusory—this new sensation having had on me the effect which love has of filling me with a precious essence; or rather this essence was not in me, it *was* me. I had ceased now to feel mediocre, contingent, mortal. Whence could it have come to me, this all-powerful joy? I sensed that it was connected with the taste of the tea and the cake, but that it infinitely transcended those savours, could not, indeed, be of the same nature. Whence did it come? What did it mean? How could I seize and apprehend it?

I drink a second mouthful, in which I find nothing more than in the first, then a third, which gives me rather less than the second. It is time to stop; the potion is losing its magic. It is plain that the truth I am seeking lies not in the cup but in myself. The drink has called it into being, but does not know it, and can only repeat indefinitely, with a progressive diminution of strength, the same message which I cannot interpret, though I hope at least to be able to call it forth again and to find it there presently, intact and at my disposal, for my final enlightenment. I put down the cup and examine my own mind. It alone can discover the truth. But how? What an abyss of uncertainty, whenever the mind feels overtaken by itself; when it, the seeker, is at the same time the dark region through which it must go seeking and where all its equipment will avail it nothing. Seek? More than that: create. It is face to face with something which does not yet exist, to which it alone can give reality and substance, which it alone can bring into the light of day.

And I begin again to ask myself what it could have been, this un-remembered state which brought with it no logical proof, but the indisputable evidence, of its felicity, its reality, and in whose presence other states of consciousness melted and vanished. I decide to attempt to make it reappear. I retrace my thoughts to the moment at which I drank the first spoonful of tea. I rediscover the same state, illuminated by no fresh light. I ask my mind to make one further effort, to bring back once more the fleeting sensation. And so that nothing may interrupt it in its course I shut out every obstacle, every extraneous idea, I stop my ears and inhibit all attention against the sounds from the next room. And then, feeling that my mind is tiring itself without having any success to report, I compel it for a change to enjoy the distraction which I have just denied it, to think of other things, to rest and refresh itself before making a final effort. And then for the second time I clear an empty space in front of it; I place in position before my mind's eye the still recent taste of that first mouthful, and I feel something start within me, something that leaves its resting-place and attempts to rise, something that has been embedded like an anchor at a great depth; I do not know yet what it is, but I can feel it mounting slowly; I can measure the resistance, I can hear the echo of great spaces traversed.

Undoubtedly what is thus palpitating in the depths of my being must be the image, the visual memory which, being linked to that taste, is trying to follow it into my conscious mind. But its struggles are too far off, too confused and chaotic; scarcely can I perceive the neutral glow into which the elusive whirling medley of stirred-up colours is fused, and I cannot distinguish its form, cannot invite it, as the one possible interpreter, to translate for me the evidence of its contemporary, its inseparable paramour, the taste, cannot ask it to inform me what special circumstance is in question, from what period in my past life.

Will it ultimately reach the clear surface of my consciousness, this memory, this old, dead moment which the magnetism of an identical moment has travelled so far to importune, to disturb, to raise up out of the very depths of my being? I cannot tell. Now I feel nothing; it has stopped, has perhaps sunk back into its darkness, from which who can say whether it will ever rise again? Ten times over I must essay the task, must lean down over the abyss. And each time the cowardice that deters us from every difficult task, every important enterprise, has urged me to leave the thing alone, to drink my tea and to think merely of the worries of to-day and my hopes for to-morrow, which can be brooded over painlessly.

And suddenly the memory revealed itself. The taste was that of the little piece of madeleine which on Sunday mornings at Combray (because on those mornings I did not go out before mass), when I went to say good morning to her in her bedroom, my aunt Léonie used to give me, dipping it first in her own cup of tea or tisane. The sight of the little madeleine had recalled nothing to my mind before I tasted it; perhaps because I had so often seen such things in the meantime, without tasting them, on the trays in pastry-cooks' windows, that their image had dissociated itself from those Combray days to take its place among others more recent; perhaps because of those memories, so long abandoned and put out of mind, nothing now survived, everything was scattered; the shapes of things, including that of the little scallop-shell of pastry, so richly sensual under its severe, religious folds, were either obliterated or had been so long dormant as to have lost the power of expansion which would have allowed them to resume their place in my consciousness. But when from a long-distant past nothing subsists, after the people are dead, after the things are broken and scattered, taste and smell alone, more fragile but more enduring, more unsubstantial, more persistent, more faithful, remain poised a long time, like souls, remembering, waiting, hoping, amid the ruins of all the rest; and bear unflinchingly, in the tiny and almost impalpable drop of their essence, the vast structure of recollection.

And as soon as I had recognised the taste of the piece of madeleine soaked in her decoction of lime-blossom which my aunt used to give me (although I did not yet know and must long postpone the discovery of why this memory made me so happy) immediately the old grey house upon the street, where her room was, rose up like a stage set to attach itself to the little pavilion opening on to the garden which had been built out behind it for my parents (the isolated segment which until that moment had been all that I could see); and with the house the town, from morning to night and in all weathers, the Square where I used to be sent before lunch, the streets along which I used to run errands, the country roads we took when it was fine. And as in the game wherein the Japanese amuse themselves by filling a porcelain bowl with water and steeping in it little pieces of paper which until then are without character or form, but, the moment they become wet, stretch and twist and take on colour and distinctive shape, become flowers or houses or people, solid and recognisable, so in that moment all the flowers in our garden and in M. Swann's park, and the water-lilies on the Vivonne and the good folk of the village and their little dwellings and the parish church and the whole of Combray and its surroundings, taking shape and solidity, sprang into being, town and gardens alike, from my cup of tea.

—from *À La Recherche du Temps Perdu, Remembrance of Things Past,*
1913, translated from the French by
C.K. Scott Moncrieff and Terence Kilmartin

A. J. Liebling on Proust

THE PROUST *MADELEINE* PHENOMENON IS NOW AS FIRMLY established in folklore as Newton's apple or Watt's steam kettle. The man ate a tea biscuit, the taste evoked memories, he wrote a book. This is capable of expression by the formula TMB, for Taste > Memory > Book. Some time ago, when I began to read a book called *The Food of France,* by Waverley Root, I had an inverse experience: BMT, for Book > Memory > Taste. Happily, the tastes that *The Food of France* re-created for me—small birds, stewed rabbit, stuffed tripe, Côte Rôtie, and Tavel—were more robust than that of the *madeleine,* which *Larousse* defines as "a light cake made with sugar, flour, lemon juice, brandy, and eggs." (The quantity of brandy in a *madeleine* would not furnish a gnat with an alcohol rub.) In the light of what Proust wrote with so mild a stimulus, it is the world's loss that he did not have a heartier appetite. On a dozen Gardiners Island oysters, a bowl of clam chowder, a peck of steamers, some bay scallops, three sautéed soft-shelled crabs, a few ears of fresh-picked corn, a thin swordfish steak of generous area, a pair of lobsters, and a Long Island duck, he might have written a masterpiece.

—from *Between Meals,* 1959

M.F.K. Fisher on Why She Writes About Food

PEOPLE ASK ME: WHY DO YOU WRITE ABOUT FOOD, AND eating and drinking? Why don't you write about the struggle for power and security, and about love, the way others do?

They ask it accusingly, as if I were somehow gross, unfaithful to the honor of my craft.

The easiest answer is to say that, like most other humans, I am hungry. But there is more than that. It seems to me that our three basic needs, for food and security and love, are so mixed and mingled and entwined that we cannot straightly think of one without the others. So it happens that when I write of hunger, I am really writing about love and the hunger for it, and warmth and the love of it and the hunger for it . . . and then the warmth and richness and fine reality of hunger satisfied . . . and it is all one.

I tell about myself, and how I ate bread on a lasting hillside, or drank red wine in a room now blown to bits, and it happens without my willing it that I am telling too about the people with me then, and their other deeper needs for love and happiness.

There is food in the bowl, and more often than not, because of what honesty I have, there is nourishment in the heart, to feed the wilder, more insistent hungers. We must eat. If, in the face of that dread fact, we can find other nourishment, and tolerance and compassion for it, we'll be no less full of human dignity.

There is a communion of more than our bodies when bread is broken and wine drunk. And that is my answer, when people ask me: Why do you write about hunger, and not wars or love?

—from *The Gastronomical Me,* 1943

Index

Text Credits

Grateful acknowledgment is made to the following for permission to reprint previously published material:

Academy Chicago Publishers: excerpt from *Blue Trout and Black Truffles* by Joseph Wechsberg. Reprinted by permission of the publisher.

American Scientist: excerpt from "The Changing Significance of Food" from *American Scientist* V. 58(2) 176-181. Reprinted by permission of the publisher.

Arizona State University: excerpts from *Platina: On Right Pleasure and Good Health: A Critical Edition and Translation of De Honesta Voluptate et Valetudine,* edited by Mary Ella Milham, MRTS vol. 168 (Tempe, AZ, 1998), pp. 121, 131, 151, 153, 183, 185, 197, 213, 215. Copyright Arizona Board of Regents for Arizona State University.

Avalon Publishing Group: "The Peasant Declares His Love" by Emile Roumer from *The Negritude Poets* by Ellen Conroy Kennedy. Copyright ©1975 by Ellen Conroy Kennedy. Appears by permission of the publisher, Thunder's Mouth Press.

E. J. Brill: excerpts from *The Aobu Tu* translated by Hans Vogel. Permission conveyed through Copyright Clearance Center, Inc.

Curtis Brown, Ltd.: excerpts from *Letters from Iceland* by W. H. Auden. Copyright ©1937 by W. H. Auden, renewed. Reprinted by permission of Curtis Brown, Ltd.

Alan Davidson: excerpt from *Dumas on Food* by Alexandre Dumas, translated by Jane and Alan Davidson, Folio Society, London. Reprinted by permission of the author.

C. Davidson & R. Ducas Literary Agency: excerpts from *The Fruit, Herbs and Vegetables of Italy* by Giacomo Castelvetro, translated by Gillian Riley, Viking, The Penguin Group (UK). Reprinted by permission of C. Davidson and R. Ducas Literary Agency.

Dover Publications, Inc.: excerpts from *Cookery and Dining in Imperial Rome* by Apicius, translated by Joseph Dommers Vehling. Reprinted by permission of the publisher.

Farrar, Straus and Giroux, LLC: excerpt from *Between Meals* by A. J. Liebling.

Photo Credits